W9-DJN-417

DISCARDED

THE LEADER

Psychohistorical Essays

THE LEADER

Psychohistorical Essays

Edited by
CHARLES B. STROZIER

Sangamon State University
Springfield, Illinois
and Michael Reese Hospital and Medical Center
Chicago, Illinois

and
DANIEL OFFER

Michael Reese Hospital and Medical Center
and University of Chicago
Chicago, Illinois

With a Foreword by
PETER GAY

Yale University
New Haven, Connecticut

Upsala College
Library
East Orange, N. J. 07019

PLENUM PRESS • NEW YORK AND LONDON

901.9
L434p

Library of Congress Cataloging in Publication Data

Main entry under title:

The Leader: psychohistorical essays.

Partly based on a conference at Michael Reese Hospital in June 1979.
Includes bibliographies and indexes.
1. Leadership—Congresses. 2. Leadership—Case studies—Congresses. 3. Psychohistory—Congresses. I. Strozier, Charles B. II. Offer, Daniel. [DNLM: 1. Leadership—essays. 2. Psychoanalytic Interpretation—essays. WM 460.7 L434]
BF637.L4L38   1985   901'.9   84-26431
ISBN 0-306-41784-7

©1985 Plenum Press, New York
A Division of Plenum Publishing Corporation
233 Spring Street, New York, N.Y. 10013

All rights reserved

No part of this book may be reproduced, stored in a retrieval system, or transmitted
in any form or by any means, electronic, mechanical, photocopying, microfilming,
recording, or otherwise, without written permission from the Publisher

Printed in the United States of America

For two mothers, Margaret Wright and Ilse Yallon
C.B.S. and D.O.

and to Michael
C.B.S.

180696

CONTRIBUTORS

JOSEPH A. BONGIORNO, M.D., is a psychiatrist in private practice and a Lecturer in the Department of Psychiatry of the Pritzker School of Medicine, University of Chicago. He has studied psychoanalysis at the Chicago Institute for Psychoanalysis. His essay on Woodrow Wilson is his first research effort. Currently, he is working on a book-length psychoanalytic study of collective behavior.

PRAKASH DESAI, M.D., is an Associate Professor of Psychiatry at the University of Illinois (Chicago) and Chief, Psychiatry Service of the Veterans Administration West Side Medical Center, Chicago. He is currently working on a book to be entitled *Health and Medicine in the Hindu Tradition.*

PETER GAY, Ph.D., is Durfee Professor of History at Yale University. He is the author of numerous books on modern European history, including *The Enlightenment* (1966), *Weimar Culture* (1968), *Freud, Jews, and Other Germans* (1978), and the recent *The Bourgeois Experience: Victoria to Freud,* Vol. I, "Education of the Senses."

THOMAS A. KOHUT, Ph.D., received his doctorate in history from the University of Minnesota in 1983 and is a graduate of the Cincinnati Psychoanalytic Institute. He is currently Assistant Professor of History at Williams College.

HYMAN MUSLIN, M.D., is Professor of Psychiatry at the University of Illinois, Chicago and a graduate of the Chicago Institute for Psychoanalysis. He has written numerous articles in the fields of psychiatry and psychoanalysis, including "Transference in the Dora Case," *Journal of the American Psychoanalytic Association, 26*, (1978); "Romeo and Juliet: The Tragic Self in Adolescence," in the *Annals of the American Society for Adolescent Psychiatry*, 1982; His most recent book is *Kohut's Analysis of the Self* (Cambridge: Current Medical Literature, 1981).

DANIEL OFFER, M.D., is Chairman of the Department of Psychiatry of Michael Reese Hospital and Medical Center and Professor of Psychiatry at the University of Chicago. He is the author of nine books in the fields of adolescent development and concepts of mental health. His latest book (with M. Sabshin) is *Normality and the Life Cycle* (New York: Basic Books, 1984).

CHARLES B. STROZIER, Ph.D., is Professor of History at Sangamon State University, Visiting Professor of Psychiatry at Rush Medical School, and Senior Research Consultant at Michael Reese Hospital and Medical Center. He is the author of numerous articles on psychohistory, published *Lincoln's Quest for Union: Public and Private Meanings* (New York: Basic Books, 1982), and is the editor of *The Psychohistory Review*. He is also the editor of the forthcoming volume, *The Self and History* (Norton Publishing Company).

JAMES A. WALTER, Ph.D., is Director of the Institute for Modern Biography, Griffith University, Australia.

MARVIN ZONIS, Ph.D., is Associate Professor, Committee on Human Development, Department of Behavioral Sciences, University of Chicago.

FOREWORD

PETER GAY

The syllabus of errors rehearsing the offenses of psychohistory looks devastating and seems irrefutable: crimes against the English language, crimes against scientific procedures, crimes against common sense itself. These objects are real enough, but their contours—and their gravity—mysteriously change with the perspective of the critic. From the outside, psychohistorians are to academic history what psychoanalysts are to academic psychology: a monolithic band of fanatics, making the same errors, committing the same offenses, all in the same way. But seen close up, psychohistorians (just like psychoanalysts) turn out to be a highly differentiated, even a cheerfully contentious, lot. Disciples of Hartmann jostle discoverers of Kohut, imperialists claiming the whole domain of the past debate with modest isolationists, orthodox Freudians who insist that psychoanalysis engrosses the arsenal of psychohistorical method find themselves beleaguered by sociological revisionists. The charges that confound some psychohistorians glance off the armor of others. Yet there are three potent objections, aimed at the heart of psychohistory, however it is conceived, that the psychohistorian ignores at his peril. It would be a convenient, but it is a wholly unacceptable, defense to dismiss them as forms of resistance. The days are gone when the advocates of psychoanalysis could checkmate reasoned criticisms by psychoanalyzing the critic.

To summarize these objections, psychohistory is Utopian, vulgar, and trivial. It is Utopian because it uses the most stubbornly individualistic of all psychologies to unlock the riddle of collective conduct and crowded events. The road from biography to history cannot properly follow the path of psychoanalysis, which, if it is a road at all, is one to the interior. And psychohistory is vulgar, because it reduces historical experiences and events to neurotic mechanisms. Indeed, if there is one objection to psychohistory that enjoys universal popularity among its critics, and almost invariably arouses anxiety among its supporters, it is this charge of reductionism. And, finally, psychohistory is trivial because we cannot psychoanalyze the dead, who do not, and cannot, behave like analysands. I should note at the outset that each of these objections has, in my judgment, some substance. It is only that their devastating conclusions do not follow.

Psychohistory has been called an illegitimate reading of history through biography—and a very peculiar form of biography at that. It is no secret that psychoanalysis is the psychology of the individual. The psychoanalytic situation, with its hermetic encounter of the lone analysand with the lone analyst, dramatizes this concentration on one person alone. The psychoanalyst, is, by choice, a depth biographer keeping his confidence, a private eye and, even more, a private ear.

But to separate the study of the past sharply into biography (the history of a single person) and history (the biography of collectivities) is to misread the respective domains of these two genres, which interact and overlap. Every biographer is something of a historian, every historian something of a biographer. With some recent social historians, who are retrospective sociologists in historians' clothes, the human subject has become almost wholly attenuated. But this, I submit, is bad history, just as biography that fails to place the individual firmly into his living context—his economic, social, religious environment—is bad biography. Each of these two genres, biography and history, no doubt has its particular perspective on the past, and each its professional deformations. There is tension between them, as well as collaboration. But the hoary commonplace that history is about human beings, about their encounters with nature, technology, power, one another, and themselves, retains all its validity. Practitioners of social history, however hostile they may be to psychoanalysis, only underscore this commitment; they aspire, after all, to what they call *histoire totale*. It is necessary to remind them that when human beings, even dead human beings, are the subject of inquiry, and when their experience is to be sounded to the depths, the psychology that will reach those depths deserves a privileged role in the making of intelligible patterns and credible explanations.

Psychoanalysis has yet another claim to the historian's sympathetic attention. For all the differentiated palette of human experience across time, space, class, and temperament—and it is these riches that make history interesting—human beings are much alike, both through their biological endowment and through the emotional gauntlet they must run, dictated by their long helplessness, their biphasic psychosexual maturation, and their inescapable confrontations with developmental crises, notably the Oedipal drama and the storms of adolescence. In short, human beings are much alike since they must all resolve similar conflicts and overcome similar obstacles; all learn to control impulses, to postpone gratifications, to surrender incestuous love objects—or to pay the penalty for failing to do so. And human beings are much alike, finally, because in each the ego is in commerce with the outside world, testing and adapting to reality. Vast as the repertory of human motives and actions may be—and written history is, as I have suggested, the record of how vast, in fact, that repertory is—this glittering array is achieved through unique combinations of relatively few ingredients. The raw materials of human nature are, in this sense, like chessmen, the principal activities of the drives and defenses like the moves in chess, the elaboration of historical actualities like individual games, each operating with a handful of basic elements, all members of a family, yet none precisely like any other. To analyze the game of chess, the expert must be committed to particularity and known universals. The historical analyst is in the same situation. He examines the figure of the unique against the ground of the general, aware, if I may borrow the concise formulation of Kluckholn and Murray, that "every man is in certain respects (a) like all other men, (b) like some other men, (c) like no other man."[1] Biography, I repeat, is a kind of history; history a kind of biography.

But the psychohistorian can draw scant comfort from this intimacy, for if biography and history are twins, they share their troubles quite as much as their styles of thinking. Both the individual's case history and the general historical record are crowded to illegibility with complex motives and contradictory external forces; both are overdetermined. Freud knew this; after all, he invented this term precisely out of his respect for complexity and contradiction. Two almost identical clusters of impulses may have dramatically different results; two very different sets of impulses may have almost identical results. Seemingly unambiguous statements mask defeated wishes pointing in an opposite direction; seemingly decisive actions disclose, upon examination, buried conflicts. Psychological constellations play more than one part at several levels of human functioning and change their part with the passage of time.[2] The historian intent on mapping the course of mind in the past needs a fine pen and a powerful eraser, for such a charting requires deftness, patience, and a thoroughgoing grounding in the mind's capabilities and in its limitations. But however difficult his work and problematic his discoveries, the historian can only profit from acting as though Clio is analyzable after all.

PETER GAY

NOTES

1. Clyde Kluckholn and Henry A. Murray, *Personality in Nature, Society, and Culture* (New York: Knopf, 1948), p. 35.
2. Robert Waelder, "The Principle of Multiple Function," *Psychoanalytic Quarterly* 5 (1930); Heinz Hartmann, *Ego Psychology and the Problem of Adaptation*, trans. David Rapaport (1939; rpt. New York: International Universities Press, 1958).

ACKNOWLEDGMENTS

In 1979, Arnold Goldberg approached us about plans for a conference that would draw together historians and psychoanalysts to consider some of the implications of the work of the late Heinz Kohut regarding leadership. Dr. Goldberg's idea was of interest to both us and Dr. Kohut.

The conference that resulted at Michael Reese Hospital in June, 1979, was an enormously stimulating event that included participants as diverse as Heinz Kohut, Peter Gay, Bruce Mazlish, Robert J. Lifton, Fred Weinstein, Michael Franz Basch, and others. We then worked with the papers from the conference, elicited other contributions, and, over four years, researched the topic of leadership on our own. This book is the result of those efforts.

A number of research assistants have assisted us in our work over the years, including Michael Creany, Patricia Michaelson, and Linnea Larson. We are also grateful to the psychiatric residents and the fellows of Michael Reese Hospital for participating in seminars on this topic and sharing with us their ideas about leadership. We are particularly grateful to our friend Herman Sinaiko for his stimulating suggestions at an early period of our own research on this topic. Peter Barglow, Jean Carney, Tamar Offer, and Raphael Offer have read the different parts of the book. We are grateful to them for their helpful comments.

We would like to thank Hilary Evans of Plenum Publishing Corporation for her direction and encouragement, and we are indebted to the Illinois Humanities Council for their partial support for this project (MG 5089-0000-0580). This project has also been supported in part by the Adolescent Research Fund: In Memory of Judith Offer, of the Department of Psychiatry of Michael Reese Hospital. Finally, our warmest thanks are to Marjorie K. Offer, who has both helped and cheered us from the beginning, and always.

CHARLES B. STROZIER
DANIEL OFFER

CONTENTS

PART I

PERSPECTIVES

CHAPTER 1

INTRODUCTION

CHARLES B. STROZIER AND DANIEL OFFER

It is fashionable to date the beginning of psychohistory in 1958 with William Langer's Presidential speech, "The Next Assignment," to the American Historical Association, and with the publication in the same year of Erik Erikson's *Young Man Luther*.[1] In one sense the year marked an important change, with the call of the president of the historical association to professional historians to consider motivation in a psychohistorical context and with the publication of what was undoubtedly the first good psychobiography, one that was based in the historical sources and was well written and intelligently conceived. The field since then has sprouted subfields, competing journals, and organizations and has gained some sense of its method. It has influenced the teaching of history at a number of institutions of higher learning and separated itself decisively from its origins as an incidental activity of psychoanalysts after hours. And, finally, psychohistory itself has perhaps influenced culture and politics. A certain psychological self-consciousness pervades contemporary political discourse.

Yet 1958 is surely an artificial turning point and remains inadequate as an accurate point of origin for an endeavor as complex, and often as baffling, as psychohistory. Historians often object to psychohistorical claims of newness. Historians have always closely studied motivation, and at times they have studied it better than most psychohistorians. A certain degree of turf war mentality lurks behind such assertions. Thus, the sympathetic and psychologically oriented historian, Frank Manuel, in 1968 countered claims that Freud was the central figure behind the "new" history by claiming that honor for Giambattista Vico.[2]

Within the psychoanalytic tradition, on the other hand, writers act as though psychohistory not only began with Freud, but continues simply as a testing ground for new theories generated by clinical psychoanalysis. Thus, literature reviews in articles published in psychoanalytic journals airily ignore virtually anything not written by practicing psychoanalysts.[3] This turf question has some serious implications for defining the field, its method and purposes, and the proper training for research within it. The analyst Kurt Eissler, for example, strenuously argues that only trained *and* practicing psychoanalysts should write psychohistory.[4] The historian Fred Weinstein describes this position gently as absurd, arguing that psychoanalytic theory *must* be handled and used as any theory on an objective basis; he thus implies that the subjective bias of practicing psychoanalysts corrupts the practitioner in its application.[5] Others, finally, have shifted the ground altogether and questioned the validity of psychoanalysis itself as the theoretical basis of psychological history.[6] Contention is the byword in this debate.

The matter of origins is central. Louise Hoffman has recently argued that the contemporary debate over Hilter and Nazism in the 1930s and early 1940s defined the assumptions, the method, and the style of psychohistory. It is a weighted heritage, she concludes.[7] But applied analytic writing in the 1930s was itself a relatively late flowering of Freudian thought. Long before 1933, Freud himself had already written most of his historical work. Furthermore, Freud's ardent followers had themselves produced a respectably large body of work on history, literature, religion, and culture generally. Surely, what guided Adler, Sachs, Rank, and others in the assessment of contemporary politics in the 1930s carried over from the early meetings of the Vienna Psychoanalytic Society between 1905 and 1911, from the pages of *Imago* after 1913, and from meetings and discussions in the various international congresses of psychoanalysis.

But can we even accurately categorize psychohistory as a twentieth-century enterprise largely inspired by Freud? Plato cast his theories of government in a surprisingly psychological mold. Some Biblical stories are prototypically psychobiographical. Plutarch's delightful tales probe the complexities of conscious and unconscious motivation within the convention of narrative. More modern political theorists—like Thomas Hobbes, Niccolo Machiavelli, John Locke, David Hume, Jean Jacques Rousseau, and many others—have often woven highly complex, if refractory, psychological theories into their systems of political behavior and government.

In this chapter, we will attempt to come to grips with this history, not in a systematic but in a reflective way. Neither of us claims any special knowledge of the long history of Western thought. Our discussion of all the material before the twentieth century began with a simple question that we thought at first could be easily answered: Was there psychohistory before Freud? Our answer is a strongly qualified "Yes." We found that some thinkers were surprisingly psychological and that anyone interested in such interpretation ignores their work at his or her own peril. Yet from Plato to Freud, to put it baldly, there is always something missing, and it is the delineation of the gaps and uncompleted thoughts that gives some clues into the special contribution of thinkers since Freud.

The story we tell here deepens considerably as it approaches the present. References proliferate as the literature expands almost to confusion. We have imposed some chronological order on this history of the field of psychohistory, an order which perhaps suits our need for coherence more than it genuinely reflects any emerging patterns in the literature. Furthermore, we have tried to highlight the work of certain important contributors to the field by way of illustration, relegating others to passing mention or inclusion in the footnotes. This chapter is not the result of a bibliographic search *per se*, nor can we fairly claim to have given everyone due time in court, so to speak. What we have written is history, and history is always selective or it is meaningless.

A new field requires time to mature. The writers we discuss have all variously and creatively moved it along. We attempt to describe in detail the special insights that have emerged in the history of the enterprise. Sometimes, what seems new now is really old hat. For example, it has been repeated *ad nauseum* since the late 1950s that a psychobiography cannot be a case history. That idea should have been put to rest after the debates of the Vienna Psychoanalytic Society, which met in Freud's home between April 17 and December 11, 1907.[8] But we have also been acutely aware that unfulfilled promises and missing opportunities must be identified, or we will all stagnate.

The "field" here deserves some definition. In general, *psychohistory* can be defined as a form of history that makes systematic use of concepts, principles, and theories of psychology in order to enhance our understanding of a particular people and of events in the past.[9] Such a definition broadly includes the application of psychoanalysis or *any* psychological theory to the past, political psychology (if historical), psychohistory proper, psychologically oriented sociology or anthropology, and psychological interpretations of literary figures now dead. The definition excludes psychological interpretations of art or literature. The definition contains psychohistory within the larger discipline of history.

Psychohistory is a way of seeing the past, but it is not the only prism through which historical data can be filtered. The story of the evolution of the modern state, for example, is not necessarily a psychohistorical one, though it may turn out that the most interesting part of the story is the psychological meaning of the nation-state in terms of the lives of its leaders and its ordinary citizens.

Leadership, however, not psychohistory generally, is the concern of this book. Many observers would dispute the distinction, agreeing with Donald B. Meyer: "The point ought to be made flatly: psycho-analytic history is biography-centered history."[10] There is no doubt that the study of leadership centers on biography. Biographical studies have dominated the field since its formal inception with Freud. Much of that work has been in the form of "pathography," which is the term used by the early Vienna group to indicate a focus on the pathology of the leader and how he or she translated private issues of conflict and confusion into the public realm. Harold Lasswell cast this idea into the form of a law of politics,[11] but the idea of a specific, pathological connection between public and private lies behind much of the scholarship on leadership. Freud and Bullitt's Woodrow Wilson (1966 [1932]) is a man obsessed with his father for whom history provides an outlet in playing out fantasies of Chirstlike greatness. Walter Langer's Hitler (1967 [1943])—indeed everyone's Hilter—is a psychotic, marching across Germany, imposing his gigantic problems on a wayward society.[12] More recently, Bruce Mazlish's Nixon (1971) forces crises to test his fragile sense of self, and after Watergate many more studies elaborated this point.[13] There is much to be said for this approach to the field. Many leaders carry their own pasts awkwardly on their sleeve and seem uniquely able to generalize their pathology.

However, there are limits to this view. From a psychiatric point of view, pathology alone tends to choke off creativity; that is, indeed, one of its sadder characteristics.[14] It is also patently absurd to label all leaders as pathological, just because the psychological study of leadership has tended to identify psychopathological aspects. The method should not define the field. There is always the example of Abraham Lincoln. Even Hitler was rather frighteningly together. It may be, in fact, completely accidental that leaders often seem so psychopathological. Finally, like the daily news, psychohistory has tended to turn to villains, rather than to heros, for its stories. This distorts the place of neurosis or psychosis in our sense of the past. It may well be that in most circumstances it is the individual leader's psychopathology that limits his or her ability to grow and creatively adapt history.

One aim of this book is to dissolve the dichotomy between psychopathology and normality in the study of leadership. The individual operates in a historical context, and the most interesting psychohistorical work on leadership to date has attempted to identify the precise nature of that elusive fit between *leader* and *led* in the full richness of the unique moment of the past. Unless a whole society is to be labelled "sick," questions of pathology are largely irrelevant. For what might awkwardly be called the psychological study of "followership" has emerged as the necessary counterpart to the psychohistorical study of leadership. The evolution of this awareness is a central theme in the discussions that follow. Furthermore, we attempt to explain how theoretical developments within psychoanalysis itself have pushed those interested in leadership toward an understanding of this connection.

To explore the subjective in others forces one to confront the nature of one's own private involvement in such a study. These issues, of course, differ for Strozier and Offer, and it would be self-indulgent to discuss them in detail. But we often discussed our personal interest in leadership and noted how important the general question of idealization was for both of us and how we each longed, in different ways, for ideal figures, for an understanding of idealization as a process, and, perhaps, for the ideal in ourselves.

NOTES

1. William Langer, "The Next Assignment," *American Historical Review*, 53 (1958), 283–304; Erik H. Erikson, *Young Man Luther: A Study in Psychoanalysis and History* (New York: Norton, 1958).
2. Frank E. Manuel, "The Use and Abuse of Psychology in History," in *Historical Studies Today*, ed. Felix Gilbert and Stephen R. Graubard (New York: Norton, 1972), p. 212.
3. Heinz Kohut, "Beyond the Bounds of the Basic Rule: Some Recent Contributions to Applied Psychoanalysis," *Journal of the American Psychoanalytic Association*, 8 (1960), 567–586; Robert Waelder, "Psychoanalysis, Scientific Method, and Philosophy," *Journal of American Psychoanalytic Association*, 10 (1962), 617–637; Heinz Hartmann, "The Application of Psychoanalytic Concepts to Social Science," in *Psychoanalysis and Social Science*, ed. Henrik Ruitenbeck (New York: E. P. Dutton, 1962); John E. Mack, "Psychoanalysis and Historical Biography," *Journal of the American Psychoanalytic Association*, 19 (1971), 143–179; Charles Hofling, "Current Problems in Psychohistory," *Comprehensive Psychiatry*, 17 (1976), 227–239. To get a sense of how different historians summarize the field of psychohistory, see, for example (and there are many more), Richard L. Schoenwald, "Using Psychology in History: A Review Essay," *Historical Methods Newsletter*, 7 (1973), 9–24; Gerald M. Platt, "The Sociological Endeavor and Psychoanalytic Thought," *American Quarterly* 28 (1976), 343–350; and two essays by Cushing Strout, "Ego Psychology and the Historian," *History and Theory*, 7 (1968), 281–297 and "The Uses and Abuses of Psychology in American History," *American Quarterly*, 28 (1976), 324–42.

4. Kurt R. Eissler, *Medical Orthodoxy and the Future of Psychoanalysis* (New York: Basic Books, 1965), p. 164.
5. Fred Weinstein and Gerald M. Platt, *Psychoanalytic Sociology: An Essay on the Interpretation of Historical Data and the Phenomena of Collective Behavior* (Baltimore: The Johns Hopkins University Press, 1973), I, 1.
6. In 1979 Charles Strozier edited a special issue of *The Psychohistory Review*, 7 (1979), entitled "Non-psychoanalytic Ventures in Psychohistory." The issue includes articles by Peter C. Hoffer, "Is Psychohistory Really History?," J. Harvey Asher, "Non-Psychoanalytic Approaches to National Socialism," Ur Wernic, "Cognitive Dissonance Theory, Religious Reality, and Extreme Interactionism," and William Merrill Downer, "A Psychological Justification of Anarchism: The Case of Paul Goodman." The issue also includes a bibliographic listing of non-psychoanalytic psychohistory put together by William Gilmore.
7. Louise E. Hoffman, "Psychoanalytic Interpretations of Adolf Hitler and Nazism, 1933–1945: A Prelude to Psychohistory" *The Psychohistory Reivew*, 11 (1982), 68–87.
8. *Minutes of the Vienna Psychoanalytic Society*, ed. German Numberg and Ernst Federn, 4 volumes (New York: International Universities Press, 1962), I: 167f, 259–69, and 267–68.
9. This definition represents Charles Strozier's adaptation of Faye Grosby's definition. See Faye Grosby, "Evaluating Psychohistorical Explanations," *Psychohistory Review*, 7 (1979), 6–16.
10. Donald B. Meyer, "A Review of *Young Man Luther: A Study in Psychoanalysis and History*," in *Psychoanalysis and History*, ed. Bruce Mazlish (New York: Grosset & Dunlap, 1971), pp. 178–79.
11. Harold D. Lasswell, *Psychopathology and Politics* (Chicago: University of Chicago Press, 1930).
12. Walter C. Langer, *The Mind of Adolf Hitler* (New York: Basic Books, 1967 [1943]).
13. Bruce Mazlish, *In Search of Nixon: A Psychohistorical Inquiry* (New York: Basic Books, 1972); Eli S. Cheson, *President Nixon's Psychiatric Profile* (New York: Peter H. Wyden, 1973); David Abrahamsen, *Nixon vs. Nixon: An Emotional Tragedy* (New York: Farrar, Straus & Giroux, 1976); and most recently, Fawn Brodie, *Richard Nixon: The Shaping of his Character* (New York: Norton, 1981).
14. Lawrence Kubie, *Neurotic Distinctions of the Creative Process* (New York: Noonday Press, 1977).

CHAPTER 2

LEADERS IN ANCIENT TIMES
Joseph, Plato, and Alcibiades

CHARLES B. STROZIER AND DANIEL OFFER

JOSEPH

The story of Joseph is one of the most fascinating, detailed, and complex stories in the Bible. Although no direct archaeological evidence relates the Israelites to Egypt, it is assumed that the Israelites who emmigrated from Canaan (Palestine) to Egypt in search of a more fruitful land were the Hyksos, semitic tribes who invaded Egypt in 1730 B.C. and ruled Egypt for 150 years.

It is likely that the story of Joseph is that of a leader who belonged to a marginal group (a nomadic tribe) that ruled a stable society which had been in existence for over a thousand years.

According to the Bible, in his adolescence, Joseph was his father's favorite child because "he was the son of his old age" (Genesis 37:3). Jacob, his father, made him a coat of many colors, which caused much envy and jealousy among his brothers. They developed strong hateful feelings toward Joseph, though he did not understand why. Joseph was apparently pleased with himself and his position in the family. He had two blatantly self-centered dreams in which everyone was to serve Joseph. This even annoyed his father.

Later, Joseph was sent by his father to see whether everything was all right with his brothers. As he approached them, they said to each other, "Behold, this dreamer cometh" (Genesis 37:19). Not only did he stand out as the favorite; he fantasized about his superior place in the world. The brothers considered killing him, but did not, and in the end sold Joseph as a slave to a passing tribe for twenty pieces of silver. They went back home and told their father that Joseph had been killed by a beast.

Joseph was sold to an Egyptian officer named Potiphar. Jospeh was a loyal servant and worked his way up to become the overseer of Potiphar's household. Here Joseph's story in the Bible makes a detour, and we are told that Joseph was "of beautiful form and fair to look upon" (Genesis, 39:6). (We might wonder whether we see here the influence of the Greeks.) The wife of his master took to him and tried to seduce him. Joseph, ever loyal, refused, and she became infuriated with him and accused him of trying to rape her. The consequence was that Joseph ended up in jail.

The above story is amazingly similar to the one found in the "Ordinary Papyrus" from the Nineteenth Dynasty (ca. 1300 B.C.). The story entitled "The Tale of the Two Brothers" states:

> Once upon a time there were two brothers. . . . The name of the elder one was Anubis, the younger was called Bata. Anubis owned a house and a wife and his younger brother lived with him as if he were his own son. He drove the cattle out to the fields and brought them home at night and slept with them in the cowshed. When ploughing time came round, the two brothers were ploughing the land together. They had been a few days in the fields when they ran out of corn. The elder brother therefore sent the younger one off: "Hurry and bring us corn from the city." The younger brother found his elder brother's wife having a hairdo. "Up," he said, "and give me some corn, for I have to hurry back to the field. My brother said: 'Quick, don't waste any time.'". He loaded up with corn and wheat and went out with his burden. . . . Then said she to him: "You have so much energy! Every day I see how strong you are. . . . Come! Let us lie down for an hour!—It may give you pleasure, and I shall also make you fine clothes." Then the young man was as angry as a southern panther at this wicked suggestion that had been made to him. He said to her: "What a disgraceful proposal you have just made. . . . Never do it again and I shall say nothing to anyone." So saying, he slung his load on his back and went out to the fields. The wife began to be frightened about what she had said. She got hold of some grease paint and made herself up to look like someone who had been violently assaulted. Her husband . . . found his wife lying prostrate as a result of the [pretended] outrage. Her husband said to her: "Who has been with you?" She replied: "No one . . . apart from your younger brother. When he came to fetch the corn he

found me sitting alone and said to me: 'Come, let us lie down for an hour! Do up your hair.' But I paid no attention to him. 'Am I not your mother! and is your elder brother not like a father to you!' I said to him. But he was afraid and struck me to stop me telling you about it. If you leave him alive now I shall die." Then his brother grew as wild as a southern panther. He sharpened his knife . . . to kill his younger brother. (Keller, 99–100)

In jail, Joseph's talents helped him again as he ran the prison for its keeper. Through brilliant dream interpretation, he was able to leave the prison. Joseph understood people well and was able to present himself as a natural leader of men. Hence Pharaoh turned to him and, when Joseph was thirty years old, Pharaoh appointed him vizier of Egypt. Joseph was a most able leader and guided the Egyptian people through tense and difficult times.

The Biblical story goes on in detail to describe how Joseph and his brothers resolved their past conflicts. When famine reigned over the Middle East, the Israelites needed food and Joseph's brothers went to Egypt to obtain it. Since Joseph had planned well ahead of the famine, people from all over the Middle East went to Egypt to buy food. When Joseph encountered his brothers, he recognized them, but they did not recognize him. Joseph remembered his adolescent dreams and what his brothers had done to him. He accused them of spying and jailed them. Through a number of complex transactions, Joseph instilled panic in his brothers to avenge himself, driving them to desperation and hopelessness. Only after they were completely at his mercy and totally powerless did he reveal to them that he was their brother. In the end, Joseph, the leader among his brothers, turned out to be the noble, powerful, all-giving, and forgiving person.

Jacob, joined with the whole tribe as they migrated to Egypt, where with Joseph as their leader they began the formation of a new and great nation, Israel. Joseph arranged for the Israelites to settle down in Goshen, a land that was extremely fertile and particularly well suited for raising cattle. His brothers and their kin settled there comfortably and multiplied.

Meanwhile, Joseph had consolidated his power over Egypt. He had exchanged the food that he had stored during the years of plenty for money, cattle, horses and, finally, rights to the land. He then arranged a new system of taxation, under which twenty percent of the gross income of the people went to Pharaoh and the rest was retained by the people. The Egyptians, as the Bible tells us, despised cattle breeders, and it is unlikely that under ordinary circumstances such a person as

Joseph would have risen to such prominence. As Keller (1969) put it:

> Only under the foreign overlords, the Hyksos, would an "Asiatic"
> have [had] the chance to rise to the highest office in the state. Under
> the Hyksos we repeatedly find officials with Semitic names. On
> scarabs dating from the Hyksos period the name "Jacob-Her" has
> been clearly deciphered. "And it is not impossible," concludes the
> great American Egyptologist James Henry Breasted, "that a leader of
> the Israelite tribe of Jacob gained control for a time in the Nile valley
> in this obscure period. Such an occurrence would fit in surprisingly
> well with the migration to Egypt of Israelite tribes which in any case
> must have taken place about this time."

After Jacob's death, Joseph's brothers were afraid that "Joseph will
hate us, and will fully requite us all the evil which we did unto him"
(Genesis 50:15). They went to him, treated him with tremendous admiration, and asked for his forgiveness. As a matter of fact, they treated
Joseph as if he were their God—a far cry from the way they had treated
him in the past. Joseph was embarrassed by the way his brothers
revered him, and told them, "Fear not; for am I in the place of God?"
(Genesis 50:19). He comforted his brothers and assured them that he
would not avenge past wrongdoings. Joseph went on to live to a ripe old
age without any problems that we know about.

Joseph's story, like all biblical stories, has been studied for over
three thousand years by a vast number of scholars. We do not intend to
discuss the story of Joseph, except from a very limited psychohistorical
perspective. There is no information about Joseph as a child, except that
he lost his mother at a young age and that he was his father's favorite.
Joseph's adolescent self-centeredness so irritated his brothers that they
considered killing him. The story of Joseph, as we have pointed out, is
mixed with earlier myths, and it is very hard to separate one myth from
another. The use and abuse of power, the place of revenge and violence,
spying, cheating, stealing, forgiveness, graciousness, reverence, and
dreams of grandeur are all part of the story of Joseph, which even
describes a new system of taxation that is organized particularly to help
those in power. The story's components are not that different from what
we see among leaders today: money, power, sex, violence, and wisdom.
Finally, Joseph was an outsider to Egypt, and, because he saw it more
clearly as such, he was able to undertake certain programs which produced newer systems of government. The insiders, as wise as they
were, could not comprehend what was necessary to do in Egypt under a
crisis. In this case, only an outsider, Joseph, was able to understand
Pharaoh's dreams (his internal problems) and offer new solutions for
them. The new leader integrated tradition with a revamped system. For
Joseph and the Egyptians, this worked exceedingly well.

PLATO

Plato was perhaps the first systematic theorist of the psychological basis of leadership. The remarkable insights of the *Republic* probe the varieties of leadership styles, how these styles respond to the needs of followers, the relationship between childrearing and adulthood, and political behavior, and offer an astute psychobiographical analysis of the tyrant.

These ideas are spelled out most clearly in Books VIII and IX of the *Republic*. In the dialogue between Socrates and Glaucon, Socrates describes the different forms of government: the aristocratic, the oligarchic, the democratic, and the tyrannical. Most of the earlier sections of the *Republic* develop in detail Plato's sense of the good and just man and how he rules in an aristocratic republic that rewards the good. In these two books of the *Republic*, Plato analyzes the forms of government that depart from this ideal. It is not a historical model, which describes the evolution of governmental form over time, but an abstract study of how the state can diverge from the ideal. Plato acknowledges exceptions— for example, a purchased kingdom or a mixed form of government—but he argues that the principal competing types of the state are the oligarchic, the democratic, and the tyrannical.

Plato argues that what mediates the movement from one form of government to another is the changed collective experience of childhood. For example, the aristocracy of the good and just cannot last. "Not only for plants that grow from the earth," states Socrates,

> but also for animals that live upon it there is a cycle of bearing and barrenness for soul and body as often as the revolutions of their orbs come full circle, in brief courses for the short-lived and oppositely for the opposite; by the laws of prosperous birth or infertility for your race, the men you have bred to be your rulers will not for all their wisdom ascertain by reasoning combined with sensation, but they will escape them, and there will be a time when they will beget children out of season.[1]

These children come to neglect their elders, their music, their gymnastics, and their culture. They become adults avid for wealth and all the sensual pleasures; their homes (as adults) will be "literal love nests."[2] Money comes to occupy the center of their existence and they strive only to acquire wealth. This characterizes an oligarchy, a form of government in which the rich control and the poor are excluded. The citizens in such a state never turn their thoughts to true culture.[3] And where do you look, asks Socrates, to explain the emergence of such citizens? "To guardianships of orphans, and any such opportunities of doing injustice with impunity."[4]

Oligarchy, however, contains the seeds of its own destruction, for among the huddled, poor, and disenfranchised masses are youth of vigor and strength. They observe in battle, for example, the cowardice and weakness of the pampered rich. They talk to each other and learn that all the poor are in the same situation. Resentment builds and eventually the poor band together and kill the rich by force of arms or by some form of terrorism. Then the masses appropriate the wealth and take control of the government. Democracy ensues.

In democracy, each man leads his life as he pleases. Possibly, "this is the most beautiful of all politics; as a garment of many colors, embroidered with all kinds of hues, so this, decked and diversified with every type of character, would appear the most beautiful."[5] However, such a form of government tramples underfoot the good man who from childhood has pursued truth and beauty. Such men get lost in the shuffle, for in a democracy, everyone is equal, there is no discrimination, and equality is assigned equally to equals and unequals alike.[6] The common youth tastes the pleasures of wealth and indulges all his appetites; he drinks or plays the flute or exercises or seemingly occupies himself with philosophy as whim or the moment dictate.[7]

The very lack of discrimination inherent in democracy opens the way to despotism, by which people are held in the grip of the "most cruel and bitter servile servitude."[8] The problem, essentially, is one of pleasure:"'Of our necessary pleasures and appetites,' Socrates tells Glaucon,

> "there are some lawless ones, I think, which probably are to be found in us all, but which, when controlled by the laws and the better desires in alliance with reason, can in some men be altogether got rid of, or so nearly so that only a few weak ones remain, while in others the remnant is stronger and more numerous." "What desires do you mean?" he [Glaucon] said. "Those," said I, "that are awakened in sleep when the rest of the soul, the rational, gentle and dominant part, slumbers, but the beastly and savage part, replete with food and wine, gambols and, repelling sleep, endeavors to sally forth and satisfy its own instincts. You are aware that in such case there is nothing it will not venture to undertake as being released from all sense of shame and all reason. It does not shrink from attempting to lie with a mother in fancy or with anyone else, man, God, or brute. It is ready for any foul deed of blood; it abstains from no food, and, in a word, falls short of no extreme of folly and shamelessness."[9]

The tyrant lives out these fantasies; that is, he enacts what must be restrained by good law but which, Plato recognizes, is all too human: "There exists in every one of us, even in some reputed most respectable, a terrible, fierce and lawless brood of desires, which it seems are revealed in our sleep."[10]

The tyrant's hubris lies in his excesses and in his lack of control: "Then a man becomes tyrannical in the full sense of the word, my friend, 'I said,' 'when either by nature or by habits or by both he has become even as the drunken, the erotid, the maniacal.' "[11] The tyrant is in his waking life "what he rarely became in sleep."[12] And again: "He [the tyrant] is, I presume, the man who, in his waking hours, has the qualities we found in his dream state."[13]

Plato's theory of leadership thus describes a movement along a continuum of control, from the prevalence of the good and virtuous (controlled and adaptive ego strengths) in an aristocracy, to the dissolute and wanton pursuit of pleasure (the emergence of normally repressed impulses and the breakdown of creative sublimations) in oligarchies and democracies, to the lawless and unbridled passions (pure id) of despotism. His argument is psychologically astute, for it recognizes the place of the tyrant's passions in the dream of the good and the just. Hubris is excess or, in our terms, enactment. Just laws build in control so that virtue can flourish. But the good is fragile. Children, especially, can be born out of season and mediate the unravelling of the controls of the inner demons.

ALCIBIADES

Plutarch (A.D. 46–120) was a historian, who discussed the leading political figures of ancient times in his monumental work entitled *The Lives of the Noble Grecians and Romans*,[14] which encompasses biographies of fifty-one of the noblest Greeks and Romans of the five centuries before Christ. Each *Life* gives a detailed description of the military, political, and personal achievements of its subject and devotes attention to his style of leadership, his motivation(s), and the interplay of his personality with the character of his followers. Plutarch, who seems to have had a strong platonic conviction of right and wrong, discussed the leaders of ancient times from a moralistic point of view and was quick to add his own impression of how good or bad each leader was as a human being. He often attributed the success or failure of a particular leader to how good, virtuous, or respectful of laws that leader was. The *Lives* shows Plutarch's great awareness of how an individual leader's psychodynamics, or even psychopathology, organizes his style of leadership. Personal characteristics, such as ambition, virtue, cruelty, revenge, commitment, and innate talent all played a major part in the success or failure of leaders in ancient times. Plutarch described every conceivable psychological characteristic known to man, blending narration of achievements with a discussion of psychological traits in his own personal style. We regard Plutarch as the first psychohistorian in the Western world.

In terms of modern psychology, it is of interest that the only factors which Plutarch clearly omits from his discussions are those concerning childhood. He says little about the childhoods of the political figures he treats in the *Lives,* making only general statements concerning their lineage. Although unconscious factors are not discussed as such, Plutarch often offers dreams or other psychological mechanisms to illustrate the complexities of the phenomena he discusses.

Although Freud lived eighteen centuries later, Plutarch's psychology is definitely a conflict psychology, in terms of his examination of the human situation. He presents his heroes as continually struggling with two conflicting emotions or states, of which one is usually good and the other evil. Man struggles not only between the virtues, but also between two different and conflicting emotional states.

In order to illustrate Plutarch's method, we shall use his discussion of Alcibiades, surely one of the most interesting political leaders of ancient times. He illustrates, in our opinion, a controversial yet brilliant leader.

Alcibiades was born in Athens in 450 B.C. and died in Phrygia (now Turkey) in 404 B.C. He was born with "a silver spoon in his mouth," of noble origin (he was distantly related to the famed Pericles), a most promising, intellectually brilliant, physically strong, extremely handsome, and very courageous young man, a marvellous orator with an excellent sense of humor, but also a self-centered and impulsive individual. The only known fact about his childhood is that his father, Clinias, was killed in the battle of Coronae when Alcibiades was only three or four years old. Pericles, who was busy in Athenian politics, became his guardian, and one wonders how much time he had for Alcibiades. Considering the kind of outstanding qualities that nature bestowed on him, it was not surprising that the famed Socrates took a keen interest in him and took him under his wing early in Alcibiades' youth.

There is no question that Alcibiades was an extremely gifted leader. He was a military genius, who never lost a battle regardless of whose side he was on. It seems, however, that whenever he had achieved an ambition and become revered by his fellow men, he would do something impulsive which gratified his immediate needs but which was self-destructive in the long run. One can only wonder what would have happened to Athens if the military had followed Alcibiades' advice in the war with Sparta. But by that time his reputation had become so tarnished that even though his military genius was intact, the Athenians no longer believed in him.

Let us examine his life in more detail. In his youth, according to Plutarch's account, Alcibiades possessed a thirst for knowledge, yet he was easily caught by pleasure and overcome by temperamental feelings. While in grammar school, he was known to have struck a teacher. When, as a child, Alcibiades once wanted to speak to his guardian, Pericles, and was told that he could not because Pericles was busy counseling how to give his accounts to the Athenians; Alcibiades said as he went away, "Were better for him to consider how he might avoid giving up his accounts at all."[15] He once gave a box on the ear to a wealthy and noble man, Hipponides. He had no quarrel with Hipponides; he did it only as a jest, because he had told his peers he would do it. He later felt ashamed of his action and went to the nobleman's home, took off his clothes, and asked Hipponides to beat him up as much as he pleased. Hipponides laughed and forgave him; as a matter of fact, Alcibiades later married his daughter. To use current terminology, it seems that Alcibiades was an impulsive youngster who was looking for love and acceptance and was without consistent adult guidance.

Alcibiades' vanity and ambition made him easy prey for those who wanted to use him. He would get inflated ideas about his political strength, and it took the patience of Socrates to humble and correct him and to show him how far from perfection in virtue he was.

As Plutarch said, "He possessed the people with great hopes, and he himself entertained yet greater."[16] When Alcibiades entered public life, he was thought to have great advantages; his noble birth, wealth, courage, and charisma were unmistakable. In 420 B.C. he became a general and opposed the aristocrat Nicias. He led an Athenian armada to Sicily and won the first battle easily. However, he was accused by his enemies of profaning the busts of Hermes throughout the city. He was recalled to Athens for trial. He escaped to Sparta, where he was highly regarded and helped the Spartans win the war against Athens. He changed his personal habits to conform to the Spartan way of life, giving up "high living" and easily gaining the Spartans' respect and affection. However, Alcibiades could not leave well enough alone. While the Spartan King Agis II was away on a military expedition, Alcibiades had an affair with the king's wife and had a son by her. As a result, he had to flee Sparta. He joined the archenemy of the Greeks, the Persians. He charmed the Persian king, who hated Greeks passionately, and helped the Persians in their wars with the Greeks.

Later, in 411 B.C., Alcibiades returned to Athens and helped her in some dramatic military victories. Forgiven by the Athenians for his past activities, he was welcomed in Athens as a hero. "Nevertheless," says Plutarch, this public joy was mixed with some tears, and the present happiness was allayed by the remembrance of the miseries they [the Athenians] had endured."[17] There remained much suspicion of Alcibiades, and upon the first opportunity his enemies invented a malicious story about him which, according to Plutarch, was factually incorrect. Alcibiades had to flee again, this time to Turkey, where he was later assassinated, supposedly by the Spartans. Sparta conquered Athens, and the one leader who might have prevented this had to escape shamefully. As Plutarch said,

> If ever a man was ruined by his own glory, it was Alcibiades. For his continual success had produced such an idea of his courage and conduct, that if he failed in anything he undertook, it was imputed to his neglect, and no one would believe it was through want of power.[18]

Alcibiades was probably the most gifted Athenian leader of his generation, during an era which is considered the golden age of Athens. He was, however, an impulsive, self-centered man and a pleasure-seeker who lived from moment to moment during peacetime. He showed his courage and talent best during crisis periods. He was not a cruel person, and although a traitor to his homeland, he nonetheless rose to Athens's help when he believed her survival was at stake. He was a man who could be quite generous at times, but his unpredictability made people mistrust him. In addition, his numerous talents created intense jealousy and hatred among some. He believed in his own right to succeed without modulating and moderating his own fantasies. Were his seeds of self-destruction too strong for him to overcome? Or would he have succeeded under different circumstances? It is possible that he was simply too gifted for his own good, as well as for that of his fellow men, and that his inordinate talent did not allow him to develop a sense of proportion. Things came so easily for him that he might have believed that it was his divine right to lead and govern. All this may have prevented him from dealing with failures which were of his own making. The crises which he did create did not seem to teach him anything, but rather only strengthened his sense of superiority over others. His child-like belief in his own invulnerability caused him to exaggerate his capacities as well as to underestimate his personal enemies. His continuous search for glory, together with his unmasked ambition, formed a deadly combination which allowed for no compromise with his followers.

Nothing seemed impossible for him, but in the end, he simply ran out of impossible tasks and was assassinated.

NOTES

1. Plato, *Republic,* trans. Paul Shorey, 2 volumes (Cambridge: Harvard University Press, 1963), II, 245–246.
2. Ibid., 251.
3. Ibid., 255.
4. Ibid., 275.
5. Ibid., 287.
6. Ibid., 291.
7. Ibid., 301–303.
8. Ibid., 333.
9. Ibid., 335–337.
10. Ibid., 339.
11. Ibid., 343–345.
12. Ibid., 349.
13. Ibid., 353.
14. Plutarch, *The Lives of The Noble Grecians and Romans,* trans. John Dryden, (New York: Modern Library, 1964).
15. Ibid., 237.
16. Ibid., 244.
17. Ibid., 257.
18. Ibid., 259.

THE HEROIC PERIOD IN PSYCHOHISTORY

CHARLES B. STROZIER AND DANIEL OFFER

Most fields have their time of great beginnings when "classics" are produced and bold ventures are made into the unknown areas of investigation that were perhaps once glimpsed but never fully explored. Freud, for example, always said that the poets had long intuitively understood his ideas, which he simply made available in scientific terms for the average mortal. Works that evolve from heroic periods appear glorious at the time and only later tarnish somewhat. Thus the first English novels of the eighteenth century interest professors of literature more than they do the average reader, and Max Weber requires patient determination on the part of the contemporary student of sociology. There are some nice exceptions to this general rule—Plato surely reads better than any modern philospher—but the rule still holds. Furthermore, classic periods characteristically generate obsession over method as the new search proceeds. There is no single treasure on a lost island, the existence of which can be keyed on a simple map; the islands in a sense themselves must be created in a whole new world of cartography.

It is the standard view that Freud and his circle put so much emphasis on understanding history, art, literature, religion, and culture generally because, in that early period, they lacked sufficient numbers of patients to discuss psychoanalytic issues among themselves with any degree of scientific rigor. Their real interests were clinical and theoretical, while psychohistory and psycholiterature were merely surrogates.[1] But such a view unduly minimizes the deep commitment of the early Freudians to explore the hidden motives and deeper meanings of everything human. The world of the consulting room mattered in special ways (it was the laboratory), but the data it yielded lacked broad theoretical significance unless also applied to culture in the broadest sense. Psychohistory for the early Freudians was not trivial; everything hung on it.

Freud's own decade of splendid isolation and his break with Wilhelm Fliess merged into the conscious shaping of a movement in 1902. It was then that he first asked a number of colleagues influenced by his work to attend meetings in his house on Wednesday evenings. For the first four years, no record exists of the proceedings. From 1906 on, however, Otto Rank dutifully kept thorough notes on the discussions, which continued on a regular basis until 1911 and after that fitfully until 1933 (after 1918 there is no record of the scientific discussions). Rank's notes, wonderfully enough, were saved from the Nazis by Paul Federn. Herman Nunberg and Paul Federn's son, Ernst, later transcribed, translated, edited, and published the notes in four volumes. These *Minutes of the Vienna Psychoanalytic Society* thus provide a unique glimpse into the first group for applied psychoanalysis.

The discussions were diverse and often heated. On December 4, 1907, Isidor Sadger presented some psychoanalytic thoughts on the poetry of Konrad Ferdinand Meyer. Max Graf led the discussion by dismissing Meyer as an insignificant poet and Sadger as "quite careless in supporting his hypotheses and theses." Wilhelm Stekel labeled Sadger's work as "surface psychology" and expressed the fear his work would "harm our cause"; according to Stekel, Sadger's presentation was "nonsense," not to mention inelegant: "the relationship to his mother should have been indicated just once and discretely, not emphasized in such an obtrusive manner." Otto Rank tried to find some redeeming virtues in Sadger's presentation but was quickly drowned out by Paul Federn, who was indignant about Sadger's failure to discuss Meyer's sexual development. "Sadger has not said a single word about the poet's sexual development," Federn opined,

> because one just does not know anything about it; therefore, one cannot write a pathography. Meyer must have had significant sexual experiences. A neurotic person [that is, Sadger] has recognized from Meyer's work the incestuous relationship to his sister. Meyer was probably an onanist and was ashamed of this before his mother.

Fritz Wittels, sensing that things were getting out of hand, expressed chagrin at "the personal outburst of rage and indignation on the part of Stekel and Federn." Freud also advised moderation but went on to

express the view that "Sadger's investigation has not clarified anything." Freud then gave his own thumbnail sketch of Meyer's personality, his development, and the meanings of his poetry. A chastened
Sadger had the last word. He had hoped for more than invective and
insult, he said. Furthermore, he had learned nothing from the substantive criticisms. "It is not possible accurately to deduce a poet's real
experiences from his works because there is nothing to distinguish the
real from the illusory; one does not know where truth ends and poetic
imagination begins."[2]

A little less than a year later—on October 14, 1908—it was Stekel's
turn to be chastised. His presentation dealt with a play by Franz Grillparzer, *Der Traum, ein Leben* ("A Dream is Life"). We learn from Rank's
notes that Stekel apparently approached the play as a source of data
from understanding the suffering and neurosis of Grillparzer himself.
Stekel concluded that Grillparzer was a compulsive neurotic. The discussion was, at first, gentle, by the standards of this group. Federn saw
in the presentation "the whole Stekel, with all his faults and his merits.
With his customary lack of critical judgment, Stekel jumbles up everything, and is utterly arbitrary about details." Reitler, however, liked the
presentation and mentioned several interesting aspects of it. He was
echoed by Wittels, Steiner, Rie, Sadger, and Rank.

Then Freud spoke. Not only did he disagree with the diagnosis, he
felt there was "not the slightest evidence that Grillparzer was an obsessional neurotic." Furthermore, Freud felt Stekel had "misunderstood"
the question of Grillparzer's sexuality and his method was too "radical"
and wildly indiscriminate. Freud's critical views seemed to influence the
remaining commentators—Albert Joachim, Adolph Deutsch, Edward
Hitschmann, and Alfred Adler—who were all, except for Deutsch, quite
outspoken in their dislike for the paper. Joachim doubted Stekel's method, on the grounds that "an artist's creating resembles only in part that
of the neurotic." Hitchmann sarcastically criticized Stekel's argument.
How, he wondered, could Grillparzer feel constrained in love as an
adult because he had not possessed his mother as a child, when "very
many men do not possess their mother, and yet do not become sexually
impotent"? Adler ended the attack by charging that Stekel had ar-
bitrarily lined up single elements in the Grillparzer play and then completely botched the interpretation. Stekel, in his "last word," thanked
only "the professor" and noted that the paper had fulfilled its purpose
because it had served as the occasion for Freud's reply.[3]

Such extraordinary deference to Freud, as well as the harsh bickering among the members of the group, suggests that the interaction of its
participants is as interesting a psychohistorical model of leadership as
anything they discussed. Freud's presence was everywhere. The group

was meeting in his house to discuss his ideas on his terms. The bickering, one senses, was done to gain approval from Freud, whose nod one way or the other in the middle of a discussion shifted its direction decidedly. Failure to perform well in Freud's opinion appears to have resulted in expulsion, though the exact reasons for the fluidity of membership remain in doubt.[4] Certainly, it was exacting to stay in such a group, meeting weekly, under constant scrutiny, and feeling always obliged to defer to Freud.

And there was that urn. Until 1908, the name of each member of the group was written on a piece of paper and placed in an urn. After the presentation, everyone present was obliged to comment in the order in which his name was randomly drawn from the urn. The idea was Freud's, who wanted to avoid letting any one person monopolize discussion and to encourage some self-discipline in the members. The pedagogical meaning, however, was that "the professor" was subtly grading his pupils/followers on a weekly basis specifically in relation to their understanding of his theories. It is no wonder the members of the group spoke of the tyranny of the urn. Federn even reported later that many members of the group were sneaking out of the meetings after the presentation and before discussion to avoid having their name drawn.[5] It is no wonder that the first proposal in the 1908 "Motions Concerning the Reorganization of the Meetings" was to abolish the urn. In the meeting during which the motions were discussed, February 5, 1908, there was some sharp exchange on most of the proposals. The first motion (to abolish the urn), however, carried unanimously.[6]

From our comfortable perspective, it is rather easy to see the underlying tension in the Vienna group and, as is often done in biographies of Freud, to unmask him for imperiously imposing his personality on the group and forcing submission to his ideas. This aspect of the early psychoanalytic group lent it the quality of a religious, or at least an ideological, movement. Strenuous disagreement was allowed, even encouraged, but real dissent required a complete split and separation from Freud. There was a clear and forceful leader in this group, a leader, furthermore, who manipulated his followers and enforced submission. The followers psychologically bought into this process as they idealized Freud the man and the exciting new ideas of psychoanalysis. In Freud's own subsequent formulation of such relationships, the followers came to share a common ego ideal in Freud and in this sense blended their differing and contentious personalities into a group that was given psychological coherence by the leadership of Freud.

Nevertheless, it is worth remembering that Freud was the one with original ideas in this group. There was also the reality of external derision for psychoanalytic theory. It took, perhaps, a measure of enforced group cohesion to keep things moving forward and to remain focused on relevant topics of research and discussion. Nor were the members of the group wholly naive regarding the tyranny of Freud's leadership role. They rebelled against the urn. The meetings even moved out of Freud's home in 1908. Many presentations sharply diverged from Freud's ideas, and so much remained unexplored that neither Freud nor his followers could easily define a single, orthodox line to follow. Stekel, for example, in these early years, was always refreshingly odd. The group process, whatever else it did, also fostered a remarkable creativity in the group.[7]

One example is the meeting of November 25, 1908. The presenter was Otto Rank, who outlined his ideas on the myth of the birth of the hero. This impressive study, later a book, examined the curious similarity between the founding myths of diverse nations and the recurring elements in the hero's birth and childhood, namely, that he is of noble birth but is early on cast out, usually in water, then rescued and raised in humble circumstances by kind foster parents, and later rises from his obscurity and achieves fame and glory. Rank argued that these common themes in mythology have reference in the universality of childhood fantasies. After some desultory discussion, Freud made a number of strikingly brilliant observations that later spawned at least two of his books—*Totem and Taboo* and *Moses and Monotheism*—as well as the theory of anxiety that he came to formally only in the 1920s.[8]

In fact, it was not uncommon for the presentation to be searching and wide-ranging. On May 8, 1907, Adolf Deutsch discussed a young poet, Walter Calé, who had recently committed suicide. Deutsch saw Calé as "characteristic of all brooding young autoerotics" and of those who are melancholy. Deutsch found proof of the connection between Calé's "nervousness" and his melancholy in his play, *Klingsor*, composed when he was seventeen, in which Klingsor castrates himself to acquire power. Deutsch also discussed Calé's love poems to his sister, and he notes that it was perhaps a consummated relationship, since there is so much guilt and atonement in the poetry. Deutsch guessed that Calé transferred his love for his mother to his sister, love which was probably consummated but offered no way out of its inherent conflicts. "He [Calé] could neither escape to another woman," Deutsch concluded, "nor find salvation in a homosexual love. Thus he chose suicide."[9] The discussion of Deutsch's presentation was desultory, except for Freud's comments, which elaborated on the influence of the mother on all subsequent relationships for men. Freud's evidence for this general point came from Goethe, and he concluded:

> Such conditions of love are found in everybody; all of them go back
> to infantile life. The path of love—that is, or the normal psychosis—
> is chosen in order to avoid other paths which would otherwise lead

to more serious neuroses. The histories of marriage are extremely interesting: many marry to punish themselves.[10]

Poetry and poets in general fascinated this first psychoanalytic group, and no one had more interesting comments to make on the subject then Freud. For example, on January 13, 1909, Freud severely criticized the inimitable Stekel for claiming that all poets were hysterics. Freud noted that Stekel misunderstood the nature of repression, which was, in his opinion, "a general property, not only of all neuroses, but also of other psychic processes." Furthermore, Freud noted, some great writers, like Zola, have been paranoiacs or obsessional neurotics, and many have been quite decidedly normal, like Schiller. We really know nothing about the sexual precociousness of poets, Freud concluded, for we know so little about love or sexual precocity.[11] In this discussion, Freud used the evidence from literature to make a number of important theoretical observations on hysteria, repression, psychosexual development, and normality. Sometimes nonclinical evidence went the other way, so to speak, and was introduced as relevant data in an otherwise purely theoretical discussion. For example, on November 21, 1906, Philipp Frey presented "On the Megalomania of the Normal Person." This topic prompted Max Kahane to discuss the megalomania of poets, actors, and artists, as well as of nations and even religions, i.e., of the Jews as the "chosen people." Freud added, perhaps with tongue in cheek, that he had long been struck with the megalomania of scholars whose attainments fall short of their expectations. "They replace their actual shortcomings," he noted, "with exaggerated self-esteem."[12]

Literature was the most important nonclinical source of data for these early analysts.[13] But, in a real sense, the world was theirs to investigate. On January 27, 1909, Hugo Heller presented "On the History of the Devil," which was actually a review of a book on the subject. Heller opened up the topic for psychoanalytic discussion when he noted that the chief interest of the subject of the devil is that it provides an arena in mass psychology for testing Freud's theories of individual psychology. The discussion that followed ranged from ideas of the devil as "a compendium of all that was condemned by the growing civilization," as a screen, in Adler's words, for an emphasis on the lewd male sexuality of the devil and the grossly distorted female sexuality of witches, both of which seem to derive from the father and mother (Sadger), to the notion that the devil is more purely genital, that is, is a penis (Wittels), to the idea that

> The Devil, in the completed shape in which he stands before us today, represents, one might say, the personification of the unconscious and repressed instincts, of the repressed sexual components of man, down to the last detail (e.g., anal erotism) (Freud).[14]

At times the group dealt directly with politics and leaders other than cultural or literary figures. On April 10, 1907, Fritz Wittels presented a paper on Tatjang Leontiev, a Russian revolutionary figure who had tried to assassinate a top czarist figure. His presentation might well be considered, for better or worse, the beginning of psychojournalism, a subfield of psychohistory kept alive in much of political science and in the CIA. Wittels compared Leontiev to a long list of female assassins, beginning with biblical figures (including Jael, who killed Sissera by driving a nail through his temple, and Judith, who beheaded Hologernes) and proceeding through, oddly enough, Joan of Arc. The choice of antecedent, however, is a little clearer in light of Wittels' interpretation. Jael's nail, for Wittels, "is a penis symbol." The case of Judith, who used a sword to behead Hologernes in anticipation of his raping her, is similar: This act liberated

> the cry of the flesh to accomplish also a praiseworthy deed. What gratification under the cloak of an idealistic motive. . . . She may also be a virgin because blood must flow during the deed which she plans to commit. When her father was leading her to her wedding, she looked up to him and said, "Surely, Mannasseh looks quite different." Here, for the first time, the importance of the father is indicated. We can readily assume that in all these cases the girl's first sexual affection for her father plays its role; for this love is indeed always rejected.[15]

The discussion indicated that the group had a more reasonable sensitivity to political reality than Wittels' presentation would suggest. Both Adler and Freud, were disturbed at Wittels' failure to assess adequately the political context of a revolutionary figure. Adler stressed that ideology cannot be divorced from emotional life; ideology, he continued, cannot explain everything, though ideology itself can be analyzed. Freud was concerned with the harshness of Wittels' condemnation of assassins and noted the limits of such unmasking of unconscious motives. A sound interpretation, he said, requires a certain tolerance for such hidden emotions. Nevertheless, Freud had begun his comments affirming the basic line of thought in Wittels' interpretation. "It is the suppressed erotism," he said, "which puts the weapon in the hand of these women. Every act of hate issues from erotic tendencies. Repudiated love, in particular, renders this transformation possible."[16]

Two years later, these general issues were joined again when Adler gave a presentation on the psychology of Marxism. The available summary of Adler's paper is unusually thin, which makes it difficult to characterize. But it seems that Adler stressed the instinctual basis of altruism, which "spreads over innumerable relationships in life." The defensive nature of altruism as a reaction formation links psychoanalytic and Marxian thinking on consciousness. "Among the proletariat," Adler continued, "it [the referent is vague, unfortunately] exists with regard to every kind of degradation, and is the affect that lies at the root of class consciousness."[17] Freud warmed to Adler's way of thinking and elaborated somewhat on the tension between repression and civilization that foreshadows *Civilization and its Discontents* two decades later.[18] Otherwise, the discussion drifted off into prosaic thoughts like those of Federn, who noted that Marx and Freud both offered ways for people to free themselves from Christianity.[19]

The content of the Vienna group's discussion thus ranged far and wide, though the purpose was always focused—to apply Freud's thought to culture, art, literature, and history. From the very beginning, it was apparent to the members of the group that they faced special problems of method. The term that emerged early on to designate the way that they were approaching the study of the individual poet, artist or historical figure was "pathography," or, as the editors of the *Minutes* put it, "a biography written from a medical point of view with particular attention to psychic anomalies."[20] The term "pathography" was in common intellectual coinage then, but it clearly captured the assumptions and method of the Vienna group with particular accuracy. Isidor Sadger, for example, made a number of presentations in the early years on the sexual and emotional pathology of poets as part of his larger medical study of hereditary predisposition.[21] Freud, as usual, set the tone. In his presentation near the end of 1909 on Leonardo da Vinci, he noted parenthetically but obviously (for this group) that: "We shall, of course, first inquire into the man's sexual life in order, on that basis, to understand the peculiarities of his character."[22]

The methodological notion is that the rules of the clinic spill over to culture. Sadger, noted unabashedly that he wrote pathographies "purely out of medical interest, not for the purpose of throwing light on the process of artistic creation, which, by the way, remains unexplained even by psychoanalytic interpretation."[23] Freud guarded against any mechanistic applications of his ideas on the neuroses to classify culture material, but he never questioned that psychoanalytic theory can be used to illuminate "pathographic material."[24] The only one of the Vienna group ever to raise a serious methodological objection to the group's approach to psychobiography was Max Graf, who once distinguished a case history from a psychological portrayal. "The case history," he said, "is a pathography and it is only possible where the sources are rich *and* when pathology exists. Pathography, however, tells little of the creative process." To understand that, he noted, "requires the artistic sensitivity of Freud himself."[25] It was an astute observation which, however, lost its methodological punch in Graf's apparent desire to ingratiate himself with Freud.

Nevertheless, there was some sensitivity to the limits of applying psychoanalytic theory. The group thus knew they were searching for clinical relevance in the nonclinical world. If they were not exactly humble about that, they were often cautious. No one could get away unscathed in talking about repression in reference to a nation's psychic life.[26] Furthermore, Freud recognized a fundamental methodological distinction between his enterprise and that of what we should now call the social sciences and humanities. Freud believed that psychology was ultimately grounded in biology and chemistry. He abandoned his "Project for a Scientific Psychology" only becuase he knew too little of brain function and neurological processes at the cellular level to carry forward his investigations fully. Instead, he turned to a world of methaphors in psychology. His life's work, as he said later with a degree of false humility, was only a detour. History and literature, however, are not way stations to a deeper, more fundamental reality in the natural sciences. Freud knew that, even if he sometimes acted otherwise, and whether or not the group seemed to realize it at all.

Freud's Vienna dicusssion group spawned numerous psychohistorical investigations in the following two decades. Freud himself drew direct inspiration from the discussions for at least five books: *Totem and Taboo* (1913), *Group Psychology and the Analysis of the Ego* (1920), *Civilization and its Discontents* (1930), *Woodrow Wilson* (1967), and *Moses and Monotheism* (1936). The work of the followers was directed into *Imago*, which was founded in 1912 and edited from then until 1927 by Otto Rank, the secretary of the earlier group. *Imago*, subtitled *"Zeitschrift für der Psychoanalyze auf der Geisteswissenschaften"* deserves special consideration.

Imago was published continuously between 1912 and 1937. Its emphasis at first was on literary topics, with frequent mention of religion and only occasional forays into history and issues of leadership. In this respect *Imago* closely reflected the orientation of the early group (of which, most of the authors represented in *Imago* had been members). Thus, in the first decade of publication, *Imago* published only 5 articles (out of a total of 138) that dealt with issues directly relevant to the concerns of this book. This figure would be approximately tripled if one were to include articles on religion and anthropology. Freud, for example, published *Totem and Taboo* in several parts in *Imago* as it emerged. Alice Balint submitted *"Der Familienvater"* in 1913, arguing that the prairie Indians were unable to resolve their Oedipus complex successfully and were therefore stuck, as a culture, in early adolescence. For the most part, however, *Imago* continued in its publication of formal articles in contrast with what had been looser and more wide-ranging in the Vienna discussion group. Isidor Sadger wrote for it a series of articles on poets that reflected his long-standing interest in pathographies. Ernest Jones wrote a two-part article on the psychology of salt. Theodore Reik analyzed humor. Lou Andreas-Salomé wrote on the "female type." The few gems we have in these years merit close scrutiny.

In the very first issue of the *Imago* in 1912, Carl Abraham wrote a psychoanalytic study of Amenhotep IV in which he focused attention on Amenhotep's religious activities, which, he argued, can be seen as the successful sublimation of the Egyptian monarch's aggression toward his father.[27]

Like that of many dynasties, Abraham wrote that Amenhotep's family history showed increasing decadence after initial strength. His forefathers were warriors who established a great Egyptian empire. His father, Amenhotep III, was a weak ruler whose prowess was as a hunter. The physically weak Amenhotep IV, last in the direct line, was a dreamer, whose history resembled that of Freud's neurotics.

Amenhotep IV's mother, Teje, surpassed his father in intelligence, energy, and beauty and she managed the government as Amenhotep III grew old, active as regent after he died. Abraham argues that Amenhotep IV's libido was clearly fixated on his mother and that, as in many such cases, the mother was substituted for by an adored wife, Nefertiti. Amenhotep IV never took a harem, contrary to custom, even when Nefertiti bore only daughters, and in surviving inscriptions and artwork he emphasized monogamous love. After Amenhotep III's death, Teje had begun to favor the worship of Aton over the traditional high god Amon. Amenhotep IV carried this further, completely replacing the god of his fathers with a new, single god: Aton. Typically, the father was rejected and replaced by an even more powerful figure. Aton was created by Amenhotep IV as a spiritual (not anthropomorphic) god of peace and accompanied by an ethos of peace and the sublimation of sadistic human offerings. He was represented as a sun whose rays ended in hands embracing the king. Amenhotep IV changed his name to Ikhnaton and called himself the son of Aton, just as neurotics often fantasize that they really have highborn fathers.

The only aggression in Amenhotep's reign, Abraham continues, was that against his father. He persecuted the Priests of Amon and had Amon's name erased from all inscriptions—which, of course, included inscriptions naming his father. When Teje died, Amenhotep buried her not beside his father, but in the tomb in which he expected to be buried himself. In fact, Amenhotep IV rejected much of the tradition his father had supported, even moving the capital city north toward the old lower Egypt.

Abraham concludes that Amenhotep IV religion of one god (to replace one father), a peaceful god of love (a father sharing his own personality), represents a successful sublimation. His choice of Aton in particular is significant: the sun is often a father figure (it is a single one, unlike the myriad stars, and its warmth represents love), and Aton was related to Adonis, who like Amenhotep IV, was young, died young, and preferred beauty to war. And, like the neurotic, Amenhotep IV lived in a dream world, ignoring the reality of evil and the necessity of protecting his empire.

Two years later, Ludwig Jekels produced another psychobiographical sketch in the pages of *Imago*.[28] This one dealt with the turning point in the life of Napoleon I. Jekels' concern in his article is to explain Napoleon's abrupt shift from Corsican to Frenchman. As a child, Napoleon had hated the French conquerors and invented schemes to overthrow them. He idealized Paoli, an older patriot who had been regent of Corsica before the French Occupation. But Napoleon returned to Corsica in 1793, when the king of France was out of power and the French had declared war on England. At that time Paoli was dishonored for his connections with England. Then, Napoleon abruptly accused Paoli of treason, took the side of his rival Saliceti, and, since the populace still supported Paoli, had his house burned and left Corsica. Jekels expressed disagreement with the traditional political explanation for this sudden shift of loyalties on the part of Napoleon. He claimed, instead, that a purely political explanation fails to explain the speed or intensity of the change in Napoleon's loyalties.

In this regard, Jekels argued that Napoleon's patriotism resulted from his bond with his mother, and that the earth itself, for Napoleon, was a mother figure. Thus, Napoleon's ideal was the patriotic woman of Sparta (his own mother was a Corsican patriot), and he insisted that it was wrong for sexual love to replace patriotism in the modern era. In general, the women in Napoleon's life were often mother substitutes, women who were older than he and often widows. Napoleon's mother was rumored to have had an affair with Marbeuf, the French Governor, who had befriended the family. As in both family and politics, outsiders conquered. Jekels notes that Napoleon in general hated women, with the great exception of Josephine, whose infidelity he accepted, although he demanded chastity in other women. While Napoleon was ambivalent toward his own father, he identified especially with Charlemagne, who also founded a dynasty and planned to conquer Spain and Italy. (Jekels notes that Napoleon's father's name was "Charles Marie.") Napoleon also took his father's role in the family after his father died and supported the family, even though he was the second son.

Jekels concluded that Napoleon's fixation on his mother and ambivalence toward his father are clear. The ambivalence led him to have two kinds of father figures—those of love and those of hate—Paoli, on the one hand, and Marbeuf and the king on the other. After the king was executed in January 1793, Napoleon was much more a Frenchman. The father who had kept him from his mother but had shared her with foreigners was now gone; now his Oedipal complex urged him to possess that mother. France before had symbolized Marbeuf (a rival) to Napoleon; now it meant his mother. Paoli had been the idealized father who protected his mother (Corsica) from a stranger. But after Louis was killed, Napoleon wanted all his father figures to fall, especially since Paoli supported the English, who had played the role of bringing foreigners to the mother. Napoleon thus turned against Paoli, thereby imitating his own father, who had abandoned Paoli when he (the father) worked with the French occupiers. From then on, Napoleon had no more patriotism for Corsica but had a series of mother substitutes (Italy, the Near East) he was driven to possess and authority figures he was driven to defeat. Thus, Jekels neatly links an event in Napoleon's personal history with significant large-scale political developments of the French Revolution. That the connections in Jekels' article are arbitrary and superficial goes without saying.

It was six more years before *Imago* published another psychohistorical article in 1920. This one was by Emil Lorenz and dealt with the question of political mythology.[29] Lorenz's concern was the psychology, or inner dynamics, of politics, and how in the quest for power rational and irrational motives mix.

A state, Lorenz argued, is founded both upon a sense of community among its citizens and upon a set hierarchy with a leader at its apex. Lorenz saw two forces at work, both of which mirrored the Oedipus complex: ambivalence toward the leader, who is a father figure, and love for the nurturing "motherland." In this regard Lorenz cited Livy's description of Brutus, who recognized that "the mother" mentioned in an oracle was the land, and proceeded to kill the tyrant ruler and to take his place, so that the ruler became the son and husband of the earth.

Then, oddly, Lorenz examined a series of plays by Schiller to develop his argument. These plays deal with regicide, revolution, and freedom fighting. In general, Lorenz saw the freedom fighter as the son of the land, fighting the father-tyrant and taking his place. He notes the frequency with which the freedom fighter is also an idiot figure (Brutus, Tell, Don Carlos), just as the hero of fairy tales is often the youngest or dumbest of the group. Lorenz believed that this relates to the child's game of pretended ignorance.

Lorenz went on to repeat that all rulers, priests, and magicians are father figures, and that the earth is the "mother" of all people, who are thus brothers. During revolutionary times, there is a return to the potency of the mother. If the people have a strong relationship to the land, libido freed by revolution can end up as loyalty or have other positive qualities. Where is no such strong relationship, however, the hatred directed at the ruler/father can lead to horrors like the barbarism of the French Revolution. Lorenz also argued that the negativism and the misogyny of assassins and revolutionaries is caused by their overpowering bond with their mothers.

Finally, Lorenz delineated three historical phases in the development of political realities. At first, monastic tribes had male leaders, but females were also worshipped. Then, stationary cultures were characterized by bonds to both the land/mother and the leader/father. Finally, mass movements arose when there was overpopulation and land could be bought and sold. These developments could lead to socialism and a new, leaderless, "female" community.

The scope of Lorenz's comments on politics was not to be repeated for some time in the pages of *Imago*. In the next couple of years there was a return to the more familiar and comfortable use of psychoanalytic theory in interpreting individual leaders. Thus, in 1921 J. C. Flügel wrote an interesting study of the character and life of Henry VIII.[30] According to Flügel, Henry VIII's marital problems were caused by three powerful and conflicting desires, all derived from the Oedipal complex: first, he required and hated rivals in love affairs; second, he desired and was repulsed by incestuous relationships; and third, he demanded that his women be chaste. Henry's Oedipal complex was particularly powerful because he was the son of a king and had seen his father neglect a beautiful wife; also, his mother's Yorkish relatives viewed her offspring as more legitimate rulers than the Tudor Henry VII. Henry VIII's feelings were transferred to his older brother, Arthur, whose widow, he married. Henry's father had also considered marrying Katherine of Aragon, thus making Henry, Henry's father, and Henry's brother sexual rivals.

When Henry became king, he achieved a balance between his egotistic and sexual desires, as exemplified by his self-assurance and his need for the pope's approval, respectively. However, the egotistical side of his character became dominant after his first divorce, when, as head of the Church of England, he became his own father/pope/God figure. His horror of Katherine seems to have been genuine—she was, after all, his sister—but he chose another sister as his next wife (he had had an affair with Anne Boleyn's sister Mary). Furthermore, while Anne had led Henry on for years, refusing to sleep with him, Henry grew bored with her almost as soon as they were married. He needed some hindrance to keep him interested, which Flügel argues is a fairly obvious oedipal need. The accusations which condemned Anne were Henry's own projections: that she had slept with her brother (as Henry had wanted to commit incest) and that she had planned to kill him (as Henry had wanted to kill his father and brother).

His next wife, Jane Seymour, was also a relative, whom Henry had met in her brother's house. While she was probably not a virgin, Henry shut his eyes to her past history. Jane died soon after the marriage. His next marriage, to Anne of Cleves, was political and was ended when Henry no longer needed a Protestant alliance. His next wife, Katherine Howard, was also beheaded for infidelity, this time undoubtedly real; Henry had blinded himself to her past sexual history and went through a personal crisis when he had to face the truth. Finally, Katherine Parr, twice widowed, was a nearly perfect match, given Henry's oedipal drives: she had been engaged to Jane Seymour's brother (and was thus a "sister"), and she shared his brother's wife's name. The historical record lends credence to Flügel's speculations on Henry VIII.

The next year William Boven published a study of Alexander the Great, which returned to the more exaggerated speculation of the earlier period.[31] Boven's goal was to discover the source of Alexander's megalomania, and he argued that Alexander conquered Asia basically as a compensatory effort to conquer his father.

Alexander was close to his mother, Olympias, who was reputedly involved with magic in certain erotic cults. There were rumors that she slept with strange beasts. She also hated her husband, Philip, who was both autocratic and unfaithful to her. Alexander was a promising boy—smart, talented, and brave—and competed actively with his father, taking satisfaction in being a better warrior.

When Philip took a new wife, Alexander's position as heir was threatened and he and his mother Olympias went into exile. Eventually, Alexander returned and regained his father's graces before the latter was murdered. Alexander began his reign with energy, first murdering any possible pretenders to the throne, and then proceeding with his ambitious conquests.

Boven contends that Alexander was in fact avenging his mother on his father. He notes that Alexander was famed for his kindness to women. On the other hand, he spontaneously murdered an old friend for praising Philip (again "killing his father"). As his megalomania grew,

Alexander claimed to be a son of Zeus, which was an obvious rejection of Philip and was perhaps based on Olympias's, cult activities. Eventually, Alexander placed himself with Heracles and Dionysius, below no one but Zeus himself, and he wanted his mother also to be given a place among the gods. Alexander's final triumph, then, over his father, Philip, came in the conquest of Asia, which he equated with his father.

In that same first decade of *Imago's* publication, a number of writers published psychoanalytic studies relating to leadership in other journals and some in full-length books. It was a time of general fertility in applied psychoanalytic work, after the closed period of the Vienna meetings but before the vast expansion of work after the late 1920s. For example, Hans Sachs wrote a short analysis of a dream that Bismarck had in 1863. Sachs published his article in the *International Zeitschrift für Psychanalyse* in 1913.[32] In the dream that Bismark reported in his journal, he was riding on an Alpine path that got progressively narrower, with a cliff on one side and a gorge on the other, until there was no room to go forward, turn around, or dismount. Bismarck got angry, hit the cliff on his left with his whip and called on God for help, at which point the whip got infinitely long and the cliff fell away like a curtain to reveal a road, a landscape like Bohemia with Prussian troops. The dream ended with Bismarck wanting to tell the king about it immediately.

On one level, Sachs interprets the dream as a masturbation fantasy: the whip is held in the left hand, meaning something is forbidden, and it grows to enormous length. But on another level, he argues that Bismarck was comparing himself to Moses, for, like Moses, he was trying to free an ungrateful people. The bible story in which Moses knocked against a rock and water sprang out is also partly sexual: Moses, acting against God's will, got the water but was punished. Bismarck's wish to tell the king what had happened was like bragging of a sexual conquest or asking for punishment—but he was protected because of the overt political message.

The Napoleons fascinated the early Freudians. Ernest Jones in the *Journal of Abnormal Psychology* in 1913, wrote about Louis Bonaparte, who he argued was worthy of study because he helped cause his brother Napoleon's downfall.[33] Napoleon, intending to bring Holland more completely under his control, had made Louis king of Holland in 1806. When Napoleon wanted a blockade against England, which would have been a great sacrifice for Holland, Louis took an independent, pro-Dutch position. Napoleon eventually absorbed Holland in the greater France, but chronic discontent persisted there until his overthrow.

Jones claims that Louis' incompetent political behavior was the result of introjection, and it mirrored his personal life and his relationship with his brother. Louis, Napoleon's favorite brother, had been educated by him personally, and was on his staff at an early age. When he was twenty, though, an attack of venereal disease led to a character change; from then on, he was a moody hypochondriac and complainer who constantly resigned from positions of leadership to go to spas. Napoleon's attitude toward Louis—first his overestimation, then his increasing annoyance—was in fact reasonable and consistent, but was interpreted by Louis as the vacillation of an overfond, overstern parent.

Louis' homosexual attraction to Napoleon was his main conflict. He was noticeably effeminate, which he counteracted by sexual exploits. Napoleon married Louis off to Josephine's daughter. The marriage was a failure, for Louis was jealous of Napoleon's fondness for his eldest son, who was rumored to be Napoleon's own. Louis sued for divorce at the same time Napoleon was divorcing Josephine, a decision which Jones sees as an indication of his feelings of identity with Napoleon. He was extremely bitter when Napoleon finally did have a son of his own.

In Jones' view, Louis' jealousy and delusions of persecution stemmed from his repressed homosexuality. In such cases, the original love turns to hate, and the hater then assumes that the love object hates him in return. Louis' alternating love and hatred for Napoleon were consistent with his syndrome, and his tendencies affected his behavior. For example, after having shown jealous suspicion that his wife had slept with Napoleon (which was probably not true), Louis claimed years later that Napoleon had never been unfaithful to Josephine, although that was known to be false. Jones concludes that Louis' obsession with his personal relationship with Napoleon kept him from being a competent leader.

In general, the widening scope of applied psychoanalytic work in the period from roughly 1912 to the mid-1930s seems to have represented an increase in the quantity of work that was done without significant advances in methodology or theoretical approaches.[34] In general, the interpretations now read as somewhat wooden and do not appear to have introduced new perspective. It was up to Freud to break new ground in psychoanalytic theory and in applied psychoanalytic work before psychohistory and the psychological study of leadership could move forward again after its creative beginnings in the first decade of the century.

NOTES

1. *Minutes of the Vienna Psychoanalytic Society*, ed. German Numberg and Ernst Federn, 4 volumes (New York, International Universities Press, 1962), I, xxviii.
2. Ibid., 254–58.

3. Ibid., II, 2–12.
4. See, for example, Freud's letter, ibid., I, 202–203.
5. Ibid., 299.
6. Ibid., 298–303.
7. Heinz Kohut, "Creativeness, Charisma, Group Psychology: Reflections on the Self-Analysis of Freud," in *The Search For the Self: Selected Writings of Heinz Kohut, 1950–1978*, ed. Paul H. Ornstein, 4 vols. (New York: International Universities Press, 1978), II, 793–843.
8. *Minutes*, II, 68–72.
9. Ibid., I, 190–91.
10. Ibid., 193.
11. Ibid., II, 103–104.
12. Ibid., I, 52–56.
13. Note in addition to the material already discussed, ibid., I, 111–18; II, 185–94; III, 188f., 210f., and 227f.
14. Ibid., II, 117–124; note also the discussion of magic, II, 126f.
15. Ibid., I, 160–61.
16. Ibid., 164.
17. Ibid., II, 173.
18. Ibid., 174.
19. Ibid., 174–78.
20. Ibid., I, 169.
21. Ibid., 98.
22. Ibid., II, 338–52.
23. Ibid., I, 267–68.
24. Ibid., 179–80.
25. Ibid., 259–69.
26. Ibid., 8, for example.
27. Karl Abraham, "Amenhotep IV. Psychoanalytische Beiträge zurn Verständis seiner Persönlichkeit und des monotheistischen Aton-Kultes," *Imago*, 1 (1912), 334–360.
28. Ludwig Jekels, "Der Wendepunkt im Leben Napoleons I," *Imago*, 3 (1914), 313–381.
29. Emil Lorenz, "Der Politische Mythos. Probleme und Vorarbeiten," *Imago*, 6 (1920), 402–421.
30. J. C. Flügel, "Charakter und Eheleben Heinrichs VIII," *Imago*, 7 (1920), 424–441.
31. William Boner, "Alexander der Grosse," *Imago*, 8 (1922), 418–439.
32. Hanns Sachs, "Ein Traum Bismarcks," *Internationale Zeitschrift für Psychoanalyze*, 1 (1913), 80–83.
33. Ernest Jones, "The Case of Louis Bonaporte, King of Holland," *Journal of Abnormal Psychology*, 8 (1913), 289–301.
34. Some additional studies of leadership by the early figures around Freud include: Paul Federn, *Zur Psychologie der Revolution* (1919); J. C. Flügel, *Men and Their Motives: Psychoanalytic Studies* (London, 1934); Eich Fromm, "Politik und Psychoanalyse," *Psychoanalytische Bewegung*, 2 (1930), 305–313; the English version of E. Hitschmann's essays, *Great Men: Psychoanalytic Studies* (New York): International Universities Press, 1956); Ernest Jones, "Psycho-Analyze Roosevelts," *Zentralblatt für Psychoanalyse*, 2 (1912), 675–677; W. Lange-Eichbaum, *Genie Irrsim, und Ruhn* (Munnich, 1928); Oskar Pfistar, *Sie Frömmigkut des Grafen Ludwig von Zimzendorf* (Leipzig, 1910); Geza Roheim, "Killing the Divine King," *Man*, 15 (1915), 26–28; Hans Sachs, *Die Lebensgeschichte des Caligula* (Berlin, 1930). By the 1920s, and well into the 1930s, it became quite popular to undertake psychoanalytic studies of leaders. This category includes those influenced by Freud but not in direct contact with him, the early Vienna group, or a part of *Imago*.

A few representative authors (this is not a complete listing) includes: Hill Berkeley, "A Short Study of the Life and Character of Mohammed," *International Journal of Psychoanalysis*, 2 (1921), 31–53; F. Chamberlain, *The Private Character of Queen Elizabeth* (London, 1921); L. Pierce Clark, *Lincoln: A Psycho-Biography* (New York, 1933); N. Ach, *Über die Determinationpsychologie und ihre Bedeutung für des Euherproblem* (Leipzig, 1933); R. Behrendt, "Das Problem Führes und Mosse und die Psychoanalyse," *Psychoanalytische Benegung*, 1 (1929), 134–154.

REFERENCES

German, French, and Italian authors, not related to *Imago*, from *Psychological Abstracts* 1927–1939; *Psychological Index* 1894–1930; *Index of Psychoanalytic Writings*, ed. A. Grinstein, 5 volumes (New York: 1956).

Ach, N. *Uber die Determinationspsychologie und ihre Bedeutung für das Fuhrerproblem* (Leipzig: 1933).

Behrendt, R. "Das Problem Fuhrer und Masse und die Psychoanalyse," *Psychoanalytisehe Bewegung*, 1 (1929), 134–154.

Bergler, E. "Die Biographik macht der Psychoanalyse Konzessionen," *Psychoanalytische Bewegung*, 5 (1933), 501–512.

Bergier, E. "Motifs inconscients de l'attitude de Napoléon à l'égard de Tallyrand," *Revue Française Psychanalyze*, 6 (1933), 409–457.

Binet-Sanglé, C. *La Folie de Jésus* (Paris: A. Maloine, 1908).

Bloch, L. "Die Sexualethik Luthers," *Die neue Generation*, 9 (11), Feb., Mar., 1913.

Carrard, S. "Psychologie der Führung." *Psychologische Rundschau*, 1 (1929), 301–307.

Deri, M. "Caligula," *Psychoanalytische Bewegung*, 2 (1930), 400–407.

Fenichel, O. "Psychoanalyse der Politik," *Psychoanalytische Bewegung*, 4 (1932), 255–268.

Freund, H. "Helmut von Gerlach. Eine Politikeranalyse," *Internationale Zeitschrift für Individualpsychologie*, 7 (1929), 351–353.

Friedlander, R. "Wilhelm II. Eine psychologische Studie," *Die Umschau*, 1919, No. 13–17.

Gerling, R. "Dr. Martin Luther," *Zeitschrift für Menschenkunde*, 2 (1926), 6–18.

Hammer, W. "War Mohammed geisteskrank, fallsüchtig, oder mettersüchtig?" *Zeitschrift & Psychotherapie*, 8 (1922), 170–200 (another source has this as 8 (1924), 341–362).

Hentig, H. von. *Robespierre* (Madrid: Entorial Espana, 1930); and *Machiavelli* (Heidelberg: Carl Winters, 1924.

Kornfeld, H. "Die simulierte Geistesstörung König Davids," *Psychiatrie-Neurologie Wochenschau*, 9 (1907), 450–451.

Krauss, F. "Ein Traum König Karls," *Internationale Zeitschrift für Psychoanalysis*, 6 (1920), 347–350.

Ley, A. "Les méthodes de pathographie historiques et biographiques," *Journal belge de neurologie et de psychiatrie*, 34 (1934), 438–444.

Liertz, R. "Seelenkundliches zum Charakterbilde König Ludwigs II von Bayern," *Alligemeine Zeitschrift für Psychiatrie*, 82 (1925), 56–80.

Lindworsky, J. "Die charakterologische Bedeutung der Exerzitien des hl. Ignatius von Loyola," *Jahrbuch der Charakterolosie*, 1 (1924), 271–188.

Lomer, G. *Ignatius von Loyola* (Leipzig: J. A. Barth, 1913). (Note: Abstract in Dooley on English list.)

Ludwig, E. *Wilhelm der Zweite* (Berlin: E. Rowohlt, 1926).

Oppeln-Bronikowski, F. "Eros als Schicksal bei Friedrich dem Grossen und bei Stendhal." *Psychoanalytische Bewegung*, 2 (1930), 314–325.

Ostwald, W. *Grosse Männer* (Leipzig: Akademische Verlags, 1909).

"H. P." "Napoleon als Psychoanalytiker," *Zentralblatt für Psychoanalysis*, 4 (1914), 411–412.

Pick, R. "Zum Führerproblem," *Internationale Zeitschrift für Individuale-Psychologie*, 4 (1926), 368–371.

Portigliotti, G. "L'erotismo di papa Allesandro VI," *Rude Psicologie*, 11 (1915), 55–69.

Schaefer, H. *Jesus in psychiatrischer Beleuchtung* (Berlin: Ernst Hofmann, 1910).

Schestow, L. "Alexander und Diogenes," *Almanach*, 1931, 117–119.

Schneiter, C. "Ein Traum Julius Caesars," *Zentralblatt für Psychoanalysis*, 1 (1913), 80–83.

Vorberg, G. "Martin Luthers skatologische Ausdrucksweise und ihre Beziehung zur Persölichkeit," *Fortschrift Sexual Psychoanalysis*, 2 (1926), 526–528.

SIGMUND FREUD AND HISTORY

CHARLES B. STROZIER AND DANIEL OFFER

Freud's own formal efforts at applied psychoanalytic work covered an enormous range after the early period of incubation. Only music did not interest him. Just two of his books touched directly on questions of leadership: *Group Psychology and the Analysis of the Ego* (1921) and, with William Bullitt, *Thomas Woodrow Wilson: A Psychological Study* (1966 [1932]).[1] Leadership, if somewhat more broadly considered, however, was a major concern of Freud. His extensive theoretical writings on the Oedipus complex in a sense describe the psychological process of leading and following in a family. A study like that of Leonardo da Vinci in 1910 focuses on a major leader in the world of art. *Totem and Taboo* (1913) argues that the origins of civilization lay in the struggle with the clan leader of primitive cultures. *Civilization and Its Discontents* (1930) explores the complex mechanisms of guilt and repression in modern life that fuel the dynamics of mass behavior. And, finally, in his grand study of Moses, *Moses and Monotheism* (1939), Freud returned at the end of his own life to a leader who helped shape the beginnings of western civilization.

It would be futile and redundant, given the extensive literature on Freud, to review these writings in any systematic way. All are readily available and familiar to the literate public. We will attempt here only a few cursory generalizations that will cull from Freud's work the most relevant ideas for our purposes. Such an overview and analysis can only proceed on the assumption that the basic argument of the book in question is broadly familiar to the reader. Any other approach would swell an already large section to distinctly outsize proportions.

In terms of leadership, probably the single most important generalization to make about Freud's work is the centrality of the family model for him. The father of the family defines the psychological world of leadership; all else in metaphor. For Freud himself, this had great personal significance in his understanding of his own relationship with his father, Jacob, who died in 1897. It was his father's death that prompted Freud's own self-analysis. Of the many insights that emerged from that experience, none was of greater significance than his own ambivalence toward his father and, by extension, toward figures of authority in general. *The Interpretation of Dreams*, if read as an autobiography, shows Freud's intense unconscious struggle with the multiple meanings of leadership in his own experience.

The extent to which Freud's major dreams in *The Interpretation of Dreams* center on the interrelated issues of Freud's own rightness in response to criticism, and his ambitious assertiveness toward figures of authority, for example, is remarkable. In the Irma dream, Freud constructed an elaborate defense for himself in response to his preceived criticism from his friend, Otto, who had reported to Freud on the dream day that Irma, Freud's patient, was "better, but not quite well."[2] Freud's dream blames Irma, because she is recalcitrant, Dr. M., his senior colleague, whom Freud emasculates but who confirms his diagnosis, and Otto, who has really caused the problem anyway because he thoughtlessly gave a injection with a dirty syringe.[3] In the preamble to the Count Thun dream, Freud explains the slight he felt when the Austrian politician marched past him on the railroad platform on the way to an audience with the emperor. Count Thun waved aside the ticket inspector with a curt motion of his hand and without any explanation. Freud then situated himself on the same platform, hummed a rebellious tune from an opera, recalled the French comedy with the line about the great gentleman who had taken the trouble to be born, and pushed the train officials (without success) for a compartment with a lavatory. He also dreamed of revolution and associated to his dream of urinating in his parents' bedroom, to which his father's response was to say, "The boy will come to nothing."[4] As Freud noted, "This must have been a frightful blow to my ambition, for references to this scene are still constantly recurring in my dreams and are always linked with an enumeration of my achievements and success, as though I wanted to say, 'You see, I *have* come to something.'"[5]

Freud, however, realized in his self-analysis how his own—and therefore everyone's—rivalry with the male figure of authority in the family was rooted in his libidinal attachment for his mother. The favored son of a young mother, he was to say, has a special kind of self-confidence. The tension in mediating the young boy's love for his mother and the rivalry with his father are captured in the complex that Freud labeled after the story of Oedipus Rex. In the first formulation of the Oedipus complex (in *The Interpretation of Dreams*), Freud uses Hamlet's story to illustrate the deadening effect of overpowering ambivalence (Hamlet is "sicklied o'er with the pale cast of thought"). Hamlet can act in all ways except one: he cannot take "vengeance on the man who did away with his father and took that father's place with his mother, the man who shows him the repressed wishes of his own childhood realized."[6] The sense one has here, as well as in case histories like Little Hans, Dr. Paul Schreber, and the Rat Man, is that the boy's attraction for the mother has a thin edge of danger, but that the real family source of ambivalence, struggle, and competition lies in the relationship with father.

For it is the father, who is everyone's own private leader, who mediates the delicate transition from inner to outer, from psychology to politics, from the family to culture. Erikson, whose father abandoned his mother before his birth and who later, in his thirties, adopted himself as his own father (Erik, son of Erik), said of fathers, "A man must confront his childhood and, above all, give an account of his conflicts with his father."[7] And, further, leaders, who were once children, "*have* to become their own fathers and in a way their father's fathers while not yet adult. This spells special conflicts and special tasks."[8] If the mother regulates the private sources of the self—love and sex most of all—one can only become something in a public world in relation to the father. A nice clinical expression of this idea in Freud is the case of Little Hans, who literally could not leave home (mother) because of his phobia that the father/horse would bite him for falling down. The world was too dangerous even to enter until Hans could resolve his conflicts with his father.[9]

Hans was later reincarnated in Woodrow Wilson, whose excruciating ambivalence toward papa shaped (disastrously, in the view of Freud and Bullitt) the mapping of Europe in the Treaty of Versailles. Whatever indelicacies of exposition justify the attribution of actual authorship to Bullitt, there is equally no question that the ideas expressed in the book belong to Freud. Wilson thus never worked through the gnawing resentments that lay buried under his intense idealization of his impressive and articulate father; he simply acted them all out, first in the Princeton fight with Dean West, then with the world at Versailles. By then, time and disease had aggravated his own grandiosity and his ambivalence toward his father. He became the Jesus of the world in lieu of God and his dead father. The stage for his theatrical enactments shifted, but the psychological conflicts that cast the play never altered. Wilson's behavior was neurotic in Freud's view precisely because it carried the private family issues of the son's ambivalence toward the father directly into the public realm.

In Freud's view, the general family issues with the father cluster around certain core conflicts which can be clearly identified and form the basis for the prediction of behavior. For Freud, these conflicts were largely instinctive and drive-related in nature. They cannot be avoided. The libidinal attachment to the mother that generates rivalry with the father is, in a sense, encoded. Because they come so early and are so central, such conflictual beginnings necessarily carry over to the public realm. To paraphrase Lincoln, we cannot escape our own history. Freud's world is, in essence, one of conflict, in which normality is firmly rooted in pathology. The hidden and renounced in everyone are the pathological products of an average and expectable family environment. We may grow beyond our origins, but only with difficulty, and we are always subject to regression in the face of difficulties, and to what Freud called the return of the repressed.

Freud's is not a very hopeful model. As he commented in his introduction to the Wilson book,

> Fools, visionaries, sufferers from delusions, neurotics and lunatics have played great roles at all times in the history of mankind and not merely when the accident of birth had bequeathed them sovereignty. Usually they have wreaked havoc; but not always. Such persons have exercized far-reaching influence upon their own and later times, they have given impetus to important cultural movements and have made great discoveries. They have been able to accomplish such achievements on the one hand through the help of the intact portion of their personalities, that is to say in spite of their abnormalities, but on the other hand it is often precisely the pathological traits of their characters, the one-sidedness of their development, the abnormal strengthening of certain desires, the uncritical and unrestrained abandonment to a single aim, which give them the power to drag others after them and to overcome the resistance of the world.[10]

This pathological model also defined for Freud the misty orgins of culture itself. In *Totem and Taboo*, Freud argued that the powerful father dominated the primal horde and retained for himself sole possession of the women while excluding the young males. Resentment and envy eventually drove the other males to band together and kill the father.

This deed required massive repression and atonement, which Freud felt was the basis for religion and civilization. Freud's conclusions to the book stressed that these phylogenetic beginnings of civilization resulted in the neurotic's inhibition of action, in sharp contrast with primitive man, who is uninhibited and whose "thought passes directly into action," according to Freud. In other words, first there is historical reality, which for various reasons requires repression and the creation of new psychological structures. Culture and civilization as we know them evolve from this process. The residue of the historical event, however, appears imbedded ontogenetically in everyone's experience. The drives, according to Freud, activate ingrained phylogenetic memories which become, for the individual, fantasies of what the human race once acted out.[11]

Carl Jung pushed these ideas to their ultimate conclusion. But even with Freud, one cannot understand the individual in the family or in civilization generally without close attention to the deeply embedded unconscious memories from the group's collective past. As Kohut has often argued, Freud's model is an elegant and consistent whole. It all hangs on drives and the notion of pathology as a "normal" part of the soul (die Seele). What is true for the individual is likewise valid for the group. Ontogeny and phylogeny must logically and psychologically be interrelated. The problem is how to define the link. Fathers, presidents, and kings, must lead, and individuals and groups follow, largely in response to internal messages from long lost events. We are free, perhaps, but not quite as free as we might imagine.

Another feature of the family model for leadership in Freud's thinking was that it centered on maleness. For Freud, the leader in the family and politics, not to mention the broader spheres of culture, art, and civilization, is always male. Freud always examines the unfolding of the Oedipus complex from the boy's point of view, adding only parenthetically that the analogue of the boy's conflicts occurs in girls. Only in Lecture 33 of his *New Introductory Lectures* did Freud systematically review the question of femininity, which he considers a "riddle."[12] He argues that the clitoris is an atrophied penis, and that psychologically femininity seeks passive aims.[13] The real dilemma, however, for girls as opposed to boys, is the task of shifting libidinal excitation from the clitoris to the vagina and the special complications of exchanging the maternal for the paternal love object as the Oedipus complex unfolds. All this, in Freud's view, profoundly affects superego formation in girls, "which cannot attain the strength and independence which give it cultural significance."[14] Basically, it seems from Freud's argument, because psychosexual development is more complicated for females, they are more prone to neurosis. It is not a huge step in logic to assume that they would also be unfit to fill positions of leadership, either in the family or in politics.

Freud's most important and, in fact, his only systematic discussion of leadership was the 1921 monograph, *Group Psychology and the Analysis of the Ego*. The opening paragraph makes clear Freud's intention to use clinical psychoanalytic insights to understand group phenomena. It states the assumption that governed the Vienna meetings:

> In the individual's mental life, someone else is invariably involved, as a model, as an object, as a helper, an an opponent; and so from the very first individual psychology, in this extended but entirely justifiable sense of the words, is at the same time social psychology as well.[15]

Freud then dissects at length Gustave Le Bon's *Psychologie de Foules* (1895) as a way of separating his own views from those of the most significant thinker to date on the same issues. What most interested Freud about Le Bon's work was his idea of a primitive group mind. Groups, for Freud, reduce differences to their lowest common denominator, so that the individual seems to be lost in an almost hypnotic way. A group is impulsive, changeable, and irritable. As Freud had noted in *Totem and Taboo*, a group "cannot tolerate any delay between its desire and the fulfillment of what it desires. It has a sense of omnipotence; the notion of impossibility disappears for the individual in a group."[16] Furthermore, a group never doubts its sense of rightness or strength. It is both intolerant of differences and somewhat ironically obedient to authority. It demands leaders who are strong and even violent, seeking domination and oppression from them. "A group," for Freud, "is an obedient herd, which could never live without a master. It has such a thirst for obedience that it submits instinctively to anyone who appoints himself its master."[17] Freud discusses other theorists on the subject—such as W. McDougall, author of the 1920 study, *The Group Mind*—but finds nothing as evocative as Le Bon's study.

In a general sense, the fundamental fact of group behavior for Freud lies in the interrelated ideas of intensification of affect and inhibition of intellect as the psychological influences on individuals in groups.[18] Both these aspects of group behavior are derived from the libidinal ties that bind people together in the mass: ". . . a group is held together by Eros, which holds together everything in the world."[19] To lose one's place in the group is terrifying, precisely because such loss threatens one's basic libidinal organization; group fear is thus directly analogous to anxiety in the individual.

> Fear in an individual is provoked either by the greatness of a danger or by the cessation of emotional ties (libidinal cathexes); the latter is the case of neurotic fear or anxiety. In just the same way panic arises either owing to an increase of the common danger or owing to the disappearance of the emotional ties which hold the group together; and the latter case is analogous to that of neurotic anxiety.[20]

The question then becomes how to define more precisely the exact nature of the libidinal ties among individuals in groups. This leads Freud to a discussion of identification, which "endeavors to mould a person's own ego after the fashion of one that has been taken as a model."[21] Identification describes both the first form of a tie with an object and a regressive substitute for a libidinal object relation. It may also, however, represent a "new perception of a common quality shared with some other person who is not an object of the sexual instinct."[22] It is in this "new" sense that identification serves as the basis of group cohesion. In this, and indeed in any of the meanings of identification, the loved object is placed within one's own ego as an ideal. In individual psychology, one can observe the force of such developmental structuralization in various breakdown products as homosexuality, depression, hypnosis, and the normal state of being in love (where the object is intensely idealized). In groups, there is a pooling of ego ideals in regard to the figure of the leader: "*A primary group of this kind is a number of individuals who have put one and the same object in the place of their ego ideal and have consequently identified themselves with one another in their ego.*"[23]

The leader of a group is thus heavily invested by all members of the group, whose attachment to their leader provides the raison d'être for their emotional survival. As such, a group revives the primal horde and its psychology is "the oldest human psychology."[24] A group regressively re-creates the original bonds in human affairs. In a phylogenetic sense, individual structuralization that establishes one's own object sources as an inner voice (the ego ideal) represents a differentiation of the primitive relation of group members to the idealized leader. It seems, however, to be a historical process marked by frequent backsliding.[25] We keep forming groups and creating idealized leaders.

In Freudian terms, therefore, leaders are not altogether welcome in human society. We suffer under them and bear the consequence of their actions. Collective pooling of ego ideals in a group forces regressive idealization of the external leader that is primitive and archaic in its form and meanings. Freud never addresses the specific role of the leader in enhancing this process. The leader seems to be created largely out of collective need, an almost accidental by-product of group process. Furthermore, the leader's power is immense, for the psychological bondage of groups to him gives license to all peremptory needs of the leader himself. Considering that Freud wrote this well over a decade before Hitler's rise this was an extraordinary insight.

NOTES

1. S. Freud and C. Bullitt, *Thomas Woodrow Wilson: A Psychological Study* (New York: Houghton Mifflin, 1966 [1932]).
2. Sigmund Freud, "Group Psychology and The Analysis of the Ego," in Vol. XVIII of *The Standard Edition of the Complete Psychological Works of Sigmund Freud*, ed. James Strachey (London: Hogarth Press, 1955).
3. Sigmund Freud, *The Interpretation of Dreams*, ed. James Strachey, one-volume paperback (New York: Avon Library, 1900), p. 139.
4. Ibid., 139–154.
5. Ibid., 241–247.
6. Ibid., 298–299.
7. Erik H. Erikson, *Gandhi's Truth: On the Origins of Militant Nonviolence* (New York: Norton, 1969), p. 123.
8. Ibid., 102.
9. Sigmund Freud, "Analysis of a Phobia in a Five-Year-Old Boy," *Standard Edition*, X (1909), 3–149.
10. Freud and Bullitt, *Wilson*, p. xvi.
11. Sigmund Freud, "Totem and Taboo," *Standard Edition*, XIII (1913), 9–162.
12. Sigmund Freud, *New Introductory Lectures on Psychoanalysis*, ed. James Strachey, paperback edition (New York: Norton, 1933), p. 113.
13. Ibid., 114–115.
14. Ibid., 129.
15. Sigmund Freud, "Group Psychology," *Standard Edition*, XVIII, 69.
16. Ibid., 77.
17. Ibid., 81.
18. Ibid., 88.
19. Ibid., 92.
20. Ibid., 97.
21. Ibid., 106.
22. Ibid., 108.
23. Ibid., 116.
24. Ibid., 123.
25. Ibid., 123.

ERIK H. ERIKSON, EGO PSYCHOLOGY, AND THE GREAT MAN THEORY

CHARLES B. STROZIER AND DANIEL OFFER

Of all the people influenced by Freud, Erik Erikson most creatively bridged psychoanalysis and history. He began as an artist, but in the 1920s was drawn into analysis with Anna Freud and eventually graduated from the last class of the Vienna Psychoanalytic Society in 1933. On the boat coming to America shortly afterwards, Erikson shared his essay on Hitler with the diplomat and historian George Kennan, who helped him to translate it into English. In America, Erikson soon established his reputation as a child analyst and became acquainted with people like Margaret Mead. In the late 1930s and 1940s he conducted a series of studies that culminated in his first book, *Childhood and Society* (1950). Since then, his interests have always included both the clinical and the historical.[1]

The range, not to mention the depth, of Erik Erikson's psychohistorical investigation is remarkable. There are three full-length biographical studies, of Martin Luther, Mohandas Gandhi, and Thomas Jefferson.[2] One is almost tempted to add Sigmund Freud to that list, for surely Erikson's scattered essays on the founder of psychoanalysis make up a monograph (though to pull the essays together would make for a rather disjointed book). In different articles and in parts of various books, Erikson has also dealt with William James, George Bernard Shaw, Albert Einstein, Adolf Hitler, Maxim Gorky, and, most recently, Jesus of Nazareth.[3] It is an impressive body of work, one focused on

49

issues of leadership but ranging across all the topics that concern the field of psychohistory today.

The sometimes bewildering diversity of Erikson's applied analytic work should not obscure an articulated theory of leadership that emerges in his writings. There is, first of all, the notion that the leader himself—there are no women in Erikson's corpus—is to be understood psychologically in terms of various vicissitudes in the eight stages of the life cycle. In theory, at least, a given life history unfolds epigenetically according to a psychosocial plan, and a hierarchy of "virtues" accrues to those who pass muster at each stage of life. Erikson's famous chart, in which developmental progress is plotted diagonally, attempts to capture as well the enduring effects of fixation, arrest, and regression.

The chart, however, also expresses the essential idea that growth and change occur throughout the life cycle. Nothing is immutable. Erikson's detailed discussion of Gandhi's mid-life crisis is perhaps his most complete elaboration of this concept. As a young man in South Africa, Gandhi had perfected his political style in *Satyagraha* (pressure for social and political reform through friendly passive resistance). But he had never used the hunger strike and had not yet developed resonance with the hundreds of millions of Indians yearning for political integrity and freedom from the British. Gandhi's first foray into this market was ambivalent and apparently inconsequential. He chose for his first Indian action a minor textile strike in Ahmedabad in 1918, which he infused with religious zeal and moral purpose by declaring a fast until death unless the workers received a thirty-seven percent increase in salary. Gandhi doubted the validity of his actions from the outset—he had to agree with the charge that the fast was more blackmail than legitimate—and in the end he reluctantly accepted a purely face-saving compromise to the strike. His personal punishment exceeded anything meted out by the owners, for he shortly suffered what amounted to a nervous breakdown. But like Abraham Lincoln, Gandhi learned from mistakes. In this great crisis of generativity, Gandhi found a proper voice with which to speak to his followers. He redefined Satyagraha. He discovered his own capacity for political and moral commitment. Neither he nor the British were ever again quite the same.

Most of Erikson's work, however, has focused on adolescence and its concomitant crisis of identity. Some would even say that he helped create the identity crisis as almost a rite of passage for adolescents, who seem to wear their crises on their sleeves, whether Edwardian or leather. But it is worth stressing that the detailed cases Erikson provides to illustrate the precise meaning of the identity crisis are historical. Martin Luther, one of the first examples Erikson cites, remains the most interesting. In 1505, on his way home from college while contemplating the choice of bride and career his father had made for him, Martin heard God call him to the faith during a thunderstorm and fled into the Augustinian order. In the monastery a kindly superior, Father Staupitz, listened patiently to Martin's compulsive confessions, guided him to think critically about the Scriptures, and, it seems, fell in love with him.[4] Martin weathered many emotional storms within himself during his "moratorium" before he posted his ninety-five theses on the Wittenberg Church door in 1517.

A less well known, but equally fascinating case that Erikson discusses to illustrate the identify crisis is that of George Bernard Shaw. At twenty, Shaw broke loose from an oppressive family and a good future in business and left Ireland to avoid the danger of success in business, which would be unequal to the enormity of his unconscious ambition.[5] He went to England, where he spent the next few years filling up five pages a day with turgid prose that led to five unpublished novels. It was, he said, his "professional apprenticeship."[6] As Erikson notes, Shaw managed to abandon unacceptable work without relinquishing the work habit. As Shaw himself noted, he worked as his father drank, and in the process he found a solid anchor in his mastery of the symbolism of paternal impotence.[7] Erikson concludes in one of his best passages on the place of work in identity formation:

> Man, to take his place in society, must acquire a "conflict-free," habitual use of a dominant faculty, to be elaborated in an occupation; a limitless resource, a feedback, as it were, from the immediate exercise of this occupation, from the companionship it provides, and from its tradition; and, finally, an intelligible theory of the processes of life which the old atheist, eager to shock to the last, calls a religion.[8]

Erikson elaborated his thoughts on Hitler in two works—*Childhood and Society* and *Young Man Luther*. Today, after all the psychohistorical writing on Hitler, Erikson's asides remain poignantly original. The adolescent Hitler was a troubled but intensely creative young man. He had one friend, August Kubizek, with whom he used to walk the streets of Linz. Hitler would talk passionately of art and literature, pausing occasionally to read his friend passages of his poetry from a small black book he always carried with him. But most of all, young Hitler talked of architecture and his dreamy plan to rebuild the city. "That house there was in a wrong position," he told Kubizek; "it would have to be abolished." Kubizek continued:

> "That street needed a correction in order to give a more compact impression. Away with this horrible, completely bungled tenement block! Let's have a free vista to the Castle." Thus he was always

rebuilding the town. . . . He gave his whole self to his imaginary building and was completely carried away by it. Once he had conceived an idea he was like one possessed. Nothing else existed for him—he was oblivious to time, sleep and hunger. . . . He could never walk through the streets without being provoked by what he saw. Usually he carried around in his head, at the same time, half a dozen different building projects, and sometimes I could not help feeling that all the buildings of the town were lined up in his brain like a giant panorama. . . . He felt responsible for everything that was being build.[9]

Erikson notes, quoting Trevor-Roper, that one of Hitler's last projects in the bunker as his world collapsed around him was to design a new opera house and picture gallery for Linz. And Erikson concludes:

This account illustrates the eerie balance between destructiveness and constructiveness, between suicidal Nothingness and dictatorial Allness, in a young man who at fifteen "felt responsible for everything that was being built," that is, was dominated by an overwhelming conscience and a kind of premature integrity such as characterizes all ideological leaders; he had selected, with deadly obsessiveness, *his* medium of salvation: architecture. Maybe, maybe, if he had been permitted to build, he would not have destroyed.[10]

The eloquence of Erikson's writing tended for many years to mute critical assessment of his ideas. At worst, he was ignored; *Young Man Luther*, for example, was never reviewed in the *American Historical Review*. His political status as the ideological guru for a generation in cultural turmoil also tended to deflect dissenting voices. Nevertheless, there are problems to note in Erikson's psychobiographical and psychological theories. He is always bafflingly diffuse. Joel Kovel once referred to Erikson's "identity salad."[11] And at times—too many times—Erikson is theoretically vague. For example, the chronology of adolescence in Erikson's work has a decided middle-age spread. In *Young Man Luther*, he notes: "My main interest is in the fact that at about the age of thirty—an important age for gifted people with a delayed identity crisis—the wholeness of Luther's theology first emerges from the fragments of his totalistic reevaluations."[12] Furthermore, as Frank Manuel points out: "There is no theory of social change in Eriksonian psychology, any more than in Freud's, except for the assumption that each new generation strives to surpass the older one, to innovate upon its works, risking oedipal ambivalence in the process."[13] It is also hardly self-evident that emotional growth best proceeds through crisis. This argument is most plausible for conceptualizing the normative meanings of the life cycle and has been developed in detail by the Offers.[14] It may be that the leader's creativity is special and requires a kind of baptism by developmental fire. "Greatness," says Erikson, "depends on the preservation and continual corroboration of something which most ex-children lose."[15] But it is worth reflecting that Martin Luther perhaps became great despite his crisis of identity rather than because of it.

There is a good deal more to Erikson's theory of leadership than the psychobiographical account of great men's conflicts. Pathology, where it exists, must be confronted. But the capacity to lead, create, and inspire has sources that lie outside conflict.

One important source of the leader's effectiveness is his manipulation of symbolism. For example, in his book on Thomas Jefferson, *Dimensions of a New Identity*, Erikson once elaborates on the relationship between body symbolism and political rhetoric. In a digression orginating in Erikson's fascination with Jefferson's abiding interest in the upright human body, he tells a fable:

> It was the time of the New Deal. Here was a great and wealthy country having undergone a traumatic economic depression which, as I can now see, must have seemed to paralyze that very self-made identity and put into question its eternal renewal. At that lowest period, a leader appeared who himself could not stand on his own feet because, alas, he was paralyzed from the waist down. But on the arm of a son or an aide, he appeared always erect; and his mood seemed to belie the catastrophe that had befallen him, and as his voice ringingly arose above any emotional depression, he was able to lift the spirit of the masses, and they marched—behind the man in the wheelchair. Happy days were here again.[16]

A man impressively taller than most of his contemporaries, Jefferson had described the natural bridge as "springing, as it were, up to heaven"[17] and referred to the British as in America's bowels and therefore to be expelled.[18] Jefferson's imagery was a part of, and helped to create, some central American symbols. To stand erect is to be proud, strong, and American. What counts, Erikson notes, "is to be out front, and to be well equipped up front."[19] What is easily dispensable is the "shit" behind, from Indians to blacks to the Vietnamese at My Lai.

Bodily symbolism and its connection with political rhetoric is, in fact, a central theme in Erikson's theory of leadership. Take, for example, the way Erikson handles Gandhi's intense struggles with darkness, sexuality, and sin.

> One can see, then, why Gandhi, in all his preoccupation with sexuality and with dirt, with race and with poverty, gradually recognized the fact that civilized man can overcome his pride in his

pseudospecies only by learning to differentiate rationally and com-
passionately between matters of unhygienic contamination and matters of mere symbolic uncleanness—a modern sense of discrimination which would no longer reject India's Untouchable castes upon
whom all dirtiness had been ritually projected for centuries. But he
also saw that "cleanliness," once it becomes a matter of pious compulsion, can be as dirty as its opposite; even an hypocritical moral-
ism can be as dirty as sin.[20]

Erikson also notes carefully the way Gandhi's phallic maleness, his compulsive walking, and his virile near-nakedness were absorbed in his
decisive wielding of political influence. And yet his aggressive maleness
alternated with powerful images of maternal care. The spinning wheel
was the central symbol of the *Ashram*. Gandhi cared for his followers as a
woman tends to her brood. And in *Brahmacharya*, Gandhi perhaps disavowed his God-given organ of such singular potential but managed in
the process to bring together a personal need and a national trend of
Indian religiosity.[21]

The creative manipulation of bodily symbols need not serve psychohistorically healthy ends. Luther, for example, said: "I am like ripe shit,
and the world is a gigantic ass-hole. They probably will let go of each
other soon."[22] Erikson confronts this pathology directly.

In its excess, Luther's obscenity expresses the needs of a manic-
depressive nature which has to maintain a state of unrelenting paranoid repudiation of an appointed enemy on the outside in order to
avoid victimizing and, as it were, eliminating itself.[23]

Luther, who raised human consciousness to new heights, also left an
abiding sense of badness and sin in his theology. He "settled a personal
account by providing a public accounting," as Erikson puts it.[24]

The centerpiece of Erikson's theory is that the leader articulates the
latent issues of his age in his personal struggles. In probably his most
famous paragraph, Erikson describes the connection between *public* and
private in Luther:

Millions of boys face these problems [struggles with the father] and
solve them in some way or another—they live, as Captain Ahab
says, with half of their heart and with only one of their lungs, and
the world is the worse for it. Now and again, however, an individual
is called upon (called by *whom*, only the theologians claim to know,
and by *what*, only bad psychologists) to lift his individual patienthood to the level of a universal one and to try to solve for all
what he could not solve for himself alone.[25]

The "collective patienthood" Erikson evokes here is the crisis of Western Christendom over man's relationship to God the Father, which

found its direct political analogue in struggles with earthly fathers, princes, and popes. Luther did the dirty work of his age, Erikson concludes, and we have all benefited from an enhanced sense of self ever since.

It is at this critical juncture where psychology and history meet that Erikson's theory is most vulnerable. Notions of universal or collective patienthood are not exactly the kind of precise formulation of past group experience that historians warm to. Furthermore, for some time there has been a tendency for Erikson's work to become less clear on just this point. *Young Man Luther* at least attempts to identify some specific correlations between the private man and the public issues at the beginning of the sixteenth century. Since *Young Man Luther*, Erikson has become steadily murkier, grander, more philosophical, and less historical. In *Gandhi's Truth*, it is never quite clear what latent meanings in the group the Mahatma articulates. The "group" moves from the special needs of South African Indians to the unique and complex political strivings of Indians, to everyone everywhere. This last meaning is the most confusing:

> When I came to Anmedabad, it had become clear to me (for I had just come from the disarmament conference of the American Academy of Arts and Sciences) that man as a species can no longer afford any more to cultivate illusions either about his own "nature" or about that of other species, or about those "pseudospecies" he calls enemies—not while inventing and manufacturing arsenals capable of global destruction and while relying for inner and outer peace solely on the superbrakes built into the superweaponry. And Gandhi seems to have been the only man who has visualized *and* demonstrated an overall alternative.[26]

After Gandhi (1969), Erikson turned to Thomas Jefferson (1979), who articulated the dimensions of a new American identity. But what does that mean? "The earth belongs to the living," he quotes Jefferson as saying, and he cites Jefferson's comment, "God forbid that we should ever be twenty years without . . . a rebellion."[27] Erikson's analysis of this is quite far fetched:

> Twenty years is about the span of human development needed for the individual to acquire a sense of identity firm and informed enough to act: which requires enough experience to acknowledge the power of facts and the facts of power; enough practical idealism to attach infantile ideals to live persons and issues; and enough rebellious commitment to the future to leave behind some of the internalized debt of infantile guilt.[28]

Elsewhere in *Dimensions of a New Identity*, Erikson elaborates on Jefferson's ideal of the self-made man in terms of America's immigrant experience;[29] he explains Jefferson's love for the mulatto Sally Hemmings as somehow fundamentally expressive of black and white in America; and he concludes with a vague idea about Jefferson and American adulthood:

> And Jefferson, one could summarize, could not have been as great (and yet tragically aware) a figure, were it not for the inner circumstance that the oppressive conscience which he shared with past generations was in important respects balanced by ideal images personified in his youth by genuinely adult and competent figures. This, I believe, is the most poignant lesson for today of any restudy of such a man.[30]

Erikson's study of Jesus of Nazareth—of which only one short paper has appeared so far—ranges loosely from Galilee to Freud and Gandhi and is as much concerned with the ultimate meaning of life as it is with the historical Jesus. In fact, the tension between Erikson the philosopher (one is tempted to say preacher) and Erikson the historian strains the essay beyond reasonable limits. On the one hand, Erikson discusses at tedious length the work of the form critics within theology, who have sought to identify the earliest and most "authentic" of Jesus' sayings. Erikson's analyses closely examine each saying or parable in terms of how the form critics have judged it, but then they often take off on flights of fancy, leading just as easily to Freud as to the diaspora or the American frontier:

> As we now approach such unique space-time configurations as *Diaspora*—configurations which can have quite ambiguous connotations for a nation's sense of existence—we might briefly reconsider the spatial sense established by the all-important fact in American history of a *frontier*. As an overall gestalt, the frontier gradually moved westward and northward until it joined the Pacific Ocean, and yet it still figures in many life plans and ventures, as well as, of course, memories—not to speak of habitual media themes. Let us not overlook, in passing, the configuration of immigration which for so long—as it does in Israel today—expressed the eagerness of the new homecomers to have "made it," no matter what may have made them leave where they came from. "Frontier" has obviously played a significant role in the implicit images of "new deals" as well as the explicit slogan of a "new frontier." The same is true (or, significantly, *has* been true) for the American imagery of war, which always assumed that armies are *ex*peditionary forces expected to fight on *foreign* fronts and not meant to wait for a potential enemy ever to *in*vade. The personal sense of fate which depends on such shared space-time configurations can consist of the simplest of all defensive attitudes, such as who can do what to me—and what can I

do to them if they do it. Radical changes in such habitual expect-ability and the totally new threat of total nuclear vulnerability are absorbed only very, very slowly into either the individual sense of existence or, indeed, the psychosocial and national identity. They demand and are in fact waiting for nothing less than a kind of revelatory reorientation of the whole world image as based on the acceptance of the undeniable facts of developing technology and on the capacity for new modes of ethical adaptation.[31]

Each insight here is interesting, perhaps, but so loosely connected as to make the whole almost incomprehensible. In his best work, Erikson uses the aside to heighten the tension in the narrative. Here he seems all asides.

But the problem may be even more basic and reflect an inner shift that has taken Erikson out of psychohistory and into religion. He reads like a preacher here:

> [I] have now counterposed a few examples of the style and the logic of Jesus of Nazareth's original sayings with some of the dimensions of the human sense of *I*. I did so because I share the belief that the elemental sayings that emerged in the millennium "before Christ," and in Jesus' own short life, all deal with dimensions of human consciousness in a new manner nowadays expressed in the terms of individuality and universality, that is, a more aware *I* related to a more universal *We*, approaching the idea of one mankind.[32]

Isaiah Berlin once used the old story of the hedgehog and the fox to explain the inner dynamics of Tolstoy's life and thought. The fox in the story knows many things; the hedghog one big thing. Some great foxes would include Confucious, Shakespeare, and Jefferson; some great hedghogs would be Jesus, Dante, Dostoyevsky, and Lincoln. Tolstoy, says Berlin, was a fox who always wanted to and thought he should be a hedgehog. Erikson, one might say, has been creative when he has man-aged to keep the hedgehog in him under wraps. Like Freud before him, however, Erikson was taken over by the hedgehog sometime in his ninth decade of life. Now, alas, he is all hedgehog.

NOTES

1. There is one (inadequate) biography of Erikson: Robert Coles, *Erik H. Erikson: The Growth of His Work* (Boston: Little, Brown, 1970).
2. Erik H. Erikson, *Young Man Luther* (1958); *Gandhi's Truth* (1968); and *Dimensions of a New Identity* (New York: Norton, 1974).
3. For William James, see *Identity: Youth and Crisis* (New York: Norton, 1968), pp. 150–155; for George Bernard Shaw, ibid., pp. 142–150; for Albert Einstein, "Psychoanalytic Reflections on Einstein's Centenary," in *Albert Einstein: Historical and Cultural Perspec-*

tives, ed. Gerald Holton and Yehuda Elkam (Princeton: Princeton University Press, 1979); for Adolf Hitler, *Childhood and Society* (New York: Norton, 1963 [1950]), pp. 326–58, and *Young Man Luther*, pp. 105–110; for Maxim Gorky, *Childhood and Society*, pp. 359–402; for Jesus, "The Galilean Sayings and the Sense of 'I'," *Yale Review*, 70 (1981), 321–362.

4. Erikson, *Young Man Luther*, p. 169.
5. Erikson, *Identity*, p. 143.
6. Ibid., 144.
7. Ibid., 145.
8. Ibid., 150.
9. Erikson, *Young Man Luther*, pp. 105–106.
10. Ibid., 107–108.
11. Joel Kovel, "Erik Erikson's Psychohistory," *Social Policy*, 4 (1974), 63.
12. Erikson, *Young Man Luther*, p. 201.
13. Frank E. Manuel, "The Use and Abuse of Psychology in History," in *Historical Studies Today*, ed. Felix Gilbert and Stephen R. Graubard (New York: Norton, 1972), p. 225.
14. Daniel Offer and Judith Offer, *From Teenage to Young Manhood* (New York: Basic Books, 1975).
15. Erikson, *Gandhi's Truth*, p. 107.
16. Erikson, *Dimensions*, p. 98.
17. Ibid., 87.
18. Ibid., 89.
19. Ibid., 90.
20. Erikson, *Gandhi's Truth*, pp. 196–197.
21. Ibid., 402–403.
22. Erikson, *Young Man Luther*, p. 206.
23. Ibid., 246.
24. Ibid., 250.
25. Ibid., 67.
26. Erikson, *Gandhi's Truth*, p. 51.
27. Erikson, *Dimensions*, p. 72.
28. Ibid., 72–73.
29. Ibid., 76–77.
30. Ibid., 125.
31. Erikson, "The Galilean . . . ," pp. 332–333.
32. Ibid., 358.

THE GROWTH OF PSYCHOHISTORY

CHARLES B. STROZIER AND DANIEL OFFER

Erikson's *Young Man Luther* opened a whole new phase in psychohistory. It became a highly controversial and visible endeavor for the literate public: one *New Yorker* cartoon in the mid-1970s pictured the locked door of a psychiatric unit with the label "Psychohistorian" above a small window. Among professional historians, profound skepticism developed along with ambivalent curiosity. No convention program after about 1970 was worth its salt without one or more avowedly psychohistorical sessions. The leading historical journals began publishing articles that made clear their dependence on psychoanalytic theory. Interest in psychohistory among psychiatrists and psychoanalysts was less dramatic or intense and also less ambivalent. Psychoanalytic applications to history had had a longer established and more secure place; such applications now simply increased. In 1962, Bruce Mazlish published the first collection of psychohistorical essays, an approach to publishing in the field that has since become quite popular.[1] Periodic reviews of the literature and assessments of the "state of the art" became *de rigeur* for anyone who claimed to be "in" psychohistory.[2] Nearly everyone had studied the field to as far back as 1958, when Erikson published *Young Man Luther* and William Langer summoned historians to their "next assignment." Some, however, especially psychoanalysts such as Heinz Kohut and Robert Lifton, took a broader perspective, and gradually historians, too, began to place psychohistory in a longer time frame.

All this assessing and reviewing of psychohistory was a direct response to a rapid expansion of the field after 1960. Psychologically informed biography, which had always been at the heart of the field, expanded considerably. But now systematic and psychoanalytic reflections on motivation touched other areas of research. Robert Lifton explored the collective response to the bomb in Japan and to the Vietnam War in America, the mass support of Mao, and, more recently and as yet unpublished, the doctor response to Nazism.[3] Other investigators, including Peter Loewenberg, Rudolph Binion, Kai Erikson, Charles Strozier, and Peter Gay, found different ways to go beyond biography, but the goal remained the same—to deal psychologically with broad historical concerns.[4] A particularly interesting expansion of the field in the last two decades has been in what is called "the new social history." John Demos pioneered such investigations with his 1971 study of American colonial family life, *A Little Commonwealth*, which has been followed recently by his study of witchcraft, *Entertaining Satan*.[5] Once issues in family history were opened up, psychohistory quickly found a creative link with the burgeoning field of women's history; for example, Carroll Smith-Rosenberg, in her noted 1975 paper on nineteenth-century female friendships, argued that special conditions of mothering defined the emotional climate for a unique female world of love and ritual.[6]

The growth of psychohistory and the responses to it have been so extensive that it is often difficult to find one's bearings. There are now several competing orientations in psychohistory, from Freudian to Eriksonian to Liftonian to Kohutian. Many have also argued recently about the irrelevance (or inadequacy) of psychoanalysis altogether and call for psychohistorical empiricism or for a reliance on such theories as that of cognitive dissonance or a blending of psychohistory with the French school of collective mentalities.[7] It was inevitable that something as dynamic and avowedly psychological as psychohistory has generated two curious developments on the fringes: the irresponsible, even at times unethical, use of psychology in history, and the disavowed, yet significant, incorporation of psychology into apparently traditional research. One might say there are three categories to study: psychohistory proper, its abusers, and closet psychohistorians.

The closet psychohistorians suggest the pervasive impact of psychohistory. In 1980 David Stannard issued a diatribe against everything psychohistorical in a book titled *Shrinking History: On Freud and the Failure of Psychohistory*, which originally carried the working title of *Freudian History*.[8] The book received widespread attention because of the deserved reputations of Stannard and the publisher, the Oxford University Press. The book argued that from psychohistory's earliest endeavors—Stannard began with Freud's 1910 essay on Leonardo da Vinci—"individual writings of would-be psychohistorians have consistently been characterized by a cavalier attitude toward fact, a contorted attitude toward logic, an irresponsible attitude toward theory validation, and a myopic attitude toward cultural difference and anachronism."[9] To buttress this claim, Stannard reviewed precious few actual works of psychohistory, and those he touched upon were treated superficially.[10] His real concern was that the theoretical foundation of psychohistory is profoundly unscientific, and that the problem lies in psychoanalysis itself, in its groundless assumptions and faulty method of treatment. This approach to the subject took Stannard into a murky assessment of the theoretical effectiveness of psychoanalysis and a confidently assertive definition of scientific investigation and the meanings of logic.

Psychohistorians reacted to Stannard's book with predictable outrage.[11] Even John Leonard, in the *New York Times*, was appalled at Stannard's vehemence and his disdain of metaphor, which "for many of us is liberating."[12]

But by far the most interesting point to make about David Stannard concerns the psychohistorical nature of his own work. His 1977 study, *The Puritan Way of Death: A Study in Religion, Culture, and Social Change*,[13] is a model of the sensitive use of psychology applied to an important area of social history. On the very first page of this book, Stannard quoted Freud, and later he noted that we live in a post-Puritan, post-Einsteinian, post-Darwinian, and post-Freudian world "that in conquering the ignorance and stripping the supernaturalism from man's vision of his universe, his species, and his self has uncovered new mysteries of an even more troubling nature."[14] He freely and intelligently speculated on the psychological connection between the Puritan conceptions of the child as deprived and ungodly and the "emotional distance between his offspring and himself;"[15] on contemporary American funerals as "something of an unconscious protest by the alienated and isolated urban American family that has had to absorb the impact of death on its own;"[16] and on the psychological themes in Puritan sermons of loss, depression, helplessness, guilt and inwardly-turned hostility, and the idealization of the dead.[17] The footnotes to the book abounded in references to the relevant psychiatric, psychological, and psychoanalytic literature—from William James to John Bowlby—and to other psychohistorians to whom Stannard was indebted, including John Demos and even the much maligned Lloyd DeMause.

David Stannard seemed unaware of what his two hands were doing. An even more interesting example of someone in the closet

would be Gary Wills. No one has ridiculed psychohistory more resound-
ingly than Wills.[18] He calls the endeavor "psychobunk" and Lloyd De-
Mause, its most flamboyant spokesman, "Mickey DeMause." And yet
there is no better psychological study of leadership than Wills' 1968
book, *Nixon Agonistes*, which was an acute analysis of Nixon's personality, that asked—and answered—relevant psychological questions.
There were no footnotes to Freud, but *Nixon Agonistes* showed how
profoundly biographical writing has been affected by psychohistory.
Furthermore—and this sharply separates Wills from the array of second-rate psychohistorians writing about Nixon—*Nixon Agonistes* explored systematically the link between leader and follower. Without
being facile, Wills showed how curiously representative Nixon was in
1968. One only regrets Wills' disavowal.

Long ago, Erikson noted that historians often introduce psychological observations with a kind of "virginal apology" and that they imply
"to divorce themselves from the professional psychology they so heartily distrust."[19] Their apology often sanctions facile psychological observations that are themselves grounded in nothing beyond intuition.
Some historians simply separate themselves from any open use of professional psychology. James Thomas Flexner, who was surpassingly un-
psychological in his four volumes on George Washington, felt free to tell
us what young "George" felt on any given occasion, even though such
intuitive leaps must be purely speculative.[20] The historian and most
eminent Lincoln scholar, Don E. Fehrenbacker, who is openly disdainful
of psychohistory, seemed to feel that he had a license based on nothing
beyond common sense and a rich imagination to explain Lincoln's guilt:

> There is no evidence that Lincoln suffered from a sustained sense of
> guilt, either real or neurotic. Yet at times his responsibilities as Presi-
> dent must have weighed as heavily as the guilt of any assassin, and
> the latest casualty lists must have seemed like accusations. It is not
> altogether unlikely that in the gloom of some sleepless night he
> beheld blood upon his hands or found a prayer faltering on his
> lips. . . . For such a man there could never cease to be sorrow on the
> bosom of the earth.[21]

The historian Robert G. L. Waite was rather more humble in his psychological dealings with Hitler. From quite traditional beginnings in history,
Waite turned to psychology (and consulted Erikson, among others) because "the career of Adolf Hitler raises questions that can be answered
neither by psychology nor by history working alone."[22] That kind of
honesty and boldness is as refreshing as it is rare. Usually historians
make extraordinary leaps of psychological intuition without the slightest
quiver, while simultaneously holding psychohistorians to the strictest
standards of empirical validation for any statement of motivation.

A field in some ways is defined on its fringes. Those in the closet demonstrate better than any bibliographic listing the impact of psychohistory. The abusers, on the other hand, illustrate just how irresponsible psychohistory can become in the wrong hands. There is, of course, lots of bad psychohistory around, just as there is lots of bad social history, or economic history, or political history. But the abusers of psychohistory are a special case of badness that deserves attention, because in their exaggerations, unfounded inferences, and shaky grasp of either history or psychology, the abusers reveal the methodological aspects of psychohistory that most need to be watched and curtailed.

Lloyd DeMause and his followers who generally publish in *The Journal of Psychohistory* are abusers. There are exceptions, of course, and in DeMause and his followers one often encounters a surprising spark of creativity. But the flame of exaggeration always seems to engulf it. For example, DeMause began writing over a decade ago on the interesting idea that the history of childhood should be explored in its own right. That became "the discovery" that the history of childhood followed evolutionary patterns that are "lawful," and that the new field of childhood history is the basis for studying patterns of personality and behavior of both individuals and groups in history.[23] Or again, most researchers in psychohistory feel that for ethical and sound reasons of training, a personal acquaintance with therapy is relevant to the use of psychoanalytic ideas in understanding others. This hardly distinguishes psychohistorians as a breed apart, and undoubtedly many can work effectively in history or psychohistory without it; some would even argue that personal therapy is a bad idea for psychohistorians.[24] The consensus, however, is that for most mortals analysis or some therapy is a useful beginning point for work in a complicated and uncharted field that avowedly pursues the subjective. In DeMause's hands, an issue that should be treated cautiously becomes a perverse certainty:

> I no longer believe that most traditional historians are emotionally equipped, even with training, to use their feelings as psychohistorical research tools, although there is a whole new generation of psychohistorians just now beginning to write who *are* able to do so. To expect the average historian to do psychohistory is like trying to teach a blind man to be an astronomer, so averse are they to psychological insight into themselves or their historical material from *any* school of modern psychology.[25]

To exaggerate a valid point is one kind of problem. DeMause and his followers, however, systematically search out the unfounded inference. Jimmy Carter, for example, according to David Beiser, felt "repressed anger" toward his mother. The evidence: "the autobiography

[Carter's *Why Not the Best?*] devotes less space to her than to his father."[26] DeMause, as well, seems to have it in for Carter's mother, who, because of her "distanced and often distorted messages," made her son "susceptible to the hidden group fantasy needs of the nation."[27] The evidence for Miss Lillian's "distance" is nonexistent. But even if she were a distancing type—whatever that is—there would still be no theoretical or empirical basis for the leap from her distance to Carter's presidential style that makes him the special repository of the nation's fantasy needs. The evidence for such hidden fantasy needs comes from DeMause's peculiar and decidedly idiosyncratic analysis of Carter's speeches, the daily press, and television commentary. He calls his method "fantasy analysis" and seems convinced that it is scientific. In 1978 he was so certain of its utility that he predicted that the United States would be in a major war in 1979.[28]

Finally, there is the basic problem that DeMause and his followers have an insecure grasp of both psychoanalytic and historical methodology. In theory they are rigorously Kleinian, which has always occupied an important, but marginal, place in psychoanalysis. No one can really disprove the Kleinians, but neither can their beliefs in very early oral and aggressive fantasies be proven. Certainly, few clinicians, who are in the best position to test such ideas, work with Kleinian notions, except in a passing way, and then only with severe cases of psychosis. DeMause is equally off base in his understanding of history. Radical empiricism, as he calls it, is one thing, but historical evidence is always refractory, and it has been a century since serious historians talked of iron laws governing human affairs. Psychological theory legitimately frames questions of motivation in history that define the psychohistorical endeavor. But in the last analysis, psychohistory is nothing more or less than history. Without a sense of narrative; without an appreciation for the rational and the irrational; without the traditions that bind as well as the forces that disrupt, and the enormous complexity of social and political institutions, one is left observing only a few trees in a very large forest to which one is blinded.

The worthwhile research in psychohistory is quite abundant now after some two and a half decades. Take, for example, the field of Hitler and Nazi Germany.[29] Here research, for obvious reasons, dates back to World War II, and, as Louise Hoffman has recently indicated, there was an ongoing contemporary psychological assessment of Nazism in the 1930s.[30] During the war, American intelligence operations—headed by "Wild" Bill Donovan at the Office of Secret Services—hired a small army of analysts and psychologists to investigate Hitler. The most famous of these studies was Walter C. Langer's *The Mind of Adolf Hitler*, which was written in 1943 as a secret war-time report and published in 1973.[31] In the immediate aftermath of the war, a number of psychologically informed scholars turned their attention to Hitler, his immediate circle, and Nazi Germany in general.[32] A steady stream of books and articles followed in the next few decades, the most important of which have been written by James H. McRandle, Alexander Mitscherlich, Peter Loewenberg, Rudolph Binion, Robert G. L. Waite, and Saul Friedländer.[33] One might even say that the study of Nazi Germany has been dominated by psychohistorians. As an extreme event in human history, Hitler and Nazi Germany lent themselves to the (perhaps unfortunate) psychoanalytic tendency to generalize about normality by studying the pathological.

However, psychohistory has not been restricted to the field of Nazism. In the last couple of decades, European history in general has been opened up to psychological scrutiny, including many studies of Russian, French, and English history.[34] Erikson, as discussed earlier, wrote a fine book on Gandhi in 1968, which is now part of a literature of psychological studies of Indian culture.[35] But the most striking new contextual direction in psychohistory since 1960 has been the application of psychology to aspects of American history. Several recent anthologies make this trend obvious, as does the content of frequent special issues in *The Psychohistory Review*.[36] John Demos has clearly established his preeminence in the area of colonial history, though his research is not part of the study of leadership. In that area, the best work has been done on presidents, including Thomas Jefferson, Abraham Lincoln, Theodore Roosevelt, Franklin Roosevelt, John Kennedy, Lyndon Johnson, Richard Nixon, and Jimmy Carter. Many of these studies have been theoretically pedestrian, but a few have pushed psychohistorical methodology into new areas.[37] In this work, one unfortunate tendency has been to focus unduly on events and figures close to the present, indeed on those alive and sometimes actually in office. Such work is methodologically and ethically suspect. Psychojournalism can never define the field of psychohistory.

In the last two decades, Robert Jay Lifton has written a series of books that present a creative psychohistorical model for approaching leadership and followership that departs in significant ways from the Freudian or Eriksonian paradigms which have dominated the field. Lifton conducted interviews and studies of four specific groups of people whose historical exposures have a bearing on important characteristics of the present era: Chinese and Westerners who underwent Chinese "thought reform" or brainwashing, Japanese university students during the early 1960s, Hiroshima survivors of the atomic bomb, and antiwar

Vietnam veterans.[38] The focus was on themes, forms, and images that are in significant ways shared, rather than on the life of a single person as such. Lifton's approach required considerable innovation in interview method.

For more than twenty years, Lifton has struggled with modifications of the psychiatric and psychoanalytic interview in order to approach and understand various kinds of people who have not sought therapeutic help but have been sought out by him. Lifton has developed a free interview style: it remains probing, encouraging the widest range of associations, and includes detailed life histories and explorations of dreams. But it focuses on the specific situation responsible for bringing the interviewee and interviewer together (most of the interviews have been individual ones) and takes the form of something close to an open dialogue emerging from that situation.

The relationship the two develop is neither one of doctor and patient nor one of ordinary friends, although at moments it can seen to resemble either. Lifton has wrestled with what to call the subject in that relationship. "Research subject" seems unsatisfactory because it suggests someone merely studied or investigated in a more or less passive way. "Patient" is entirely inappropriate, and "client" is not much better. "Historical actor" and "pivotal person" come closer, but they have their own ambiguities. Progress in psychohistory may, in part, depend on such innovations in method. Once developed in the study of contemporary matters, such innovations could also be applied to the study of the past, although their usefulness lies mainly in relation to the search for and the interpretation of various kinds of records and documents.

The psychohistorical interview emphasizes shared exploration, mostly of the world of the person sought out but including a great deal of give-and-take and more than a little discussion of the author's own attitudes and interests. It requires a combination of human spontaneity and professional discipline. One's way of combining the two is always idiosyncratic and always less than ideal.

The "shared themes approach," as Lifton calls his approach to psychohistorical method, was used in six months of research in Hiroshima in 1963 on the psychological effects of the atomic bomb. The work centered mainly on intensive interviews with seventy-five bomb survivors, about half of them chosen at random from an official list. The other half were specially selected because of their active involvement over the years in atomic bomb issues and problems. Most of the interviews were tape-recorded, and the book written about the work, *Death in Life*, took shape mainly from those interviews, making extensive use of direct quotations to illustrate the death-haunted responses that were encountered. But in both the research and the book, Lifton moved outward from interviews with individual survivors to examine groups that they formed, leaders emerging from among them, and social currents in Hiroshima that the survivors created and were affected by. This approach required close attention to the post-atomic bomb history of the city and to the relation of that special history to the rest of Japan and to the world at large, as well as to the city's own earlier heritage. Significant parts of that history consisted of creative struggles by writers, painters, and filmmakers from both within and without the city to come to terms with Hiroshima. These historical creative struggles were deeply bound up with issues of memorialization and commemoration and with efforts to move beyond the bomb while remaining true to its dead.

Through a detailed elaboration of the ethos of the survivor, Lifton was able to unite the individual psychological and historical currents observed. He compared survival of the atomic bomb to survival of other massive death immersions—Nazi persecutions, the plagues in the Middle Ages as revealed through records and natural disasters—and the deaths of close friends and family members. He then, in that and in subsequent studies, raised questions about the general importance of the survivor ethos of the present age and of the degree to which people have become historically prone to the survivor's retained death imprint, to his death guilt and his psychic numbing or desensitization to death-dominated images, and to his struggle for significance or what the author calls his "formulation." Those questions now intrude into virtually all of Lifton's work, and they haunt the contemporary imagination.

In *Revolutionary Immortality,* Lifton discussed Mao Tse-tung's relationship to the Chinese cultural revolution in terms of Mao's many experiences of individual and revolutionary survival. Mao's use of the survivor state was related to his extraordinary accomplishments as a leader, and the general relevance of death symbolism was considered in the broadest historical perspective in relation to the Chinese cultural revolution. By connecting certain psychological characteristics of Mao's personal and revolutionary style with the predominant themes of the cultural revolution, Lifton attempted to combine the "great man" and "shared themes" approaches.

The central thesis of the book revolved around Mao's anticipation of his own impending death and his own and his followers' fear of the death of the revolution. What Lifton saw as the overwhelming threat that Mao faced was not so much death itself as the suggestion that his revolutionary works would not endure. By revolutionary immortality, then, was meant a shared sense of participating in permanent revolutionary ferment and of transcending individual death by living on indefinitely within continuing revolution, as expressed in Trotsky's principle of permanent revolution. That vision took on unprecedented intensity in the Chinese Communist experience. The quest for revolutionary immortality provided a general framework within which the political and economic struggles and antibureaucratic and antirevisionist assaults of the cultural revolution could be examined without being reduced to a particular psychological or psychopathological trait of any one person.

Also related to that quest was a pattern that reflected the excruciating Maoist struggles with technology. The author called that pattern "psychism," by which he meant an exaggerated reliance on psychic power as a means of controlling the external environment or an attempt to replace the requirements of technology with pure revolutionary will. Technology was desperately sought but feelings were cultivated. In that pattern of psychism, there was once more a coming together of Mao's personal revolutionary style, including what Chinese Communist commentators referred to as his revolutionary romanticism, and a number of larger currents surrounding the cultural revolution. The concept of psychism, like that of revolutionary immortality, was an attempt to say something about precisely that psychohistorical interface.

Revolutionary Immortality was not based on the kind of detailed interview approach described in relation to Lifton's Hiroshima work. Rather, it was a brief interpretive essay that drew heavily on documents and observations by others of the cultural revolution and on the writings of Mao. It included only on a very limited number of interviews with participants and observers of the events described. As compared with the Hiroshima study, the Mao study was more tenuous and more vulnerable. In Lifton's latest (and forthcoming) study of the physicians in Nazi Germany, he has returned to the use of interviews with "historical actors" to understand psychologically the meaning of important events in recent history.

NOTES

1. Bruce Mazlish, *Psychoanalysis and History*. The other important collections of essays published during the last two decades include: *Explorations in Psychohistory: The Well-fleet Papers*, ed. Robert Jay Lifton (New York: Simon & Schuster, 1974); *Varieties of Psychohistory*, ed. George M. Kren and Leon H. Rappaport (New York: Springer, 1976); *Psychoanalytic Interpretation of History*, ed. Benjamin Wolman (New York: Basic Books, 1971); and four collections edited by Lloyd DeMause (all of dubious value): *The History of Childhood* (New York: The Psychohistory Press, 1974); *The New Psychohistory* (New York: The Psychohistory Press, 1975); (with Henry Ebel), *Jimmy Carter and American Fantasy: Psychohistorical Exploration* (New York: Psychohistory Press, 1977); and *Foundations of Psychohistory* (New York: Creative Roots, 1982). The promises and problems of

collections without a theme are illustrated in *New Directions in Psychohistory: The Adelphi Papers in Honor of Erik H. Erikman*, ed. Mel Albin (Lexington: Lexington Books, 1980); and Robert J. Brugger, *Our Selves, Our Past: Psychological Approaches to American History* (Baltimore: Johns Hopkins University Press, 1981). Various journals, especially *The Psychohistory Review*, regularly publish collections of essays on a special topic, and less specialized journals, such as the *American Historical Review* or the *Journal of Interdisciplinary History*, occasionally devote whole issues to psychohistory.

2. It is only possible to mention here a few representative titles, arranged in chronological order. The best of the lot, an essay seldom read by historians but frequently cited and discussed by psychoanalysts, is Heinz Kohut, "Beyond the Bounds" (1960). Other essays include: Heinz Hartmann, "The Application of Psychoanalytic Concepts to Social Science," *Essays on Ego Psychology* (New York: International Universities Press, 1964), 90–98; Erik H. Erikson, "Psychoanalysis and Ongoing History," *American Journal of Psychiatry*, 22 (1965), 241–250; Richard Bushman, "On the Use of Psychohistory: Conflict and Conciliation in Benjamin Franklin," *History and Theory*, 5 (1966), 225–240; John Klauber, "On the Dual Use of Historical and Scientific Method in Psychoanalysis," *International Journal of Psycho-Analysis*, 49 (1968), 80–88; Erik Erikson, "Autobiographic Notes on the Identity Crisis," *Daedulus*, 99 (1970), 730–759; John E. Mack, "Psychoanalysis and Historical Biography," *Journal of the American Psychoanalytic Association*, 19 (1971), 143–179; Bruce Mazlish, "Autobiography and Psychoanalysis: Between truth and Self-Deception," *Encounter*, 35 (1970), 28–37; "What is Psychohistory?" *Transactions of the Royal Historical Society*, Fifth Series 21 (1971), 79–99; review essay of Mitzmon's *The Iron Cage*, *History and Theory*, 10 (1970), 90–107; Hans-Ulrich Wehler, *Geschichte und Psychoanalyse*, (Köln: Kiepenfeur und Witsch, 1971); Arnold Toynbee, "Aspects of Psychohistory," *Main Currents*, 29 (1972), 44–46; George Rosen, "Psyche and History," *Psychological Medicine*, 2 (1972), 205–207; Robert Detmeilar, "Retreat From Environmentalism: A Review of the Psychohistory of George III," *History Teacher*, 6 (1972), 37–46; Fritz Schmidt, "Problems of Method in Applied Psychoanalysis," *Psychoanalytic Quarterly*, 41 (1972), 402–419; Philip Pomper, "Problems of a Naturalistic Psychohistory," *History and Theory*, 12 (1973), 367–88; Arthur Mitzman, "Social Engagement and Psycho-History," *Tydschrift voor Geschiedenis*, 87 (1974), 425–442; Perry Lewis, "Psychology and the Abolitionists: Reflections on Martin Duberman and the Neo-Abolitionist of the 1960s," *Reviews in American History*, 2 (1974), 309–321; Peter Loewenberg, "Psychohistorical Perspectives in Modern German History," *Journal of Modern History*, 47 (1975), 229–279; Fred Weinstein and Gerald Platt, "The Coming Crisis in Psychohistory," *Journal of Modern History*, 47 (1975), 202–228; Bruce Mazlish, "On Teaching History," *AHA Newsletter*, 14 (1976), 5–8; William M. Banks, "Psychohistory and the Black Psychologist," *Journal of Black Psychology*, 2 (1976), 25–31; Robert Pois, "Historicism, Marxism, and Psychohistory: Three Approaches to the Problem of Historical Individuality," *Social Science Journal*, 13 (1976), 77–91; Gerald M. Platt, "The Sociological Endeavor and Psychoanalytic Thought," *American Quarterly*, 28 (1976), 343–359; Fred Weinstein, "Benjamin Nelson's Contribution to Psychosocial Perspectives," *Psychohistory Review*, 5 (1976), 4–10; Bruce Mazlish, "Psychohistory and Politics," *Center Magazine*, 10 (1977), 5–14; Joseph I. Shulin, "Robespierre and the French Revolution: A Review Article," *American History Review*, 82 (1977), 20–38; George M. Kren, "Psychohistorical Interpretation of National Socialism," *German Studies Review*, 1 (1978), 150–172; Donald J. Winslow, "Current Bibliography on Life-Writing," *Biography*, 1 (1978), 76–81; Paul W. Guyser, "Psychoanalytic Method in the Study of Religious Meanings," *Psychohistory Review*, 6 (1978), 45–50; Terry H. Anderson, "Becoming Sane With Psychohistory," *Historians*, 41

(1978), 1–20; Stephen D. Rockwood and Geoffrey Cocks, "The Use and Abuse of Psychohistory," *Journal of Psychohistory*, 5 (1977), 131–138; Patrick G. Russell, "Psychohistory: An Object Relations Approach" (Unpublished PhD dissertation, The Ohio State University, 1980); and Bruce Mazlish, "The Next 'Next Assignment': Leader and Led, Individual and Group," *Psychohistory Review*, 9 (1981), 214–137.

3. Robert Jay Lifton, *Death In Life: Survivors of Hiroshima* (New York: Vintage Books, 1967); *Revolutionary Immortality: Mao Tse-tung and the Chinese Cultural Revolution* (New York: Vintage Books, 1968); *Home From the War: Vietnam Veterans, Neither Victims Nor Executioners* (New York: Simon & Shuster, 1973). Note also *The Broken Connection: On Death and the Continuity of Life* (New York: Simon & Schuster, 1979; paperback, Basic Books, 1983).

4. Peter Loewenberg, "The Psychohistorical Origins of the Nazi Youth Cohort," *American Historical Review*, 76 (1971), 1457–1502; Rudolph Binion, *Hitler Among The Germans*, (New York: Elsevier, 1976); Kai Erikson, *Wayward Puritans: A Study in the Sociology of Deviance* (New York: Wiley, 1960); Charles B. Strozier, *Lincoln's Quest For Union: Public and Private Meanings* (New York: Basic Books, 1982); Peter Gay, *The Bourgeois Experience*, Vol. I of *Education of the Senses* (New York: Oxford University Press, 1984).

5. John P. Demos, *A Little Commonwealth: Family Life in Plymouth Colony* (New York: Oxford University Press, 1970); and *Entertaining Satan: Witchcraft and the Culture of Early New England* (New York: Oxford University Press, 1982).

6. Carroll Smith-Rosenberg, "The Female World of Love and Ritual: Relations Between Women in Nineteenth-Century America," *Signs*, 1 (1975), 1–29.

7. Special Issue, *Psychohistory Review* (1979); Lloyd DeMause, *The New Psychohistory*, p. 4; Patrick Hutton, "The Psychohistory of Erik Erikson From the Perspective of Collective Mentalities," *Psychohistory Review*, 12 (1983), 18–25.

8. The publisher, Oxford University Press, shared the galleys of the book with Charles Strozier before publication.

9. Stannard, *Shrinking History*, p. 147.

10. Note, for example, ibid., the discussion of Erikson, pp. 22–24 and of John Demos, pp. 119–121.

11. Note the discussion forum of Stannard's book organized by Charles Strozier, *Psychohistory Review*, 9 (1980), 136–161.

12. John Leonard, book review of *Shrinking History*, *The New York Times*, 26 May, 1980, Book review section.

13. David E. Stannard, *The Puritan Way of Death: A Study in Religion, Culture, and Social Change* (New York: Oxford University Press, 1980).

14. Ibid., 33.

15. Ibid., 60.

16. Ibid., 138.

17. Ibid., 138.

18. Gary Wills, *Chicago Sun Times*, 20 Jan. 1978.

19. Erikson, *Young Man Luther*, p. 110.

20. James Thomas Flexner, *George Washington*, 4 volumes, Vol. I: *The Forge of Experience* (Boston: Little, Brown, 1965), p. 31, for example.

21. Don E. Fehrenbacher, "Lincoln and the Weight of Responsibility," *Journal of the Illinois State Historical Society*, 68 (1975), p. 53 and p. 58.

22. Robert G. L. Waite, *The Psychopathic God: Adolf Hitler* (New York: Basic Books, 1977), p. xiii.

23. DeMause, *The New Psychohistory*, p. 4.

24. Fred Weinstein and Gerald Platt, *Psychoanalytic Sociology*, p. 1, note 1.

25. DeMause, *The New Psychohistory*, p. 23.
26. DeMause and Beisel, *Jimmy Carter*, p. 63.
27. Ibid., 26.
28. Ibid., 9.
29. Two excellent reviews of the literature have appeared in the last decade: Hans Gatzke, "Hitler and Psychohistory: A Review Article," *American Historical Review*, 78 (1973), 394–401; and Peter Loewenberg, "Psychohistorical Perspectives. . ." Note also Saul Friedländer, *History and Psychoanalysis* (New York: Holmes and Meir, 1978).
30. Hoffman, "Psychoanalytic Interpretations. . ."
31. Walter C. Langer, *The Mind of Adolf Hitler: The Secret Wartime Report* (New York: New American Library, 1973).
32. Henry V. Dicks, "Personality Traits and National Socialist Ideology: A Wartime Study of German Prisoners of War," *Human Relations* (1950), 111–154 (this became, later, *Licensed Mass Murder: A Socio-psychological Study of Some SS Killers*, (New York, 1972); Eugene Lerner, "Pathological Nazi Stereotypes Found in Recent German Technical Journals," *Journal of Psychology*, 13 (1942), 187–92; Bertram Schaffner, *Father Land: A Study of Authoritarianism in the German Family*, (New York, 1948); Paul Keczkemeti and Nathan Leites, "Some Psychological Hypotheses on Nazi Germany," *Journal of Social Psychology*, **26,** part 2 (November, 1947), 141–83; 27, part 1 (February 1948), 91–117; 27, part 2 (May, 1948), 241–70; 28, part 1 (August, 1948), 141–64; David C. McClelland, *The Roots of Consciousness* (New York, 1964).
33. James H. McRandle, *The Tracks of the Wolf* (Evanston: Northwestern University Press, 1965); Alexander Mitscherlich, *Society Without The Father: A Contribution to Social Psychology*, trans. Eric Mosbacker (New York: Schocken Books, 1970); Peter Loewenberg, "The Psychohistorical Origins . . . ," and "The Unsuccessful Adolescence of Heinrich Himmler," *American Historical Review*, 76 (1971), 612–641; Rudolph Binion, *Hitler Among the Germans*; Robert G. L. Waite, *The Psychopathic God*; Saul Friedländer, *L'Antisemitisme Nazi: Histoire d'une psychose collective* (Paris: Le Senil, 1971).
34. For example, Robert C. Tucker, *Stalin as Revolutionary, 1829–1929*, (New York: Norton, 1973); and Bruce Mazlish, *James and John Stuart Mill: Father and Son in The Nineteenth Century* (London: Hutchinson, 1975). The best bibliographic listing of psychohistorical material in European history is Friedländer, *History and Psychoanalysis*.
35. See, for example, Gordon Fellman, "Leaf in a Storm: Jayaprakash Narayan as Politician and as Saint," *Psychohistory Review*, 9 (1981), 183–213; and the essay by Muslin and Desai in this volume.
36. Brugger, ed. *Our Selves, Our Past*; Albin, ed., *New Directions*. Note two special issues of *The Psychohistory Review*: "American Culture," 10 (1982) and "Psychological Studies of the James Family," 8 (1979).
37. Strozier, *Lincoln's Quest for Union*; Erikson, *Dimensions*.
38. Robert Jay Lifton, *Thought Reform and the Psychology of Totalism: A Study of 'Brainwashing' in China*, (New York: Norton, 1971); *History and Human Survival* (New York: Random House, 1970); *Death in Life*; and *Home From the War*.

CHAPTER 7

NEW DIRECTIONS
Heinz Kohut

CHARLES B. STROZIER AND DANIEL OFFER

The most recent and relevant ideas to emerge in psychoanalysis have been those of Heinz Kohut (1913–1981). Unlike cult figures such as Erikson who left mainstream psychoanalysis for the university, Kohut proudly bore the title "Mr. Psychoanalysis." From the late 1940s until the mid-1960s, he faithfully and diligently (and rather quietly) kept the psychoanalytic flame alive within the tight world of psychoanalytic orthodoxy, serving on numerous committees for the Chicago Institute (where he was on the faculty) and for the American Psychoanalytic Association. In the mid-1960s and throughout the 1970s, Kohut published a series of papers and books that challenged many stale ideas in psychoanalysis and offered alternative ways of thinking about human behavior developmentally and in depth.[1] His goal was to redefine psychoanalysis and revitalize it, not to break free from it as so many others who seriously challenge the theory have done. In time Kohut was to call his work the psychoanalytic psychology of the self.

Kohut is important for future directions in psychohistory in several ways. Like Freud, he has developed a consistent and interesting way of conceptualizing human behavior that is both theoretically relevant and methodologically feasible for expanding our understanding of the past. Furthermore, Kohut has reflected often on psychohistory and written many diverse asides and even whole pieces on historical issues (though some are as yet unpublished).[2] His main historical interests concern the

subject of this book—leadership. He has written on the new meanings
of psychobiography in terms of self-psychology, on the underlying psychological issues in group behavior, and, most importantly, on the *relationship* between leader and follower and their mutual interdependen-
cies and interactions.

Throughout his writings, Kohut has often found it useful to provide
brief sketches of historical figures to illustrate some point. For example,
in his now classic paper, "Forms and Transformations of Narcissism"
(1966), he cited Winston Churchill as an example of the interplay of the
grandiose self, the ego, and the superego in determining personality.
Churchill, as a child, had attempted to jump across a ravine to escape
pursuing playmates. It was days before he regained consciousness and
months before he began walking again. Nor was this episode an isolated
event in Churchill's life. He seemed to possess an uncanny ability to
extricate himself from apparently hopeless situations. Kohut suspects
that for many of his early years, Churchill's grandiosity was not completely under control, though later, "when he reached the peak of his
responsibilities the inner balance had shifted."[3] As a child, however,
Churchill almost died at the hands of his impulsive grandiosity. According to Kohut, he jumped the ravine because, deep down, he thought he
could fly.[4]

Such grandiosity can take many forms, as Kohut has often noted in
his various asides on Hitler. In his 1971 discussion of mirror transferences, Kohut noted how frequently the fantasy of magical-sadistic
control over the world enters into thoughts of certain kinds of patients.[5]
More specifically, Kohut speculated about Hitler's "healed-over psychosis," with which he emerged from his lonely period of isolation between
1907 and 1913. At the center of that psychosis was "the fixed idea that
the Jews had invaded the body of Germany and had to be eradicated."[6]

In such psychobiographical asides, Kohut never attempted to provide a complete analysis of the figure in question or to write what Erikson has labeled a "life history." The evidence from the biographies of
Churchill and Hitler is used selectively and for illustrative, rather than
analytical, purposes. In the process, Kohut suggested some new lines of
psychobiographical investigation, even though his primary interest was
to enrich his discussion of basically clinical material. The model clearly
was Freud, who drew creatively on literary, historical, anthropological,
and political examples to enliven his discussion of theoretical issues.
Kohut, as Freud, recognized the limits of such an approach.

But there is more methodological meat to Kohut's psychobiographical vignettes than is immediately apparent. For one thing, Kohut's careful attention to narcissistic issues opens up categories of evidence from a

much later period in a figure's life than we are accustomed to handling in psychohistory. Although any serious writer strains against the regressive pulls into his figure's childhood (because in the end there simply is no evidence from a dead person's infancy), a theoretical emphasis on drives and object relations far too often forces the psychohistorian into facile reconstruction of developmental issues. Kohut avoids this tendency. Thus his example of Churchill's grandiosity is firmly based on the leader's own concrete autobiographical report.

Freudian drive theory leads the unwary biographer into the very private and largely inaccessible realm of a significant figure's loves and hates, unconscious fantasies, and symbolic interactions with his or her contemporaries. Kohut's approach on the other hand—indeed his whole psychology of the self—permits the observer to interpret what we actually see: a figure's goals and ambitions, his ideas, and all the complex interactions characterizing his life's work.[7]

Kohut's concept of the group self as a way of thinking about large and complex groups, even whole nations, is rather more elusive. At first sight, it seems little more than a rarified abstraction and evokes familiar problems of talking about the idea of a national personality. Kohut, however, used the idea of the group self,—defined as the sum total of those clusters of interconnected experiences of each individual that prevail in consequence of his temporary or continuous submersion into the group—to define the underlying psychological basis of group cohesion and fragmentation. According to Kohut, the strivings of the group self are just as complicated as those of the individual self—and directly analogous to it. Thus, groups form and remain together in part because they share an ego ideal, as Freud first described in 1921. Kohut argued that groups also share a kind of "subject-bound grandiosity," or a grandiose self, which provides an important cohesive glue.[8] Groups also share ideals—the religious, cultural, and political threads woven into the fabric of our heritage—as important bases for the cohesion of the group self. One particularly interesting application of this idea was Kohut's discussion of the psychoanalytic group self's idealization of Freud. Such a shared ideal, he argued in 1976, provides a solid safeguard against narcissistic tensions (such as shame) and protects against narcissistic disequilibria (such as envy, jealousy, and rage).[9]

This conceptualization of group behavior provides a range of insights into some very old issues. For example, the idealized group image of late nineteenth-century Germany centered around all-powerful, authoritarian, politically and militarily omnipotent images that fused together patriarchal family patterns with antidemocratic political traditions. Such idealization spawned political passivity and was in turn fed by rapid military victories, the growth of an empire, and economic dynamism. The other constituents of Germany's group self centered on grandiose notions of world domination and cultural preeminence. The humiliating loss in the First World War then created extreme, rageful responses because the whole basis of the German group self's cohesion was threatened. Fragmentation, which historically expresses itself as political, social, and economic chaos, resulted. In time, a strutting little corporal provided brittle but desperately sought narcissistic nourishment for Germany's bruised self. What followed was a frantic search for revenge as "Hitler exploited the readiness of a civilized nation to shed the thin layer of its uncomfortably carried restraints."[10]

Kohut, however, seldom thought of the group self except in the context of its leaders. He thus sought avowedly to pursue a historical understanding of politics and culture that reflected his clinical findings of the way in which objects and selfobjects are always and necessarily intertwined. As he himself expressed it some years ago:

> There is an important difference between group processes in history and that of the individual in psychoanalysis. In the clinical situation it is in regard to a single person—the analyst—around which the transferences establish themselves and are worked through. In the arena of history, however, it is either the leader who mobilizes the transferences or a leading group that fills this role. Furthermore, primitive and unstable identifications in the historical field take place always in relation to a single dominant figure who by his presence is able to give instant relief to the diseased group self, while the slow process of working through that leads to a stable firming of a diseased group self requires the interpretative presence of many active and influential minds. What moves society toward health is the creative work of individuals in religion, philosophy, art, and in the sciences concerned with man (sociology, political science, history, psychology). These leaders are in empathic contact with the illness of the group self and, through their work and thought, mobilize the unfulfilled narcissistic needs and point the way toward vital social changes. It follows that during crisis in the group self there is an absence of creativity in religion, philosophy, art, and in the sciences of man. The absence of creative experimental art during such periods is a striking phenomenon. Creativity in all fields is choked off. There is no one in empathic touch with the diseased group self. This points toward the increasingly worsening condition of the group self.
>
> The example of Hitler and the Nazis, was—and is—an example of chronic weakness in the German group self. Would other nations have been able to respond to the attacks on group self structures to which the German nation was exposed in the pre-Hitler period by

successfully mobilizing all their inner resources? Was the acute destruction of its structure less severe, less widespread than the corresponding aspects of Germany's illness? Germany had suffered external defeats. The German nation lacked the conviction to sustain group cohesion in face of defeat. It was too recently established as a nation to feel secure. It had not successfully asserted itself and taken the responsibility for its destiny. It was still weak and relied on being told by external forces not only what to *believe* but also what it *was*.

It does not seem to me that the blow of having lost World War I and of having to pay reparations should be considered as the psychological basis for Germany's readiness to espouse the Hitlerian remedy for its self-pathology. The Nazis clearly exploited German sensibilities in order to harness the ensuing narcissistic rage in the service of their vengeful atrocities and of a vengeful war. Nevertheless, we are not dealing here with the primary manifestations of a diseased group self but with the secondary symptoms of an underlying self disorder. The disease itself, as would be the case with an individual patient, was silent. What the skilled psycho-historian must look for now, in retrospect, is evidence for a sense of group depression, a lack of vitality, and a sense of discontinuity in time and of fragmentation in space. Behind the noisy rage was a despair that the demands for respect and the legitimate needs for a merger with powerful ego ideals were not only responded to in action but before Hitler received no effectively communicative recognition through words or by other symbolic means. Basing myself openly and unashamedly on the profound insights about man's self and its experiences and reactions that are obtained in individual psychoanalytic treatment of patients with self pathology, I suggest that the psychological illness of pre-Hitler Germany was not caused by the external adversities to which Germany was exposed at that time. Of course they mattered, especially since these adversities occurred not only in the realm of power and greatness via defeat and poverty but also in the realm of ideals. But the real issue was the absence of an empathic matrix that would have recognized and acknowledged the emotional needs of the German group self exposed to such external adversities.[11]

Change occurs slowly in the substantive scholarship of a relatively new field. Neither Kohut's work nor anyone else's offers a theoretical panacea. Certainly, there are no scales to fall from the eyes of anyone seriously interested in asking good questions about motivation in history. But we must know our past to have a future. The contributions that follow in this volume suggest the range of Kohut's impact on recent work in the field. We need further integration of such research, the clarification of purpose for the field in general, and the determination to keep intellectually alive on that fragile bridge linking history and psychology. The challenge is before us. In the playful words of Maurice Sendak, "Let the wild rumpus start."

NOTES

1. Heinz Kohut, *The Analysis of the Self: A Systematic Approach to the Psychoanalytic Treatment of Narcissistic Disorders* (New York: International Universities Press, 1971); *The Restoration of the Self* (New York: International Universities Press, 1977); *The Search for the Self: Selected Writings of Heinz Kohut: 1950–1978*, two vols., ed. Paul H. Ornstein, (New York: International Universities Press, 1978).
2. Heinz Kohut, *The Self and History*, ed. Charles B. Strozier, (New York: Norton, 1985).
3. Heinz Kohut, "Forms and Transformations of Narcissism," *Journal of the American Psychoanalytic Association*, 14 (1966), 257.
4. Kohut returned to Churchill in "Creativeness, Charisma, Group Psychology: Reflections on the Self-Analysis of Freud," in *Freud: The Fusion of Science and Humanism*, ed. John E. Gedo and George H. Pollock, *Psychological Issues*, Monograph 34/35 (New York: International Universities Press, 1976), p. 411.
5. Kohut, *Analysis of the Self*, p. 150.
6. Ibid., 256.
7. Note John Demos's comments in "The Self In History," ed. Charles B. Strozier, *Newsletter of the Group for the Use of Psychology in History*, 3 (1975), 3–10.
8. Heinz Kohut, "Thoughts on Narcissism and Narcissistic Rage," *The Psychoanalytic Study of the Child*, 27 (1972), 397–398.
9. Kohut, "Creativeness, Charisma. . . ," p. 389.
10. Kohut, "Thoughts on Narcissism" pp. 362 and 367.
11. The following quote is from an unpublished manuscript of Kohut's that will appear, perhaps somewhat modified, in *The Self and History*, ed. Charles B. Strozier.

PART II

STUDIES

LINCOLN AND THE CRISIS OF THE 1850s
Thoughts on the Group Self

CHARLES B. STROZIER

Psychohistory has long struggled to find ways of bridging individual and group experience. It has been a field painfully focused on biography, which is interesting but, in the minds of most historians, ultimately trivial. The individual case may or may not illuminate the whole. The idiosyncracy of personal experience can never be factored out. The leading journal in the discipline of history, the *American Historical Review*, for example, refuses to publish biographical articles except in unusual circumstances, and then only when the connection between the individual figure's life and larger historical events is made explicit.

Freud tried to extrapolate directly from psychology to history, from the individual to the group, from ontogeny to phylogeny. Thus his biographical sketches of Leonardo da Vinci, Wilson, and Moses have their direct analogue in his treatment of the origin of culture and civilization. The link is not very convincing. Erikson's titanic struggles with identity were not much more productive. He was successful in showing that a careful psychological biography could be written. The "pathographies" of Freud's day were not the only model. But Erikson's greatest weakness was his discussion of group experience and how his figures related to that experience. More recently, a few scholars have found selected points of psychohistorical access to the past that are not biographical, for example John Demos' discussion of colonial family life, Carroll Smith-Rosenberg's research on female friendship in the nineteenth century, Robert Jay Lifton's interview work on "shared themes," and Fred Weinstein's sociological work that emphasizes the psychological cost of traumatic disruption of the symbolic code.[1]

Dissatisfaction, however, prevails, and nowhere is it greater than among those interested in leadership. A leader's story is necessarily biographical, and yet the very fact of his or her role as leader only makes sense as a precipitate of the aspirations, needs, and confusions of a specific group of followers at a unique moment of the past. Hitler and Gandhi are incomprehensible outside of Nazi Germany and colonial India, respectively. Most historians solve this problem by writing "life and times" biographies. At its best, such work nicely keeps two parallel stories going simultaneously. The cost of such an approach, however, is that the biographer operates at the psychological surface. But as soon as one probes for greater psychological depth and clarity, one loses sight of the world beyond the leader and the historical context, without which the leader makes no sense.

The work of Heinz Kohut, especially as it relates to leadership and the group self, offers some intriguing suggestions for resolving this dilemma. With anything new (and tentative), there are inevitably questions of method and terminology that arise. Chapters one through eight of this book discuss in some detail these issues in the general context of the history of psychohistory. To avoid redundancy, therefore, in this chapter discursive definitions will be avoided. What is attempted instead is a specific application of self-psychology to one small piece of the past: Abraham Lincoln and the 1850s in the United States. The individual is not writ large here (as in Erikson's work), nor does the group's experience simply reflect the stages of an individual life (as in Freud). Rather, there is a complicated, interdependent tie that connects the leader's experience with the psychological agenda of the group. The two exist, in a sense, symbiotically. History, psychology, and sociology must necessarily be woven together.

LINCOLN, SLAVERY, AND THE HOUSE DIVIDED

In 1858, Lincoln was a political figure little known outside of Illinois. For four years, he had vigorously opposed the prospect of slavery's extension into the territories, made politically feasible in Stephen A. Douglas's doctrine of popular sovereignty that was introduced in the Kansas-Nebraska Act (1854). Lincoln believed strongly by 1858, that Stephen Douglas was the principal spokesman for a disastrous set of policies dealing with issues that the country faced. The country's founders, in Lincoln's view, had reluctantly accepted slavery as a southern institution. They recognized its existence and even validated its perpetuation with the three-fifths compromise. Such constitutional protection had justified federal laws governing the return of fugitive slaves for over half a century. It was thus illegal and unconstitutional to talk of abolition and the mobilization of a national effort to end the South's peculiar institution. Lincoln hated the realities of tracking down fugitive slaves but reluctantly accepted the practice. He told Joshua Speed in 1855:

> I also acknowledge *your* rights and *my* obligations, under the Constitution, in regard to your slaves. I confess I hate to see the poor creatures hunted down, and caught, and carried back to their stripes, and unrewarded toils; but I bite my lip and keep quiet.[2]

Nevertheless, Lincoln believed that the Constitutional recognition of slavery in the South by no means meant that the founders approved of an institution that excluded a whole race from the benefits of the principles outlined in the Declaration of Independence. The only way the founders had to secure passage of the Constitution was to allow slavery to exist. But just as God defines ethical perfection, Lincoln continued, so the Constitution sets up a standard for legal action. "If we cannot give freedom to every creature," Lincoln argued in the summer of 1858, "let us do nothing that will impose slavery upon any other creature."[3] Slavery, Lincoln stated again and again in the 1850s, was morally wrong, a "monstrous injustice," as he called it in 1854.[4] "I have always hated slavery I think as much as any abolitionist," he proclaimed in 1858.[5] Furthermore, this powerfully negative judgment of slavery, he argued, lay behind most of the founders' thinking when they accepted the three-fifths compromise. It took one hundred years of agitation, Lincoln once noted, to abolish the slave trade in Great Britain.[6] Men like Thomas Jefferson and George Washington had been tied to slavery economically but were politically and morally opposed to it. Life as they knew it in the South seemed inconceivable without slaves, but all had hoped for a better day when slaves could be freed and returned to Africa, and the ideals of life, liberty, and the pursuit of happiness genuinely engaged. Lincoln recognized the inconsistencies in this position but accepted the muddle as all too human. His great hero was Henry Clay, who could eloquently criticize those who would blow out the moral lights around us while sipping a mint julep served by a black house slave.

Thus, the heart of Lincoln's opposition to slavery was moral and Constitutional. The people of the South, he said, had an "immediate

FIGURE 1. Lincoln, the circuit lawyer, photographed at Beardstown, Illinois on May 7, 1858. (Source: Illinois State Historical Library, Old State Capitol, Springfield, Illinois 62706)

and palpable and immensely great pecuniary interest" in their institution, but for those in the North "it is merely an abstract question of moral right, with only *slight* and *remote* pecuniary interest added."[7] However, the abstract issue for Lincoln was not as far removed from political reality as the term might suggest. "When the white man governs himself that is self-government; but when he governs himself, and also governs *another* man, that is *more* than self-government—that is despotism."[8] The moral issue was abstract only in that the Declaration of Independence defined a standard of equality that did not explicitly include the Negroes. The founding documents defined republican institutions and established the criteria for assessing the ethics of political action in modern society. The documents, however, were complex, varied, contradictory—and human. Lincoln argued vehemently after 1854 in favor of the abolitionists to the extent that they opposed the extension of slavery while he also argued for the return of fugitive slaves. "Stand with anybody that stands RIGHT," he thundered. "Stand with him while he is right and PART with him when he goes wrong. Stand WITH the abolitionist in restoring the Missouri Compromise; and stand against him when he attempts to repeal the fugitive slave law."[9]

Lincoln also had strong economic views on the poisonous effect of slavery on white workers. "As I would not be a slave," he wrote, "so I would not be a master. This expresses my idea of democracy."[10] In general, Lincoln was a decided economic optimist. When he wrote about inventions or technological progress, he became almost boyish in his buoyant, hopeful, assertive enthusiasm. "All creation is a mine," he began his first lecture on discoveries and inventions, "and every man a miner." Lincoln went on to stress the uniqueness of man, who may work like animals, but, unlike them, improves on his workmanship.[11] Lincoln's view of technology was clearly optimistic; it was almost somewhat naive. He seemed to accept unquestionably that technological progress carried with it moral improvement. And that is the link to slavery. The slave was kept apart from the just rewards for his labor. That degraded him and his master and perverted democratic institutions. Our republican form of government as defined by the Constitution required free labor, which in turn brought opportunity, progress, hope. Slavery dashed all to the ground.[12]

Yet the evil of slavery went along, in Lincoln's thought, with a mournful sense of racial inequality between white and black.[13] For there is no denying that at this point in his life Lincoln in the 1850s was convinced blacks were inferior and did not deserve social or political equality with whites. He made that point often, though most vociferously at Charleston in 1858: "I am not, nor ever have been in favor of bringing about in any way the social and political equality of the white and black races." Lincoln would not make voters or jurors of blacks, nor qualify them to hold office, nor allow them to intermarry with whites. He believed that the physical differences of the races would always keep them from living together on equal terms and that whites would always be superior. Just because he did not want a Negro woman to be his slave did not mean he wanted her for a wife; he could just leave her alone.[14]

These are not pleasant statements. As the historian Kenneth M. Stampp has recently put it, Lincoln's speech at Charleston represents Lincoln's "fullest and most explicit declaration of belief in white supremacy."[15] Charleston, however, was not an isolated event in Lincoln's struggle with the issue of racial equality. Clearly, before that audience leaned South in sentiment, Lincoln was rather more explicit in stating his white supremacist views. It has been frequently noted that Lincoln altered his emphasis on these matters, depending on which part of Illinois he found himself in; indeed, during the debates, Stephen Douglas himself charged Lincoln with inconsistency on exactly this issue. But it would be naive to ignore the essential racism that informed Lincoln's thought wherever he spoke. In Peoria in 1854, he frankly acknowledged that his own feelings would not allow him to entertain the notion of political and social equality between the races. And, he added as a shrewd politician, "If mine would, we well know that those of the great mass of white people will not."[16] Even in Chicago, Lincoln stressed the numerous categories of inequality between white and black in the same breath that he claimed minimal rights of life, liberty and the pursuit of happiness for Negroes in America.[17] The Declaration of Independence, Lincoln noted in Springfield in 1857, never intended to assert that all men are equal in all respects. Such a notion is patently absurd, in any event. The Declaration simply defined basic rights and clarified a "standard maxim for free society" that, although never attained, could be admired, striven for, and perhaps, in time, approximated.[18]

The fact that Lincoln held back from the notion of full equality for blacks does not necessarily cast doubt on the sincerity of his insistence that they be granted minimal rights under the Constitution. For example, when Lincoln argued that the Declaration of Independence defined a standard maxim for free society, he was nudging his fellow citizens toward giving rights to blacks that they did not then possess. In the 1850s such an assertion had overtones of abolitionism, which was the label that would most harm Lincoln politically (and the one that Stephen Douglas was most eager to pin on him). Lincoln made tortuous, indeed specious, distinctions after 1854, but he recognized the humanity of blacks. They were people, albeit inferior in some odd and almost incomprehensible way. Our sensibilities tend to emphasize the prejudices that remained in the man we generally admire as a paragon of American virtue. But in the 1850s white supremacy was taken for granted; what was remarkable was that Lincoln had the courage to brand slavery *wrong*, oppose its extension into the territories on moral and political grounds, and risk association with abolitionism. As Frederick Douglass pointed out, Lincoln was always devoted entirely to the welfare of whites. He was willing to postpone, deny, or sacrifice the rights of blacks. He came to the presidency opposed only to the spread of slavery. His patriotic dreams embraced only whites. He supported the Fugitive Slave Law and would have eagerly suppressed any uprising. Whites were his natural children; blacks were his only by adoption. Yet, Douglass concluded, "measuring him by the sentiment of his country . . . he was swift, zealous, radical and determined."[19]

It was not easy for Lincoln to resolve his genuine and growing hatred of slavery with his white supremacist views. Furthermore, to abolish slavery was not only unconstitutional but also impractical, for what would happen to the slaves? They would become unequal members of a society in which they could never fully participate: "If all earthly power were given me," said Lincoln in 1854, "I should not know what to do, as to the existing institution. My first impulse would be to free all slaves, and send them to Liberia—to their own native land."[20] Lincoln saw acutely that colonization of blacks would be expensive, dangerous and time-consuming, but he also felt it might be the only viable solution. There seemed to be only two alternatives: free the slaves and keep them in America as "underlings" or make them fully equal. Both alternatives seemed to him impossible from a white perspective.[21] And so he toyed for years with colonization schemes, as absurd and offensive in retrospect as they seemed sensible and humane at the time. In 1852 he eulogized Clay's efforts since 1816 to return blacks to Africa:

> May it indeed be realized! . . . If as the friends of colonization hope, the present and coming generations of our countrymen shall by any means, succeed in freeing our land from the dangerous presence of slavery; and, at the same time, in restoring a captive people to their long-lost father-land, with bright prospects for the future; and this too, so gradually that neither races nor individuals shall have suffered by the change, it will indeed be a glorious consummation.[22]

Lincoln himself was an active member of Springfield's Colonization Society, to which he spoke on January 4, 1855.[23] When Lincoln talked of the "ultimate extinction" of slavery in the "house divided" speech, he may have had colonization in the back of his mind.[24]

The confusions, contradictions, and specific distinctions built into Lincoln's thought about the interrelated issues of slavery and racial equality in the 1850s reflected the fact that his primary concern lay elsewhere—with the preservation of the union. For the political issue in the slavery question was not abolition but extension, and on that question Lincoln saw the country hurtling toward civil war. The Constitution was vague in what it intended to happen regarding slavery in newly acquired territories. A sensibly worked out compromise in 1820 had seemed to settle the matter forever. However, the huge acquisitions from Mexico after 1848 and renewed tensions between North and South on a variety of other fronts fatefully reopened the whole issue of slavery's spread. After much agony and near war, a second compromise was tried in 1850. It seemed secure at first but quickly fell apart under pressure from the man most responsible for putting it together—Stephen Douglas. Douglas was an opportunist, inordinately ambitious, and very interested in the railroads. As chairman of the Senate Committee on the Territories, he wanted to push through a bill in 1854 that would quickly organize Kansas and Nebraska. Effective state government would then make possible the construction of a transcontinental railroad. In one blow, Douglas hoped to solve the most vexing political issue of the day and, of course, assume leadership of the country for his labors.

The key, he felt, lay in allowing the states to decide for themselves whether they would be free or slave. To justify this side-stepping of the issue of slavery, Douglas invoked the concept of popular sovereignty. For Douglas, popular sovereignty was a convenient and perfectly legitimate evasion of the moral passions that inflamed the debate over slavery. He personally did not care whether slavery was voted up or down. Let the people decide. For Lincoln, however, popular sovereignty was a grossly inappropriate concept for dealing with the question of slavery in the territories. The founders, he felt, never intended to allow slavery to extend beyond its original location in the states of the South. If left alone, slavery would in time wither away. But slavery must not be given a new lease on life in the territories. Thus the democratic principle of local self-government in the territories had to give way to the larger concern for legitimate government and the principles of the Declaration of Independence.

PARANOIA AND THE GROUP SELF

On June 16, 1858, in the sultry heat of the legislative chamber, Abraham Lincoln spoke to the assembled members of the State Republican Convention. That afternoon the convention had nominated him as its candidate for the United States Senate. Lincoln spoke to accept the nomination and to outline his sense of current issues and future agendas.

The speech began with a rhetorical flourish—constituting some seven percent of its total—that has immortalized the speech in our political history:

If we could first know *where* we are, and *whither* we are tending, we could then better judge *what* to do, and *how* to do it.

We are now far into the *fifth* year, since a policy was initiated, with the *avowed* object, and *confident* promise, of putting an end to slavery agitation.

Under the operation of that policy, that agitation has not only, *not ceased*, but has constantly *augmented*.

In *my* opinion, it *will* not cease, until a *crisis* shall have been reached, and passed.

"A house divided against itself cannot stand."

I believe this government cannot endure, permanently half *slave* and half *free*.

I do not expect the Union to be *dissolved*—I do not expect the house to *fall*—but I *do* expect it will cease to be divided.

It will become *all* one thing, or *all* the other.

Either the *opponents* of slavery will arrest the further spread of it, and place it where the public mind shall rest in the belief that it is in the course of ultimate extinction; or its *advocates* will push it forward, till it shall become alike lawful in *all* the States, *old* as well as *new*— North as well as *South*.[25]

There were, however, two distinct parts to the "house divided" speech. The familiar opening flourish built psychologically on Lincoln's own experiences, feelings, and needs. His rhetorical domestication of politics nicely expressed his own deepest concerns and could be grasped clearly by a country dangerously close to civil war. But the heart of the speech—and what most of it dealt with—outlined a remarkable Southern conspiracy to nationalize slavery. Lincoln developed his theory in the context of a brief history of recent events, which, if examined dispassionately, he argued, showed clear "evidence of design" and "concert of action." Lincoln felt the conspiracy was hatched early, for the "first point gained" was the Kansas-Nebraska Bill of 1854, which had opened up the territories to slavery on the spurious grounds of popular sovereignty. Then, in 1856, came the election of President Buchanan, a weak but decidedly pro-Southern Democrat. Thus was the second point gained. The third and final point came immediately following Buchanan's inauguration when the Supreme Court announced its decision on the Dred Scott case. In this decision the "machinery" of the conspiracy reached full operating condition. It declared that no black slave or his descendant could ever become a citizen; that neither Congress nor a territorial legislature could exclude slavery from any territory; and that it was up to the separate slave states to deal with whether a slave was made free by passing into free states. In theory, at least, this part of the decision virtually endorsed southern kidnapping of free Northern blacks.

"Several things will now appear less dark and mysterious," Lincoln commented, "than they did when they were transpiring." And he continued:

> We can not absolutely know that all these exact adaptations are the result of preconcert. But when we see a lot of framed timbers, different portions of which we know have been gotten out at different times and places and by different workmen—Stephen [Douglas], Franklin [Pearce], Roger [Taney] and James [Buchanan] for instance—and when we see these timbers joined together, and see they exactly make the frame of a house or a mill, all the tenons and mortices exactly fitting, and all the lengths and proportions of the different pieces exactly adapted to their respective places, and not a piece too many or too few—not omitting even scaffolding—or, if a single piece be lacking, we can see the place in the frame exactly fitted and prepared to yet bring such piece in—in such a case, we find it impossible to not believe that Stephen and Franklin and Roger and James all understood one another from the beginning, and all worked upon a common plan or draft drawn up before the first lick was struck.

Lincoln's interpretation of events dramatically shifted the attention from Kansas and the other territories to Illinois and the free states of the North. We may go to sleep pleasantly in the belief that Missouri will be voted free, Lincoln argued, but "we shall awake to the reality, instead, that the Supreme Court has made Illinois a slave state." And as if that were not enough, Lincoln further argued that the country could also look forward to the reopening of the slave trade with Africa. If it is a sacred right of white men to own slaves, then how can it be less a sacred right to buy them where they can be bought cheapest? That clearly was Africa rather than Virginia.

The conspiracy argument of the speech clarifies significantly the force of the opening flourish. The house, in Lincoln's view, will not endure divided. Either slavery will be nationalized and our free institutions will crumble, or the North will arrest the spread of slavery and put it on a course of ultimate extinction. Many observers immediately saw in this stark vision a call for war to end slavery. To see the inevitable so clearly appeared to hurry it along. Thus Charles Lanphier, editor of Springfield's *Register* (a Democratic paper), lambasted Lincoln for his bellicosity.[26]

Lincoln, however, neither retreated from his conspiracy theory nor relinquished it easily. He was irritated that Douglas chose largely to ignore the charge.[27] Lincoln returned to conspiracy throughout the debates with Douglas in the late summer and fall of 1858.[28] As late as September 16, 1859, Lincoln told an audience in Columbus, Ohio that the Republican party must stand firm against the conspiracy to revive the African slave trade, pass a congressional slave code, and push through an extension of Dred Scott that would explicitly make slavery legal throughout the United States. These developments are not immediately upon us, Lincoln noted. But beware:

> They are not quite ready yet. The authors of these measures know that we are too strong for them; but they will be upon us in due time, and we will be grappling with them hand to hand, if they are not now headed off.[29]

And as late as June 12, 1863, he wrote: "The insurgents had been preparing for [the war] more than thirty years, while the Government had taken no steps to resist them."[30]

It is dramatically obvious in retrospect how wrong Lincoln was in his conspiracy theory.[31] For as he formulated it, the conspiracy went well beyond the schemes of southern fanatics. The leaders, in Lincoln's view, were the preeminent political figures of the day: president of the United States, James Buchanan; chief justice of the Supreme Court, Roger B. Taney; and, of course, Stephen Douglas. Because Douglas was generally acknowledged as the most important Democratic senator, Lincoln's sense of the conspirators' base of operations included all three branches of government: executive, judicial and legislative. There appears to have been some collusion between Buchanan and Taney over the Dred Scott case, but beyond that, it is most unlikely that an elaborate conspiracy among Douglas, Buchanan and Taney could have hatched in 1854, developed in 1856, and matured in 1857. For one thing, Buchanan and Douglas hated each other. Douglas had expected to receive a prized position in the Buchanan administration but was instead unaccountably snubbed and isolated entirely from any position of influence. Douglas then opposed Buchanan on the Lecompton Constitution, and Buchanan retaliated by trying to remove Douglas's patronage base in Illinois. This political battle preoccupied the state in the months before Lincoln delivered his house divided speech. There is also only meager evidence of radical Southerners calling for a revival of the slave trade. It is hard to imagine the leaders of the three branches of government actually planning such an act. Nor was a national slave code envisioned by serious politicians. There had been enough trouble with the Fugitive Slave Law, which was a part of the Compromise of 1850. Lincoln had not only lost perspective but he had also misinterpreted the drift of politics.

Lincoln's misperception of events in 1858 seems paranoid. Why he responded to the rush of events with such miscalculated fervor is perplexing. It is quite possible he was simply seizing the public's mood and giving it voice. Certainly, he was a reasonable man. There is little in his early development that even hints at paranoia. He was then—and later—noted for his generosity toward his enemies, his warmth and understanding. It is clear that he sensed the crisis and made it his own. He articulated its latent meanings as few others could. He gave it shape, if not direction. The fact is that paranoia pervaded people's minds. Lincoln responded empathetically to their deepest fears. "He knew the American people better than they knew themselves" said Frederick Douglass.[32]

Lincoln's apparent paranoia fed on and reflected a widespread, indeed rampant, paranoia throughout the land. His opponent in the Senate race, Stephen Douglas, returned Lincoln's charges with his own, rather more deviously conceived, exaggeration of the implications of Lincoln's program for the country. During the debates, Douglas exhorted his listeners to vote for Lincoln,

> If you desire negro citizenship, if you desire to allow them to come into the State and settle with the white man, if you desire them to vote on an equality with yourselves, and to make them eligible to office, to serve on juries, and to adjudge your rights, then support Mr. Lincoln and the Black Republican party, who are in favor of the citizenship of the negro.[33]

Lincoln repeatedly tried to answer Douglas by pointing out that he was neither an amalgamationist (in favor of bringing the races fully together) nor an abolitionist; that just because he wanted to grant a Negro woman her legitimate rights did not mean he wanted to marry her; and that his moral opposition to slavery in no way represented an abolitionist desire to forcibly free the slaves.[34] It is hard to believe Douglas was not aware of these distinctions, but then it is equally difficult to understand the meanings of Lincoln's conspiracy theory, which put Douglas at the center of a malevolent plot to nationalize slavery.

Politics in America breeds competition, suspicion, and overstatement. Individuals of roughly comparable ability and party-backing struggle against each other for elected office. At stake are their own fortunes and those of their parties as well as those of the literally thousands of hangers-on who expect to benefit from victory. In America the political system as it evolved in the Jacksonian era put unusual stress on the competitive personal aspects of vying for elective office. A long tradition of virulence legitimated the most outrageous charges and counter-charges. In the fiercely contested election of 1828, for example,

Andrew Jackson was called the son of a prostitute and a Negro, a usurper, a gambler, a cockfighter, a brawler, a drunkard, an illiterate, and a person unfit for high office. His wife, furthermore, was called an adulteress. John Quincy Adams, it seems, was a panderer, who had bought the presidency, was opposed to American institutions, and had grossly misspent public funds during his administration. Even Henry Clay was not spared. He was described as a traitor who had instigated the assassination of William Morgan to prevent the exposure of freemasonry. If 1828 is an extreme example, it is not an unrepresentative one. At all levels of government, this attacking, competitive style prevailed. And the people loved it. Speeches, parades, kegs of whiskey—all helped stir partisan feeling. People endured two-hour-long speeches as the norm and then read a fiercely loyal summary and analysis of the speeches in their violently partisan paper of choice the next day. It was the kind of environment that encouraged political battles and forced extreme positions on otherwise mild men. Something in American politics of the time pushed opponents to their limits.

Until the 1850s, however, the dominant theme in this process was the coarseness of the attack, which seemed to be prompted less by paranoia than by the burning desire to win. For example, as head of the New York Regency, Martin Van Buren was a decidedly unlovely figure in the 1820s and 1830s, but he was not paranoid. Something new appeared on the scene in the 1850s. The dark shadow of paranoia that has always lurked on the fringes of American politics and culture came to block out the sun entirely. Suspiciousness reached extreme proportions. A basically conservative man such as Lincoln shuddered in terror at an imagined conspiracy to nationalize slavery. A less attractive but impressively shrewd politician such as Douglas became increasingly brittle and vulnerable. He might or might not have believed all that he attributed to Lincoln in 1858, but he certainly felt legitimately hounded by President Buchanan in their fight over control of the Democratic party after 1857.[35] Douglas also came under mounting pressure from the Southern wing of the party, which wanted no compromise on anything relating to slavery. Furthermore, what Lincoln and Douglas experienced and felt was repeated in a host of leaders throughout the country. A man such as William Seward, who had resisted compromise in 1850, came to see the inevitability of open conflict to resolve the issue of slavery. Seward, interestingly enough, felt almost as strongly against nativism—the powerful movement that affirmed old ideals of the nation and vigorously opposed the recent immigration from Europe. It has been suggested that Seward lost out to Lincoln in the Republican Convention of 1860 because he (Seward) had offended nativists over the years.[36]

The case of the abolitionists is a fascinating example of the changes in politics and culture from the 1830s to the 1850s. Abolitionists had long reacted with moral outrage and a mounting sense of frustration to the continued existence of slavery. In the 1830s, when the movement began, a strong religious fervor encouraged abolitionists to commit themselves to a variety of reform movements (especially temperance) and remain peaceful, even pacifistic, in their means. As Lawrence Friedman has persuasively argued, however, the degree of genuine pacifism that infused the abolitionists of the 1830s is open to some question.[37] The basic issue the abolitionists failed to grapple with was whether violence was acceptable if used defensively. All agreed the goal was political reform through moral persuasion. The problem, however, was that few considered how to react to violence if directed at themselves. They soon discovered that this question of whether defensively employed violence was consonant with their moral and religious beliefs was the central dilemma they faced. Thus Elijah Lovejoy, an abolitionist editor in Alton, Illinois, saw two printing presses destroyed. On the day of arrival of his third press he and a group of followers were huddled inside the warehouse with guns to ward off attackers. Lovejoy himself, though he never fired a gun, died with a bullet through his heart in the melee that followed.

The reaction to Lovejoy's death provides an interesting litmus test of how genuinely pacifistic the abolitionist movement was in the 1830s. Most abolitionists never really questioned the propriety of Lovejoy's willingness to counter violence with violence. The issue for them was the brutality of the scene, the evils of slavery, the devastating power of the mob. Only Sarah Grimké and a handful of other abolitionists strongly objected to Lovejoy's decision to defend himself. Lovejoy, Grimké felt, had seriously compromised the moral integrity of the reform movement by his willingness to defend the press with his guns.

In the 1830s this debate was remote from the political mainstream. However, the easy accommodation to defensive use of violence was to have fateful consequences for the abolitionists. When they lost their firm commitment to pacifism, in a sense they lost their moral innocence. Pacifism was clearly desirable, but the overriding concern was the end of slavery. And that goal became increasingly elusive for the abolitionists. They watched with growing alarm as the political power of the white-led South, based in slavery, seemed to grow stronger over the years. Moral reform had backfired. Southern power was spreading everywhere, and its bellicosity was growing more shrill every day. The abolitionists felt a mounting sense of suspicion, disorientation, frustration, and anger from 1848 on, which resulted in a loss of cohesion within their movement, that rapidly affected the means they felt were appropriate and necessary to end slavery. Tactics were reconsidered. The old moral pacifism gave way to an accommodation to violence as the only way to end the curse of slavery. John Brown's attack on some pro-slavery settlers in 1856 thus helped reshape attitudes and prepare the ground for his attempted raid on Harper's Ferry in 1859. The articulate black leader, Frederick Douglass, had been informed by Brown of the raid on Harper's Ferry (though Douglass warned him against the plan), and abolitionist William Lloyd Garrison applauded Brown's courage and commitment.

The interesting thing about the example of the abolitionists is that it illustrates how extreme suspiciousness can effectively undermine firmly held beliefs and even passionately valued moral codes. It is said that when the firing on Fort Sumter—the start of the war—was announced in the Senate, a woman cheered lustily from the balcony; she was an abolitionist and for her only war could mean the end of slavery.[38] For the spiritual children of Lyman Beecher, the start of war was a long way from their 1830s program of moral reform through committed pacifism. Mounting frustration had fed abolitionists' fears of Southern power, making them increasingly combative and eventually violent. The more the abolitionists felt out of control (especially after 1848), the more they were filled with rage.

Freud first noted how psychological symptoms often spread. Thus obsessions that begin in a relatively circumscribed form usually become a way of thinking. The Rat Man, for example, first feared that the rat punishment described by the sadistic Captain Nowak would be imposed on his father and the Rat Man's friend, Gisela. But the devastating fears he experienced in connection with rats spread to all facets of his life, and his obsessive rituals to ward off danger had to increase proportionately. In the transference, Freud arrested the spread and focused the fears, anxieties, and conflicts on himself.[39] The same spreading phenomenon is true for phobias and can be true for hysterics (for example, Anna O.).[40] The point is that the underlying conflict, once expressed in a specific form of symptomatology, will invent new variations on the same theme if for some reason the conflict itself is exacerbated. This notion of spreading symptomatology has relevance for an attempt to grasp the underlying issues of the 1850s in what might be called the group self. We must, however, make something of a translation from classical psychoanalysis to self-psychology. For it is not the relationship between conflict and symptom that concerns us, but the meaning of the fragmentation of experience of the group self. As individual members of small, defined groups—abolitionists, Irish immigrants in Boston, Southern white aristocrats—experience intense feelings of suspiciousness, competitiveness, rage, and envy, the effects of a larger group-fragmentation anxiety become evident. Nor does this issue have to be as complicated as it seems. As all of us undoubtedly know, fear and hatred feed on themselves, swallowing up dissenters in any community. A smart, empathic leader, such as Churchill, knows how to arrest the spread of such fear; an equally smart and empathic leader, but one with different motives, such as Hitler, knows how to foster spreading fear and hatred in the group self.

The suspicousness of the 1850s in America was indeed widespread. The transformation of the abolitionist movement in the process of its accommodation to violence refracted the image of Southern white bellicosity and increasing preparedness for war, For Southerners also felt they were under attack. They saw abolitionists crusading against the essence of their way of life, spurring slave revolts and poisoning minds everywhere.

> The antebellum South," Kenneth M. Stampp has recently noted, "was a land troubled by a nagging dread of slave insurrections; indeed, it is impossible to understand the psychology of white Southerners, or the events of the sectional conflict, without taking this fact into account.[41]

George Fitzhugh, a conservative Southern ideologue who sarcastically described the abolitionists as devoted to the "uncouth, dirty, naked little cannibals of Africa,"[42] also expressed the projective fantasies behind the paranoia: "Whilst they dare invoke anarchy in Europe, they dare not inaugurate New York Free Love, and Oneida Incest, and Mormon Polygamy. The moral, religious and social heresies of the North are more monstrous than those of Europe."[43] Furthermore, the white Southern sense of abolitionism was psychologically and politically expansive: it included anyone who was not actively on the side of the South. Lincoln, for example, was perceived as part of the abolitionist conspiracy to destroy the South; he would contain slavery to kill it and work determinedly to keep slaves out of the territories. Many Southerners saw the election of Lincoln in 1860 as an act of aggression deliberately perpetrated against themselves. Within a month and a half after the election, South Carolina seceded; and before Lincoln left Springfield for Washington on February 11, 1861, the seven states of the deep South had seceded. After 1858, the South even turned on Stephen Douglas, who attempted to stand between North and South and find some compromise ground that would focus attention on unity, growth, and the rail-roads and away from slavery, secession, and war. In the debates with Lincoln, it became clear that Douglas was not an unquestioning support-er of the South. The South regarded Douglas' reservations as treason to their cause and, without southern support, Douglas's 1860 presidential hopes were doomed.

One of the many clinical signs of a disorder in the self is the pa-tient's grandiose isolation: the cold, detached, uninvolved individual, whose brittle grandiosity serves to protect the vulnerable nuclear self against crumbling. For example, one of the patients the psychoanalyst Heinz Kohut discusses, Mr. I., began his analysis with a grandiose presentation of his exploits. He described in detail his numerous girlfriends, paintings, and poems, and his wish to be the best patient ever. The direct expression of these fantasies, especially that of being uniquely interesting, opened up the raw feelings that lay beneath: his awkwardness in social situations, his sense of inferiority to people with status and money, and his "big Jewish nose" that had once been oper-ated on at his father's insistence. He had been a sickly child, with many colds, sore throats, and coughs, as well as bronchitis. Beneath the gran-diose exterior of Mr. I. lay massive self-contempt and a low sense of self-esteem. His compulsive sexual activity was not the expression of a healthy self-assertiveness, nor could it be best conceptualized in classic psychoanalytic terms as an essential sexual conflict. It reflected vul-nerabilities in the self.

The clue in distinguishing normal assertiveness or neurotic conflict from grandiose isolation as a disturbance in the self is the brittle texture of the grandiosity. This idea has relevance for the group as well. For the endangered group self and the individuals who make up such a group, exaggerated notions of absolute rightness help hold together—with a Band-Aid, so to speak—the fragmenting nuclear self. The example of Nazi Germany comes to mind immediately, but the United States in the 1850s is in some ways more suggestive of an endangered group self. Most participants in the political turmoil of that decade developed a heightened—and constantly growing—sense of their own rightness. Even Lincoln grew increasingly and somewhat rigidly certain of his views. At first his position was tempered and moderate. In 1854, in a speech in Peoria, Lincoln went to some length to express his under-standing of the South's position: "Before proceeding," he interjected after an assault on slavery and its extension,

> let me say I think I have no prejudice against the Southern people.
> They are just what we would be in their situation. If slavery did not

> now exist amongst them they would not introduce it. If it did now
> exist amongst us, we should not instantly give it up.[44]

By 1857 Lincoln had stopped trying to empathize with the South and
instead focused his attention on what the founders really intended in
the Declaration of Independence as a way of supporting his own position. "They meant to set up a standard maxim for free society," he said
in Springfield in response to the Dred Scott decision,

> which should be familiar to all and revered by all; constantly looked
> to, constantly labored for, and even though never perfectly attained,
> constantly approximated, and thereby constantly spreading and
> deepening its influence, and augmenting the happiness and value of
> life to all people of all colors everywhere.[45]

The generosity of Lincoln's outlook, however, gave way to the assertive
sense of noble and moral rightness in the "house divided" speech (the
opening flourish) that was psychologically the counterpart of the deep-
seated fears of a conspiracy to nationalize slavery (the bulk of the
speech). Events had pushed Lincoln to assume an increasingly shrill
tone in asserting his own moral and political rectitude.

The evolution of Lincoln's articulate, pained and sensitive thoughts
on slavery from empathic opposition to a belief in conspiracy that was
closely tied to his own sense of moral correctness suggests the broader
significance of these issues for the group self. Indeed, it was characteristic in the 1850s to assert loudly how right one was and how wrong
everyone else was. It was this holier-than-thou quality that so alienated
society from the abolitionists. Their self-protective response to this alien-
ation was to withdraw even further, which in turn heightened both their
sense of superiority and of being under seige.[46] The vocal Southern
whites similarly grew progressively assertive and grandiose in their
claims for the superiority of Southern life. George Fitzhugh, for example, became a passionate defender of slavery after 1854 and an equally
vigorous critic of free society and Northern ideas of personal liberty.[47]

Perhaps a second, well-known clinical case will help illustrate how
diffused grandiosity connects psychologically with extreme suspiciousness that borders on paranoia. One response of the endangered
self is to stake out an emotional territory that far exceeds its legitimate
rights. Having made such a grandiose claim on the world, one is open
to, and wary of, anticipated encroachments and attacks on the self. Mr.
E., another case Kohut discusses at length, used to contemplate redoing
the entire architecture of the city where he lived, when he rode through
it on his bicycle as a child. In an eerie way these fantasies paralleled the
adolescent experience of Adolph Hitler. Mr. E.'s report to his analyst of

his architectural fantasy followed an association to the dreaded and boring childhood feeling of being stranded with his mother, who could never respond to him. "It was like always just waiting for her to die," he reported. He would feel extremely lonely in these situations and play "from morning to dark" with his toys. "I thought I would go to pieces," he said. "Just thinking of it again makes my skin tingle and my spirit go blah." He recalled that when he felt that way he would rub his face on the pavement until it was sore. Then he recalled his bicycle riding and his fantasy of redesigning the city.

Frustrations and disappointments are inevitably experienced by a patient as vulnerable as Mr. E. Such patients feel perpetually exposed to attack, which must be warded off by various defensive means. Their vulnerability, in other words, makes them wary and suspicious, which not infrequently borders on (or leads to) a full-blown set of paranoid delusions. Their cold aloofness is a protective shield masking the rage beneath. When their extraordinary demands meet with criticism or lack of response—not easily separated in the minds of such patients—they are devastated. One response to such an injury is to attack. Thus once, at the end of the last session of the week, the analyst cut Mr. E. off in the middle of some difficult and painful associations, suggesting that the topic could be picked up again on Monday. Over the weekend, Mr. E. dreamed that he had been waiting for the analyst to finish with another patient; it seemed like an endless amount of time. "Then he turned and shot more times than he needed to at someone who was behind him. "He meant," he said, "that the person was already dead, and yet he continued to shoot him."[48]

Mr. E.'s dream of killing the analyst came as a direct response to the injury he felt at being cut off during his painful associations. But he himself had established his vulnerabilities to this injury by his own grandiose expansion of the self that demanded, impossibly, a mirroring response of his inner state from the unseen figure behind the couch. When the analyst inevitably failed to meet these extraordinary demands and abruptly ended the hour, Mr. E. experienced the resulting frustration as a violent intrusion on himself. And so he struck back.

If this sequence of feelings illustrates how, in issues of the self, grandiosity relates to suspiciousness, it also suggests how peevishness and a pervasive, wary antagonism breed on the vulnerabilities of the self. Mr. E. was clearly a demanding patient who responded harshly (and often self-destructively) to "failures" from the analyst. His anger and sense of antagonism toward the world appeared everywhere. The collective analogue to this aspect of Mr. E. lies in the sectional, class, and racial conflicts that increasingly devastated mid-nineteenth-century

America. The American colonies were, of course, separate entities, but they were culturally homogeneous and constitutionally united in their common relationship to England. After the Revolution, each state surrendered a measure of its sovereignty to the newly formed federal government. States' interests, nevertheless, as well as local or even parochial interests, remained the most significant center of initiative. For the next few decades, sectional rivalry continued as an important theme. The noisy struggle over tariffs, for example, pitted the North and West against the South; banking issues tended to forge a West–South alliance against the North; and issues of internal development tended to isolate the South, which benefited relatively little from such projects. Such divisions were clearly important and kept the new country politically, socially, economically, and culturally heterogeneous.

The basis for a cohesive group self, however, was being forged. A firm idealization of the Constitution and the Declaration of Independence fed on idealizing cultural needs after the Revolution. Parson Weems' *Life of Washington* (1802), for instance, created George Washington as a mythic hero, admired for his role in shaping the war and our political institutions but revered primarily for his personal, moral virtues; it was Weems who invented the story of the cherry tree. Collectively affirmed idealizations, in turn, supported a strong sense of agreement on such things as the extension of the suffrage, the value of internal development, and the importance of such republican virtues as openness, honesty, integrity, health, abundance, and strength. After the Revolution, almost all agreed, furthermore, that the Indians should be forced off their lands, blacks kept on the plantations in a condition of slavery, and the class status quo left unchanged. In the period after 1825, the imposing figure of Andrew Jackson heavily influenced the gradual erosion of state sovereignty and the emergence of a federal government that was relatively effective and increasingly powerful. In 1828, for example, the so-called tariff of abominations infuriated South Carolina, which feared that high tariffs would ruin its declining economic state. John Calhoun then formulated the first fully developed theory of the right of secession. The South Carolina Legislature responded by voting to secede if the tariff was not repealed. Jackson, himself a Southerner, would not tolerate such divisive sectionalism. In 1832 he mobilized troops for a movement into South Carolina while he also pushed the Force Act through Congress. The issue was compromised and left many raw feelings, but a crucial point had been demonstrated. The new American self was not to be easily undone by internal strife.

The Jacksonians generally succeeded in sidestepping the issue of race. Neither major party opposed slavery *per se,* which meant that both Democrats and Whigs agreed to preserve intact a system that kept some three million blacks in bondage. The Constitution recognized the legitimacy of slavery, and the South increasingly built its economy around the institution; the racism of Northern whites and the abundance of land muted any latent discontent with existing political and social arrangements. To someone like Lincoln, it was not surprising that Southerners could believe slavery was wrong and still own slaves. Because the economic and social system of the South was built on slavery, anyone who lived there would necessarily participate in the prevailing patterns of behavior. The crucial point for Lincoln was whether one recognized the essential wrongness of slavery and hoped it would die a natural death; one's correct attitude about the future of slavery need not inform present actions. There were, to be sure, Northern dissenters from this easy accommodation to the existence of slavery, but the voice of opposition was generally still and went unheeded politically.

The tensions and splits in the group self were, however, fundamental, and the course of events after 1848 increasingly eroded the assumptions of the Jacksonians. The major challenge came from the acquisition of vast new tracts of land after the Mexican War. No one knew what laws should govern settlement of these lands. The South felt it had the right to extend slavery wherever and whenever it desired, whereas Northern and Western opinion grasped with a new understanding the significance of slavery spreading indiscriminately into the territories. The debate over the war itself focused the issues. The national parties that had so effectively buried sectional discord for some twenty-five years soon gave way to ideological alliances that had little to do with traditional Whig or Democratic positions. The Compromise of 1850 papered over these basic changes in the political climate, but their full meaning struck home after the passage of the Kansas-Nebraska Act in 1854. The Whig party quickly dissolved and the Democrats divided into warring factions. Disgruntled Northerners—old Whigs, Democrats, nativists, free-soilers—coalesced around the Republican party, which in 1856 nominated John Charles Fremont in an intensely ideological campaign.

The rapidity of these changes astounded contemporaries and continues to amaze historians. In a matter of a few years a largely stable, cohesive society disintegrated into separate and warring factions. The developments of the 1850s naturally had antecedents. Southern white culture had long since acquired distinctive characteristics that made it extremely sensitive to slights and eager to defend its rights.[49] On the other side, the abolitionists were insistent about the righteousness of their cause, and many were willing to forgo their earlier pacifism in order to achieve their goal. But it was politics and society in a new key in the 1850s. A terrible sense of urgency infected all aspects of public life. The confused party situation between 1854 and 1856, for example, created high levels of anxiety for everyone and prodded even the ordinary citizen to sort through political priorities; for the reflective, the period often became the turning point of their adult lives. Lincoln before 1854 was a comfortable Whig, who opposed Jackson and Jacksonian leaders, favored strong banks and internal developments, and idealized Henry Clay. He seldom thought much about slavery, though he clearly felt it was wrong. Suddenly, after 1854, the rules changed, and Lincoln became a different person.

FIGURE 2. A photograph of Lincoln taken not long before his death. It captures visually the lines in the Second Inaugural Address: "With malice toward none, with charity for all." (Source: National Portrait Gallery, Smithsonian Institution)

Sectional rivalry now disintegrated into rhetorical, and, at times, bloody regional warfare. Congressman Preston Brooks of South Carolina beat Senator Charles Sumner senseless on the Senate floor on May 22, 1856 over derogatory remarks the latter had made about his relative, Senator Andrew P. Butler. John Brown's "Holy Crusade" on slavery took shape as paramilitary action that avowedly aimed at revenge and fomenting social revolution in the South. Brown's great disappointment in the raid on Harper's Ferry was that the blacks in the area never rose up to fight in response to his call; what he failed to realize was that they had never heard it in the first place. The passion of rhetoric escalated on all sides, from George Fitzhugh and Jefferson Davis to Charles Sumner, William Lloyd Garrison, and John Brown. Even traditional political rivalries acquired a shrillness that suggested underlying themes of larger significance.

As the crisis intensified in the 1850s, there were a variety of compensatory responses to the imminent collapse; there was a fervent spirit of revivalism sweeping the land.[50] Periods of religious enthusiasm were not new in American history, but the oddly conservative character of the "New Light" movement in the 1740s gave way, after 1820, to a more expressive religiosity that featured the week-long revivals of Charles Grandison Finney. In Illinois in the 1840s, Peter Cartwright, a noted preacher, was able to move large crowds to hysteria and religious ecstasy, though he proved less able in his political efforts to defeat Lincoln for Congress in 1846. After 1852, at least in Illinois, something of an unconscious dread of the underlying meaning of the revivals became intertwined with the process of building the nascent field of psychiatry. Thus the records of the first mental institution in the state, Jacksonville State Hospital, list for eight percent of admissions between 1852 and 1860 the following closely interrelated set of causes for illness: religious enthusiasm, excessive reading of the Bible, church difficulty, spiritualism, Millerism (adherence to William Miller's Second Adventist Church), and "Spiritual Rappings."

These records suggest a confusion of cause and effect, of symptom for real illness. Nevertheless, the categories of diagnosing mental illness in the state's first institution for the insane reveal a deeply ingrained fear of intense religiosity as potentially pathological.[51]

The fragmenting self struggles desperately to heal its widening split and to restore cohesion. If the spreading revivalism was one such attempt, another, of broader cultural and social significance, was the cult of domesticity that came to define the idealized style of family life in the 1850s. Changes in values leading to this cult became apparent after 1820 but greatly intensified in the 1850s. For women, the cult sharply defined ideal virtues—piety, purity, passivity and domesticity—and their loath-some opposites. The home itself became a haven or refuge from the outside male jungle of work and politics. Children were the exclusive responsibility of women in their accepted role as mothers. Sexuality *per se* was severely repressed, but a warm sentimentality suffused all the essential relationships, especially that of mother and child.

Themes in family history, even their indirect expression in popular literature, seldom appear or disappear in as short a period as a decade. However, one book and its warm reception suggest a unique intensifica-tion of the cult of domesticity in the 1850s. Harriet Beecher Stowe's *Uncle Tom's Cabin* appeared in serial form in 1851 and was published in book form the following year. Its characters are etched in our consciousness by now: Eliza and George, Tom, St. Clare, Little Eva, Miss Ophelia, and Simon Legree. The dramatic appeal of the story aroused millions to the evils of slavery in the wake of the reopened debate after 1848. But it is worth noting that the central themes of *Uncle Tom's Cabin* deal with family and domestic issues. The "message" and central point of the book is that blacks are fully human, indeed at times more upright, Christian, responsible, and worthy than their dissolute white masters, and the proof of that central point is that blacks, like whites, have families and family ties. Eliza and George, for example, are models of fidelity, integrity and mutual respect in an age haunted by these issues. Eliza is the ideal mother. Her escape from the Shelby plantation with young Harry to avoid being sold is achieved at a great cost. The planta-tion is the only home she has ever known, and her escape means leaving her "loved and revered" husband. "But," Stowe notes, "stronger than all was maternal love, wrought into a paroxysm of frenzy by the near approach of a fearful danger."[52]

Finally, the complex relationship between fragmentation anxiety—the fear of disintegration—and compensatory maneuvers to heal splits in the group self is perhaps nowhere better illustrated than in the course of nativism in the 1850s. On the one hand, nativist feelings of hatred for Catholics, Irish, Germans—or, more simply, anyone or anything for-eign—came to dominate politics in many parts of the country. Building on the tradition of anti-masonry from the early 1830s, the tensions be-tween native-born Protestant whites and Catholic foreigners reached major proportions in the early 1850s. The nativist movement had by then already generated its own literature (for example, *The Awful Dis-closures of Maria Monk*) and would soon establish its own party, the Know-Nothings. It was a party of hate, as Lincoln saw more clearly than most of his contemporaries.[53]

The importance of nativism cannot be overemphasized. It blended curiously with free-soil, antislavery sentiment, for nativists hated the aristocratic white South as much as they did Catholic foreigners. As historian David Potter has recently put it, both nativism and antislavery

> reflected psychologically a highly dramatized fear of a powerful force which sought by conspiratorial means to subvert the values of the republic: in one case this was the slavocracy, with its "lords of the lash," in the other, the Church of Rome with its crafty priests and suble Jesuits.[54]

In social terms as well, nativist feeling seemed to govern essential human relationships and define normative behavior. In the Jacksonville asylum's records, for example, at least forty percent of the patients between 1852 and 1860 were foreign-born, and that figure could be much higher.[55] These patients were, on the whole, young female domestic servants, recently arrived, lonely and different. "Homesickness" is not infrequently cited as the "supposed cause" of illness in the admitting records.

And yet nativist sentiment built as it destroyed and affirmed essential values as it intolerantly castigated others. It was a curious kind of populism, typically American, terribly important, often profoundly misunderstood. Thus in many areas nativism carried the spirit of reform, whether it was against slavery or for temperance. Furthermore, a powerful nationalism informed all nativist programs and politics. The fact that the Know-Nothing Convention in June, 1855 disintegrated into sectional rivalry is less surprising (or interesting) than is the "Union Degree," exalting nationalism, that the group had instituted in its ritual. As many as one million, five hundred thousand members of the Know-Nothing Party took the Union Degree and pledged themselves against sectional forces from either North or South.[56]

The most important and dangerous by-product of a fragmenting self is rage. Rage can express itself in almost infinitely variable ways, turning on the self one moment, on a loved figure the next. Freud all but missed rage, both because of the kind of patients he saw and because of his larger theoretical interests in aggression and the death instinct. Kohut's work, however, helps us appreciate the central position of rage in human existence and its relationship to the dissolving self.[57] The loss of cohesion in the self generates rage in its wake. The rage can express itself in a kind of affect storm (for example, a child's temper tantrum) or it can become quite elaborately organized, defining an angry, hostile, and vulnerable style that attempts to ward off further fragmentation. For the group there are fascinating analogues to these characteristics of rage in the individual: the fury of war perhaps most accurately expresses the collective version of the temper tantrum, while elaborately structured systems of hate, fear, and suspicion can become built into social institutions in the same way a narcissistic patient so often organizes himself or herself around rage.

As the crisis of the 1850s matured, anger pervaded American life. War increasingly seemed inevitable. There is no easily discernible turning point in this process, which is not surprising since it is inherently irrational. Thus the Compromise of 1850 appeared to settle the interrelated issues of slavery and the territorial expansion of the country but actually foreshadowed the dramatic realignments of the political parties four years later. A number of events in 1856 revealed the mounting rage in the group self breaking through—the caning of Charles Sumner, for example—but then all was quiet again, and there was even a degree of consolidation during the early part of Buchanan's administration.

John Brown's own rage escalated with that of the group self as the raid on Harper's Ferry in 1859 sent tremors of real war through the country. And finally, the blustering and strutting of the secession crisis, from Lincoln's election to his inauguration, fed the deepest levels of rage as the self split into two parts. That Lincoln and his contemporaries tended to think of the spirit of the Union in terms that are understandable in the framework of self-psychology suggests how deeply invested they were in the national concept. Its dissolution over a decade unraveled the fragile idealizations of the past—those collective strands of value that bound the self—and prompted an eruptive, peremptory grandiosity. The rage that this process generated in the end could only be absorbed by war itself.

CONCLUSION

One of the striking characteristics of the 1850s is the absence of effective leadership. The Presidents between 1848 and 1860 were a succession of bland nonentities—Zachary Taylor, Millard Fillmore, Franklin Pierce, and James Buchanan. The parties themselves seemed adrift at their point of greatest crisis. Only Stephen Douglas had real stature, but his fight with Buchanan after 1857 only further divided the Democratic party. Certainly the Whigs had no one of note to lead them in the early 1850s. Henry Clay was dead; Daniel Webster was dead; gone after a brief tenure was President Taylor, only the second Whig President ever elected to that office. Then, as the Republican party took shape after 1854, the great problem was that no one spoke for it. Its growth was a spontaneous coalescence at the local level of groups that quickly realized they had a great deal in common with other groups elsewhere. There was no leader. The raucus convention in Philadelphia in 1856 nominated John Charles Fremont, whose essential weakness of character would become painfully clear to Lincoln in the early years of the Civil War. There were articulate and powerful political leaders in the land, but they either lacked power (Stephen Douglas), or commitment to the Union (Jefferson Davis), or were fanatics (John Brown). the fatal lack of leadership in this critical decade greatly accentuated the unbinding of the group self. The process is ironically dialectical: the loss or absence of a leader for the group in crisis tends to further the process of fragmentation, which in turn makes the need for an idealized figure that much more burning. Thus, out of total collapse, civil war, and six hundred thousand dead came our nation's greatest hero, who also, it happened, was quite an effective leader.

NOTES

1. John Demos, *A Little Commonwealth: Family Life in Plymouth Colony* (New York: Oxford University Press, 1971); Carroll Smith-Rosenberg, "The Female World of Love and Ritual: Relations Between Woman in Nineteenth-Century America," *Signs: Journal of Women in Culture and Society*, (1975); 1–29; Robert Jay Lifton, *Death in Life: Survivors of Hiroshima* (New York: Random House, 1967) and *House From the War* (New York: Simon & Schuster, 1973); Fred Weinstein, *The Dynamics of Nazism: Leadership, Ideology and the Holocaust* (New York: Academic Press, 1980).
2. Roy P. Basler, ed., *The Collected Works of Abraham Lincoln*, 8 vols. (New Brunswick: Rutgers University Press, 1953), II, 320.
3. Ibid., 501.
4. Ibid., 255.
5. Ibid., 492.
6. Ibid., 482.
7. Ibid., 349–52.
8. Ibid., 266.
9. Ibid., 273.
10. Benjamin Quarles, *Lincoln and the Negro* (New York: Oxford University Press, 1962), p. 35.
11. *Collected Works*, II, 437–42.
12. Gabor Boritt, *Lincoln and the Economics of the American Dream* (Memphis: Memphis State University Press, 1978); Eric Foner, *Free Soil, Free Labor, Free Men: The Ideology of the Republican Party Before the Civil War* (New York: Oxford University Press, 1970), p. 45; Quarles, *Lincoln and the Negro*, pp. 30–38.
13. The issue of Lincoln and race has been hotly debated since Lerone Bennett, "Was Abe Lincoln a White Supremacist?" *Ebony* 23 (1968), 35–38, 40, 42. Herbert Mitgang replied to Bennett quickly and self-assuredly, "Was Lincoln Just a Honkie?" *New York Times Magazine* (February 11, 1968), 34–35, 100–107. In fact, quite a lot of scholarship preceeded Bennett's 1968 article. See, for example, Edward Magdol, "Owen Lovejoy's Role in the Campaign of 1858," *Journal of the Illinois Historical Society*, 59 (1959), 403–16;

Quarles, *Lincoln and the Negro* (1962); and Arvarh E. Strickland, "The Illinois Background of Lincoln's Attitude Toward Slavery and the Negro," *Journal of the Illinois State Historical Society*, 55 (1963), 474–94. See also Leon Litwack, *North of Slavery: The Negro in the Free States, 1790–1860* (Chicago: University of Chicago Press, 1961); and Martin Duberman, ed., *The Antislavery Vanguard: New Essays on the Abolitionists* (Princeton: Princeton University Press, 1965). Since 1968 a number of important works have appeared on this issue. The best general study is Foner, *Free Soil*; a careful analysis is George W. Fredrickson, "A Man But Not a Brother: Abraham Lincoln and Racial Equality," *The Journal of Southern History* 41 (1975). Compare Stephen B. Oates, *Lincoln's Journey to Emancipation: Our Fiery Trial* (Amherst: University of Massachusetts Press, 1979). The historiographical story is nicely summarized in Arthur Zilversmith's presentation of the topic of Lincoln and race, February 12, 1980, Abraham Lincoln Colloquium, State Historical Library, Springfield, Illinois that will appear in the forthcoming *Papers* of the Abraham Lincoln Association, vol. II.

14. *Collected Works*, III, 145–46; see also II, 405–498.
15. Kenneth Stampp, *The Imperiled Union: Essays on the Background of the Civil War* (New York: Oxford University Press, 1980), p. 128.
16. *Collected Works*, II, 256.
17. Ibid., 520.
18. Ibid., 405–6.
19. Frederick Douglass, "Oration in Memory of Abraham Lincoln, Delivered at the Unveiling of the Freedmen's Monument in Memory of Abraham Lincoln in Lincoln Park, Washington, D.C., April 14, 1876," *The Life and Writings of Frederick Douglass*, 8 volumes, ed. Eric Fonet (New York: International Publishers, 1955), 4, 312. Compare Christopher Breiseth, "Lincoln and Frederick Douglass: Another Debate," *Journal of the Illinois State Historical Society*, 68 (1975), 9–26.
20. *Collected Works*, II, 255.
21. Ibid., 255–56.
22. Ibid., 132.
23. Ibid., 298–99; Earl Schenck Miers, ed., *Lincoln Day By Day: A Chronology, 1809–1865*, 3 vols., (Washington: Lincoln Sequicentennial Commission, 1960), II, 114.
24. Frederickson, "A Man But Not a Brother," p. 50, makes this point, repeating, without credit, Harry V. Jaffa, *Crisis of the House Divided: An Interpretation of the Lincoln-Douglas Debates* (Seattle: University of Washington Press, 1959), p. 61.
25. Collected Works, II, 461–62.
26. Illinois State *Register*, June 19, 1858, p. 2.
27. *Collected Works*, II, 20–22.
28. For example, ibid., III, 20.
29. Ibid., 404.
30. Ibid., IV, 263.
31. Almost all commentators on Lincoln and on the 1850s agree with the observation. Don E. Fehrenbacher, *Prelude to Greatness: Lincoln in the 1850s* (Stanford: Stanford University Press, 1962), p. 80, noted that there is "no evidence of any organized movement in 1858 to push slavery into the free states, or of any disposition among members of the Supreme Court to attempt such folly." (For a complete discussion of the Dred Scott case, see Fehrenbacher, *The Dred Scott Case: Its Significance in American Law and Politics* (New York: Oxford University Press, 1978). James G. Randall, *Lincoln the President: Springfield to Gettysburg*, 2 volumes (Gloucester, Mass.: Eyre and Spottiswoode, 1945), 1, 108, termed Lincoln's conspiracy theory "quite fanciful and nonexistent." Allen Nevins, *The Emergence of Lincoln*, 2 volumes (New York: Scribner's, 1950), I, 362, called Lincoln's theory a "partisan analysis" which "in the eyes of posterity, was pitched on

a disappointingly low plane." And in the view of David Donald, *Liberty and Union* (Lexington, Mass.: D. C. Heath, 1978), p. 71, "These utterances in the house divided speech reveal more about the state of Lincoln's mind and the receptivity of the Northern audiences that cheered his speeches than they do about historical reality." There has been one major dissenter to this interpretation, Harry Jaffa, *Crisis of the House Divided: An Interpretation of the Lincoln-Douglas Debates* (Seattle: University of Washington Press, 1959), pp. 81, 277–78. Jaffa, however, marshalls evidence regarding only the Dred Scott decision. Lincoln's theory went well beyond that. Jaffa's interpretation has been echoed by George W. Frederickson, "A Man but Not a Brother: Abraham Lincoln and Racial Equality." *The Journal of Southern History*, 41 (1975), p. 45, "It is important to recognize that the years after 1854 not only saw an effort to extend and nationalize slavery but also provided the occasion for a torrent of racist propoganda." In support of this assertion, Frederickson footnotes his own *Black Image in the White Mind: The Debate on Afro-American Character and Destiny, 1817–1914* (New York: Harper Torchbooks, 1971), pp. 44–164; and Eugene H. Berwanger, *The Frontier Against Slavery* (Urbana: University of Illinois Press, 1967), pp. 123–37. These sources, however, support only Frederickson's notion that there was a "torrent of racist propoganda." His idea that there was an effort to nationalize slavery remains unproven. Oddly enough, Richard Hofstadter, *The Paranoid Style in American Politics and Other Essays* (New York: Knopf, 1966), passes over Lincoln and the 1850s.

32. Frederick Douglass, "Oration in Memory of Abraham Lincoln" 4, 318.

33. *Collected Works*, III, 9.

34. Ibid., 16, 29, 145–46, 221–22, 248–49, 299–300.

35. See Christopher Breiseth, "Lincoln, Douglas and Springfield," *The Public and Private Lincoln: Contemporary Perspectives*, ed. Cullom Davis *et al.* (Carbondale: Southern Illinois University Press, 1979), pp. 101–20.

36. David M. Potter, *The Impending Crisis, 1848–1861*, completed and edited by Don E. Fehrenbacher. (New York: Harper & Row, 1976), p. 246. See also Kenneth M. Stampp, *An Imperiled Union: Essays on the Background of the Civil War* (New York: Oxford University Press, 1980), pp. 156–57.

37. Lawrence J. Friedman, "Antebellum American Abolitionism and the Problem of Violent Means," *The Psychohistory Review*, 9 (1980), 26–32.

38. Bruce Catton, *This Hallowed Ground* (New York: Simon & Schuster, 1955), p. 23.

39. Sigmund Freud, *The Standard Edition of the Complete Psychological Works of Sigmund Freud*, ed. James Strachey (London: Hogarth, 1962), X, 153–230.

40. Ibid., II, 21–47.

41. Stampp, *An Imperiled Union*, pp. 242–43.

42. George Fitzhugh, *Cannibals All!! or Slaves without Masters*, ed. C. Vann Woodward (Cambridge: The Belknap Press of Harvard University Press, 1852), p. 252.

43. Ibid., 11.

44. *Collected Works*, II, 73.

45. Ibid., 91.

46. Lawrence J. Friedman, "Garrisonism, Abolitionism, and the Boston Clique: A Psychosocial Inquiry," *The Psychohistory Review*, 7 (1978), 6–19.

47. Fitzhugh, *Cannibals All!!*; see also Fitzhugh, *Sociology for the South or the Failure of Free Institutions* (New York: Burt Franklin, 1854).

48. Arnold Goldberg, ed., *The Psychology of the Self: A Casebook, Written with the Collaboration of Heinz Kohut* (New York: International University Press, 1978), p. 282.

49. Steven M. Stowe, "The 'Touchiness' of the Gentleman Planter: The Sense of Esteem and Continuity in the Antebellum South," *The Psychohistory Review* 8 (1979), 6–15.

50. Fehrenbacher, *Prelude to Greatness*, p. 14.

51. Admissions records of the Jacksonville State Hospital, 1852–1860, Illinois State Archives.
52. Harriet Beecher Stowe, *Uncle Tom's Cabin* (New York: Collier Books, 1966 [1852]), p. 104.
53. Even Mary Lincoln despised the Irish and leaned toward the Know-Nothings. See Justin G. Turner and Linda Levitt Turner, Eds., *Mary Todd Lincoln: Her Life and Letters* (New York, Knopf, 1972), p. 46. Compare Lincoln's own views, *Collected Works*, II, 323.
54. Potter, *The Impending Crisis*, p. 252.
55. Approximately forty percent of the patients clearly indicated to the staff of the hospital when admitted that they had been born abroad. However, for those whose place of origin is listed as an eastern state—a sizable number—many could well have been born abroad but lived in the East long enough to establish residency before moving to Illinois. I suspect for example, that many Irish immigrants named Massachusetts or New York as their place of origin.
56. Potter, *The Impending Crisis*, p. 254. Note David Bryon Davis, *The Slave Power Conspiracy and the Paranoid Style* (Baton Rouge: Louisiana State University Press, 1969).
57. Heinz Kohut, "Thoughts on Narcissism and Narcissistic Rage," in *The Search for the Self: Selected Writings of Heinz Kohut 1950–1978*, ed. Paul H. Orenstein, 2 vols., (New York: International Universities Press, 1978), 2, 615–58. See also Charles B. Strozier, "Heinz Kohut and the Historical Imagination," *Advances in Self Psychology*, ed. Arnold Goldberg (New York: International Universities Press, 1980), 397–406.

THE TRANSFORMATIONS IN THE SELF
OF MAHATMA GANDHI

HYMAN MUSLIN AND PRAKASH DESAI

The mystery of Mohandas K. Gandhi resides in his transformation from a painfully shy boy, saddled with innumerable fears and intensely attached to his mother, to the man who is universally regarded as the great liberator of India. The Mahatma, who effected what could be called a milestone in the history of the human race, always had, as he said, shyness as his shield. Even the title "Mahatma" made him uncomfortable: "Often the title has deeply pained me; and there is not a moment I can recall when it may be said to have tickled me."[1] Mahatma (*maha* + *atma*) means the great Soul, a very special human being. The title was bestowed on Gandhi by Rabindranath Tagore, the poet laureate of India. Here, aiming not at a solution to the mystery of Gandhi but only at an enhanced appreciation of the complexity of the man, we will explore his self-development, particularly the content of the ideals which set his psychological compass. To this end, we will focus on the psychological dimension of Gandhi's unfolding self-experience rather than on the various social, cultural, political, and economic conditions that made Gandhi an ideal leader in the eyes of the Indian masses of South Africa and India at the time of the eclipse of the British Empire. We are concerned, then, with the inner reality of Gandhi's self-transformation, not with the historical circumstances that challenged him to ascend to leadership.

In attempting to trace Gandhi's development from his youth through his emergence as the leader of the beleaguered Indians in South Africa, we will rely largely on Gandhi's own words in his autobiography, *The Story of My Experiments with Truth.* The autobiography describes those significant figures of his early life—a saintly mother, a revered father, two older brothers and an older sister—who are crucially implicated in his unfolding life-story. To the end of his days, Gandhi assigned his parents a central role in his development; serving them was an activity that was his greatest gratification.

Gandhi was born in 1869 in Porbandar, a town on the western pennisula of India. His staunchly religious family belonged to a sect known as Vaishnavas; in fact, the dwelling alongside the family house was a Vaishnava temple dedicated to Lord Krishna.

Gandhi's mother, Putaliba, was, to all observers, a saintly woman. Lacking formal education and illiterate, she was a deeply religious person who sought contact with God through the practice of vows and especially through fasting. Putaliba's day began at six o'clock in the morning, when she recited her daily prayers over the course of two hours. Although Putaliba's beliefs were eclectic, she was impressed with the tenets of Jainaism, which emphasized good works and the sanctity of all life (*Ahimsa*). She was rigid in her emphasis on daily devotions and fasts; the use of intoxicants, meat, and unlawful visits to women were all unacceptable to her. While devoted to her youngest son, Mohandas, she apparently had little time to attend to his daily care; these tasks were relegated to the boy's sister, Raliat, and later to a woman servant, Rambha.[2]

Gandhi was often described as a child who was difficult to control because of his excess energy and curiosity. He was also described as a frightened child, fearful of thieves, ghosts, and serpents. His fear of goblins and spirits emerging in the dark led him to sleep with a candle. He was, by his own admission, further frightened of censure from authority figures and of boisterousness and rowdiness. His nursemaid was obliged to calm him nightly, sometimes by attempting to have him repeat the name of God (Ramanama) as a mantra.[3] Going to school was a special hardship for young Mohandas; he would run home not only when school was over, but even during recess, unable to participate in the games of his friends for fear of bodily injury. The general impression we gain from Gandhi's descriptions of his childhood is of a self-experience consisting of a pervasive feeling of fragility and a resulting incapacity to experience himself as a vigorous boy.

These findings point to the special nature of Gandhi's relationship with his mother and mothering figures, which eventuated in a self lacking in assertiveness. Putaliba's capacity to respond to her youngest child's emerging phase-appropriate grandiosity apparently was limited, perhaps by her many responsibilities, perhaps by her religious preoccupations.[4] In any case, young Mohandas's need to rush home and merge with his family sanctuary point to his fragile self and continuing need for protection. His mother was herself perplexed over Mohandas's inability to assert himself during his later childhood, even when he was physically provoked.

Although the Hindu system of belief is filled with ghosts and goblins, little Mohandas's persisting need for the protection of his family sanctuary was highly unusual. A Hindu household is ordinarily filled with many responsive people; the child moves from one lap to another, from one shoulder to another, with ease and comfort.[5] The experience of first going to school is not devoid of psychological challenge, but it is ordinarily an occasion for joy, accompanied by traditional rituals. Thus, Gandhi's manifest need for the reassurance of his family points to the absence of that psychological structure which enables a child to calm and sooth himself.

Gandhi always spoke with awe and reverence of his relationship with his father. As he observed in later life: "I did not talk much with him. I was afraid to speak."[6] Kaba Gandhi married Mohandas's mother, his fourth wife, when he was forty, and fathered Mohandas when he was forty-seven. He was a prime minister in Porbandar and subsequently in Rajkot, where the family moved when Mohandas was seven. Widely known as an outstanding administrator and judge, he was also regarded as short-tempered and intransigent in political matters when he felt his cause was just. Kaba Gandhi's house, where Mohandas was raised, amounted to a miniature court, where the number of guests who sat down to dinner was seldom less than twenty,[7] including the family, secretaries, and officials. In Mohandas's eyes, Kaba was an important presence, the head of the clan. He arranged marriages, secured jobs, and was called on to intercede in all domestic matters concerning members of the clan. From early in life, then, Gandhi's notion of acceptable interaction with his father pertained to service: he had to serve his father in order to receive parental approbation. One of Gandhi's early memories concerned his attraction to his father's book, *Shravana Pitribhakti Nataka*, which was a play about the protagonist's devotion to his parents. Once, when a visiting theater troupe staged this play, they enhanced its dramatic impact by showing stereoscopic pictures of Shravana carrying his aged blind parents in a shoulder sling. Gandhi witnessed the production and later observed:

> The book and the picture left an indelible impression on my mind. "Here is an example for you to copy," I said to myself. The agonized lament of the parents over Shravana's death is still fresh in my memory. The melting tune moved over me deeply, and I played it on a concertina which my father had purchased for me.[8]

It is with justification that Pyarelal claimed that Gandhi exalted the ideals of filial devotion. Perhaps by his total devotion to his parents, especially in the service of his father, he was able to gain a measure of approval while simultaneously emulating the standards of his distinguished father. But even in his deeply moving memory, it was the lament of Shravana's parents over the death of their son that remained the most vivid, reflecting a craving to be loved while being of service. In a letter to his second son, Manilal, written when he was forty years old, Gandhi wrote:

> As soon as a child attains the age of discretion, he must learn to go about with a full sense of responsibility and make a ceaseless, conscious effort to develop his character . . . . I remember when I was less than your age, my greatest joy was to nurse my father. I have not known what fun and frolic are since my twelfth year.[9]

It may be said that Gandhi's active involvement with his father began directly after his arranged marriage at the age of thirteen. He had entered into the marriage under his father's protection: "Everything that my father did then struck me as beyond reproach."[10] As he was rushing to the wedding ceremonies, Kaba Gandhi was involved in an accident in which his cart was overturned, and he received severe injuries from which he never recovered. From this point until Kaba Gandhi's death three years later, Mohandas assumed the duties of his nurse. He would begin each day by bringing his father his washbasin and water for his ablutions, helping him to the lavatory, washing and bathing him, dressing his wounds, and giving him his medicine. At night, he would massage his father's legs, retiring to his apartment and his wife only when his father no longer needed him. He experienced all these activities as a service of love, indicating that these nursing ministrations permitted him to be meaningfully engaged with his idealized father.

During his fifteenth year, an incident occurred which revealed the special qualities of Gandhi's relationship with his father. Mohandas and a friend had stolen a piece of gold from one of his brother's armlets to repay a debt. Some time later, the fact of the thievery, as well as its subsequent cover-up, began to weigh heavily on his mind, and he resolved to confess the crime to his father. He trembled when he handed his written confession to his father, assuming there would be a violent explosion that would end with his father striking himself on the forehead. Instead, his father cried, and Gandhi joined him with tears in a scene that became a catharsis of love. Forty-one years later, when Gandhi recounted this incident, he still remembered it as an occasion when his exalted and explosive father demonstrated sublime for-

giveness and he was gathered into his father's bosom and not destroyed. As he said, "This sort of sublime forgiveness was not natural to
my father. I had thought he would be angry, say hard things, and strike
his forehead."[11]

Still another dramatic memory that unfolded in Gandhi's autobiography concerned the death scene of his father. Gandhi, then sixteen, was deprived of the final contact with his father. Instead, Kaba
Gandhi died in the arms of his brother, Mohandas's paternal uncle. This
event transpired because Gandhi had, on this single occasion, been
relieved of his caretaking duties by his uncle, who apparently wished to
spare the youth the tiring chore of the nightly leg massage. In the Hindu
family, it is vitally important for children—especially sons—to be with a
dying parent, just as it is vitally important for the dying parent to be
with his children. It is an article of Hindu tradition that the giving and
receiving of the final transfusion from one generation to another occur
during these very moments. (Mariott has described the Hindu world-
view, and its manifestations in interpersonal transaction, as a fluid system with interpersonal permeability.[12]) It is the death of a parent that
threatens generational continuity.

Following his father's death, Gandhi railed at himself for the weakness of his flesh, because he had eagerly left his father's sickroom to
make love to his wife, Kasturba. The interlude was short-lived; he was
called back to his father's sickroom after only five minutes with his wife.
During this brief respite, however, his father had died. In his au-
tiobiography he poignantly recalled his grief and remorse at the time:

> So, all was over! I had but to wring my hands. I felt deeply ashamed
> and miserable. I ran to my father's room. I saw that if animal passion
> had not blinded me, I should have been spared the torture of separa-
> tion from my father during his last moments. I should have been
> massaging him, and he would have died in my arms. But now it was
> my uncle who had had this privilege. He was so deeply devoted to
> his elder brother that he had earned the honour of doing him the last
> services![13]

Denied the "privilege" of this final engagement, Gandhi was deprived of the final act of merger with his idealized father. Throughout
his life, he related this incident as a manifestation of his shameful wish
to have carnal union with his wife, omitting his sense of deprivation and
attendant narcissistic rage at being denied the last measure of the long-
coveted reward for his filial devotion. To put this matter differently, we
may say that Gandhi did not receive a final infusion of strength from his
dying father, the idealized figure of his childhood. In all likelihood, his

subsequent struggle with his parents' religion was a measure of this final disappointment in his father. To his dying day, Gandhi sought merger with the God of his childhood. His family religion, the Vaishnava faith, never appealed to him, cynical as he was of the genuineness of both its priests and its adherents. To his mother, he often complained of the hypocrisy of any religion that systematically excluded certain people from its fold, such as the Vaishnava's exclusion of the Untouchables. His criticisms of the family religion extended to all forms of organized religion; he was critical of the Christian missionaries who poured abuse on the Hindus. His complaints and questions about religion and religious practices derived from his own disappointment in not being exposed to proper spiritual experiences and "good books."[14] As he said of his religious teaching: "I may say that I failed to get from the teachers what they could have given me without any effort on their part."[15] Gandhi's father, although not directly implicated, must be considered one of those teachers who failed to give young Mohandas what he needed.

From this point—the death of his father—to the end of his days, Gandhi would engage in a continuing quest for the "word," unfortunately in combination with another lifelong dynamic—his resistance to the "word." Speaking of the *Bhagavad Gita*, he would, in fact, say: "It is my perpetual regret that I was not fortunate enough to hear more good books of this kind read during that period."[16] His nursemaid, Rambha, encouraged him to memorize religious sayings, but Gandhi mentions neither his father nor his mother as reading with him or to him. Perhaps as an adaptation to a milieu which offered inconsistent ideals that were often contradictory and left him in a state of uncertainty, what he had developed was a keen ability to perceive and focus on contradictions. From the schoolteacher who asked him to copy from a classmate the spelling of the word "kettle" during a high school inspection to the mother who admonished him to "fight back," situations were always arising in which he perceived a fundamental contradiction and proceeded to shame those who seemed to endorse a contradictory position. In these youthful events and in Gandhi's perceptions of them, we see in nascent form the Gandhi who would defiantly pit himself against adversity as if to compensate for his sense of fragility. He became an experimenter, testing himself and his strength in repeated attempts to master his surroundings.

Gandhi's complaints about his disappointments in receiving direction and guidance from his teachers was, in our view, the expression of a persistent and intense inner concern about his sense of personal adequacy. Thus, as he noted, he was frightened of incurring his teacher's displeasure and would rush home each day to avoid simple contact with his schoolmates. His fear of his mentors stimulated him to be meticulous in his school preparations, but he suffered greatly lest he be caught unprepared. He was careful to be totally honest and obedient in all his dealings with authority, often to the chagrin of his schoolmates. His self-doubts apparently influenced his valuation of his academic performance as well as his social interactions. Indeed, for a long time, he derived no reassurance at all from his achievements in school: "I used to be astonished whenever I won prizes and scholarships."[17] This problem stayed with him throughout his student days, even as a law student in London. Thus, we see the young Gandhi as a distressed person at many levels, phobic of the dark where hidden ghosts might appear, anxious about his own aggression and the aggression of others, and in constant need of support for his diminished self.

Because he was frightened by the boys in high school, Mohandas had need of a bodyguard to shield him from harassment. He found him in the person of a Muslim boy, Sheikh Mehtab, one of the first of a long line of mentors and potential gurus with whom he attempted to form an attachment throughout his life. Ultimately, this list would include Ruskin, Tolstoy, his Indian mentors Mehta and Raychandra, and his English teachers Dr. Oldfield and Dr. Allison. Mehtab, his leader during adolescence, was a distinct counterpart to Mohandas. As Mohandas was frightened of ghosts, thieves, and snakes and unable to venture into the dark, so Mehtab boasted that he could "hold in his hand live serpents, could defy thieves and did not believe in ghosts."[18] For a short time, Mehtab also introduced Gandhi to meat eating, a major instance of rebellion against the tenets of the Vaishnava sect. Owing to the influence of the Jaina religion, perhaps nowhere in India was meat eating regarded with such horror as among the Vaishyas of Gujarat. Indeed, Gandhi's subservience to his young mentor was so complete that he allowed Mehtab to take him, the married man of fifteen, to a brothel. The relationship with Mehtab continued even after the death of Gandhi's father.

After the death of Kaba Gandhi, the family conferred with a respected family friend, Mavji Dave, about Mohandas's future. He advised that Mohandas journey to London to become a barrister, the occupation which would best prepare him for a Diwanship, the administrative position held by his father. Gandhi, now eighteen, was under the protection of his elder brother, who, ultimately, with their mother's reluctant permission, helped him go to London. By this time he had been married for five years and was the father of an infant son. Leaving his wife and son was difficult for Mohandas, but he experienced leaving his mother as tragic.[19]

The transition to life in London was an understandable hardship for the young man from colonial India, who was without adequate command of the English language or knowledge of English manners and dress. It was made somewhat easier by a new guide, Dr. P. J. Mehta, who advised him on many matters, including living arrangements, dress, and attitude. It was during his London years that Gandhi began his lifelong involvement with the principles of Hinduism. It was also in London that Gandhi, albeit with intense trepidation, began to display more assertiveness in academic studies, in public service, and in social intercourse.

Reading of Gandhi's London years, one is struck by his unremitting search for direction in each of his activities, not dissimilar to his quest for guidance and direction in his earlier years. In his legal pursuits, he had originally been under the guidance of the family advisor, Mavji Dave, who was replaced in London by Dr. Mehta. In his religious quest, he was guided by several advisers, including several teachers of Theosophy; it was also at this time that he first became involved with the *Gita*, another guiding light. In his pursuit of Vegetarianism, he was aided by Dr. Allison and Dr. Oldfield, two English physicians who befriended him. Although he suffered greatly with his inner experience of ineptitude, he was able, especially with the support of Dr. Oldfield, increasingly to assert himself and assume an active role in the Vegetarianism movement. In fact, he published ten brief articles in the local Vegetarian journals. By the end of his stay in London, having completed his legal studies and gained admittance to the bar, Gandhi could be said to have expanded his self in several directions, even as he admitted that "there was no end to my helplessness and fear."[20]

It was during his London years that Gandhi was first able to experience himself as a competent student and to complete a major course of study without tutoring. Indeed, he even went beyond the required studies and read Roman law in Latin, an unnecessary and ardous task that he embraced in the spirit of pitting himself against adversity. Only a short time had passed since he had viewed himself as an inept student in Samaldas College in India. It will be remembered that Mohandas had had difficulty in his early student days with all manner of schoolwork, including multiplication tables, geometry, and Sanskrit. Reading, apart from its role in his studies, had not been a routine activity for him; in London, he read widely and began his initial study of the Gita. Still another manifestation of his self-development was his involvement with the Vegetarianism movement, in which he became a prominent member of the executive committee of his local society and authored several papers. Although his stay in London did place him in several situations in which his anxiety about exhibiting himself continued to manifest itself, he was able for the first time to express his leadership skills; he started a local Vegetarian club and even arranged for his own farewell party.

Even as he demonstrated a new assertiveness in certain areas, however, he remained in contact with Dr. Mehta throughout his stay in London, and it was Mehta who arranged many things—rooms, study arrangements, clothiers—for him. Other valued advisors were Dr. Oldfield, who introduced him to Vegetarianism and the Vegetarian Society, and Dr. Allison, who functioned as an intellectual guide. Thus, Gandhi's continuing involvement with idealized parent figures revealed him to be still in need of, or in quest for, internal regulatory structure; it was this *intrapsychic* need that manifested itself in his need for external guidance and support. In the context of this continuing search for idealizable leaders, however, he managed to become a leader himself, a barrister, even as he continued to experience himself as personally ineffective. We may say that his self-structure was gradually becoming more firm, and that he was beginning to internalize certain aspects of the ideals of his "fathers" in constituting his own adult self.

Soon after returning home to India, Mohandas was informed that his venerated mother had died just weeks before. Thus, once again in his young life, Mohandas had been deprived of the infusion from a dying parent. His grief was intense, but he did not decompensate. His return to India was, nonetheless, fraught with failure from the outset. Immediately after his return, Mohandas attempted to establish himself as a barrister in Bombay. He failed in his debut in the small claims court, however, because he was unable, out of anxiety, to conduct his assigned hearing. Following this failure and his persisting inability to obtain cases, he joined his brother in Rajkot, where he essentially worked as a law clerk until his departure for South Africa two years later. His self once more in a state of apparent vulnerability, Gandhi again attempted to merge with yet another target of idealization.

We refer to the poet and merchant Raychandra, a Jaina and the son-in-law of Dr. Mehta's elder brother. During the two years of Gandhi's stay in India, Raychandra functioned as an ideal of knowledge and spirituality. Gandhi acknowledged his influence in this way: "Three moderns have left a deep impress on my life, and captivated me: Raychandbhai by his living contact; Tolstoy by his book, *The Kingdom of God is Within You;* and Ruskin by his *Unto this Last.*"[21] Raychandra was a highly successful merchant in jewels, but he viewed his business life as peripheral to his spiritual life. According to Gandhi, he not only possessed a profound intellect, but he was the embodiment of a great religious leader. Through his example and his teachings, he encouraged Gandhi to become involved in the Jaina system of thought centering on the doctrines of Ahimsa. For two years, as a disciple of Raychandra, Mohandas "scrutinized his life minutely at close quarters."[22] In the end, however, he rejected Raychandbhai as his guru: "And yet in spite of this high regard for him, I could not enthrone him in my heart as my Guru. The throne has remained vacant and my search still continues."[23]

In conversation with Pyarelal, Gandhi commented that his disappointment in Raychandra stemmed from the fact that he mixed business with religion, that he disregarded ordinary rules of health, and that he believed in the observance of orthodox caste rules. Once again Gandhi experienced contradictions, once again he experienced a disillusioning lack of perfection in a leader and had to reject Raychandra as his guru. In his relations with Raychandra, Gandhi could not restrain himself from arguing, from questioning, from criticizing; in short, he could not enter into a guru–pupil relationship.

According to the tenets of Hinduism, the institution of Guru holds a unique place, since, as Gandhi knew, true knowledge is considered impossible without a guru. The guru is the master who commands surrender of the pupil's whole being. In the guru–pupil relationship, then, there can be no doubting, no questioning. Once such surrender is effected, the pupil will be molded into the image of the guru.[24] It follows, then, that Gandhi's rejection of certain aspects of Raychandra's life and doctrine made it impossible for him to enthrone Raychandra as his guru. On examining the knowledge and virtues which Gandhi and others ascribed to Raychandra, it seems likely that Gandhi experienced a resistance to becoming immersed in a relationship with the merchant. In fact, his previous disappointing relations with other idealized objects had not permitted him to undertake such an involvement without the anxiety and misgivings that ultimately coalesced in rejection. His "search," as he put it, was destined to continue in a ceaseless manner, since his resistance could not be overcome. Thus, while he continued throughout his life to form many diluted idealized relationships, he never permitted any of these relationships to deepen. At the age of fifty-six, he wrote that "My search still continues."[25] Gandhi thereby became the victim of his own repetitive search for an idealized parent able to impart to him the strength he needed to firm up his self. He was left to derive "pieces" of guidance from many sources, without being totally receptive to any single source, be it religion, religious figures, social leaders, or philosophers. Each was destined to be rejected in small or large measure. Thus, his later admission:

> I believe in the Hindu theory of the Guru and his importance in spiritual realization. I think there is a great deal of truth in the doctrine that true knowledge is impossible without a Guru. An imperfect teacher may be tolerable in mundane matters, but not in

spiritual matters. Only a perfect *gnani* deserves to be enthroned as Guru. There must, therefore, be ceaseless striving after perfection. For one gets the Guru that one deserves. Infinite striving after perfection is one's right.[26]

When Gandhi arrived in South Africa, he was filled with relief at having escaped circumstances that had been demeaning to him both professionally and socially.* His legal activities had proven disappointing, and his social life had not been uplifting in any respect. In sum, his environment—particularly at the time of his mother's death—had not provided him with the support and guidance that he had previously received in London. Furthermore, his interaction with Raychandra resulted in an unsatisfying stalemate; he would continue to receive religious direction from Raychandbhai for some time, but, as he said, the throne reserved for his guru—an idealized parent—was destined to remain empty. In point of fact, the short stay in India appears to have reactivated Gandhi's earlier self-distress.

Gandhi's entry into the world of South Africa was dramatic. Almost as soon as he landed, he was embroiled in disputes with a hostile environment. He was traveling as a first-class passenger to Pretoria to assume his duties as a barrister when he was suddenly ordered out of his first-class accommodations by an indignant railroad official who had suddenly discovered this person of color occupying the suite of a white man. When the young barrister refused to leave, he was forcibly taken out of the seat by a guard. Later, on that same journey to Pretoria, Gandhi was beaten on a coach because he was again not in a proper place for a "coolie"—the designation given to Indians living in South Africa. Thus was Gandhi initiated into the major social problem of the Indians in South Africa. Confronted with a group of people viewed as inferior and subjected to oppression, Gandhi's identification with them shortly became his *Dhruv Laksha*,† his trigger to action.

What thereby transpired in Gandhi would subsequently be construed as a signal moment in world history. As he later recounted,

> I began to think of my duty. Should I fight for my rights or go back to India, or should I go on to Pretoria without minding the insults, and

---

*Hindu ascetics have been known to travel to the Himalayas to meditate and prepare themselves for closeness with God. Usually after some family crisis, a young man may venture off into the forests and spend years meditating in isolation. This meditation represents a form of penance, *Tapas*, a self-purification or "inward brooding" that aims at achieving communion with God. (See Wendy O. O'Flaherty, *Asceticism and Eroticism in the Mythology of Shiva*.)

†*Dhruv* is the Indian word referring to a permanent guide, literally the Polar Star, and *Laksha*, the setting of the sight.

> return to India after finishing the case? It would be cowardice to run
> back to India without fulfilling my obligation. The hardship to which
> I was subjected was superficial—only a symptom of the deep dis-
> ease of colour prejudice. I should try if possible to root out the
> disease and suffer hardships in the process.[27]

Suffering hardship in order to transform himself henceforth was essential. As Hindus have always known, intense heat separates gold from its
impurities.

Thus Gandhi, in a seemingly sudden emergence of assertiveness,
proclaimed with certainty his wish to live up to the ideals of service to
his community, and to accept the suffering and sacrifice such adherence
would entail. Through this resolve, he began to make contact with
"every Indian in Pretoria."[28] He undertook to study the social and
working conditions of his people and to learn at first hand of the in-
justices Indians were suffering. He quickly arranged for a public meeting with his countrymen where he gave an inspiring speech on ethics in
business. (We recall that Gandhi's last public presentation in the law
courts of Bombay had resulted in a personal disaster: he could not, at
that time, speak at all.) He also suggested the formation of a grievance
association and volunteered as much of his own time as necessary to
make representations to the authorities on the Indians' behalf. His activities did not stop at these public meetings; he offered to teach English
to whoever so desired. Through these and other activities, Gandhi
rapidly became acquainted with a large number of Pretorian Indians and
was instituted as their Ombudsman. His activities had created a milieu
in which his public of suffering Indians inevitably viewed him as a
valued leader. Psychologically, we propose that Gandhi entered into a
set of relationships from which he derived the necessary support for his
depleted self, and that his need for admiration and confirmation was
met by his followers' appreciation of his leadership.

On another front, Gandhi again became involved with people and
books in his continuing quest to establish viable ideals. His contact with
his former mentor Raychandra continued, partly, through correspondence. He began meeting with a law colleague who was a staunch lay
preacher and even began attending the daily Christian prayers at his
friend's church; daily prayer would become a lifelong ritual for Gandhi.
Shortly thereafter, he met and befriended still another Christian, a
Quaker, who instructed him in Christian theology. Gandhi would meet
with this friend every Sunday and present him with his "religious diary
for the week," a compilation of notes on his assigned readings. Thus did
Gandhi institute yet another relationship in which he became the dis-
guised disciple. In addition, his own reading in a variety of areas now
served a major appetite for knowledge which, he noted, "had become

almost insatiable."[29] He became increasingly attracted to Hinduism, without the resistance he had previously experienced.

After three years of pursuing a part-time career in public service, Gandhi determined to become what he termed a full-time public worker. He returned to India to retrieve his family and came back to South Africa in 1897 to fight even more actively for the needs of his people. He established a periodical, the *Indian Opinion,* and began devoting himself exclusively to the community. In 1904 he established his own community, the Phoenix settlement, influenced by Ruskin's book, *Unto This Last,* which emphasized the value of the commune in bringing together people from many walks of life. This community came to be known as the "Tolstoy Farm," once again in recognition of the ideal of living an ascetic and altruistic life.

Two momentous events in Gandhi's life occurred at this time. He became a convert to the codes of *Brahmacharya* and also gave birth to the principle of *Satyagraha.* In Gandhi's view, the vows of *Brahmacharya,* which were vows of restraint against the egress of any type of instinct, for example sadism or sexuality, were preparatory to establishing *Satyagraha* as a method of pursuing his struggles against his and his countrymen's oppressors. *Satyagraha* literally means truth force; in operation, it came to signify nonviolent, rather than merely passive, resistance.

FIGURE 1. Gandhi toward the end of his life.

Brahmacharya and Satayagraha would dominate Gandhi's life until the end of his days.

Gandhi subsequently stated that he had been preoccupied with Brahmacharya since 1900, but took the vows of self-restraint and became a true *Brahmacharyi* after his service in the nursing corps during the Zulu War. Only at that time, in other words, did he become a true adherent of Brahmacharya, literally a mode of life or course of conduct adapted to the search for *Brahman.*

For Gandhi, the five cardinal observances for one striving for self-realization derived from a devotional song (*"Vaishnava Jana to tene Kahiye,"* by Narsinha Mehta). They were Ahimsa (nondestructiveness), truth, nonpossessiveness, nonstealing, and Brahmacharya. In the manner of the Hindu ascetic, the striver must take vows of self-restraint, especially against the egress of sexuality, if he is to "shake the throne of his oppressors." We propose that these precepts and related practices of Hindu faith became transmuted into internal self-structures that provided Gandhi with continuing sources of calming and soothing and with ideals that directed him to a life of compassion. Those rituals emphasizing the ascetic way of life—his weekly "silences," his fastings, and his experiments with naturopathy—provided Gandhi with still another permanent source of calming.

In its total import, Gandhi's transformation represented a softening of his ancient resistance to the teachings of his elders and a corresponding attraction to the values of his heritage, especially Brahmacharya. With this transformation, one facet of his quest for values seemed to be coming to an end: he now could allow himself to merge partially with Hindu values. Thus his inability to accept totally the precepts of any ethical or moral code continued. Even granting this reluctance, however, his self-movement toward a Hindu set of values represented an increased capacity to accept the values of his elders, which he had rejected all through his childhood, especially following the disappointment surrounding the circumstances of his father's death. But in returning to the values of his elders, he was obliged to reject his identification with the values of the West. He began to shun all facets of modernity, including the social changes that had been a part of his life. He rejected modern medicine on behalf of naturopathy, mills and factories on behalf of hand-spinning and use of the hand loom, modern science on behalf of antiquity, the English language on behalf of the vernacular, and so on. Thus, as his occasionally frenetic quest for ideals abated, his involvement with the symbols of his parents' interests and teachings became increasingly possible. Moreover, as his life after the age of thirty-seven shows, he seemed genuinely to internalize these values: consider the shame he experienced when he failed to realize these values later in his life's work.[30] Another vital aspect of Gandhi's transformation consisted of a newfound appreciation of the values of his mother as guidelines for his own life. It was suddenly clear in his mind that "woman is the incarnation of Ahimsa."[34]

To summarize to this point: following long years of searching for values and gurus, Gandhi turned to the values of his elders, the very values he had spurned in his long retreat (or rebellion) from the ways of his people. An important aspect of his turning was an idealization of the values of his mother. He gradually began to internalize these values, thereby making them his own. Thus, Gandhi effected a self-cure, which took the form of a firming up of his values and an enhancement of his overall self-cohesion. He proceeded to assume his historical role in the political and moral battles of India.

DISCUSSION

This paper has studied Gandhi's development up to the time when his self, psychoanalytically understood, had firmed up to the point at which Gandhi could become the great liberator of the Indian masses. Associated with his search for a guru and for religious, philosophical, and social maxims to live by, was his dissatisfaction with the many teachers with whom he had contact and the many religious and philosophical points of view that he had attempted to embrace. In fact, as we have seen, Gandhi had struggled with much of what was presented to him since his childhood. Our discussion will center on the structure-seeking with which Gandhi was involved throughout his development.

We have accepted as valid Gandhi's composite account of his childhood experience—that he was concerned with fears of aggression from both human and supernatural sources and that these fears of his surroundings did not permit him to immerse himself in his milieu with vitality or assertiveness. The self that emerges from his descriptions is filled with a sense of vulnerability: the young Gandhi could not experience himself as the master of his environment. In our view, the admiring and supporting mirroring functions adequate to his unique constitutional needs were not available, so that Gandhi's experience of himself as a "coward" is understandable. That pole of the self that encompasses an individual's ambitiousness, from early expression of grandiosity to adult assertiveness, requires a self/selfobject unit in which the selfobject functions as the admiring mirror. The phenomenon of internalization in the developing self requires the repeated experience of so-called optimal frustrations sufficient to enhance the imago of embryonic self-mirroring functions to the point where they become a permanent source of nurturance. This is normally accomplished through "transmuting internalizations" that follow on the heels of optimal frustrations.[35] In Gandhi's case, the type of archaic self/selfobject dyad conducive to the optimal unfolding of the grandiose self was never established; that is, there was a deficiency in the mirroring affirmation of his exhibitionistic strivings. Thus, the young Gandhi who rushed home from school suggests a child who did not experience the joys of childhood assertiveness, the joys of game playing, of running, or of rowdiness. Seemingly, he had no opportunity to experience those affirmative responses to his assertiveness that are necessary if a child is to experience himself in a confident, positive manner. Had he received consistently supportive mirroring of his self, we may surmise he would have moved through life with abandon, because at an early age he would have acquired an inner source of well-being—the internalized feeling of admiration that is integral to the vitality of a cohesive nuclear self. As it was, the Gandhi who experienced himself throughout his childhood as unequal to the challenges of his environment persisted in his attempt to eke out of his environment the mirroring support he needed to fill out his self. Such support was never entirely forthcoming, and, as we know, Gandhi suffered throughout much of his life from the experience of ineptitude.

Perhaps the single most striking impression one gains from Gandhi's description of his life pertains to the intensity of his search for, and disappointment in, leaders. At fifty-seven, speaking of his search for a guru, he confessed that "the throne remains vacant."[32] This heartfelt admission encompassed Gandhi's pressing need for a teacher of life with whom, and from whom, he could finally absorb the strength he needed to experience the inner cohesiveness he so desired. Unfortunately, as we have seen, he had a limited ability to allow the idealization process to become established. Thus, his poignant statement that "the throne remains vacant" alludes to his resistance against merger with the very type of idealized figure from whom he could ultimately have internalized missing self-structure and thereby experienced enhanced self-esteem. It was resistance against such mergers that led Gandhi to focus quickly on the imperfections of all those mentors who presented themselves as potential selfobjects for idealization. Ultimately, he settled on God, an image of perfection with whom he had to see "eye to eye."

It seems clear that Gandhi emerged from his relationship with his mother figures—Putaliba, his sister, his nursemaid—without adequate filling out of that pole of his structure which dealt with ambitions, and that he was consequently unable to become the type of vigorous person whom he admired. He experienced himself as defective, frightened of all manner of physical violence and destructiveness of his surroundings, including imagined serpents, thieves, and goblins. Thus, Gandhi was in dire need of a compensatory source of strength to fill out his inadequate self. From Kohut we have learned that in patients subjected to an inadequate mirroring selfobject, a compensatory archaic idealized selfobject may serve to buttress self-regard through the specific selfobject functions provided by such an idealized parent.[33] Now what or who in Gandhi's environment was available to him as a target for idealization? Who could become the idealized parent who would permit Gandhi to experience the archaic self/selfobject merger whereby he could begin to absorb the strength that comes from identifying with both the precepts and the calming, soothing presence of the idealized figure? On the surface, many figures presented themselves as targets for the idealization process. Apart from his father, there were older brothers, a sister, a mother, and a nursemaid. More peripherally, there was an assortment of religious and secular teachers and, more peripherally still, there was the religion itself and the godhead, Lord Krishna, with whom Gandhi could ally himself.

With his father, the prime minister, Gandhi had a special relationship: he was the favored younger child whom his occasionally bad-tempered father never struck and, in fact, consistently cherished. Gandhi's reverance for his devoted father is well documented; it is equally well documented that he regarded his father as a pedestalized figure who, in actuality, could devote little time to him. It follows that Gandhi's father could not serve as a target for idealization, a source of power with whom Gandhi could merge. Gandhi had learned that he could receive nurturing from his father by being of service to him. His father's teaching consisted of his own exemplification of a way of life characterized by strength and honesty and, above all, by commitment to his family and to his community. Perhaps for a boy less troubled by self-doubts, the elder Gandhi might very well have been adequate as an idealizable parent. For young Mohandas, however, the elder Gandhi's ministrations were not sufficiently empathic. It is clear, nonetheless, that Gandhi was able to identify with his father in several important respects: he did, of course, develop high standards and an exacting, if not rigid, conscience. He certainly identified with his father's mission as a public servant and leader of men.

To summarize our discussion to this point, the Mahatma experienced a failure in the mirroring phase of his self-development and a further failure in the development of an idealized parental imago. This "compensatory" selfobject relationship in repair of a primary deficit in his mirroring selfobject relationship was not adequate to fill in his defective self-structure.[39] Thus, Gandhi emerged from his early life desperately seeking self-structure and at the same time resisting—out of previous disappointments—total commitment to new selfobjects potentially able to make good this deficit.

What of the other figures who might have served as targets for idealization for the young Mohandas? While his mother, nursemaid, and older sister were committed to his welfare, they achieved but partial success as selfobjects. His brothers, too, were apparently involved in his care, but their ability to commit themselves to Mohandas was limited. From all these figures to whom he was devoted, then, he derived neither adequate intrapsychic guidelines nor sufficient strength to provide the basis for the sense of vitality and assertiveness which he felt lacking in himself. We have already noted that Gandhi was further unable to immerse himself in the particular religious milieu of his upbringing.

Later in adolescence, when Gandhi served as a nurse to his father, his caretaking role became a major organizer in his life. When his father died and he was not present to receive the final infusion of paternal strength, he reacted not only with despair, but with a wholesale rejection of religious precepts. Displacing his disappointment in his father, he proceeded to express anger at his teachers for withholding what they could easily have given him—the "special knowledge," as he called it. His father's death and his reaction to this event crystallized Gandhi's quest for the special qualities he felt he lacked, especially a sense of vigor and a sense of confidence uncolored by self-doubts. It was a quest that would occupy him throughout his life, certainly until the end of his stay in South Africa, when he entered the fifth decade of his life.

As we have noted, during his stay in London Gandhi was involved in a search for a way of life and for ideals to which he could adhere. To this end, he was able to establish relationships with several men who offered support and guidance; this pattern of seeking self-structure through others had by then become well established. In particular, it was Gandhi's relationship with the members of the Vegetarian Society and their leader, Dr. Otfield, that enabled him to complete his legal studies in an impressive way, despite his continuing feelings of ineptitude.

When we next find Gandhi in India, his fortunes had again taken a negative turn: he had lost his mother, his law career was at a standstill, and he again experienced a serious loss of self-esteem. Once more a relationship with a potentially idealizable leader came onto the horizon in the form of the scholar-merchant Raychandra. Here again, Gandhi edged toward the establishment of a self/selfobject dyad, only to extricate himself from the situation by invoking the rationalization that his mentor's spiritual life was contaminated by his worldly interests. By this time, however, Gandhi's rejection of Hindu religious teachings seemed at an end. Already, in London, he had begun to study the Gita.

When the offer to become a barrister in South Africa came at the end of this two-year stay in India, Gandhi was glad to leave his homeland. Almost immediately upon entering South Africa, a dramatic and lasting self-transformation took place: Gandhi became a leader. In announcing that *he* would lead the fight to uphold the rights of the much maligned Indians living in South Africa, Gandhi's transformation took the external form of the striving to be an admired leader. We may understand Gandhi's transformation to be, in part, a reaction to the recent blows to his self-esteem that accompanied the deaths of his parents, the failures in his legal career, and his departure from his supportive mentors in London. We may surmise that Gandhi's reaction to the first insult that he suffered in South Africa—the rebuff on the train—represented the unfolding of a rage that over a long period had been taking shape in him in response to many disappointments, both recent and past. Gandhi, in other words, was vulnerable to insult when he arrived in South Africa; his initial response to the insult on the train was in part a transference response—an expression of narcissistic rage evoked by yet another unempathic rebuff. It is clear from Gandhi's capacity to act in a goal-directed manner that he was by then able to channel his aggressive energies into a burst of adaptive assertiveness.

The Gandhi who came to South Africa, then, was a man intensely in need of support for a self enfeebled by losses and failures and, as we have seen, correspondingly vulnerable and reactive to rejections and insults. The deprived masses of Indians in South Africa served an important selfobject function for Gandhi's weakened self, and collectively became a source of admiration for Gandhi's self of service. In his virtually instantaneous transformation into a revered presence, the most admired Indian in South Africa, Gandhi experienced a bracing antidote for his flagging self. Yet the subsequent behavior of the young barrister, recently deprived of parents and other sources of self-nutriments and suddenly caught up in leading and teaching the deprived countrymen who revered him, lends weight to our belief that Gandhi effected a "self-repair" in South Africa. This self-repair consisted of the consolidation of healthy self-esteem that followed Gandhi's response to the need of his countrymen for a leader whom they could extol. In embracing this role, his enfeebled self received the necessary infusion of esteem from grateful masses who were thereby telescoped into one mirroring selfobject. Thus Gandhi's self-transformation consisted of his becoming the charismatic leader, the leader filled with the rectitude of his mission, who receives the daily supplies of admiration and reverence that are normally reserved for the pedestalized leader. We further submit that the specific activities of the self of service which Gandhi so energetically offered to his beleaguered countrymen represented a reenactment (that is to say, a transference) of his ancient dealings with his father. When he served his father as a devoted nursing son, we recall, his father rewarded him with gratitude. Just so did the South African Indians reward him for his nurturant ministrations.

Alas, Gandhi's needs for self-value were not totally fulfilled through his service to his countrymen in South Africa any more than they had been totally fulfilled by his father in India. Side by side with Gandhi the revered leader of the Indian masses, there persisted Gandhi the frustrated seeker of his "own" sources of strength. This development resembles the transference pattern often encountered in those who, having suffered a disappointment in their archaic selfobjects, continue to initiate bonds with potential selfobjects; however, once the bond is established, they break off the ties, because in their transferences they experience real, threatened, or imagined disappointments.

Thus, while becoming a leader himself, Gandhi continued to become involved with potentially idealizable leaders and with philosophic and religious teachings, continually evading commitment to either a single idealized selfobject or a single idealized religion. By 1906, the year when he committed himself to the vows of Brahmacharya and the founding of the Satyagraha political movement, Gandhi was an established figure on several continents. Although he propounded the vows of Brahmacharya as tenets of self-restraint that he could live with, they were in fact *his* particular version of the ideals of Brahmacharya. Gandhi's capacity to form a relationship with an idealized leader or idealized religion continued to be fraught with resistance; along with his political activities, his quest for the perfect guru continued. The succession of philosophers, religionists, friends, and advisors who continued to come into his orbit was impressive, indeed. It is not accidental that Gandhi settled on the Gita as one of his guiding compasses. Apart from the fact that the Gita is a highly revered and most influential religious text, it also epitomizes the struggles of a young warrior, Arjun, who, gripped with depression, seeks and finds a spiritual guide. The Gita is a dialogue between the warrior, Arjun, and his mentor, Lord Krishna, in which Lord Krishna cannot persuade Arjun to go to war against his kin until he presents himself in his godly image (*Vishwarup Dorshan*) for Arjun to see with his own eyes. Lord Krishna then invites Arjun to shed all fears and attachments and to merge with him. The powerful message about merger with God as the ultimate salvation in life, the ultimate means of attaining self-realization, surely attracted Gandhi to the Gita (The *Bhagavad Gita*).

So what can be said of Gandhi's self at the time of his reentry into

India? By then, sufficient consolidation of his self had mobilized his capacity to accept and express his ambitions as a reliable feature of his self. This newfound capacity would be fully and consistently realized only with his ascendance to leadership in South Africa. The other pole of his self, the pole of ideals, always noisily manifest in his involvement and rejection of a succession of potential gurus, had become sufficiently (if not completely) consolidated to the point that his ideals of the public servant—the ideals of his father—were now more operational. Although he had tentatively embraced the ideals and teachings of Raychandra, Thoreau, Tolstoy, and Ruskin, he now devoted himself to the Hindu teachings—albeit his own version of these teachings—of Brahmacharya, especially the notion of self-restraint coexisting with the preservation of one's vigor and vitality. Finally, then, in his acceptance of Brahmacharya, Gandhi came closer to the self-values of the Hindu ascetic, such as his early mentor, Raychandra, and the religious figures his mother had exalted since his childhood days.

Notwithstanding the dramatic self-transformation Gandhi underwent, it is clear that he continued to feel incomplete. In his own testament, he related that he continued his experiments in truth seeking, even as he failed to attain the position from which God could be viewed "eye to eye." Psychoanalytically, we would equate these experiments with his unending quest for the idealized parent: "What I want to achieve—what I have been striving and pining to achieve these thirty years—is self-realization, to see God face-to-face, to attain *Moksha*."[34]

NOTES

1. Mohandas K. Gandhi, *An Autobiography: The Story of My Experiments With Truth* (Boston: Beacon Press, 1957), p. xii.
2. Ibid.
3. Ibid.
4. Mahatma Gandhi Pyarelal, *The Early Phase* (Ahmedabad: Navjivan Publishing House, (1965), I.
5. Prakash N. Desai, "Psychoanalysis and the Hindu Psyche," Unpublished paper presented at the Institute for Psychoanalysis, Chicago, October, 1980.
6. Pyarelal, *The Early Phase*, p. 202.
7. Ibid., p. 192.
8. Gandhi, *An Autobiography*, p. 7.
9. Pyarelal, *The Early Phase*, p. 207.
10. Gandhi, *An Autobiography*, p. 10.
11. Ibid., p. 28.
12. M. Marriott, "Hindu Transactions: Diversity Without Dualism," in *Transactions and Meaning: Directions in the Anthropology of Exchange and Symbolic Behavior* ed. B. Kapferer (Philadelphia: Institute for the Study of Human Issues, 1976).
13. Gandhi, *An Autobiography*, p. 30.

14. Ibid., p. 33.
15. Ibid., p. 31.
16. Ibid., p. 33.
17. Ibid., p. 15.
18. Ibid.
19. Gandhi, *An Autobiography*, p. 44.
20. Ibid., p. 80.
21. Ibid., p. 90.
22. Pyarelal, *The Early Phase*, p. 274.
23. Gandhi, *An Autobiography*, p. 89.
24. J. S. Neki, "Guru-Chela Relationship: The Possibility of a Therapeutic Paradigm," *American Journal of Orthopsychiatry*, 45 (1973), 273–290.
25. Gandhi, *An Autobiography*, p. 89.
26. Ibid., p. 89.
27. Ibid., p. 112.
28. Ibid., p. 125.
29. Ibid., p. 158.
30. Erik H. Erikson, *Gandhi's Truth* (New York: Norton, 1969).
31. Robert Payne, *The Life and Death of Mahatma Gandhi* (London: The Bondley Head, 1969), p. 59.
32. Gandhi, *An Autobiography*, p. 89.
33. Note especially Heinz Kohut, *The Analysis of the Self* (New York: International Universities Press, 1971) and *The Restoration of the Self* (New York: International Universities Press, 1977).
34. Gandhi, *An Autobiography*, p. xii.

REFERENCES

G. M. Carstairs, *The Twice-Born: a Study of a Community of High-Caste Hindus* (Bloomington: Indiana University Press, 1957).

S. Kakar, *The Inner World: A Psychoanalytic Study of Childhood and Society in India* (Delhi: Oxford University Press, 1981), second edition.

Wendy O. O'Flaherty, *Asceticism and Eroticism in the Mythology of Shiva* (Oxford: Oxford University Press, 1973).

Wendy O. O'Flaherty, *Women, Androgynes, And Other Mythical Beasts,* Chapter on Sexual Fluids (Chicago: University Chicago Press, 1980).

The Bhagavadgita, Trans. S. Radhakrishnan (New York: Harper & Row, 1948).

A. Roland, "Psychoanalytic perspectives on personality development in India," *International Review of Psychoanalysis*, (1980), VII, 73–88.

WOODROW WILSON REVISITED
The Prepolitical Years

JOSEPH A. BONGIORNO

Woodrow Wilson has fascinated and puzzled generations of students and scholars. On the one hand, he was a man of remarkable strengths and talents. He was a respected historian and political scientist, a prodigious worker, and—at his best—a brilliant leader and innovator, first as president of Princeton University (1902–10) and later as governor of New Jersey (1910–12) and president of the United States (1912–20). He developed rich life-long friendships, he was capable of humor (including humor about himself), and he was a devoted son, husband, and father. On the other hand, beginning in adolescence, he suffered several emotional breakdowns and near-breakdowns. At his worst as a leader, he lost his humor, demanded complete loyalty and compliance, refused compromise, stubbornly adhered to his causes, and thereby contributed greatly to his own defeats.

These contradictions have been difficult to explain. Alexander and Juliette George propose that Wilson was unconsciously angry with his abusive, critical father, that he displaced this anger onto his leading opponents, and that he acted out this conflict under the guise of moral crusades. Sigmund Freud and William Bullitt propose that he unconsciously longed passively for his father, that he unconsciously hated his younger brother, and that he precipitated the battles at Princeton and as president of the United States because of a variety of transferences and identifications. Edwin Weinstein proposes that Wilson's adult problems

133

were mainly caused by brain dysfunction due to longstanding cerebrovascular insufficiency and repeated strokes, by an overly close relationship to his insecure, depressed mother, and by a pathological vulnerability to guilt.[1]

In the following essay, I examine episodes and materials from
Wilson's earliest years to the end of his presidency of Princeton. I propose that under certain circumstances Wilson suffered problems in the
regulation of tension and self-esteem and was vulnerable to the kinds of
regression that Heinz Kohut has described in his studies of the self. I
hope to demonstrate that this more plausibly explains Wilson and his
struggles than do explanations based on structural conflict or neurological impairment. I propose further that most of the time Wilson's
vulnerability lay dormant and that other aspects of his personality played the leading or central roles. Under particular kinds of stresses, however, Wilson responded—so humanly—not from his strengths but from
his vulnerability, which temporarily became the leading edge of his
personality. And I finally propose that considerations of self help explain not only Wilson's weakness, but also his greatness. I rely as much
as possible on primary sources.[2]

PARENTS, CHILDHOOD, AND ADOLESCENCE

Thomas Woodrow Wilson was born on December 28, 1856, in
Staunton, Virginia. He was the third child of Dr. Joseph Ruggles Wilson,
an eminent Presbyterian minister, and of Janet Woodrow Wilson, herself the daughter of a Presbyterian minister. Woodrow had a sister five
years older and another three years older than he. A brother was born
when Woodrow was ten. Woodrow went by his first name, Thomas (or
Tommy), until he was twenty-five.

Janet Woodrow was the fifth of eight children. When she was five,
her mother died of illnesses contracted during the rough sea voyage by
which the family had emigrated from Scotland to the United States.
Janet and the other children were then cared for by a maternal aunt,
whom their father soon married and with whom he had more children.
He may have lost interest in the children of his first marriage: he remembered none of them in his will, and Janet mentioned him only once in
her correspondence, although she maintained close ties with her brothers and sisters. She was proud of her ancestors and probably exaggerated their accomplishments. As an adult, she was subject to frequent
physical ailments for which no medical basis was found and which were
probably psychosomatic symptoms of depression. In her letters to

FIGURE 1. Janet Woodrow Wilson about 1874. (Published with permission of Princeton University Library.)

Woodrow during his school years, she showed special concern about his physical ailments, and these were likely a frequent subject of discussion between them. She was blindly loyal to Woodrow and sided totally with him, even in his disputes with college professors where he was at least partly at fault. And, finally, she expressed disappointment with his decisions to spend parts or all of his school vacations away from home, but she wrote of her sadness and disappointment by stating that these feelings were his father's or brother's. In 1917, nearly thirty years after she died, Woodrow wrote glowingly of her unusual grace, refinement, and perceptiveness. Her reserved bearing made her true lovableness apparent only to her family. Even so many years after her death, he could still feel "the touch of her hand and the sweet steadying influence of her character."[3]

Joseph Ruggles Wilson was a dynamic minister and a deeply ambitious man. The seventh son of Scottish-Irish immigrants, he had graduated first in his class from Jefferson College and later did some of his theology studies at the Princeton Theological Seminary. He held a series of increasingly eminent pastorates and rose high within the hierarchy of the Presbyterian Church of the Confederate States of America. This rise culminated in 1870 when the General Assembly, the church's highest decision-making body, named him a professor of rhetoric at the prestigious Columbia Theological Seminary in Columbia, South Carolina. Accomplished in spoken and written rhetoric, he quickly became a popular and successful teacher. At last he had the eminence and success he so eagerly desired.

But he soon precipitated a conflict that led to the greatest disappointment in his career. In October, 1872, the parishioners of the local First Presbyterian Church, for whom Dr. Wilson was doing a profitable ($1,500 per year) part-time ministry, decided that they needed a full-time minister: he had to give up his part-time position in July of 1873. That fall he asked the seminary faculty to declare attendance at campus Sunday chapel services compulsory for students. Campus services conflicted with those at the First Presbyterian Church, and parishioners and students alike protested. Wilson was acting at least in part out of personal pique about the loss of his job and of the supplementary income. In January, 1874, after weeks of deadlock, the seminary faculty agreed with Wilson and declared the campus services compulsory. Student protest and noncompliance with the ruling led to the suspension of thirteen students. That spring the decision was appealed to the General Assembly. During the three days' debate, Wilson made an unimpressive defense of his position. The General Assembly finally voted, by a small margin, to reverse the faculty's ruling, although it made special efforts to be conciliatory to Wilson. Wilson quickly resigned. He claimed that the assembly had stripped him of the authority necessary to carry out his professorial duties. He accepted a well-paying pastorate in Wilmington, North Carolina, and in subsequent years he rose in prestige in the southern church and was elected to the church's highest position. Yet he never fully recovered his self-confidence and self-esteem after this defeat.[4]

Woodrow's childhood was dominated by his father. In the evenings, the family listened as Dr. Wilson read aloud passages of literature and scripture and led them in singing hymns, and on Sundays the family attended the services at which he officiated. Woodrow's earliest memory was of seeking an explanation from his father after hearing someone say that Lincoln had been elected and that there would be war. Dr. Wilson took Woodrow's education into his own hands. Woodrow did not learn the alphabet until he was nine and did not read until he was eleven. Weinstein plausibly explains this lateness, which has been variously attributed by other biographers to the slow recovery of organized education in the South or to the passive-aggressive expression of his anger at his father, as the result of a developmental dyslexia caused by mixed cerebral dominance. When Woodrow finally began his formal studies, Dr. Wilson heavily emphasized self-expression. He demanded that Woodrow use precisely the correct word, that he rework compositions three or four times, and that he rewrite passages from the classics in order to express the ideas better than the original authors. There was an intense closeness between the two. They took long walks together, and Woodrow served as an assistant and a confidant. All his life Woodrow revered his father and praised his father's influence on him. Some relatives thought Dr. Wilson treated Woodrow cruelly with his wit and jokes. A cousin recalled that one morning Woodrow, then a young adolescent, arrived late to breakfast. Dr. Wilson explained to the visiting relatives that Woodrow must have been detained by his excitement at finding a new whisker. Another cousin recalled that Dr. Wilson was proud of Woodrow, especially after his talents began to show, "but only a man as sweet as cousin Woodrow would have forgotten the severity of the criticism to the value of which he so often paid tribute, in after life."[5]

A shy boy and adolescent, Woodrow had trouble making friends at fourteen when his family moved to Columbia. A classmate remembered him as being "extremely dignified" but not a brilliant student. "He was not like the other boys. He had a queer way of going off by himself." Yet he was popular and had a way of being helpful to the younger students.[6]

Woodrow underwent two years of turmoil and change between the autumn of 1872, when he was nearly sixteen, and the autumn of 1874. This period began about the time that Dr. Wilson received notice that he would have to give up his cherished job at the First Presbyterian Church, and it ended several months after Dr. Wilson's defeat before the General Assembly and his move to Wilmington. Ray Stannard Baker, the author of a respected eight-volume biography of Wilson, considers this period one of the most important of Woodrow's life. Woodrow became much more religious and befriended an older youth, Frank Brooke, a student at the seminary. Brooke, Woodrow, and others met in private religious services in Brooke's room and later in a small chapel on the campus. These services had great impact on Woodrow. Years afterward, while President of the United States, he said at the doorway to this chapel, "I feel . . . as though I ought to take off my shoes. This is holy ground . . . I have never heard greater speaking in my life than I heard from that rostrum." In July of 1873, he became a member of the local First Presbyterian Church of Columbia—the same month his father had to resign from that church. That autumn Woodrow went off to Davidson College in North Carolina. Poorly prepared for study, he still did fairly well in his coursework. He played baseball and had his first experiences with debate. At the end of the year, he began to have problems with his health, though there is no record of what his health difficulties were. That autumn he was unable to return to Davidson and he withdrew from school.[7]

He remained at home for the next fifteen months. Although he was not a recluse, he spent much of his time reading or walking the docks of Wilmington alone. He also made a few uncomfortable calls on young ladies. He and his father spent a lot of time together and grew even closer. Woodrow befriended another young man, with whom he discussed books at length. Woodrow was interested in great men and especially the causes of their greatness. During this time, Woodrow also became engrossed in learning shorthand. He had begun to study it the previous summer and now returned to it intensely, corresponding with the author of the system and amusing and puzzling his friends with his fascination and excitement.[8]

Wilson wrote down some of his fantasies during this important period. They provide a remarkably intimate look into his inner world. He usually portrayed himself as British nobility of high military rank. The documents include a promotion order, a list of officers of his Royal Lance Guards (he was in command, with the rank of lieutenant general, and assorted real friends were his subordinates), and a special order threatening to demote any officers appearing in civilian dress. In one fantasy, written as a *London Times* article, he was a vice-admiral in command of a six-vessel "flying squadron." The ships were all built "according to plans drawn by her celebrated commander Lord Wilson" and "have been pronounced by all the best judges to be the best vessels in the Royal Navy." The flagship, HMS *Renown*, was "the fastest man-of-war ever built." After a detailed description of her guns, masts, sails, and anchor, he wrote, "The *Renown* is, beyond a doubt, the fastest vessel in the *world*." The final document, written in July of 1874, soon after Woodrow returned home from Davidson, was the constitution for the Royal United Kingdom Yacht Club. The constitution was preceded by a list of thirty vessels, headed by the *Eclipse*, owned by Lord Thomas W. Wilson. Lord Wilson presided over the yacht club with authority like that of an admiral over his fleet: he had absolute veto power over all resolutions, even over those approved unanimously by the other members. Lord Wilson donated prizes for the most important annual boat race. Because of this arrangement, his own vessels did not compete.[9]

Wilson carried on his most elaborate fantasy for several months. The manuscript, no longer extant, is described in detail by an early biographer. Woodrow was an American admiral assigned to investigate the mysterious disappearance of ships which were "swallowed up" with their valuable cargoes "in the bosom of an ocean on which no known war raged, no known storms swept." One night he and his fleet sighted a suspicious-looking ship "with black hull and rakish rig." A long chase led to an "island uncharted and hitherto unknown." It appeared "bare and uninhabited," but what appeared to be a narrow inlet ending at a wall of rock turned out to be a cunningly contrived entrance to a spacious atoll-like bay, where Admiral Wilson discovered the ships of the outlaws "and the dismantled hulls of many of their victims." Admiral Wilson heroically destroyed the pirates and rescued the surviving victims.[10]

Woodrow's experiences and fantasies in these years were related at least in part to his father's disappointments in the local church and the ensuing struggle and defeat over the campus chapel services. This is suggested not only by the simultaneity of Woodrow's turmoil and his father's problems, but also by the content of his fantasies, which assume an even greater importance because he wrote them in the months leading up to his failure to return to Davidson.

Woodrow's fantasies and illness lend themselves to tentative interpretations at either an oedipal or self level. According to an oedipal interpretation, they suggest a heightening of castration anxiety and of his defenses against it. His father's distress and defeat unconsciously threatened an oedipal victory, with the attendant threats of retaliation and castration. Woodrow defended against his own aggression and competitiveness by reaction formation: he became more religious and he sought out idealizing—that is, non-competitive—relationships with Brooke, God, and the author of the shorthand system. He nevertheless revealed his aggression and competitiveness in his fantasies of war, power, conquest, and himself as the great man—that is, himself becoming or surpassing his father. Attending Davidson may have unconsciously represented an aggressive act against his father, and Woodrow had to fail or else risk retaliation. In short, an oedipal formulation would argue that Woodrow had a success neurosis.

According to a self-level interpretation, Woodrow was describing his experiences of himself. Disappearing ships, "bare and uninhabited islands," and "dismantled hulls" referred to his inner experience of emptiness and barrenness. The spacious bay, hidden in the interior of the island, represented his protected, vulnerable inner self—the sense of endangered vitality that D. W. Winnicott refers to as "the true self." The "ocean on which no known war raged, no known storms swept" suggests Woodrow's characterological appearance of imperturbable calm, although beyond that calm, as the fantasy went on to relate, lay threats and danger. [11]

Feeling empty and barren was painful and frightening to him. Perhaps Woodrow had warded off such feelings by maintaining—long beyond the phase-appropriate age—a close, over-idealizing relationship with his father. His earliest memory (the announcement of Lincoln's election) indicated idealization. His discussions of great men reflected his admiration and his concern for his father. The idealization, then, served not as a defense against competition but as a way of maintaining a whole, full sense of self. Kohut has described the need for this type of idealizing relationship and its functioning to maintain self-completeness and cohesion as a normal, transient phase of early self-development which persists in certain types of self-disturbance. Dr. Wilson's struggle and disappointments disrupted Woodrow's idealization by letting Woodrow see his fantasized omnipotent father defeated and shaken and by making his father less available emotionally to Woodrow. This traumatic de-idealization and disruption plunged Woodrow back into his painful self-experience. He tried to soothe himself by fantasies of greatness and adventure and by seeking out new idealizing relationships. He also identified with his father—in imagining himself the great man—and immersed himself into an aspect of language (shorthand), the area of his father's expertise and the area of their mutual interaction and pleasure. And finally, he returned home from Davidson and restored the relationship with his father, which had been disrupted geographically as well as emotionally. [12]

If Woodrow's self-experience was indeed so painful and his idealization needs so prolonged, these adolescent experiences and fantasies do not reveal why. Nor do they reveal which interpretation—a self-level or an oedipal interpretation—is more plausible. But central questions have been raised and serve to introduce the next period of Woodrow's life.

PRINCETON UNDERGRADUATE

In the autumn of 1875, after fifteen months at home and now late in his eighteenth year, Woodrow returned to college—this time at Princeton University (then named the College of New Jersey). His second year at Princeton, according to Baker, was "among the most important of his life: a turning point." As early as his sixteenth year, Woodrow had expressed interest in being a political leader. Now, moved by reading the speeches and essays of British orators and by reading essays on powerful democratic leadership, he decided actually to become a political leader. He devoted himself intensely to the study and practice of oratory: he went off by himself to the woods near Princeton or to his father's empty church at home and practiced verbatim the orations of great orators. Becoming more self-confident, at prayer meetings he found himself so at ease—and, apparently, excited—that he found it "hard to keep my seat." He won second prize in a sophomore oratorical contest, he organized a new debating society, and he was elected the sophomore representative to the school paper. In the midst of all these accomplishments, he wrote to his father that he had discovered that he had a mind.[13]

That spring he wrote a letter to his father, who was attending the church's General Assembly. It is the earliest of the three extant letters from Woodrow to his father and the only one from his Princeton years. He asked his father to give the assembly his respects, and he advised the assembly to heed the opinions of their stated clerk (Dr. Wilson), who "has a very inconvenient way of seeing right to the heart of any matter which comes under his observation." Woodrow went on to describe himself as "a queer fellow . . . entirely free from anything like his father's clear-sightedness" with a mind which seemed "remarkably bright and empty." He was distinguishable in a crowd by his "long nose . . . and consequential manner" and was known "as a man who can make a remarkably good show with little or no material. . . . He has a few queer ideas of his own and very few of them are his own." Woodrow's writing lacked clearness, and the "scarce ideas" he did have he expressed in a

FIGURE 2. Woodrow Wilson as a student at Princeton. (Published with permission of Princeton University Archives.)

limping, cloudy manner. Ideas in his writings appeared like oases in the desert, "except that his ideas are very seldom distinguishable from the waste which surrounds them." He was "apt to allow himself to sympathize almost too heartily with everything that is afloat and, consequently, subjects his nervous system to frequent severe and, sometimes, rather unnecessary strains."[14]

From his sophomore year on, Woodrow took charge of his own education: he worked to complete course requirements creditably but devoted his main energies to oratory, debate, and the study of history and politics. In ensuing years, he became managing editor of the school paper, for which he wrote numerous articles and editorials (invariably idealistic). He became one of the most prominent orators and debators on campus and was valued for his humor and for his extemporaneous speaking ability. His undergraduate career culminated in his senior year, when the prestigious *International Review* accepted for publication a paper which he had written on cabinet government. Through all of this, his health held up very well.

Woodrow saved many letters from his father during his Princeton years and continued to do so until Dr. Wilson's death in January, 1903. Dr. Wilson's letters provide invaluable access to their relationship. During Woodrow's Princeton years, Dr. Wilson wrote that all his life he himself had been self-deprecating, prone to melancholy, and overly introspective, and he strongly encouraged Woodrow to avoid those pitfalls. He was concerned for Woodrow's health and happiness. Although family finances were strained, he sent Woodrow what money he could, with occasional reminders to use the money only for necessities. Dr. Wilson was a mentor and teacher in Woodrow's literary pursuits, in his oratory, and in life. He delighted in Woodrow's writing style and offered pointed but friendly criticism of the essays and manuscripts which Woodrow sent home for his review. He was especially interested in Woodrow's oratory. When Woodrow had a fishbone extracted surgically from his throat, Dr. Wilson asked anxiously if it had injured his voice. The voice, he reminded Woodrow, is a speaker's principal tool and should be guarded carefully.[15]

In advising Woodrow how to conduct his life, Dr. Wilson revealed much of his own philosophy of life. Hard work was the most valuable habit his son could learn. Hard work and self-denial were the very heart of genius. It was fruitless to daydream of success and fame; rather, Woodrow should work hard and thus earn them. Disappointment and failure were the major sources of real growth, and one's handling of them was an accurate measure of one's worth and mettle. When Woodrow was disappointed about not representing his debating society at an oratorical contest, Dr. Wilson expressed the family's sympathy but added that he was rather pleased with the failure, because it would reveal Woodrow's worth. "If you shall continue to be disheartened . . . well, you can't be good for much. But if . . . you arise with new resolution . . . well, this will be prophetic of a noble and honorable manhood."[16]

Dr. Wilson often expressed his closeness to Woodrow and asked him to write as to a friend. "I am glad to have a friend in you, whose character I greatly esteem and upon whose excellence in the future I look with confidence." He repeatedly expressed pleasure in Woodrow's fine character and his literary and oratorical accomplishments. He even wondered whether major New York newspapers might be commenting on some of Woodrow's campus writings. He expressed sorrow at their being separated and complained of the infrequency of Woodrow's letters home.[17]

He explicitly stated that he had expected success from Woodrow all along and that he now expected him to work hard and to grow in the face of disappointment. In fact, it would be Woodrow's own fault if he did not become a great writer and thinker. Also, during Woodrow's second year in college, Dr. Wilson made his first allusion to a unity existing between the two of them—this time, a unity of interest. Dr. Wilson asked him to wait before buying a new overcoat unless it was absolutely essential. "Our interests are *one* [.] I will sacrifice anything for you, as I am sure you will for me."[18]

Woodrow made a remarkable comeback at Princeton. After dropping out of Davidson, he had now resumed his studies and triumphed. This capacity to recover from failure and to go on to triumph would become his hallmark. Behaviorally, his recovery evolved around becoming a scholar and orator and taking active steps toward becoming a political leader. Psychologically, his recovery evolved around his identifying with his father, his father's expectations of him, and his father's ego ideal. Woodrow's pursuit of oratory represented identification with his father: Dr. Wilson was an excellent orator; the great orators, whose speeches Woodrow practiced, represented his father; and Woodrow even delivered their speeches from his father's pulpit. Woodrow adopted as his own and identified with his father's expectations of him that he work very hard, that he be strengthened by disappointment and failure (his success at Princeton after failing at Davidson was one example of that), and that he become a great thinker and writer. Woodrow also identified with his father's ego ideal. Dr. Wilson intensely wanted power and prestige and never really recovered after he lost them at

Columbia. In becoming a scholar and aspiring to politics, Woodrow was striving to become what his father had failed to become and now wanted Woodrow to become.

How did these identifications help Woodrow to recover so dramatically? Again, one may approach this question with oedipal or self-level interpretations. At an oedipal level, perhaps Woodrow was defending against castration anxiety by identification with the aggressor: behind his father's pleasure in him he perceived—or fantasized—intense jealousy and aggression. To defend against the resulting anxiety, Woodrow identified with, or "became," this aggressive, assertive father. Or perhaps his father's pleasure assured him that his accomplishments were not viewed as competition and therefore were not liable to retaliation. His becoming what his father wanted him to become may even have represented passivity and compliance. At the self level, the identification with his father, his expectations, and his ego ideal may have defended against and compensated for a sense of deficit. Woodrow's letter to his father contained some of the imagery of barrenness of the earlier pirate fantasy (he wrote of his ideas being "scarce," "limping," and "seldom distinguishable from the waste that surrounds them"), but the barrenness was now less austere and he handled it with humor. Perhaps by aspiring to what his father had wanted to become, Woodrow regained the pleasure he had previously received in his father's approval. But now that he had made these sources of gratification his own, he internalized them by these identifications. This relief from his sense of deficit was exhilarating.

A self-formulation would be supported if Dr. Wilson could be shown to be excessively invested in Woodrow and in his accomplishments—if he needed to have Woodrow need him and to develop in these directions in order to compensate for some insecurity or sense of deficit of his own. A parent who is overinvested because of a sense of his own deficit often experiences his child as a part of himself rather than as a separate individual. Remarkably perceptive of the parent's anxiety, the child seeks out and learns behaviors which allay the anxiety. Thus enmeshed in his parent's needs, the child has difficulty developing a full, continuous, separate sense of self apart from the parent. Instead, he grows up to feel incomplete and empty unless he maintains the original relationship or establishes a similar one. It is not clear from Dr. Wilson's letters of these Princeton years whether his investment in Woodrow was excessive in these ways. There are hints that it was: the intensity of his investment, the request that they relate as friends, and the statement that their interests were one and that each was willing to sacrifice anything for the other. Further evidence appears in later letters. Admittedly these letters reflect needs from late in Dr. Wilson's life and from late in Woodrow's. But they are the earliest indicators we have.

WOODROW IN LOVE

In the autumn of 1879, Woodrow began law school at the University of Virginia. He quickly fell in love with his first cousin, Harriet Woodrow, the daughter of a maternal uncle. Harriet was pretty, outgoing, and musically talented. She and Woodrow had renewed their childhood acquaintanceship in his senior year at Princeton, and now she was attending school only a two-hour ride from the University of Virginia. Woodrow visited her so often that his absences from school got him into trouble with university authorities. And for the first time since Davidson, he encountered serious health problems, which forced him to withdraw from school in late December of his second year. The symptoms he reported to friends were an intractable cold and dyspepsia. This return home, like the one from Davidson, gradually restored his health, and he completed his law studies at home over the next fifteen months.[19]

During the summer of 1881, he stayed with Harriet and her family in Ohio while he worked with another uncle, a lawyer, as an apprentice clerk. Woodrow was delighted to be with Harriet, and in September he amazed her by proposing marriage. She refused, giving as her reason their blood relationship, but in truth she did not love him. Woodrow spent the night at a local hotel, where he wrote her a note (on a scrap of paper) to allay her concerns about their blood relationship. He left for home the following day. He wrote her a letter en route describing his high spirits and requesting that she be photographed in a particular dress and particular pose, as he fondly remembered her. There was to be only one print made, which she would send to him. Woodrow and Harriet continued to correspond over the next few days, but the ardor of his letters soon persuaded her—and probably her father—to terminate the correspondence.[20]

Although Woodrow struggled to maintain appearances, he was deeply hurt by his rejection. That December he wrote a 100-line poem, "A River's Course." In the beginning, the river chafes and rages within the bondage of its shores. Later it passes a grey abandoned castle which sits high on the pinnacle of a rocky island, its front walls scarred with the traces of earlier hate-filled assaults, its oaken dining table rotting, its alarm bell silenced with rust, and its empty halls and courts lined with cobwebs, mould, and moss. The river then passes through a city where men have no idea of the sadness, death, and pity it has known. Beyond the city, it passes a manor house where two young brothers romp and their young mother laughs with delight in their gladness. The river's heart lightened at this happy scene, it peacefully pours its waters into the sea.[21]

Three months after writing this poem, Woodrow wrote to a close friend that his love, although not easily elicited, was "all the more vehement when once aroused." He added that he had suffered greatly, especially since he believed Harriet really loved him and had rejected him only out of prejudice and duty. He was "not unmanned," although his studies and his plans to begin law practice had been delayed.[22]

Until this time, he had gone by his baptized name, Thomas. After this, he dropped it permanently (he had experimented with variations of his initials and names at the University of Virginia). He was now Woodrow Wilson.[23]

In the spring of 1882, at the age of twenty-five, Woodrow began a law practice in Atlanta, Georgia, but within a year he realized that law was not for him and decided that in the fall (1883) he would undertake graduate study in history and political science at Johns Hopkins University. That same spring (1882) he met Ellen Louise Axson and—again quickly—fell in love. Ellen was attractive, shy, artistic, and widely read. Her father was a Presbyterian minister and an old friend of Dr. Wilson. Woodrow courted Ellen that summer, proposed hesitantly in September, and won her acceptance. Woodrow was ecstatic.[24]

Except for brief periods, Woodrow and Ellen were apart for the twenty-one months between their betrothal in September of 1883 and their wedding in June of 1885. Woodrow spent two very successful years studying history and political science at Johns Hopkins University. Buoyed by the love of Ellen, he immersed himself in his studies and writing with an intensity unprecedented even for him; and in the autumn of 1884 he published a book, *Congressional Government*, which established him as a respected scholar of his time.

During their engagement, Woodrow and Ellen wrote each other hundreds of letters, and most of them remain. A beautiful collection of love letters, they provide a more revealing look into Woodrow's inner life than do any other materials. As he likely did earlier in his letters to his mother, he reported to Ellen his assorted physical concerns and worried intensely about her health. Most valuably for our interest in his inner life, he frequently wrote in detail about his feelings and his experience of himself. He described frequent periods of despondency in which he doubted his ability to do anything worthwhile. He had no faith in his talents and was convinced he was a "dull fool with a vain knack for

FIGURE 3. Ellen Louise Axson about the time of her engagement. (Published with permission of Princeton University Library.)

counterfeiting thought." He did not really have a mind; he had only the skill to conceal its absence. He was "utterly without sparkle and versatility," and his education thus far consisted of expressing "the poverty of thought" that was in him. He felt less real than other men.[25]

Woodrow found it painful to be alone. After eight years away from home, he still suffered from homesickness. When he was alone, by which he meant "shut off from *active* sympathy" of his loved ones, he took life too seriously and was unable to relax. At those times he felt the feeling side of himself repressed, and "there is nothing to do but *think*." Without the love of his family, his "disposition would sour," his heart would "starve," and his mind "become parched and arid." Without a home life, he felt "like only *half* a man . . . as if I were waiting for my *real* life to begin."[26]

He also revealed how he overcame these feelings. One way was to imagine having a message for the world and delivering it, to imagine doing immortal work. A much more important way was love. All his life the love from his family had eased his loneliness and self-doubt and provided the only way to rid himself of his morbid tendencies. And now his love for Ellen took him beyond that. Since their engagement, his work was greatly improved and his whole nature seemed expanded. For him, the idea of love as self-sacrifice was nonsense. Love was a luxury which made "sorrows light and cares easy to bear." He felt indescribably exalted that she was really so intensely interested in him. "The strength and sweetness of your love and the ardour of your sympathy and trust give me a sense of completeness, a serene confidence in the future which is beyond description, because beyond all comparison blessed." With some timidity, he asked her to put into her letters as much expression of love as she conscientously could. Such expressions were sunshine to his frosts of mood. He was especially delighted by her interest in him and her acceptance of him:

> You alone are part of that [his individual, secret, inmost life]. You alone may know me altogether, at my best and at my worst. You alone may look my heart full in the face and see without reserve the lineaments which others may only guess at. And *this*, my Eileen, is *the* delight of my love for you. I did not know what it was to live until I found you for whom to live, in whom to live. . . . That is *why* you are "all the world to me" . . . you are the keeper of all my heart's secrets.[27]

This joy of sharing his inner world with Ellen was reflected in his dreams. Barely two weeks after their betrothal, he wrote to her of a dream in which he had shown her a side of himself she had never seen—his nonsensical side. In the dream, he and Ellen frolicked through a house "with playful caresses and stolen kisses." The following summer he wrote of a dream in which she coaxed him out of independent thought and action and into a grateful slavery of love. In relating the dream, he mentioned her brown eyes, and later in the letter he mentioned the grave yet happy feeling of looking into her eyes.[28]

Shortly after New Year's Day of 1884, Woodrow had a very different dream. He had stayed at Johns Hopkins over the Christmas holidays in order to save trainfare and to study and write. He was totally alone. Trying to "escape intolerable loneliness," he had plunged himself intensely into his work and by New Year's Day found himself so nervous and fatigued that he had to stop work altogether for a few days. He called it the most severe state he had ever experienced. While in this "half-crazy condition," he had "three successive all-night dreams" of Ellen soothing him with "sweet inimitable ministrations of love." On January 3, however, still struggling to recover, he received a letter in which Ellen teased him in feigned indignation about his writing about scores of kisses and caresses. That night, *I dreamt that you were dead—* you, without whom I would not care to live, nay, whose loss would make me wish to die." In an unusually rambling letter, he told Ellen that he had vowed to himself to open himself completely to her. This meant he must abandon previous resolutions never to reveal his "private thoughts and motives" to anyone—a resolution made because of his "ignorance of women" and his "experience of selfishness with men." He was not about to abandon his vow now, but her letter made him worry that she might not accept him.[29]

Four days later—he had not yet received another letter from Ellen— he wrote that people noted how happy he was, even though he could see no difference in the mirror. At night he had dreams of her smiling at him and telling him of her love. In one dream, she was glad to see him (he mentioned that twice) and forgave him "for the one or two offenses against decorum and 'principles' into which I was betrayed by my delight at being with you." In that same letter he commented on his disgust at his own work because it was so inadequate compared to the writing style he desired:

> I have imagined a style clear, bold, fresh, and facile . . . flexible but always strong . . . that could be driven at a high speed—a brilliant, dashing, coursing speed—or constrained . . . as the case required; a style full of life, of color and vivacity, of soul and energy, of inexhaustible power—of a thousand qualities of beauty and grace and strength that would make it immortal—is it any wonder that I am disgusted with the stiff, dry, mechanical, monotonous sentences in

which my meagre thoughts are compelled to masquerade, as in garments which are too mean even for *them!*[30]

Even by January 4, Woodrow was beginning to feel better, but his total recovery was delayed by a tragic event. On January 10, Ellen's father had to be hospitalized because he had become violent. There remain no letters from this immediate period. On January 20 or 21, Woodrow joined Ellen in Georgia and stayed with her and her family until January 27. He visited his own family in Wilmington on January 28 and delayed his departure for Baltimore for two days because he was not feeling well. He related, without confirming or denying, his father's diagnosing the illness as "a sickness of *heart* at having to leave you." Woodrow regretted that he could not stay longer under his mother's nursing care but had to return to Baltimore. Once there, he was saved from being lonely by visits from his friends. Because people told him he looked ill and because he felt a responsibility to Ellen to care for his health, he consulted a physician for the first time in several years and was reassured that his malady, apparently gastrointestinal, was minor. On February 7, he reported that he was fully recovered.[31]

In these years of law school, law practice, and graduate school, Woodrow had again demonstrated his capacity to recover from failure. He had broken down in law school but recovered to complete his law studies, to practice law, and to triumph in graduate school. He was painfully disappointed in his love of Harriet Woodrow but recovered to win the love of Ellen.

An oedipal interpretation of Woodrow's breakdown in law school and of his tensions in the early days of 1884 would emphasize guilt and castration anxiety over his sexual and competitive impulses. But for the first time, an oedipal formulation runs into difficulties. That Woodrow went on to successes after his failure rules out a success neurosis. Further, he gave little indication of guilt over his attractions to either Harriet or Ellen. He wrote to Ellen freely and often of kisses and caresses. And finally at no time did he show disgust or revulsion, the presence of which would suggest the danger of gratifying a repressed, forbidden impulse. Rather, Woodrow's experiences and feelings in these years are familiar to us now from patients who have experienced some disturbances in their self development: low self-esteem, poor tension regulation, and the need for personal relationships to maintain a manageable balance in each.

Woodrow documented his low self-esteem in various ways. He experienced himself as incomplete (*"half* a man"), barren ("parched," "arid"), and depleted ("starved"). But loving personal relationships made him feel otherwise. All his life his relationships with his family made him feel better. At the University of Virginia, his relationship with Harriet, to judge from his behavior, made him feel alive and exuberant. And in his letters to Ellen he revealed that she too made him feel expanded, confident, and complete. In short, loving personal relationships profoundly improved his self-esteem.

The evidence of faulty tension regulation is dramatic. His breakdown at the University of Virginia resulted directly from his being overstimulated in his relationship with Harriet. He was so excited by her being nice to him and, presumably, by his sexual attraction to her that he travelled all over the countryside to be with her, he neglected his studies to a degree that forced the school and his father to intervene, and finally, after developing psychosomatic or hypochrondiacal symptoms, he withdrew from school. Clearly it was not guilt that incapacitated him. The only remorse he felt was over embarrassing Harriet. Rather, he could not regulate his tensions by himself and had to return home so that his family could help him manage them. His overstimulation was a combination of sexual stimulation and stimulation at Harriet's liking him and being nice to him. When he visited Harriet the next summer, he again became overstimulated and misinterpreted her kindness as love. Written in response to his rejection, his poem of the river was a transparent description of his own emotional state. His tensions had chafed and raged out of control. The abandoned castle, scarred by earlier trauma and inhabited by mould, cobwebs, rust, and rotting wood, represented his self-experience. The city represented the external world, which could not see his sufferings. The lovely young mother represented a childlike fantasy of his own mother and how he had wanted Harriet to respond: with delight in him and in his joy. This scene and the merging with the sea represented his peaceful and soothing experience with his family, especially his mother.

At first, Woodrow's experiences in Baltimore around New Year's Day of 1884 may appear open to an oedipal interpretation. Perhaps he felt guilty and anxious about sexual fantasies. Perhaps his all-night dreams of "sweet, inimitable ministrations of love" were explicitly sexual and made him feel even more guilty and anxious. He could not let himself consciously recognize the obvious coquettishness of Ellen's scolding, for that too was sexual. Instead, he projected onto her his own harsh superego, and his dream of her death fulfilled his wish to be freed from these sexual temptations.

But this line of interpretation fails to capture the tone and mood of Woodrow's dreams and of his letter. He reported the dreams as joyful and loving, and he was delighted—not guilty or ashamed—to tell her about them. Rather, these experiences in Baltimore, like the earlier ones with Harriet, seemed to result from faulty tension regulation. Being alone, he had trouble distracting himself from his sexual fantasies and tensions. His love-ministration dreams fulfilled his wish for Ellen to soothe his painful, work-disrupting, "half-crazy condition" of un-manageable tensions. Ellen's coquettishness, instead of providing the soothing which he required and had been dreaming about for the pre-vious three nights, stimulated him even further. Thus he dreamed that she was dead in order to remove the source of unmanageable tension, as distinguished from the source of sexual temptation. He concretely seized the prohibitions of her teasing in order to regulate his own ten-sions, as distinguished from projecting onto her his own harsh super-ego.

Four days later, Woodrow's tension evolved to excitement—people were even commenting on how happy he seemed. This is reminiscent of the high spirits he reported to Harriet the day after she rejected him. In part, he was resorting to a hypomanic defense against depression, but he was also experiencing a grandiosity-tinged excitement, evident in the progression of terms with which he described his desired writing style: "bold . . . always strong . . . driven at a high speed . . . inexhaustible power . . . a thousand qualities of beauty and grace and strength that would make it immortal." He did not fully recover until he spent time with Ellen (although under tragic circumstances) and with his own fami-ly and finally received medical attention and reassurance.

In his letters to Ellen, Woodrow revealed two important ways in which he tried to regulate his tensions. One was to entertain fantasies of immortal work—the successors of his adolescent fantasies of adventure and renown. But far more important and effective for him was love, both from his own family and now from Ellen. Love helped him, I propose, by fulfilling what Kohut has called the mirroring function. Every young child needs to have his worth reflected back to him, or mirrored, by his parents. In normal self-development, the child gradu-ally assumes for himself, or internalizes, this function and thereby the capacity for regulation of tension and self-esteem. No one ever inter-nalizes this function completely. Everyone's self-experience is influ-enced to some degree by the mirroring he continues to receive from the environment. But an individual whose early self-development is im-paired or unduly interfered with continues to require excessive degrees of mirroring and has difficulty regulating tension and self-esteem with-out it. Woodrow indicated repeatedly that a crucial—albeit not the only—aspect of Ellen's love was this mirroring function, and at times his need was excessive. He explicitly asked her to put into her letters as much expression of love as she could. Her being inside his "innermost life" and looking his "heart full in the face" was for him "*the* delight" of her love. He dreamed and wrote repeatedly about her joy at seeing him, about her eyes—and once even about a mirror. Her seeing him, accepting him, and loving him—her mirroring him—made him feel complete, whole, and exhilarated.[32]

Woodrow's reports to Ellen about his health and his requests for expressions of affection are reminiscent of the earlier correspondence between him and his mother. These similarities and Woodrow's difficulties with tension regulation suggest an admittedly speculative reconstruction of some of his important early childhood experiences. Woodrow's mother was likely very adept at soothing and comforting Woodrow. But somehow, probably because of her own insecurities and traumatic parent-loss background, she did this excessively and was not able to pull back when Woodrow's needs for such soothing and comforting began phase-appropriately to subside—that is, when he needed instead to begin to experience himself as a separate self. In this way, Woodrow's mother was not empathic to his real needs, and she interfered with his internalizing for himself some of these crucial tension-regulating functions. As an adult, whenever Woodrow's sense of self was seriously threatened by such tension-heightening experiences as sexual excitement, love, rejection, or solitude, he needed an important other person to soothe him by mirroring him with support and expressions of love. But his mother's loyalty and idealization of him also had positive effects. Freud wrote that "if a man has been his mother's undisputed darling he retains throughout life the triumphant feeling, the confidence in success, which not seldom brings actual success with it." Wilson's mother helped give him the confidence which carried him so far.[33]

Woodrow did not require of Ellen, nor did she offer, the near-flawless empathy and unquestioning admiration that some extremely vulnerable people demand. She often questioned his feelings and opinions and even admitted puzzlement with them. But she did so in an open, nonjudgmental way. She encouraged him to reveal himself to her and she accepted him as himself. Woodrow found that vitalizing. After their marriage in 1885, she provided him with a peaceful, happy home life. She bore him three daughters and was especially helpful during his three unhappy years teaching at Bryn Mawr College (1885–1888). In April, 1888, Woodrow's mother unexpectedly died. During his several months of deep mourning, Ellen's soothing and affection helped him get through a time which might otherwise have caused him another breakdown. Throughout their marriage, Ellen remained attentive to

Woodrow's needs, even supporting his friendships with other women because she believed she was too shy to fulfill his need for vivacious company.

WILSON AND HIS FATHER

Documents from the years between Woodrow's graduation from Princeton in 1879 and Dr. Wilson's death in 1903 reveal a great deal about their relationship and about Woodrow's self-experience. Dr. Wilson continued to serve as Woodrow's advisor. He cautioned against excessive introspection during depression, because introspection only makes depression worse.

> The true method for knowing oneself and what he is fit for, is to grapple with things outward—is to attack and conquer difficulties of whatever kind that may come up—is to learn to defy circumstances, even those that seem most adverse. In your present case, you ought to pour yourself into your daily studies as if they were your very life . . . your cure therefore for imaginary broodings is always at hand. It is conquest.

He repeatedly advised against backing down from adversity. When he suspected that Woodrow was wavering about debating another student at the University of Virginia, Dr. Wilson pointed out flaws in an essay by the student and concluded, "If you fear to enter the arena with him, you are a goose." And when Woodrow was disillusioned and dejected with his law practice in Atlanta, Dr. Wilson urged him often and strongly to give law an adequate try. "It is hardly like you, my brave boy, to show a white feather before the battle is well joined."[34]

He continued to express delight in Woodrow's accomplishments. In 1884, when he learned that Woodrow's book, *Congressional Government*, had been accepted for publication, he "fairly cried for gladness" and ecstatically congratulated Woodrow for such a triumph at such an early age—"almost unprecedented in the history of American literature." He did not know that Woodrow had dedicated the book to him until he received one of the first published copies. The dedication read, "To his Father, the patient guide of his youth, the gracious companion of his manhood, his best instructor and most lenient critic, this book is affectionately dedicated by the Author." He wrote immediately to Woodrow:

> My precious Son—
> Your book has been received and gloated over. The "dedication" took me by surprise, and never have I felt such a blow of love.

FIGURE 4. Joseph Ruggles Wilson about 1870. (Published with permission of Princeton University Library.)

Shall I confess it?—I wept and sobbed in the stir of the glad pain.
God bless you, my noble child, for such a token of your affection.[35]

He wrote several times—again, attempting to console Woodrow—
of their unity. During Woodrow's first year at law school, Dr. Wilson
wrote that they should both take heart about several rejection notices
from journals. "I say 'us' for I feel identified with you." And when
Woodrow was in trouble at the University of Virginia because of unex-
cused absences, Dr. Wilson wrote that they should both confront the
problem together: "We are as truly identified . . . as if we were one and
the same person."[36]

Dr. Wilson's letters in these years differ from earlier ones in two
ways. First, he referred to needing Woodrow: Woodrow's letters affected him as cool water "to a thirsty soul" or "to a parched throat," and
he thanked Woodrow for his love and for the immeasurable gladness it
brought him. Second, he hinted at fears of losing their relationship: if
Woodrow were to prove untrustworthy in the matter of the absences at
the University of Virginia, Dr. Wilson would be wretched for the rest of
his life; and when Dr. Wilson counseled Woodrow at the end of his first
year at Johns Hopkins to wait another year before marrying Ellen, he
wept from fear that Woodrow would hate him.[37]

Between the mid-eighties and the mid-nineties, the relationship
between the two men changed significantly. Woodrow had less emotional need of his father because of Ellen and less professional need of
him because he had become more secure and accomplished in his work.
In fact, after the three unhappy years at Bryn Mawr, Woodrow's career
soared. He spent two eminently successful years at Wesleyan University
in Connecticut (1888–1890), where he was a very popular teacher and
where he continued to publish articles and books. In 1890, he became a
professor at Princeton, where he gained a national reputation through
popular and scholarly publications, became a spokesman for the younger faculty members, and was offered the presidencies of several major
universities. In the meantime, Dr. Wilson grew disillusioned with his
Wilmington ministry. Longing for years to return to academia, in 1884
he accepted a teaching position at a struggling seminary in Clarksville,
Tennessee. He wrote that Woodrow's temperament and accomplishments now surpassed his own and asked that Woodrow suggest an
outline for his inaugural address at Clarksville because Dr. Wilson wanted his address to be "*extra* and *unusual*." In 1886, again commenting on
Woodrow's superior gifts, Dr. Wilson asked him to continue to let him
read, if no longer review, his writings in manuscript, at least for his own
pleasure.[38]

From this time, Dr. Wilson did not limit his references to union with Woodrow to times of consolation. In 1886, when Woodrow asked his advice about study abroad, Dr. Wilson questioned the value of his own advice because he was too likely to advise what he thought Woodrow wanted, "so that should you desire to visit the moon I would assuredly counsel you to go! You are my alter ego: what pleases you equally pleases me." Several months later, after reading a published paper by Woodrow, Dr. Wilson praised his style and marvelled at Woodrow's ability to make original discoveries. Woodrow would surely make more of a mark in his profession than Dr. Wilson had done in his own. He continued:

> you with your powers all in their spring-time, and possessing a truer perspicacity than that with which I was ever gifted! You are assuredly my second edition, "revised and improved" as to contents, and with a superior letter-press and binding. How I bless God that it is even so, and that no law of His forbids the pride your father takes in his larger son.[39]

The year 1888 was tragic for Dr. Wilson. He was already dissatisfied with his work at the Clarksville Seminary, and in April his wife died. His letters became depressive. He expressed often and poignantly how much he missed Woodrow. In December of 1888 and January of 1889, he berated himself for not taking time off from a religious meeting he had chaired in New York to visit Woodrow in Connecticut. "I never cease thinking of you—but since my return I seem to miss you more than ever. . . . Sometimes my heart cries out for you to an extent that can hardly be endured. . . ."[40]

In October of 1889, he recounted how he experienced his relationship with Woodrow—then and earlier:

> Ah, my son, this old heart—you fill it, and with a charm that is quite unspeakable:—so that I am made to feel that after all I can never be lonely, were every thing else stricken from my grasp, and you alone were to remain. Of course I am not forgetting . . . the other children. . . . But you were my companion more entirely than they; and are now not merely my child to whom consanguinity attaches by a tie of natural regard but my *friend* to whom community of thought binds by ligatures which are thicker than blood. I am sure that we are the two who thoroughly—most thoroughly—comprehend each other. You satisfy my intellect as I believe I am able to content yours. You gratify my pride also, and I feel assured that your corresponding emotion has its demands measurably met in me, to whom you have long been accustomed to look up with an eye that perceives in me far more than there really is of goodness and of largeness (for which I parenthetically take this occasion to thank you).[41]

He later wrote of a *"hunger"* for Woodrow and his letters. He was saved from starvation by thoughts of Woodrow, "who is dearer to my heart than all else." In another letter, he wrote that he understood that many professional duties made it difficult for Woodrow to write, but he wondered if Woodrow gave those duties too high a priority as they left so little time for loved ones. He then asked Woodrow, for Woodrow's own sake, not to cease reaching out to a "faithful heart" which was always warmly responsive to Woodrow's own warmth. He continued:

> I seriously think that, in the act of squeezing out the juices of your life, you would do well to water with many of them this age-fading plant—at least with *some* of their big drops. Ah, my son, you have plenty of friends . . . and . . . admirers . . . yet you have only one parent, the truest of all your friends, the intensest of all your admirers: and if I were you I would cultivate him still even though he may seem to need it not. . . . Your love and mine are not composed of the stuff which ever enters into the make-up of the common article. . . . Still the closest love . . . ought not to be denied certain of its natural joys.[42]

His concerns about losing his relationship with Woodrow intensified. He feared that the bronchitis he was suffering would turn into something fatal and that he would not see Woodrow again before he died. He hesitated to write Woodrow for fear of boring him. When beset with a "thin mist of bad humour," he felt very solitary and old and even imagined that Woodrow was forgetting him. And when he asked Woodrow to water with his juices the fading plant of his father's life, he also wrote, "I do not suspect for a moment—(the suspicion would kill me)—that there creeps through my darling boy's thoughts the ghost even of a chill when his old father is present to them."[43]

In 1893, Dr. Wilson gave up his position at Clarksville and supported himself thereafter with lectures and sermons. He developed relationships with a number of women, including a relationship which Woodrow was very happy to see terminate in 1894. Woodrow and Ellen were unable to persuade him to move in with them until the spring of 1901, when deteriorating health (gall bladder disease and generalized atherosclerosis) made it necessary. By the fall of 1902, he had become so senile that he could no longer feed himself; he suffered constantly, and he sometimes cried and screamed for hours. Ellen was grateful that Woodrow's work took him out of the home and out of town as much as it did. Dr. Wilson died on January 21, 1903.[44]

Materials indicating how Woodrow experienced his relationship with his father are sparse but revealing. It is clear from his father's letters that Woodrow confided in him, sought his advice, valued his esteem, and frequently expressed respect and love. Woodrow also referred to his father in letters to other people. In 1884, he wrote to Ellen, "He makes me his *intellectual* companion when I am home, and the life he stirs up in my brain is worth a whole year's course at 'the Hopkins.' Without him, therefore, our life is *narrower*." Another time he wrote that he admired "beyond measure" his father's gifts and loved him with his "heart of hearts," but he could never tell him this openly because of the same reverence an artist has for praising the work of his master. And when Woodrow's mother died in April, 1888, Woodrow, although wracked by his own grief, wrote that he was even more deeply troubled about his father, who was now left "practically without a home," with a college-age son. "My own happy little home seems to reprove me on his account, in my morbid moments."[45]

Of the many letters that Woodrow wrote to his father, only three remain. I quoted earlier the letter from Woodrow's second year at Princeton. In a second letter, Woodrow expressed grave concern over his father's bronchitis and assured him that he did not resent his father's not visiting him from New York. The third letter, written in December, 1888, was a tender, touching letter. Woodrow wrote of the pain he felt at spending Christmas away from his father. Yet, during that season of rejoicing, Woodrow rejoiced most in being his son.

> I realize the benefit of being your son more and more as my talents and experience grow: I recognize the strength growing in me as of the nature of your strength: I become more and more conscious of the hereditary wealth I possess, the capital of principle, of literary force and skill, of capacity for first-hand thought; and I feel daily more and more bent toward creating in my own children that combined respect and tender devotion for their father that you gave your children for you. . . . You have given me a love that grows . . . recognizing you as in a certain very real sense the author of all I have to be grateful for. I bless God for my noble, strong, and saintly mother and for my incomparable father.[46]

After his father resigned from Clarksville, Woodrow felt sorrow and compassion for his homelessness and isolation. When his father died in 1903, Woodrow relieved his grief—as he had done when his mother died—by immersing himself in his work. He took consolation in the thought that he still retained "as spiritual capital" all that was best of his relationship with his father. It took the heart out of him to lose his

> life-long friend and companion. . . . Now he is gone and a great loneliness is in my heart. No generation ahead of me now! I am in the firing line. The more reason to be steady and attend to the fighting without repining.

He especially valued the letter of condolence from a man whose own father–son relationship had been very close. Filial sentiment

> plays a larger part in my life than in that of most men; and there is no sympathy I would rather have than that of a man who feels an even chivalric devotion to his father and to all the honorable things that his father stands for.[47]

We may draw a number of conclusions about these two men from these materials. Dr. Wilson likely felt a painful loss when Woodrow needed him less. There was sadness and bitterness in his plea for Woodrow to continue to let him read his manuscripts. His fear that Woodrow would hate him for advising delay in marrying Ellen may also have reflected his own anger more than the likelihood of Woodrow's, and when he rebuked himself for not taking time off from his meeting in New York to visit Woodrow he probably felt angry at Woodrow, who did not visit him. Dr. Wilson may have been defending against his own envy and competitiveness toward Woodrow by reaction formation and by a retreat to passivity. But he was also revealing an intense need for Woodrow's love and idealization.

This need became more apparent during and after the tragic year of 1888. Clearly he regressed in those years because of the combined traumata of disillusionment in his work and the death of his wife. In regression, an individual mobilizes unconscious constellations of needs, wishes, and defenses which otherwise are apparent only indirectly (if at all) but which nevertheless exert great influence on his life and relationships. In his regression, Dr. Wilson consciously and explicitly revealed his need for Woodrow's idealization of him and the pleasure it brought him. He thanked Woodrow for seeing in him more good than there really was—which is, of course, exactly what idealization is. He dreaded Woodrow's becoming bored with him or—a lethal thought—experiencing a "chill" toward him because this would mean that Woodrow no longer idealized him. Dr. Wilson also revealed that he needed Woodrow to need him and to be dependent on him. That need motivated his sad plea—actually a demand—that Woodrow continue to seek out his generosity. And he also revealed explicitly the importance of his union with Woodrow, then and through the years: they were companions, bound by a "community of thought" which was "thicker than blood," they gratified each other's pride, and they thoroughly comprehended and satisfied one another. And, finally, he revealed that Woodrow vitalized him. Woodrow filled his heart, cured his loneliness, staved off his *"hunger,"* and saved him from starvation. Thus Dr. Wilson now desperately needed—and begged for—Woodrow to water with the juices of his own life "this age-fading plant."

What all of this means is that Dr. Wilson had all these needs of Woodrow—that Woodrow idealize him and need him and be in union with him—in order for Dr. Wilson himself to feel alive. These needs were amply hinted at in his earlier letters. In this regression they were painfully bared. This formulation raises some speculations about some of Dr. Wilson's puzzling behavior. Perhaps when he teased and criticized young Woodrow, to the indignation of relatives, he was attempting to modulate and defend against his own pleasure and excitement in Woodrow's development. And perhaps when he initiated and prolonged the conflict over the compulsory chapel services at Columbia, he was in part responding to the disruption of his relationship with Woodrow, who not only had left for Davidson but was also making some phase-appropriate emotional attachment outside of the family onto peers—attempts that were stressful for Dr. Wilson as well as for Woodrow. And perhaps Dr. Wilson's regression in 1888 was in part caused by Woodrow already not needing him so much any more.

What about the relationship with Dr. Wilson from Woodrow's point of view? One major question is the meaning of the obvious idealization. The Georges maintain that idealization arose from reaction formation against his unconscious aggression toward his father. When the Georges wrote their book, this meaning of idealization was almost axiomatic, but idealization is now recognized to have other possible meanings. Woodrow revealed the meaning of his. When he wrote that his father stirred more life into his brain than a whole year's study at Johns Hopkins, he meant more than intellectual stimulation; he also meant phychical stimulation. His father vitalized him. Woodrow contrasted this vitalization to the *"narrower"*—less vital, less complete—inner experience he had at other times.[48]

Woodrow revealed more than idealization. His comment about being on the firing line after his father's death suggests that he experienced his father as a protective buffer against a hostile world. And he often referred to passive receiving from his father: his father was his critic, guide, and instructor. In his most striking continuations of this imagery, Woodrow indicated that he felt molded and fashioned by his father. He called his father the master artist. Inherent in that image is the master artist directly fashioning the skills of the apprentice. And in his Christmas letter of 1888, Woodrow referred to his own strength "as of the nature" of his father's and to his father as the source of his hereditary wealth ("the capital of principle, of literary source and style, of the capacity for firsthand thought"). His father was the "author," no less, of all that he had to be grateful for. Perhaps this passivity and molding were what Freud and Bullitt were addressing when they made the interpretation—or, more accurately, the accusation—that Woodrow had homosexual longings for his father. It is highly unlikely that Woodrow desired, even unconsciously, genital contact with his father, either out of excessive libidinal stimulation as a child or as a regression from a highly-threatening oedipal situation. Rather, Woodrow longed for a psychic union with his fantasized omnipotent father so that he, Woodrow, could experience a full sense of self and thus feel complete and whole. The sexualization of such a longing and function can result in homosexuality or other perverse behaviors, but there is no evidence this was so in Woodrow.[49]

With the help of such data, I will extend my speculative reconstruction of Woodrow's childhood experiences. After his less than optimal experiences with his mother, Woodrow turned to his father with expectable idealization. Idealization of the father is an appropriate early phase of self-development. But when Woodrow entered this phase, he was already suffering a sense of deficit from his earlier experiences with his mother. Thus his relationship with his father began with—and needed to compensate for—this additional burden and thereby assumed more importance than it normally should have for maintaining Woodrow's sense of wholeness and self-cohesion. The relationship apparently succeeded in fulfilling these needs and was therefore intensely gratifying for Woodrow. It was also intensely gratifying for Dr. Wilson because it satisfied his own need to be idealized and to shape Woodrow into his desired image. Disruptions of the relationship were correspondingly painful for both. Because of these mutual gratifications and discomforts, Woodrow and Dr. Wilson both prolonged the union long after it is usually given up in father–son relationships, and this further interfered with Woodrow's developing a stable, enduring, separate sense of self. Thus Woodrow emerged from childhood with a persisting vulnerability in his sense of self, a vulnerability to being thrown back into an agonizing sense of incompleteness, with its attendant problems in regulating tensions and self-esteem, which coincided with his desperate needs at those times for soothing, loving relationships.[50]

The relationship between Woodrow and his father, however, also provided the foundation for Woodrow's strengths, and Woodrow had many. Compared with his relationship with his mother, Woodrow was able to internalize and assume for himself important functions from the relationship with his father. This relationship provided him early identifications and foundations for his ideals, principles, and ambitions. Woodrow's Christmas letter to his father was a touching and remarkably perceptive tribute to his father's special role in giving him this "spiritual capital." At times of disappointment and failure, instead of being crushed and defeated, Woodrow drew upon this capital first to stabilize himself and then to pull himself back even stronger. The "spiritual capital" from his father was the heart of Wilson's ability to rebound. And the ability to rebound was the heart of Wilson's greatness.

PRESIDENT OF PRINCETON

In June of 1902, the president of Princeton resigned, and the Board of Trustees quickly elected Woodrow to succeed him. Woodrow was delighted. At last he would be a man of action. And indeed for several years he met great successes. By means of curriculum reform, faculty improvement, and an Oxford-like preceptor program, he raised Princeton to eminence among American universities. In May of 1906, however, at the height of his successes, he suddenly went blind in his left eye. He had suffered a retinal hemorrhage. His doctors told him that he had hypertension and generalized arteriosclerosis. Ten years earlier he had experienced a period of pain, numbness, and weakness in his right hand; it had been diagnosed as neuritis at the time. He may have reexperienced some weakness in 1906, along with his eye problem. The gravity of the condition was now recognized: it was the same illness that had killed his father. One physician even advised immediate retirement. Another, however, advised a long summer's vacation and a decreased workload thereafter. Accordingly, Wilson vacationed that summer with his family in Rydal, England, the home of Wordsworth. He developed an instant and lasting friendship with a British portrait painter, Frederick Yates, and his family. After his return, Wilson wrote them that their affection and friendship were the greatest restoratives of his health.[51]

Wilson returned physically restored in September of 1906. The next four years, however, were years of conflict and defeat. He was first defeated in his attempt to replace the independent, abuse-laden dining clubs with a system of quadrangles, in which undergraduates, graduate students, and unmarried preceptors would eat and live together in a spirit of intellectual stimulation. He was next defeated in the famed battle over the location and control of the proposed graduate school.

Wilson behaved atypically (for him) in several ways after his illness. He had long believed that the quadrangle plan would require up to twenty-five years to implement. In 1906, after his illness, however, he wanted to implement it immediately. Wilson, the former faculty spokesman, neglected to consult the faculty or alumni about this huge, expensive innovation. Rather, he proposed it formally to the board of trustees in December of 1906. They approved it in the spring, and he announced the plan and its immediate implementation in June, 1907. In subsequent weeks, as faculty members protested their not being consulted and alumni protested the planned elimination of their cherished dining clubs, Wilson did not try to pacify the resistance, but rather welcomed it. "The fight is on, and I regard it, not as a fight for the development, but as a fight for the restoration of Princeton. My heart is in it more than it has been in anything else, because it is a scheme for salvation." One last unusual item was his conclusion to the formal proposal to the trustees in December, 1906:

> [The university] has already grown beyond the point where it would be possible to make of it a single unit again. The disintegration is taking place, a disintegration into atoms too small to hold the fine spirit of college life. We must substitute for disintegration a new organic process. The new body will have divisions, but all the parts will be organs of a common life. It is reintegration by more varied and more abundant organic life. This is the time to act, when the fluid mass trembles upon the verge of some sort of final crystallization.[52]

Wilson was right; the fight was on. He met a major disappointment in September, when his confidant and closest friend, John Grier Hibben, actively opposed the plan. He met another in October—and nearly resigned—when the trustees asked him to withdraw the plan because of lack of funds and because of the opposition of major benefactors. He was so rude to Hibben and Hibben's wife that day that he later apologized to them for his behavior during his "black mood." Friends were puzzled by his changed demeanor, and they feared that they may have unwittingly offended him. In December, he had a recurrence of right-arm pain and numbness. By January of 1908, he was so nervous and exhausted that he took a month's vacation in Bermuda. Ellen later said that his disappointment with Hibben was one of the greatest disappointments of his career and a cause of his breakdown at this time.[53]

In Bermuda, Wilson's friendship deepened with Mary Allen Hulbert Peck, an attractive socialite who feted him in the local society circles. For years thereafter, Wilson turned to Peck as a trusted correspondent and friend, and the relationship was one of the most important and famous of his life. Wilson's letters to her were similar to his letters to Ellen, although more subdued: he expressed intense concern for her health and welfare, he shared his private thoughts and feelings about his own problems, and he repeatedly expressed affection, gratitude, and longing for her company. Weinstein has recently argued most persuasively that in Bermuda she became considerably more than the cherished platonic friend most biographers have described and that, in fact, Wilson and Peck had a sexual affair.[54]

The vacation and Peck's attentions restored him. Upon his return, he pleaded his case to alumni groups, but in April a committee of trustees exonerated the dining clubs and thus dealt the quadrangle plan its final blow. In June, Wilson wrote that the year had gone very hard for him and that he had found it difficult all year to keep in any sort of spirits. He vacationed the entire summer in England, including several weeks with the Yates family, and he gradually freed his mind of Princeton. When he returned in September, he again felt fully restored.[55]

Wilson's final Princeton defeat was in the battle over the location and the control of the graduate school. When he first became president of Princeton, he had gotten along well with the dean of the graduate school, Andrew Fleming West, and even wrote a laudatory preface to West's pamphlet on graduate education. With time, however, Wilson became disenchanted with West's emphasis on luxurious living quarters and his apparent disinterest in serious education. In October, 1906, upon his return from Europe, Wilson learned that West had been offered the presidency of the Massachusetts Institute of Technology. Instead of seizing this chance to free himself and Princeton of West, Wilson supported efforts to persuade West to stay. West agreed, with the understanding that plans for the graduate school would be implemented straightway. When Wilson proceeded instead with the quadrangles, West felt betrayed and was an outspoken opponent of Wilson and the plan.

With time, Wilson returned so much of West's authority to himself and the trustees that by the spring of 1909 many expected West to resign. In May, 1909, however, West announced that his close friend, William Procter, the wealthy soap manufacturer, was offering a half-million-dollar donation for the new graduate school. One condition was that it be built on the peripherally located golf course rather than on the central site which Wilson wanted. Wilson objected to this condition. The graduate school would be the intellectual center of the university and therefore must not be isolated at the periphery of the campus. In October, the board of trustees overrode Wilson's wishes—as well as the recommendations of trustee and faculty committees—and voted to accept Procter's offer and the golf course site. Again, Wilson nearly resigned. A period of uneasy truce, including a reception attended by all the principals, ended on December 22, when Wilson proposed to Procter that Princeton build two graduate schools: a centrally located quadrangle-like one, supported by an earlier donation, and a second school on the golf course, supported by Procter. Procter refused. On Christmas day, Wilson wrote to the trustees that no school based on West's plans could succeed and that he, Wilson, could not agree to gifts which gave donors control of university policy. The battle was rejoined.[56]

Wilson's opponents persuaded Procter to accept the two-school proposal, believing that Wilson would now reject it and appear a fool for rejecting his own plan. When Procter's acceptance of the two-school plan was announced at the January meeting of the board of trustees, Wilson was indeed caught by surprise and blurted that the issue was not one of geography, which had thus far been his major argument, but one of ideals: the faculty could run a successful graduate school anywhere in the county. Procter's offer, he continued, was intended to carry out the ideals propounded in West's pamphlet, and a school based on those ideals could not succeed. When asked why he had written such a laudatory preface to the pamphlet, Wilson claimed that he had not read the pamphlet before doing so. He did admit to reading it in draft form and to doing so before West was offered the M. I. T. presidency. When asked how he could now reject a proposal he himself had made, he stated that certain faculty members had persuaded him that it was unworkable. A trustee expressed doubt about Wilson's honor. Wilson was incensed.[57]

At the end of January, 1910, an editor of the *New York Times* wrote to Wilson that he had heard rumors about the controversy at Princeton and thought it might be relevant to all American college life. Wilson wrote back that the graduate school controversy, like the quadrangle controversy, was really a conflict between the forces of privilege and those of democracy. The *Times* wrote an editorial along those lines, which drew the nation's attention to Princeton and represented Wilson as an exemplar of progressivism. Yet the editorial hurt him at Princeton because it was unfair to his opponents. If the trustees had known of Wilson's letter, Wilson would likely have had to resign.[58]

Wilson left for a Bermuda vacation on February 12. He pleaded for—and thrived on—letters from his wife and Peck. He was amazed to discover how exhausted he was: he slept twelve to fourteen hours a day for the first week and wrote that his sleep was disturbed by dreams of the Princeton disputes. Again, his vacation restored him.[59]

After his return in early March, Wilson took his case to several major alumni organizations. At the April meeting of the board of trustees, he asked the trustees to submit the question of the graduate school location to the faculty, where he knew he had enough support to win. The trustees heatedly discussed this proposal and finally decided to postpone the decision and to do nothing. Wilson was infuriated. Two days later, he delivered his famous "Pittsburgh speech"—a largely extemporaneous attack on the influence of wealth and the inattention of universities to the needs of the nation. He blasted the country's churches for serving only the upper social strata and not the masses. "[The churches] have more regard for pew-rents than for soul[s]." His climactic sentence was, "If she loses her self-possession, America will stagger like France through fields of blood before she again finds peace and prosperity under the leadership of men who understand her needs." Wilson had taken his case to the nation over the heads of Princeton's board of trustees and was predicting revolution.[60]

Afterwards, Wilson recognized his speech was intemperate. The trustees offered to reduce West's position to provost in exchange for Wilson's accepting the golf course site—proposals tantamount to surrender by his opponents. Wilson refused. This impasse was resolved unexpectedly on May 18, when a wealthy alumnus died and left an estimated two million dollars to be used for a graduate school. One of the executors of the will was Andrew Fleming West himself. Wilson told Ellen, "We've beaten the living, but we can't fight the dead—the game is up." He agreed to the Procter gift, to the golf course site, and to West's serving as dean of the graduate school. Ironically, as John Mulder points out, the battle over the influence of contributions was resolved by a contribution. Commencement was a celebration of West, Procter, and the dead donor. And yet Wilson had the love of many faculty, alumni, and students. At the ceremony he was met with ovations that made him weep.

That autumn, he was elected governor of New Jersey. Two years after that, he was elected president of the United States.[61]

What may we conclude from these Princeton years? The turning point in Wilson's Princeton career was his illness. Before it, he met exceptional successes. After it, he met only conflict and failure. Several important questions are raised: Just what was Wilson's physical condition? Did he have brain disease and therefore act aberrantly because of an organic brain syndrome? Or were his behaviors determined solely by psychological causes? Or were they determined by a combination of psychological and physical causes?

Wilson scholars have polarized in their attempts to answer these questions. Leading one side has been Edwin Weinstein, whose biography of Wilson I have already cited often. A neurologist, Weinstein maintains that Wilson had major strokes in 1896 and 1906 (in addition, of course, to his famous—and disputed—stroke in 1919) and minor strokes in 1904, 1907, 1908, and 1910. According to Weinstein, Wilson had atherosclerotic placques in the internal carotid arteries, the major arteries in the neck which carry blood to the brain. Small particles of these placques broke free, lodged in and occluded small arteries in the brain, and caused the destruction of brain tissue fed by these small arteries. Thus Wilson had many small cerebrovascular accidents, or strokes. One such particle lodged in Wilson's left ophthalmic artery and caused his blindness. In earlier papers Weinstein had attributed nearly all of Wilson's puzzling behaviors to the abnormal neurophysiology resulting from these strokes. In his recent book, however, he considerably softens this position and allows more of a role for psychological factors: he proposes, for example, that Wilson projected his grave health concerns onto Princeton and often acted out of worry over his illness and out of guilt over his affair with Mary Peck. But Weinstein still maintains as his central hypothesis that Wilson had repeated strokes.[62]

Leading the opposition have been the pioneering psychobiographers of Wilson, Juliette and Alexander George, who have been arguing vehemently against Weinstein's stroke hypothesis for some years. They have recently recruited an ophthalmologist, Michael Marmor. Marmor and the Georges criticize Weinstein for being so dogmatic about his hypotheses and for not presenting alternative hypotheses or differential diagnoses. Marmor also offers substantive medical arguments against Weinstein's stroke hypothesis. Among Marmor's more cogent points is that the primary materials indicate that Wilson's eye problems in 1906 were not caused by an embolus, as Weinstein maintains, but by an occluded and ruptured central or branch retinal vein, which would be more compatible with the diagnosis arrived at by Wilson's own physicians—namely, hypertension and generalized arteriosclerosis. Further, Weinstein virtually passes over the evidence that the major clinical picture was one of retinal hemorrhage, and he argues over-zealously for an embolism and clot. Marmor also points out that Wilson's clinical course—repeated episodes of transient impairment spread over many years—would be unusual for repeated strokes and, finally, that there is no evidence that Wilson suffered any cognitive dysfunction, which would be unusual in the presence of the stroke-related personality changes postulated by Weinstein. Jerrold Post, a psychiatrist, writes convincingly that Wilson's arm numbness and weakness might be accounted for by a number of orthopedic or peripheral nerve conditions, including the common "carpal tunnel syndrome."[63]

The question of organic brain disease during Wilson's Princeton years will be debated for years to come. If he did have organic brain disease, that would have compounded his psychological distress by impairing his ability to respond adaptively to his illness and to other stresses. Such an impairment would have rendered his illness even more threatening and traumatic. One might also wonder whether

Wilson's organically-based symptoms of weakness, numbness, and pain may have attracted a variety of important unconscious, symbolic meanings and thereby formed the nucleus of later conversion reactions. Wilson's symptoms in December, 1907, for example, when Hibben had defected and the trustees had refused to proceed with the quadrangles, may well have been a conversion reaction symbolizing Wilson's powerlessness and psychic peril.

For the present, I agree with Marmor and Post that Wilson's physical findings and puzzling behaviors are better explained by conditions other than repeated strokes. A psychological explanation of Wilson's behaviors does not require a stroke diagnosis at all.

The most important psychological fact is that in May, 1906, Wilson knew that he had serious physical illness—the same illness that had killed his father. As would anyone else in his situation, Wilson felt his bodily and mental integrity threatened; he felt powerless to reverse the process, and he was forced to confront the painful realities of mortality, death, and his relative powerlessness before them—realities which almost everyone struggles all his life to ignore. Also, Wilson was struck at the height of his successes and was threatened with the loss or impairment of his intellect, which was, as we have seen repeatedly, so very important to him. Understandably, he experienced anxiety and depression; understandably, he tried to soothe and make these manageable; and understandably, he resorted to older, previously abandoned means of defense and compensation—he regressed—when familiar means of defense and compensation failed. Regression is expectable in any serious illness. The extent and the type of regression depend on the individual, his premorbid personality, and what the illness means to him.

Wilson's illness likely meant to him that he did not have long to live and that he must push ahead with his plans if he hoped to see them realized in his own lifetime. But in his report to the trustees in December, 1906, he revealed an additional, more ominous meaning. When he wrote that the university was undergoing a "disintegration into atoms too small to hold the fine spirit of college life" and that it needed "a new organic process" in which "all the parts will be organs of a common life," Princeton was actually functioning very well. Wilson himself—not Princeton—was undergoing disintegration: a physical and psychic disintegration. Wilson himself—not Princeton—desperately needed a "new organic process" to make all parts "the organs of a common life." Weinstein's interpretation that Wilson was responding to a danger to his own "physical, moral, and mental integrity" does not go far enough. Wilson was responding to a danger to his psyche and self. He had identified Princeton with himself and was displacing his grave concerns about his physical and psychic survival onto Princeton. This is why the quadrangles and the graduate school became so important to him and why he became so intensely and immovably fixed on them.[64]

Wilson resorted to familiar means of defense and compensation. He sought loyalty and affection from family and friends, he tried to turn passivity into activity, and perhaps he even renewed his old quest for immortality ("fight for salvation" at least hints at immortality). He also became more idealistic and democratic than ever before. Kohut has described how ideals can compensate for a sense of depletion and power-lessness. But these familiar means were blocked: Hibben defected and the trustees refused to approve the quadrangles. Wilson's health got worse: he suffered a recurrence of right-arm pain, numbness, and weakness (conversion reaction?) and suffered a state of exhaustion and near-col-lapse. He required emergency measures to relieve his traumatic state. His affair with Mary Peck was one such measure. It is hard to imagine the agonizing fear and powerlessness which could induce him into his affair with Peck—that is, induce him to turn his back on his Presbyterian heritage and to be unfaithful to Ellen, whom he loved so completely. He was struggling, literally, for psychic survival. Mary Peck's admiration and idealization served as desperately needed soothing and mirroring and thereby revitalized him. We have already seen how the attentions of Harriet and Ellen had done so before. He again responded with gratitude and intense sexual feelings, probably even more than in his earlier rela-tionships with Harriet and Ellen because now his situation was more desperate. Also, this time he was dealing with an interested, mature, experienced woman and not a blushing schoolgirl. He succumbed to the affair.[65]

Sensational as Wilson's affair may have been, Wilson's most impor-tant defense and compensation was an intensified identification with his father's precepts and with his father himself. In his Princeton struggles, Woodrow lived out the precepts which his father had prescribed when Woodrow was a student: Woodrow now fought against melancholy by grappling "with things outward," and he now fought "adverse circum-stances" with defiance and a striving for conquest. In short, he was clutching to the "spiritual capital" from his father as if it were a life preserver. Woodrow also intensified his identification with his father: he was now suffering from the same illness that had killed his father, and he behaved in his crises at Princeton almost exactly as his father had behaved during the chapel-attendance controversy more than thirty years earlier. Dr. Wilson had precipitated and prolonged the chapel-attendance controversy, had proven stubborn and inflexible, had de-fended his case to the higher authority of the General Assembly, and had resigned when defeated. Woodrow precipitated and prolonged the quadrangle controversy, prolonged the controversy over the graduate school, proved stubborn and inflexible, defended his case to the higher authority of the alumni and the nation, considered resigning several times, and finally did.

This was different from the familiar identification with his father's strengths, precepts, and ambitions—identifications which had provided the nucleus of many of Woodrow's own strengths. Rather, this was an identification with a darker side of his father, with the stubborn, self-righteous, bullying side. Dr. Wilson had shown this side during the chapel-service conflict. He must also have shown it at times in his relationship with Woodrow, as in the criticism and teasing about which relatives later commented. The later relationship between Woodrow and his father clearly shows that these experiences did not cause the psychological deformity and repressed rage which the Georges have postulated. But Woodrow did unconsciously identify with this side of his father. It required the grave trauma of his Princeton illness and the resulting serious regression to mobilize this unconscious identification. Wilson used it to fill in and protect his terrible sense of powerlessness and fear, like a skin graft over raw, burned flesh. In one of his early letters to Ellen—one often quoted by biographers—Woodrow said that he felt as if he had a volcano inside of him. I believe he was referring to this identification with the aggressive, bullying side of his father.[66]

As a result of this regression, Wilson failed to respond appropriately to the Princeton conflicts and failed to provide the leadership which Princeton, because of Wilson's idiosyncratic behaviors, now desperately needed. Wilson's failure to lead—and not whether his positions on the quadrangles and graduate school were right or wrong—is the central psychological issue of his battles at Princeton. Wilson failed to prepare the faculty and alumni for the quadrangles, he failed to be diplomatic and flexible about the quadrangles and the graduate school, and he failed to convey to his opponents the slightest sense that he understood their point of view. Instead, he chose to fight, he antagonized his opponents and some of his friends, he wrote the imprudent letter to the editor of the *New York Times*, and he unrealistically attempted to win over the alumni with his oratory. Understandably, his opponents experienced him as high-handed and egotistical and became more firmly entrenched in their own positions. What his opponents had no way of knowing—in fact, Wilson did not know it himself—was that he was attempting to restore a desperately needed peace and order to his inner world. In attempting to do so, he resorted to means which precipitated or helped to precipitate the Princeton crises and interfered with his dealing with them once they arose. Thus encumbered, Wilson was defeated.

CONCLUSION

I have examined episodes and materials of Woodrow Wilson's life from his childhood through his presidency of Princeton University. I proposed that his early breakdowns and his problems as president of Princeton were due to a vulnerability in his self-experience. I followed his self experience through his adolescent turmoil, his breakdowns at Davidson and in law school, his experiences with love, and his crises as president of Princeton. I examined his relationship with his parents and proposed that each interfered with Woodrow's developing a sustained, lasting, independent sense of self and that each also contributed uniquely to his strengths. His mother interfered with his self-development by her incapacity to move beyond the soothing and comforting roles of motherhood. Yet her loyalty to him and her idealization of him probably helped impart to him his sense of being special and destined for great things. His father interfered with his self-development by his own intense needs to have Woodrow idealize him, need him, and achieve his own unfulfilled ambitions; Woodrow's regressive identification with his father's stubborn, bullying side also played a major role in his failures at Princeton. Yet the relationship with his father also provided Woodrow with the strengths and expectations of himself which enabled him repeatedly to rebound from defeat and which constituted the nucleus of his greatness.

Although I have emphasized considerations of the self in this paper, I do not believe that Wilson had a narcissistic personality disorder. His rich personal relationships, his capacity for humor about himself, and his powerful and vital personality indicate that he did not. Rather, I believe that he experienced weaknesses and vulnerabilities in the self sector of his personality; these vulnerabilities usually lay dormant but emerged at times of great tension and disappointment. The complex relationships between the sectors of the personality having to do with self esteem and tension regulation on the one hand and with the classical conflicts over sexual and aggressive impulses on the other are only beginning to be studied and are puzzling enough in living psychotherapy and psychoanalytic patients, let alone in a historical figure such as Woodrow Wilson.

ACKNOWLEDGMENTS

I thank Drs. Michael Hoit, James W. Anderson, Mark Levey, and David Klass for their many valuable comments on this paper; the Department of Psychiatry of Michael Reese Hospital, Chicago, Illinois for supporting the preparation of the final manuscript; Princeton University Press for granting permission to reprint excerpts from *The Papers of Woodrow Wilson;* Princeton University Library and Archives for permission to reproduce photographs; the library staff of Trinity College, Deerfield, Illinois for allowing me generous checkout privileges; and Mrs. Eva Sandberg for typing earlier drafts. I have presented portions of earlier versions of this paper at the Faculty Research Seminar of the Chicago Institute for Psychoanalysis on March 26, 1980 and to the Department of Psychiatry of the University of Chicago Medical School on September 15, 1981.

NOTES

1. Alexander and Juliette George, *Woodrow Wilson and Colonel House* (New York: Dover, 1964); Sigmund Freud and William Bullitt, *Thomas Woodrow Wilson: a Psychological Study* (Boston: Houghton Mifflin; Cambridge: The Riverside Press, 1967); Edwin A. Weinstein, *Woodrow Wilson: A Medical and Psychological Biography* (Princeton: Princeton University Press, 1981).
2. Primary materials are published in Arthur S. Link, John W. Davidson, David H. Hirst *et al.* eds. *The Papers of Woodrow Wilson,* 46 vols. (Princeton: Princeton University Press, 1966–), hereafter cited as *Papers.* In the footnotes, I use the following abbreviations for individuals: WW = Woodrow Wilson, JWW = Janet Woodrow Wilson, JRW = Joseph Ruggles Wilson, ELA = Ellen Louise Axson, and EAW = Ellen Axson Wilson.
3. Background information on JWW: Weinstein gives the most convincing portrait of JWW in the extensive Wilson literature. See Weinstein, pp. 10–13, 21–23, and 44–45. See also Ray Stannard Baker, *Woodrow Wilson: Life and Letters,* 8 vols. (Garden City, N.Y.: Doubleday, 1927–39), I, p. 18. Representative letters of JWW to WW are those of May 20, 1874, *Papers,* I, p. 50; November 8, 1876, ibid., p. 223; February 6, 16, 28, and March 7, 1877, ibid., pp. 250–252. WW's adult reminiscences: WW to William J. Hampton, September 13, 1917, quoted in Baker, I, p. 34.
4. I have summarized this account of JRW's life from John M. Mulder, *Woodrow Wilson: the Years of Preparation* (Princeton: Princeton University Press, 1978), pp. 3–28.
5. Earliest memory: "Address on Abraham Lincoln," February 12, 1909, quoted in Baker, I, p. 28. Role of JRW in WW's education: ibid., pp. 37–41. WW's late learning as result of slow recovery of organized education: Mulder, p. 31; WW's late learning as result of passive-aggression: George and George, pp. 6–7; WW's late learning as result of mixed cerebral dominance: Weinstein, pp. 15–18. Cousins's observations: George and George, p. 8.
6. Baker, I, p. 59.
7. Ibid., pp. 64–77 and Weinstein, pp. 23–24.
8. Baker, I, pp. 77–80. Editorial note, "Wilson's Study and Use of Shorthand, 1872–92," *Papers,* I, pp. 8–19.
9. Promotion: January 5, 1873, ibid., p. 22. List of officers: ibid., August 25, 1873, pp. 24–25. Civilian dress: ibid., September 1, 1873, p. 28. *London Times* article about HMS *Renown:* ibid., April 5, 1874, pp. 43–46. Yacht Club: ibid., July 1, 1874, pp. 54–56.

10. William B. Hale, *Woodrow Wilson, The Story of His Life* (Garden City, N.Y.: Doubleday, 1912), pp. 44–46. Quoted in *Papers*, I, pp. 21–22. See also editorial note, "Wilson's Imaginary World," ibid., pp. 20–22.

11. D. W. Winnicott, "Ego Distortion in Terms of True and False Self," in *The Maturational Process and the Facilitating Environment* (1960; rpt. New York: International Universities Press, 1965), pp. 140–152.

12. Idealization in self-development: Heinz Kohut, *Tne Analysis of the Self* (New York: International Universities Press, 1971) pp. 37–56 and 74–78.

13. "Turning point" and summary of oratory: Baker, I, pp. 86–93. Prayer meetings: diary entry of October 22, 1876, *Papers*, I, p. 215. Letter to father is cited in Baker, I, p. 89

14. WW to JRW, May 23, 1877, *Papers*, I, pp. 265–266.

15. Introspection and depression: JRW to WW, January 25, 1878, ibid., pp. 345–6; January 27, 1880, ibid., pp. 596–7. Overcoat: November 12, 1877, ibid., p. 318. Comments on style: March 27, 1877, ibid., pp. 254–5; July 26, 1877, ibid., p. 287; August 10, 1877, ibid., p. 288; November 5, 1877, ibid., p. 315. Fishbone: October 23, 1877, ibid., p. 304.

16. Hard work, self-denial, earning success and reaction to WW's disappointment: JRW to WW, December 22, 1877, ibid., pp. 331–2; January 25, 1878, ibid., pp. 345–6.

17. Pleasure in friendship: JRW to WW, July 26, 1877, ibid., p. 287. New York papers: May 9, 1878, ibid., pp. 375–6.

18. Expectations: JRW to WW, March 27, 1877, ibid., p. 254; July 26, 1877, ibid., p. 287; October 22, 1878, ibid., pp. 421–2. Unity of interest: November 12, 1877, ibid., p. 318.

19. Symptoms: WW to Robert Bridges, January 1, 1881, *Papers*, II, p. 9; WW to Richard Heath Dabney, February 1, 1881, ibid., p. 17.

20. Work as apprentice clerk: Henry Wilkinson Bragdon, *Woodrow Wilson: the Academic Years* (Cambridge: The Belknap Press of Harvard University Press, 1967), p. 91. Details of proposal: Editorial note, "Wilson's Proposal to Hattie Woodrow," *Papers*, II, pp. 84–85.

21. Poem: ibid., pp. 91–94.

22. WW to Robert Bridges, March 15, 1882, ibid., pp. 107–108.

23. Name and initials: Bragdon, p. 76.

24. Editorial note, "Wilson's Practice of Law," *Papers*, II, pp. 144–145. For WW's feelings of disillusionment with law and eagerness to return to studies, see also WW to Robert Bridges, April 29, 1883, ibid., pp. 343–344. WW and ELA: Editorial notes, "Wilson's Early Courtship of Ellen Axson" and "The Engagement," ibid., pp. 361–363 and 426–427.

25. Weinstein makes the important comparison of WW's letter to EAW with the correspondence between WW and his mother: Weinstein, pp. 63–65. WW's description of unhappy moods: WW to EAW, November 1, 1884, *Papers*, III, pp. 393–394.

26. Homesickness: WW to ELA, October 2, 1883, *Papers*, II, p. 449. "*Active* sympathy": March 5, 1885, *Papers*, IV, p. 335. Disposition would sour: January 9, 1885, *Papers*, III, p. 592. "*Half* a man": November 12, 1884, ibid., p. 429.

27. Immortal work: WW to ELA, November 5, 1884, ibid., p. 405 and November 1, 1884, ibid., pp. 393–394. Love of family: January 9, 1885, ibid., p. 592 and April 4, 1885, *Papers*, IV, p. 451. Nature expanded: January 16, 1884, *Papers*, II, p. 660. Love as luxury: February 5, 1884, *Papers*, III, p. 10. Love gives completeness: March 3, 1885, *Papers*, IV, pp. 324–325. Expression of love: November 5, 1884, *Papers*, III, p. 406. ELA inside his innermost life: October 28, 1884, ibid., p. 383 (Copyright 1967 by Princeton University Press. Excerpt reprinted by permission of Princeton University Press).

28. Earlier dream: WW to ELA, October 2, 1883, *Papers*, II, pp. 449–450. Later dream: July 26, 1884, *Papers*, III, p. 261.

29. WW's account of anxiety and his dream: WW to ELA, January 4, 1884, *Papers*, II, pp. 644–647. WW's "indiscreet" letter: December 25, 1883, ibid., pp. 601–602. ELA's teasing response: December 31, 1883, ibid., p. 614. The editors of the *Papers* document that WW received that letter on January 3, 1884 in footnote one, ibid., p. 657.

30. WW to ELA, January 8, 1884, ibid., pp. 653–655 (Copyright 1967 by Princeton University Press. Excerpt reprinted by permission of Princeton University Press).

31. Chronology of WW's visit to ELA and his own family: editors' footnote three, ibid., p. 662. JRW's diagnosing "sickness of *heart*": WW to ELA, January 28, 1884, ibid., pp. 663–664. Visitors and preference to stay in Wilmington: January 31, 1884, ibid., pp. 667–668. Account of medical consultation: February 2, 1884, *Papers*, III, p. 4. Recovery: February 7, 1884, ibid., p. 12.

32. Mirroring function: Kohut, pp. 105–42.

33. Sigmund Freud, "A Childhood Recollection from *Dichtung und Wahrheit*," in *The Standard Edition of The Complete Psychological Works of Sigmund Freud*, ed. James Strachey (1917; rpt. London: The Hogarth Press and The Institute for Psychoanalysis, 1955) XVII, p. 156.

34. Advice on depression: JRW to WW, January 27, 1880, *Papers*, I, pp. 596–597 (Copyright 1967 by Princeton University Press. Excerpt reprinted by permission of Princeton University Press). See also October 19, 1880, ibid., pp. 685–686. Advice not to back down: November 19, 1879, ibid., pp. 585–586; August 20, 1882, *Papers*, II, pp. 135–136.

35. Reaction to acceptance of *Congressional Government*: JRW to WW, December 2, 1884, *Papers*, III, p. 505. The dedication is quoted in WW to EAW, December 1, 1884, ibid., p. 503. JRW's response to the dedication: January 30, 1885, *Papers*, IV, p. 208 (Copyright 1968 by Princeton University Press. Excerpt reprinted by permission of Princeton University Press).

36. JRW to WW, December 22, 1879, *Papers*, I, p. 589 and June 7, 1880, ibid., p. 660.

37. "Cool water": JRW to WW, April 17, 1880, ibid., p. 650 and August 20, 1882, *Papers*, II, p. 135. Fears: June 7, 1880, *Papers*, I, p. 660 and May 17, 1884, *Papers*, III, p. 183.

38. Superior temperament and Clarksville: JRW to WW, December 17, 1884, ibid., p. 549. Superior gifts and request for manuscripts: April 5, 1886, *Papers*, V, p. 152. Mulder also noted the change in JRW and WW's relationship: p. 89. For an instance where Woodrow still did react to his father's critique, see JRW to WW, September 6 and 12, 1887, *Papers*, V, p. 584 and pp. 587–588 and Editorial note, "Wilson's Desire for a 'Literary Life,'" ibid., pp. 474–475.

39. JRW to WW, November 15, 1886 and March 12, 1887, ibid., p. 391 and p. 467 (Copyright 1968 by Princeton University Press. Excerpt reprinted by permission of Princeton University Press).

40. JRW to WW, January 5, 1889, *Papers*, VI, p. 38. See also January 10, 1889 and March 6, 1889, ibid., pp. 47–48 and 137–138.

41. JRW to WW, October 5, 1889, ibid., pp. 400–401 (Copyright 1969 by Princeton University Press. Excerpt reprinted by permission of Princeton University Press).

42. "*Hunger*": JRW to WW, March 27, 1890, ibid., pp. 560–561. October 13, 1891, *Papers*, VII, p. 311 (Copyright 1969 by Princeton University Press. Excerpt reprinted by permission of Princeton University Press).

43. Bronchitis: JRW to WW, January 10, 1889, *Papers*, VI, pp. 47–48. Fear of boring WW: October 5, 1889, ibid., pp. 400–401. Fear of WW forgetting him: March 7, 1891, *Papers*, VII, p. 174. Ghost of a chill: October 13, 1891, ibid., p. 311.

44. WW's reaction to JRW's female relationship: WW to EAW, February 7, 1894, *Papers*, VIII, pp. 462–3. JRW's terminal symptoms: EAW to Mary Eloise Hoyt, December 15, 1902, *Papers*, XIV, p. 294.

45. WW to ELA, August 16, 1884, *Papers*, III, p. 293. WW to ELA, May 14, 1885, *Papers*, IV, p. 590. Concern for JRW after JWW's death: WW to Richard H. Dabney, *Papers*, V, p. 726.

46. Bronchitis: WW to JRW, January 13, 1889, *Papers*, VI, pp. 48–49. Christmas letter: December 16, 1888, ibid., p. 30 (Copyright 1969 by Princeton University Press. Excerpt reprinted by permission of Princeton University Press).

47. Spiritual capital: WW to Payton H. Hoge, January 31, 1903, *Papers*, XIV, p. 336. Life-long friend: WW to Edith Gittings Reid, February 3, 1903, ibid., pp. 347–348. Chivalric devotion: WW to Daniel Moreau Barringer, February 2, 1903, *Papers*, XV, p. 581.

48. Idealization: Kohut, *Analysis of the Self*, pp. 37–56 and 74–78; John Gedo, "Forms of Idealization in the Analytic Transference," *Journal of the American Psychoanalytic Association*, 23 (1975), pp. 485–505.

49. Arnold Goldberg, "A Fresh Look at Perverse Behavior," *International Journal of Psycho-Analysis*, 56 (1975), pp. 335–342.

50. For the effects of similar but far more extreme narcissistic fixations of a parent on the self-formulation of a child, see Kohut, "Discussion of 'Further Data and Documents in the Schreber Case' by William G. Niederland," (1960) in Paul H. Ornstein, ed., *The Search for the Self: Selected Writings of Heinz Kohut* (New York: International Universities Press, 1978) pp. 305–308. See also a summary of Kohut's discussion of a paper by Augusta Bonnard in Jerome Kavka, "Meetings of the Chicago Psychoanalytic Society: A Report," *Bulletin of the Philadelphia Association for Psychoanalysis*, 12 (1962), pp. 174–176. Quoted in *Search for the Self*, pp. 650–651, footnote twelve.

51. For the narrative portions of this section on Wilson's Princeton years, I have relied heavily on Baker, II, pp. 129–357; Bragdon, pp. 269–384; Mulder, pp. 158–228, and Arthur S. Link, *Wilson: the Road to the White House* (Princeton: Princeton University Press, 1947) pp. 59–91. I will cite references for the key passages from these secondary sources and for all primary materials, which are collected in *Papers*, Vols. XIV–XX. WW's diagnoses and reactions to his illness: Weinstein, pp. 141–149 and 165–180; EAW to Mary Eloise Hoyt, June 12, 1906, *Papers*, XVI, pp. 423–424; EAW to Florence Stevens Hoyt, June 27, 1906, ibid., pp. 429–430; Baker, II, pp. 201–208. Healing value of affection: WW to Frederic and Emily Yates, November 6, 1906, ibid., p. 481.

52. Originally planned twenty-five years to implement: Baker, II, pp. 226–227. Welcomed fight: WW to C. H. Dodge, July 1, 1907, *Papers*, XVII, pp. 240–241. Disintegration quote: "A Supplementary Report to the Board of Trustees of Princeton University," c. December 13, 1906, *Papers*, XVI, p. 525 (Copyright 1973 by Princeton University Press. Excerpt reprinted by permission of Princeton University Press).

53. "Black mood"; Arthur Walwroth, *Woodrow Wilson*, 3rd ed. (New York: Norton, 1978), p. 112. Friends' puzzlement: Bragdon, pp. 328–329. EAW on WW's reaction to Hibben: Baker, II, p. 266.

54. Although some of Weinstein's evidence extends beyond Wilson's prepolitical years, to which I have limited this paper, his major arguments are important and deserve summary. The letters Ellen wrote to Woodrow in the summer of 1908 while he was vacationing alone in Europe are missing. It is possible Woodrow or a family member destroyed them because they contained some reference to the affair. Early that same vacation, Woodrow ended a letter to Ellen with a profuse apology (he did not specify the offense), intensely reassured her of his love, insisted it was more than emotional, and assured her that if she trusted him, all would "come right"—including what she did not understand (again, unspecified) (WW to EAW, July 20, 1908, *Papers*, XVIII, pp. 371–372). In his speeches for years thereafter, he stopped referring to the white of the American flag as a symbol of purity. In 1914, a year after Wilson became president of

the United States, Ellen died of chronic nephritis. After a deep depression, Woodrow met and quickly fell in love with Edith Bolling Galt, who became his second wife in 1916. During Wilson's engagement to Galt, one of his aides received an anonymous letter stating that Mary Peck was going to publicize a loan Wilson had made to her and was going to release to his political enemies some of his letters. In a panic, Wilson met with Galt and discussed his earlier relationship with Peck. Later that same evening he wrote to Galt that his relationship with Peck was "a folly long ago loathed and repented of," for which he felt guilty and punished and which he had tried to expiate "by disinterested service and honorable, self-forgetful, devoted love." (WW to Edith Bolling Galt, September 19, 1915, *Papers*, XXXIV, p. 451) Galt forgave him, he felt wonderfully freed after his confession, and thereafter he resumed referring to the white of the flag as a symbol of purity (Weinstein, pp. 181–194 and 291–293).

55. Difficult to keep up spirits: WW to C. H. Dodge, June 18, 1908, *Papers*, XVIII, pp. 337–338. For progress in freeing his mind of Princeton, see WW to EAW, July 10 and August 3, 1908, ibid., p. 357 and p. 388.

56. Letter which rejoined the battle: WW to Moses T. Pyne, December 25, 1909, *Papers*, XIX, pp. 628–631. Copies were sent to all the other trustees.

57. Editorial note, "Wilson at the Meeting of the Board of Trustees of January 13, 1909," *Papers*, XX, pp. 6–9.

58. Bragdon, pp. 371–372.

59. Dreams and exhaustion: WW to EAW, February 17, 1910, *Papers*, XX, p. 133. Longing for letters: WW to EAW, February 20 and 21, 1910, ibid., pp. 144–145; WW to M. A. H. Peck, February 21, 1910, ibid., pp. 150–151.

60. Pew-rents: "Woodrow Wilson is for True Democracy," *Pittsburgh Gazette Times*, April 17, 1910, quoted in *Papers*, XX, pp. 363–365. Fields of blood: "Disaster Forecast by Wilson," *Pittsburgh Dispatch*, April 17, 1910, quoted in *Papers*, XX, pp. 366–368.

61. WW's comment to his wife: quoted in Eleanor Wilson McAdoo, *The Woodrow Wilsons* (New York: MacMillan, 1937), p. 101. Irony of contributor solution: Mulder, p. 224.

62. Weinstein, *Biography*, pp. 141–168 and 176–180.

63. Juliette and Alexander George, "*Woodrow Wilson and Colonel House*: A Reply to Weinstein, Anderson, and Link," *Political Science Quarterly*, 96 (Winter, 1981–1982), pp. 641–665. A letter from Dr. Marmor appears as an appendix to that paper. The paper to which the Georges are responding is: Edwin Weinstein, James W. Anderson, and Arthur S. Link, "Woodrow Wilson's Political Personality: A Reappraisal," *Political Science Quarterly*, 93 (Winter, 1978), pp. 585–598. Weinstein's other major earlier paper: "Woodrow Wilson's Neurological Illness," *The Journal of American History*, 57 (September, 1970), pp. 324–351. Michael F. Marmor, "Wilson, Strokes, and Zebras," *New England Journal of Medicine*, 307 (August 26, 1982), pp. 528–535. Jerrold M. Post, "Woodrow Wilson Re-examined: The Mind-Body Problem Redux and Other Disputations," *Political Psychology*, 4 (1984), 289–306.

64. Weinstein, *Biography*, p. 178.

65. Ideals as compensatory structure: Kohut, *The Restoration of the Self* (New York: International Universities Press, 1977), pp. 3–4 and 82–83.

66. WW to EAW, December 7, 1884, *Papers*, III, p. 522.

MIRROR IMAGE OF THE NATION
An Investigation of Kaiser Wilhelm II's
Leadership of the Germans

THOMAS A. KOHUT

This Kaiser, about whom you are in an uproar, is your mirror image!

—Friedrich Naumann's admonition to the
German people in January 1909.[1]

Never before had a symbolic individual been so completely reflected in an epoch, an epoch in an individual.

—Walter Rathenau on Wilhelm II in 1919.[2]

In recent years Kaiser Wilhelm II has been the subject of renewed historical interest. For decades, however, historians have ignored the Kaiser while focusing considerable attention on the period of German history that bears his name. The striking, if lamentable, reality that not one full-scale scholarly biography of Wilhelm II has yet been published[3] testifies to the fact that until now historians have chosen to investigate Wilhelmine Germany while minimizing the significance of Wilhelm II. At the same time, a spate of popular biographies of the Kaiser have been written by more or less amateur historians.[4] The general public, it seems, remains curious about the Kaiser. This combination of popular interest and scholarly neglect corresponds to the mixture of adulation and irritation with which Wilhelm was viewed by his contemporaries. He seemed at once a fascinating, mythical figure of heroic proportions and an inconsequential and pathetic posturer. It is the thesis of this study that both images of the Kaiser reflect the reality of Wilhelm II's leadership of the Germans, a leadership that was dynamic and compelling yet weak and ineffectual.

This paradoxical view is based upon the distinction between the two principal leadership functions of the German Kaiserdom. Wilhelm was expected to combine what his best friend and political confidant, Philipp Eulenburg, described as "the two images of the governing statesman and the sleeping Hero-Kaiser."[5] On the one hand, Wilhelm II was to be a political leader: a framer and implementer of specific policies. He was to function as a traditional politician, basing his actions on an assessment of what would be to his own advantage and to that of the nation. In this context "political leadership" is defined primarily in terms of rational self-interest. On the other hand, Wilhelm II was to be the spiritual reincarnation of Friedrich Barbarossa, symbolically risen from his deep sleep in the Kyffhäuser grotto to restore, in the words of one contemporary speaking of Wilhelm II, "the German glory which he took with him into the depths of the mountain."[6] He was, in other words, to be a symbolic leader, an emotional and spiritual personification of the German nation. He was to function as the charismatic representative of the German people, giving exalted expression to deeply felt popular ideals and aspirations. In this context, "symbolic leadership" is defined primarily in terms of public image.

Wilhelm II, on the basis of this distinction, was a successful symbolic leader and an unsuccessful politician. This chapter seeks to demonstrate that the nature of Wilhelm's personality and, in particular, his narcissistic psychopathology made him uniquely able to function as a symbol of late nineteenth and early twentieth-century Germany. The contradictory and disjointed state of the Kaiser's psyche enabled him to reflect his regionally, socially, politically, and intellectually divided nation; and his efforts to promote psychological cohesion for himself also suited in large measure the needs of many of his countrymen. However, Wilhelm's inner disharmony and disorganization, his inability to define psychologically a homogeneous personal self-interest made him ineffective as a political leader and prevented him from being able to pursue policies reliably and consistently. This study, then, is a psychohistorical investigation of Wilhelm II's leadership of the Germans. Its purpose is not to "diagnose" the Kaiser psychoanalytically as narcissistically disturbed but rather to make sense of the significant, yet seemingly insubstantial, impact of this perplexing figure, to shed light on his relationship with his subjects, to assess his place in modern German history.

WILHELM II'S PERSONALITY IN THE LIGHT
OF PSYCHOANALYTIC SELF-PSYCHOLOGY

Within the limits of the present investigation, it is not possible, of course, to present a detailed description of the etiology and symptomatology of narcissistic psychopathology as understood by contemporary psychoanalysis. Suffice it to say that the view of narcissistic disorders adopted in this article is based upon a recent advance in psychoanalytic theory, the psychology of the self, which focuses on man's narcissistic needs.[7] From this perspective such disorders are understood to be the result of a defect or weakness in the essential structure of the personality. Narcissistic pathology is, in other words, "self-pathology": disorganization, disharmony, or debility of the self. The defective or weakened self generally has its origins in the faulty interaction between child and caretakers who were unable to provide needed psychological sustenance in early life. On the one hand, the caretakers may not have been able to provide the child with the opportunity to merge with an adult's sense of calmness and strength that would enable him ultimately to internalize a sense of security and stability. On the other hand, they may not have been able to respond to the child with affirming pride that would enable him ultimately to internalize a sense of inner self-confidence and self-esteem.

As a result of these developmental deficiencies, the narcissistically disturbed adult experiences a sense of inner imbalance and a fear of psychological fragmentation. External display of pseudoexcitement or frenzied activity can ward off feelings of inner apathy and deadness. Anxious grandiosity may cover a frightening sense of inferiority and depression. The internal fragility of the personality makes such individuals extremely sensitive to the way in which others respond to them, and their behavior is characterized by precipitous and intense reactions. Seemingly minor slights and rejections are experienced as profoundly threatening and often produce outbursts of rage, vengeful brooding, or an outwardly haughty withdrawal that covers the deeply felt sense of humiliation. Lacking basic internal security, harmony, and self-esteem, narcissistically disturbed individuals are exquisitely dependent on others for psychological survival. They seek to obtain from their environment that which is missing inside themselves. Others are primarily of interest not as separately experienced individuals but insofar as they can help to maintain, enhance, or restore psychic equilibrium. Like the child whose self-esteem and psychological balance are maintained through his feeling that he is a part of his parents and that they are a part of him, the narcissistically disturbed adult experiences himself as part of others and others as part of himself. The hollowness at the center of the personality creates an addiction-like craving for relationships with people he can admire and depend upon, in whom he can find strength and security. Or, to counteract feelings of worthlessness, he may need to exhibit himself and boastfully evoke attention in the hope that the confirming and admiring response of others will nourish his famished self. Without the continuous sustenance of such "selfobject" relationships—relationships with others (objects) that are experienced as part of the self—the narcissistically disturbed individual experiences a frightening loss of psychological continuity and cohesion.

Much of Kaiser Wilhelm II's personality behavior can readily be understood within the framework of this theoretical approach to narcissistic psychopathology.[8] It becomes possible to explain both his mythic external grandeur and his inner insubstantiality, his charismatic appeal and his ostentatious ineffectuality, in basic human terms. Those among Wilhelm's contemporaries who knew him best recognized the lack of integration at the core of his personality. Bernhard von Bülow, for example, Wilhelm's Chancellor and friend for many years, was "often concerned about his psychic balance."[9] "Wilhelm's character was full of contradictions," Bülow wrote in his memoirs.

> Prince Guido von Henckel-Donnersmark [sic] liked to say that the Kaiser reminded him of a dicebox in which the dice rattled against each other. His personality was not cohesive, self-contained, or harmonious; its various aspects did not interfuse as do even stubborn substances and elements during the process of amalgamation.[10]

Even perceptive casual acquaintances, though dazzled by the Kaiser's position and demeanor, could sometimes discern the incoherence of Wilhelm's self. After a lunch with Wilhelm in the summer of 1891, Viscount John Morley noted in his dairy:

> I was immensely interested in watching a man with such a part to play in Europe. . . . Energy, rapidity, restlessness in every movement from his short quick inclinations of the head to the planting of the foot. But I should be disposed to doubt whether it is all sound, steady and the result of a—what Herbert Spencer would call—rightly coordinated organization.[11]

The rattle of Wilhelm's inner dicebox resounds throughout this study. By way of introduction to the Kaiser's personality, however, it is appropriate to comment briefly at this point on some of the manifestations of his self-pathology. As beautifully evoked by the image of tumbling dice, Wilhelm's politically troublesome capriciousness and unpredictability can be traced to a lack of consolidation at the core of his personality. This central weakness was covered by a display of brittle self-certainty. The Kaiser did not possess the inner strength to admit that he did not know something. He felt compelled to express opinions on almost every subject, and he would commit himself to a position or policy with little or no information about it. He seemed unable to listen to the advice of his ministers, frequently interrupting and monopolizing the conversation. Politically, the Kaiser's display of self-certainty took the form of the frequent assertion of his absolute sovereignty by divine right. He declared in a speech in Königsberg in 1910, for example: "I see myself as an instrument of the Lord. I go my way without regard for the views or opinions of the day."[12] On the surface, Wilhelm's statement seems a powerful and self-confident assertion of virtually unlimited political authority. One gets the sense, however, that its primary psychological purpose for Wilhelm was to borrow from God that strength he missed within himself. Wilhelm's invocation of the deity in this context was ultimately an attempt to shield himself from his critics and to bolster his precarious sense of personal autonomy.

In general, Wilhelm's display of self-certainty can be understood as an attempt to protect his fragile self from outside attack. His extreme vulnerability was such that when he felt himself insufficiently appreciated, let alone condemned, he reacted with explosive rage or icy resentment, and his reign was marked by an unprecedented number of trials for lese majesty. The Kaiser also felt threatened by his own compelling need to depend emotionally upon his environment to supply him with direction and purpose. It was a fact often remarked upon by the Kaiser's advisers that he had the politically alarming tendency to adopt the opinions and goals of the person with whom he had last spoken. His assertion of personal and political absolutism was thus an attempt to convince others *and himself* of his psychological independence. In the final analysis, Wilhelm's declarations of absolute sovereignty were a defensive facade behind which he hungered for the approval and guidance of others. On close inspection this facade proved to be painfully transparent, and those like Philipp Eulenburg who knew the Kaiser best recognized that though Wilhelm pretended to hold other people in contempt, "he actually feared their judgement of him—without ever being able to admit that this was so." He was at heart motivated by what his friend described as "a feminine tendency to wish to please."[13] It would in fact be difficult to imagine a leader more keenly sensitive to the attitudes and responses of others or more profoundly influenced by "the views or opinions of the day" than Kaiser Wilhelm II.

Unable to internalize a sense of basic self-esteem and security through the steady interaction with empathic caretakers in early life,[14] the Kaiser relied upon "selfobjects" to direct his ambitions and determine his ideals. The very lack of selfconsolidation that resulted in Wilhelm's dependence on external emotional support, however, also gave him an extraordinary impressionability and personal pliancy that enabled him to adapt himself to his environment in ways designed to elicit the affirming and supportive responses he required. The Kaiser, in other words, was a consummate actor able to play those parts that would bring him needed psychological sustenance. Contemporaries recognized the assumed quality of Wilhelm's personality. Eulenburg liked to call him "Wilhelm Proteus" after the legendary Greek prophet who could assume any shape he chose. And when asked how she and the Kaiser had gotten along, the great French actress Sarah Bernhardt replied: "Mais admirablement, car ne sommes nous pas, lui et moi, tous deux cabotins?"[15] Of course all leaders at times attempt to hide their private personalities behind a public mask. In Wilhelm II's case, however, one gets the sense that his behavior was little more than a continuous theatrical performance and that the Kaiser was an actor without a character of his own. In his need to complete himself through interaction with his surroundings, Wilhelm actually became the parts he played. The remarkably convincing impression created by Wilhelm's dramatis personae on the casual observer can thus be traced to the integrity and intensity of the Kaiser's performances, to the fact that he could only feel harmonious when he experienced himself as being affirmed and appreciated by those around him.

Similarly, Wilhelm's craving for external reassurance was at the source of his anxious and seemingly unrestrained grandiosity. The Kaiser's driven display of himself most often took the form of flamboyant speech-making and traveling that was so frequent that Wilhelm became known as the *Reisekaiser*, or the "traveling emperor." In his private life, the Kaiser's civilian and military entourage provided Wilhelm with the same sense of affirmation that he derived from his state visits, gala receptions, orations, and parades. It is no accident that from his accession in 1888 until his death in exile in Holland in 1941, Wilhelm consistently surrounded himself with a narrow and relatively homogeneous group of self-consciously "charming" and "clever" aristocratic gentlemen. Not only did this inner circle share a similar social, political, intellectual, cultural, and even emotional outlook; they also seemed to recognize that their principal purpose for the Kaiser was to provide him with psychological support. Like the excitement of constant exposure to new people and places, the colorful and witty stories of these raconteurs kept the Kaiser entertained. Like the cheers of the crowds, the enthusiasm of the entourage for the Kaiser and their exaggerated deference to

FIGURE 1. The Kaiser, at the head of the Flag Company of the 13th Infantry Regiment, enters the city of Münster.

him bolstered Wilhelm's fragile sense of self-esteem. Philipp Eulenburg, a personality typical of those around the Kaiser, appreciated Wilhelm's vital need for external confirmation. He advised his friend Bülow in June 1897, as the latter was on his way to assume the post of state secretary in the foreign office, on how best to handle the Kaiser:

> Wilhelm II takes everything personally. Only personal arguments make an impression on him. He wants to instruct others but does not take to being instructed himself. He cannot tolerate anything that is boring. Slow, stiff, or overly serious people get on his nerves and have no success with him. Wilhelm II wants to shine and do everything himself and make all decisions. . . . He loves acclaim, is ambitious, and jealous. In order to get him to accept an idea, one must present it as if it had come from him. You must make everything easy for him. . . . Never forget that now and again His Majesty needs praise. He is one of those characters who without occasional recognition from the lips of significant people becomes depressed. You will have access to all your wishes so long as you do not neglect to express recognition of His Majesty when he has earned it. He is grateful for it like a good, clever child.[16]

Not only did Wilhelm depend upon those around him to assure himself of his own importance; he also depended upon his entourage to supply him with the direction and purpose he lacked within himself.

Indeed, several recent studies, as well as the voluminous published correspondence of Philipp Eulenburg, reveal the extent of the entourage's impact upon the Kaiser. Through Wilhelm, this narrow elite was able to exert a subtle yet pervasive political influence on the conduct of Wilhelmine government.[17]

As a result of these features of the Kaiser's personality, many of his contemporaries concluded that Wilhelm II was mentally "abnormal," meaning by this designation that the Kaiser's puzzling behavior was the product of some hereditary or physiological disorder. Bülow, however, did not regard Wilhelm to be abnormal in this sense of the term. The Kaiser, he believed, simply suffered from extreme hubris, a hubris that covered his profound insecurity:

> For Wilhelm II his hubris expresses itself in an addictive self-aggrandizement, that not only arouses antipathy, but is also politically dangerous. It is largely the product of his wish to hide the inner uncertainty, even anxiousness, that the Kaiser more frequently experiences than the world realizes. Fundamentally, he is not a brave but a fearful personality.[18]

As Bülow and Eulenburg recognized, the key to the Kaiser personally and politically was to understand his central weakness. This weakness would have deleterious political consequences for Germany. But paradoxically, in attempting to compensate for and overcome his psychic deficit, Wilhelm developed some exceptional symbolic leadership capacities. Put another way, the Kaiser's lack of a secure sense of psychological cohesion and continuity—that is, his narcissistic psychopathology—is at the heart of his historical significance.

THE KAISER, THE PRESS, AND GERMAN PUBLIC OPINION

"In politics no one does anything for another," Otto von Bismarck wrote in 1857, "unless he also finds it in his own interest to do so."[19] With this statement, perhaps the greatest political leader of the nineteenth century summed up what one biographer of the great statesman has described as his "fundamental rule of all political behavior." For Bismarck, the pursuit of rational self-interest was natural to the conduct of individuals, groups, and states; indeed, it was a part of God's divine order. As a result, the statesman was morally compelled to define the interest of state and to dedicate himself to its fulfullment.[20] Bismarck believed that "the only sound basis" for the conduct of the nation-state was "its egoism and not romanticism."[21] Personal feelings, the wishes of powerful elites or political parties, popular opinion were all to be subordinated to the realization of the state's self-interest. They were to be manipulated in the service of the rational conduct of foreign policy; they were never to be allowed to shape it. It seemed almost inevitable to Bismarck that the state would follow a foreign political course based upon its self-interest. In November 1887, for example, Bismarck assured Lord Salisbury (who was worried that the accession of the then Prince Wilhelm to the imperial throne would lead to an anti-English shift in German foreign policy) that no individual, be he Kaiser or Chancellor, could steer the ship of state off its predetermined course. You need not be concerned, Bismarck wrote the British Prime Minister, that Wilhelm will pursue an anti-English policy. "Neither this nor the opposite would be possible in Germany." Whoever is Kaiser "will and can only be influenced by the interests of the German Empire. The path that must be taken in order to uphold these interests is so urgently prescribed that it is impossible to depart from it."[22]

Unfortunately, Bismarck's prediction about the future of Anglo-German relations was mistaken, and his optimistically rational conception of the nature of political behavior proved to be out of tune with the mass politics of the twentieth century. With the accession of Wilhelm II in 1888, *Realpolitik* in Germany gave way to the politics of symbolism. When Bismarck retired in anger to Friedrichsruh in 1890—dismissed by a headstrong Kaiser who wished to steer the ship of state himself—Germany's course was no longer self-evident either domestically or internationally. What was certain was that both the youthfully impetuous Kaiser and his youthfully impetuous nation wanted the speed increased, the ship's screws turned faster. Germany had entered the Wilhelmine era.

This transformation of German political life is dramatically represented in the shift in style of leadership from Bismarck to Wilhelm II, from the Chancellor's efforts to realize the rational interests of state to the Kaiser's attention to public opinion and his popular image. Indeed many of Wilhelm's advisers, products as they were of the nineteenth-century perspective on political life, could not understand the Kaiser's preoccupation with his relationship with his subjects, particularly as it was reflected in and influenced by the press. "Complaints from everyone that His Majesty dodges political reports," Friedrich von Holstein, a longtime privy councillor in the foreign office, wrote shortly after Wilhelm's accession. "At the same time he reads thirty to forty newspaper clippings one after the other and makes marginal comments on them. A curious personality."[23]

Wilhelm's tendency, noted by his disgruntled advisers, to concentrate on newspapers as well as on political reports was a reflection of the

Kaiser's frequent sense that public opinion played a crucial role in determining political behavior. In 1895, during the Armenian crisis, the British military attaché in Berlin complained to Wilhelm that an article in the Russian paper *Grashdanin* was symptomatic of a fundamental Russian antipathy toward England that was preventing rapprochement between the two countries. The Kaiser's telling response was that the *Grashdanin*

> like the Press in Russia generally has no appreciable influence on account of its limited circulation; certainly nothing like the influence of the Press in other countries, particularly in England. It is precisely this Press and British public opinion dominated by it that we have to thank for the whole sorry scandal of the Armenian question.[24]

Wilhelm II did not attribute the bloody Near Eastern crisis to the actions of the Turks and Armenians or to the policies of the European world powers actively seeking to defend and promote their national self-interest in the foundering Ottoman Empire. He did not even blame the British Government directly for attempting to hasten and exploit the process of Turkish collapse—as did many in the German Foreign Office. Instead, the Kaiser blamed the English press because of its influence on public opinion. By the same token, he discounted the political significance of the Russian press. Because of its limited circulation, *Grashdanin* had no real impact on the great mass of the Russian people. The fact that newspapers were read by those who directed the policies of the Russian Government seemed irrelevant to the Kaiser. For him, in this instance at least, it was mass public opinion and the press (insofar as it influenced mass public opinion) that determined the nation's course and defined the nature of its leadership.

It became one of Wilhelm's principal occupations to follow the press because of the importance of public opinion to him and because of the enormous power of the press in its position as a medium between ruler and subject, simultaneously influencing and reflecting public opinion. He ascribed such major political developments as the growth of Anglo-French diplomatic and even military cooperation by early 1906 to the fact that the German press had "scolded" the two countries "together."[25] With its *influence* on popular opinion in France and England, the German press, Wilhelm believed, had produced decisive political action—one quite to Germany's disadvantage. As a *reflection* of public opinion, however, the press indicated future political action. In 1896, for example, Wilhelm anticipated that the English would soon decide to seize Germany's colonies because "the newspaper expectorations from England which announce the steady increase in anti-German feeling demonstrate that the antipathy is more deep-seated than has hitherto been believed."[26] In a way that his advisers did not, Wilhelm recognized that public opinion had become a crucial political factor in late nineteenth-/early twentieth-century Europe. Although he could proclaim and at times believe that he was completely above "the views and opinions of the day," his conduct as German emperor was often based upon the attitude that he expressed in December 1896 to the British Ambassador in Berlin that despite his personal desire to promote Anglo-German understanding, he was simply "not able to act in opposition to the interests and wishes of the German people."[27]

Both the Kaiser's recognition that he must be a "modern monarch," sensitive and responsive to the needs of his subjects, and his belief in the political importance of public opinion and the press as mediator between ruler and subject were a direct result of Wilhelm's narcissistic psychopathology. His preoccupation with the "interests and wishes of the German people"—often to the neglect of the interests of the German state—was a direct result of the enormous significance that public opinion (via the press) had for Wilhelm personally. Because it affected him so powerfully, he appears to have naturally assumed that public opinion had a commensurate impact on political life in general. In the theoretical language of psychoanalysis, public opinion via the press can be said to have served as a "selfobject" for the Kaiser: as an aspect of his external world that provided the direction and support that he could not find within himself.

Lacking a clear sense of consistent inner purpose, Wilhelm relied on public opinion—as he relied on other, often discordant, selfobjects—to shape his attitudes and organize his activities. In general, the Kaiser seemed unable to develop a position on his own. Like iron filings that only assume a recognizable pattern in the presence of a magnetic field, Wilhelm formed opinions in reaction to the opinions of others. At times the Kaiser simply adopted the views of those around him as his own. But even on those not infrequent occasions when he adopted a view diametrically opposed to that of the person with whom he was talking, Wilhelm needed the structured position of another to which he could impulsively react in defining his own point of view. It is significant in this context that so many of the Kaiser's telegrams and letters are essentially accounts of his conversations with others; his position only formulated in his descriptions of his replies. The same impulsive reactivity characterizes the principal way in which Wilhelm developed his opinions and articulated them to his advisers: namely, through extensive marginal comments on newspaper, diplomatic, and governmental reports. These marginalia reveal the degree to which Wilhelm was influenced by public opinion as it was reflected in the press. Not only can one see that the Kaiser actually read many newspapers, but it becomes clear that many of his personal opinions and political judgements were formed in direct response to press reports of popular feeling. In a psychological sense, public opinion can be described as having participated in the process of determining the Kaiser's point of view. Moreover, by following the press' reaction to him, Wilhelm was able to gauge the popular impact of his behavior. He lacked the internal capacity to evaluate the appropriateness of his actions, and he needed to rely upon the responses of his environment to regulate his impulsive activities. Like the timely intervention of aides who were able to prevent the Kaiser from embarking on a potentially disastrous political course, the negative responses of the general public expressed through the papers could lead Wilhelm suddenly to change a position to which moments before he had seemed unalterably committed.

But while public opinion helped to shape Wilhelm's ideas and direct his actions, for him its principal function, like that of his entourage, was to offer external affirmation. Despite the fact that Wilhelm II was an emperor, raised from earliest childhood to be a public figure *par excellence*, he still experienced intense gratification at being the focus of popular attention. Bülow remarks in his memoirs on how quickly the cheers of the crowds would bring Wilhelm to a state of unbridled excitement: "In the course of my time in office I seldom went anywhere with the Kaiser when he did not declare after his ceremonial entrance that it had been the most lovely reception of his life."[28] The exquisite pleasure that Wilhelm experienced on such occasions had a direct influence on his actions; when he felt himself appreciated by British public opinion and supported by the British press, for example, Wilhelm sought to pursue a warmly pro-English policy.[29]

Both Wilhelm II's belief in the enormous influence of public opinion on political life and its powerful impact on himself personally placed the Kaiser in a problematical position. The political and personal dilemma that confronted Wilhelm in his relationship to public opinion found expression in a letter to Czar Nicholas II in May 1909. Wilhelm wrote that he felt "blamed" for the tension in Europe following Austria's annexation of Bosnia-Herzegovina in October of the preceding year. "Especially the Press in general," he complained, "has behaved in the basest way against me." Despite their inaccuracy, Wilhelm believed that the newspaper attacks against him should be taken seriously since "the fact must be taken note of that the papers mostly create public opinion." He concluded:

> As sovereigns who are responsible to God for the welfare of the Nations entrusted to our care it is our duty therefore to closely study the genesis and development of "public opinion" before we allow it

to influence our actions. Should we find that it takes its origin from the tarnished and gutterlike sources of the above named infamous press our duty will and must oblige us to energetically correct it and resist it.

Personally I am totally indifferent to newspaper gossip, but I cannot refrain from a certain feeling of anxiety, that if not corrected at once, the foul and filthy lies which are freely circulated about my policies and country, will tend to create bitterness between our two people by virtue of their constant and uncontradicted repetition. Public opinion wants clear information and leading.[30]

In the first place, the Kaiser's letter to the Czar gives expression to the dilemma inherent in Wilhelm's position as an "absolute" monarch in an age of growing mass political participation. As an autocrat he was above newspaper criticism and yet obviously susceptible to it. He was theoretically accountable only to God and yet recognized that his leadership rested ultimately on his standing with his subjects. Wilhelm was confronted with the task of reconciling the facade of absolute self-certainty that seemed so necessary to his personal and political functioning with his appreciation of the powerful impact that press and public opinion had both on him and on modern political life. He had to reconcile his need to appear "totally indifferent to newspaper gossip" with his driven need to devote so much energy to the reading of newspapers.

The contradiction in Wilhelm's political position was probably inevitable given the changing realities of monarchical rule in turn-of-the-century Europe. The dilemma that confronted Wilhelm also had to be faced in one way or another by all the European hereditary sovereigns of his era. But though the Kaiser's political predicament was by no means unique, he was faced psychologically with a profoundly personal dilemma that arose directly out of Wilhelm's emotional dependence on the feelings and opinions of his subjects.

In the course of this study, considerable attention has been devoted to the three basic selfobject functions that public opinion served for Wilhelm II, and the reader may well have experienced a sense of discomfort at the emphasis placed on these selfobject needs of the Kaiser. After all, everyone needs the responses of others throughout life to help establish goals and set priorities and to assess the appropriateness of behavior. Everyone needs the affirming responses of others throughout life to feel truly alive and truly worthwhile. What makes Wilhelm unique was not that he needed selfobjects to sustain him, but that he needed them so much. Wilhelm's dilemma, in other words, was that to a significant degree he was at the mercy of popular responses to him. Just as he could feel exhilarated by the adulation of the masses, as he could feel uplifted upon entering a city by the cheers of the crowds, as he could feel gratified by favorable newspaper reaction to one of his speeches, he could feel correspondingly devastated when he felt himself unappreciated, undermined, or criticized by his subjects.

There is evidence to suggest that public condemnation contributed directly to a series of "nervous breakdowns" that Wilhelm suffered during the course of his reign.[31] The most famous of these occurred in the aftermath of the publication of the Kaiser's notorious interview with the English newspaper the *Daily Telegraph* in late October 1908, when Wilhelm's indiscrete remarks produced national indignation and the demand of the Reichstag that restraints be placed on the Kaiser's conduct.[32] One of Wilhelm's first such breakdowns occurred after he was roundly criticized for an inflammatory speech to the Brandenburg Provincial Diet on February 26, 1897. Bülow recalled that

> the Kaiser was so disappointed by the failure of his speech, which could not be kept from him, that. . .he suffered a nervous collapse. . . . He had anticipated that his "forthright" speech would be a huge success.[33]

It is not enough to say that Wilhelm simply felt criticized. On this occasion, and to a degree on all occasions when he felt out of tune with his countrymen, the intensity of his reaction indicates that Wilhelm experienced his subjects' response to his speech as a denigration of something that he had proudly created and displayed and as a devastating subversion where he had expected—indeed counted on—popular acclaim to support him emotionally. It is difficult to know with certainty how these breakdowns would be characterized in the terminology of contemporary psychiatry or what their precise precipitants may have been. They were doubtless the produce of various intersecting factors. Nonetheless, these incapacitating episodes of intense anxiety and depression do demonstrate that the supporting and sustaining responses of the Germans were essential to the Kaiser's personal and political functioning.

Although the extent of Wilhelm's dependence on public opinion placed him in a precarious psychological position, the nature of public opinion itself tended to increase Wilhelm's emotional vulnerability. The popular mood was a particularly problematical selfobject for the Kaiser to have adopted. In the first place, public opinion was, and remains, difficult to define and evaluate. Wilhelm could rarely get a direct sense of what the Germans were thinking and feeling. It was mainly through the medium of the press, in its capacity as a reflection of public opinion, that the Kaiser could experience his vitally important relationship with his countrymen. This relationship was subject to countless distortions. No matter how many articles the Kaiser read, he never was actually exposed to public opinion in the press. He was only exposed to news-paper opinions and reportage.

Not only did Wilhelm feel compelled to base himself on an inevita-bly distorted press image of public opinion; public opinion was also based upon an inevitably distorted press image of the Kaiser. "It is remarkable," Zedlitz-Trützschler, Wilhelm's Court Marshal for many years, noted in his diary in 1904,

> how sensitive the Kaiser is to the press. In and of themselves harmless inaccuracies and untruths about his life can greatly upset him when they are reported to him or when he comes across them in his own reading.[34]

Wilhelm's distress at the publication of misinformation about himself can be attributed to his concern that Germans would develop miscon-ceptions about him that could lead to a skewing of the popular re-sponses on which he so depended. These problems of conception were compounded by the fact that the divisions in Wilhelmine Germany meant that at any given moment there existed many different—often incompatible—public opinions. Wilhelm, with his internal inconsisten-cies, had come to rely upon a selfobject that itself profoundly lacked consensus. Furthermore, the frequent dramatic shifts of the German popular mood during the course of Wilhelm's reign added to the incon-sistency of the support that it provided the Kaiser. Unable to function for any length of time without the support of his subjects, Wilhelm's leadership bears the mark of these features of German public opinion. The confusion of the Kaiser's aims, his inability to pursue policies stead-fastly and consistently, his frequent precipitous changes in course are in part to be attributed to the ill-defined, inevitably distorted, contradictory character of public opinion as it was reflected in the press. Finally, it should be pointed out that the directions in which Wilhelm was pro-pelled via his reliance on German public opinion were very different from those in which he was propelled by the other selfobjects, like his entourage or his relatives, on which he also depended. The inconsisten-cy of the Kaiser's political views and conduct was thus increased by the inconsistency of the environment on which he relied to help him organize and direct his activities.

But if Wilhelm's dependence on public opinion contributed to the ineffectiveness of his political leadership, in his efforts to deal with the political and personal dilemma that arose out of his dependence he demonstrated an interest and skill in swaying public opinion unprece-dented for a leader of his era, let alone for a hereditary monarch. Wilhelm sought to overcome his sense of helplessness in his relationship with his subjects by attempting to control the feelings and opinions of the Germans primarily through the medium of the press, now in its capacity as an influence on public opinion. As he stated so emphatically in his letter to the Czar: "Public opinion wants clear information and leading." If Kaiser and country were in fundamental agreement, Wilhelm was not confronted with the paradox of being an absolute monarch whose leadership depended upon popular support since it was only when he and his subjects were out of step that the Kaiser realized that it was they and not he who set the pace. In fact, by using the press to encourage the German public to adapt itself to his policies and priorities, Wilhelm diminished his dependence on his countrymen and increased his political authority. Psychologically, too, by exerting his control over public opinion, Wilhelm was acting to insure the sustaining and supportive responses of his subjects, thereby reducing his sense of emotional helplessness and vulnerability. By establishing a measure of control over the feelings and opinions of the Germans, the Kaiser increased his control over himself and over his political and psychological destiny. As a direct result of his narcissistic psychopathology, Wilhelm came to develop a style of symbolic leadership that was more contemporary than traditional, more propagandistic than dynastic; it was a style of leadership suited to modern mass society.[35]

In its crudest form, Wilhelm's "leading" of public opinion involved the effort to prevent the publication of newspaper or journal articles that he deemed misleading, inappropriate, inaccurate, or malicious before they could corrupt the popular image of Wilhelm or of his policies. He constantly put pressure on his aides to suppress critical articles and prosecute "hostile" editors and was constantly irritated that there were limits on the government's authority to censor the German press.[36] Where it was not possible to prevent critical or erroneous articles from appearing, the Kaiser sought "energetically to correct" any possible popular misconceptions by publishing government denials or bulletins, and by using press leaks, friendly persuasion, or pressure to get his point of view expressed in those papers sympathetic to the government. At a particularly sensitive period in Anglo-German relations, for example, the Kaiser, annoyed at the publication of several articles in Germany critical of the English royal family, ordered that with the upcoming visit of the Prince of Wales "our Press must in the last 8 days before his arrival print only amicable articles about his trip."[37] Not only was the Prince to be spared embarrassment at the hands of the German press, but the German people were to be encouraged to share Wilhelm's enthusiasm for the visit. In general, during those periods when the Kaiser felt favorably disposed toward the English, he sought to foster a similar sense of mutual goodwill on the part of the German and English people.

When friendly articles toward Germany were printed in the English newspapers, Wilhelm ordered that they be translated and reprinted with approving commentary in the German press,[38] and he had officials of the government, academicians, and sympathetic journalists write essays for the papers, expressing the myriad economic, cultural, diplomatic, and military advantages for Germany of close friendship with England. He encouraged organizations, such as the Hamburg Chamber of Commerce, which had vested interests in improved relations between the two countries, to hold rallies and meetings to promote Anglo-German friendship.

The effort to engender popular support for a policy or position of the Kaiser by influencing the press and organizing public demonstrations found its clearest and most effective expression in the systematic propaganda campaign directed by Wilhelm and Admiral Tirpitz to create widespread German enthusiasm for the development of the navy. After the defeat of the government's naval bill in the Reichstag in March 1897, Wilhelm—although hurt and angry and thinking of instigating of a coup d'état—took decisive action to transform German public opinion and thereby end the discrepancy between his own desire for naval increases and his subjects' apparently manifest indifference to naval development. To a report that increasing numbers of middle-class Germans were beginning to recognize that German commerce could not flourish without a powerful navy, Wilhelm ordered: "This mood must be methodically exploited and strengthened by the Press. At the same time the people must be oriented and incited against the Reichstag."[39] Approximately three months later, on June 18, 1897, Wilhelm appointed Tirpitz State Secretary in the Naval Office. Wilhelm's order, however, had expressed the principle that would animate one of the first effective propaganda campaigns in the history of modern politics. Together, the Kaiser and Tirpitz through concentrated mass political action were able to achieve what more traditional political lobbying had failed to accomplish. The government, in conjunction with powerful industrial and commercial circles, skillfully manipulated the press, abetted various popular naval and colonial leagues, and generally spent vast amounts of financial and political capital to produce a groundswell of popular support for the development of the German navy. Within a year, the Reichstag had passed a naval law setting forth the long-range expansion and modernization of the navy. What the Kaiser had described as "the struggle for the fleet" had been won with astonishing ease.[40]

If Tirpitz and the Kaiser shared an appreciation of the political importance of public opinion, there was a difference in the approach the two men took in attempting to influence it. For Tirpitz, the propaganda campaign on behalf of the navy was a way to increase the naval budget, enlarge the navy, and, perhaps in the surge of patriotic fervor for naval development, to distract Germans from growing domestic tension. Although Wilhelm also yearned for the creation of a glorious German fleet, his attempt to influence public opinion was less calculated and more emotional. At heart, he was motivated by the need to make his subjects feel what he himself experienced. They were to share, affirm, and reflect his enthusiasm for the navy. By "leading" public opinion to support the government's naval building program, the Kaiser sought to create an identity of political and psychological outlook between himself and the Germans.

That Wilhelm's attempt to influence his subjects through the press was ultimately a subtle yet significant form of emotional communication with them is revealed by his order in early February 1896 that an article in the English newspaper the *Speaker* be translated and published in the German press. The article was a critical account of the successful British campaign against the Ashanti in West Africa. It concluded with the statement: "The most powerful nation in the world had crushed a naked African savage, and had celebrated its victory by treating him, his family, and his envoys considerably worse than it would have ventured to treat a party of pickpockets"—to which Wilhelm had noted in English in the margin "as it treats everybody."[41] At first glance, it seems incomprehensible that the Kaiser would want this article, on a subject apparently irrelevant to German concerns, circulated throughout the country. Wilhelm's reaction to the article and his desire that it be reprinted becomes understandable, however, in the context of the events following the Krüger telegram. On January 3rd, a month before the Kaiser's order regarding the *Speaker*, Wilhelm had sent a telegram to President Paul Krüger of the South African Republic, congratulating him on the Boer defeat of a band of British irregulars led by Leander Starr Jameson. The publication of the Kaiser's telegram produced a storm of anti-German feeling in England. Wilhelm was personally criticized by his English relatives and condemned in the British press. There were calls for an alliance between England and her traditional enemies, France and Russia, against Germany. Wilhelm was completely unprepared for the British reaction. He felt hurt and angry, and he even feared that because Germany did not possess a powerful navy, the English might be planning a surprise attack.[42] Wilhelm felt vulnerable and, as his marginalia to the *Speaker* indicates, treated with contempt by "the most powerful nation in the world"—a phrase in the article that Wilhelm had underlined. At such a time it was especially important for the Kaiser to have the support of his countrymen. By exposing his subjects to the *Speaker*'s article on the Ashanti campaign, he hoped that their reaction would mirror his. If the Germans could share his experience of being treated with disdain, they might also conclude that a mighty navy could bring England to accept and respect Germany as another world power.

As described earlier, the very lack of inner consolidation that made Wilhelm so dependent on the support of his environment also gave him the psychological flexibility to assume the roles that would bring him the responses he needed. In his interaction with his subjects, the Kaiser was able to take on those characteristics that he sensed were expected of him. Only three years into Wilhelm's reign, the Portugese diplomat, Eça de Queiroz, wrote of him:

> In this sovereign what a variety of incarnations of Royalty! One day he is a Soldier-King, rigid, stiff in helmet and cuirass, . . .regarding the drill-sergeant as the fundamental unity of the nation. . . Suddenly he strips off the uniform and dons the work-man's overall; he is the Reform-King attending only to questions of capital and wages, . . .determined to go down in history embracing the proletariat as a brother whom he has set free.
>
> Then all unaware he becomes the King by Divine Right. . . driving over the frontiers all who do not devotedly believe in him.
>
> [Then he becomes the] Courtier-King, worldly, pompous, thinking only of the brilliancy and sumptuosity of etiquette. . . The world smiles and presto! he becomes the Modern King. . .treating the past as bigoted, . . .determined to construct by the aid of Parliamentarism the largest amount of material and industrial civilization, regarding the factory as the supreme temple, dreaming of Germany as worked entirely by electricity.[43]

On a more individual level, Wilhelm's versatile theatricality, coupled with his broadly based general education and his innate intellectual capacity to grasp and retain vast amounts of information, enabled the Kaiser to establish an immediate personal contact with his subjects. Wilhelm variously presented himself as composer, painter, art historian, anthropologist, archeologist, historian, theologian, engineer, military strategist, sea captain, ship's architect, businessman; the list of his interests and activities goes on and on. The Kaiser, it would seem, had the capacity to be all things to all people. Whether in personal conversation or in "the variety of his incarnations of Royalty," Wilhelm was able to engage his subjects individually. From worker to aristocrat, most Germans at one time or another felt personally connected to their Kaiser. Like his travels throughout Germany, which gave his countrymen the opportunity to see him face-to-face, the diversity of his interests and his many royal roles narrowed the gap between ruler and subject. Through a sense of shared interests and aspirations, a special emotional bond linking Wilhelm to the Germans contributed to the success of his leadership.

Reflecting the fact, however, that his adaptability was a manifestation of inner instability, Wilhelm could not maintain or integrate his incarnations of royalty; his knowledge lacked depth; his interests proved ephemeral. Although his versatility was impressive to the general public, those who had extended contact with the Kaiser knew him to be a dilettante. As his longtime chief of the naval cabinet, Admiral von Müller, noted in his diary:

> No thoughtful observer from this period can be in any doubt that the Kaiser understood much, very much very superficially, that he was very self-absorbed and believed that he could make judgements about things which he actually neither could nor needed to make judgements about.[44]

Lord Esher recorded in his diary on September 27, 1908 that the British statesman, Sir Edward Grey, after many years' experience in dealing with the Kaiser, had become convinced that Wilhelm's diversity was a sign not of strength but of emotional weakness. Grey, Esher wrote,

> is not an admirer of the German Emperor. He thinks him not quite sane, and very superficial. This has always been my view. That he is picturesque and has a certain gift for language is true, but he is not a consistent or persistent thinker.[45]

As with so many other features of the Kaiser's personality, the diversity that enhanced his symbolic leadership contributed to the ineffectiveness of his political leadership by working to dissipate his energies, divide his attention, and encourage his inconsistency.

In considering the Kaiser's leadership, attention has been focused on the communication between Wilhelm and the Germans. Wilhelm, it has been argued, was not an effective political leader, a leader able to set an independent course and, through the power of his ideas and the influence of his political activity, to bring the nation into step behind him. Rather, what is significant about the Kaiser, and indeed marks his place in history, was his ability to sense vague, inchoate popular emotions, to experience them intensely himself, and to reflect them back to his subjects in a comprehensible and exalted form. In a way, one could describe the Kaiser's effective leadership as more a "followership" of sorts. There was, however, a significant transformation of popular feeling, an articulation and glorification of popular feeling, that makes "leadership" the appropriate characterization. In mirroring the nation, the Kaiser presented the Germans with a defined and enlarged image of themselves. The essence of this process of leadership, then, consisted of Wilhelm's capacity to experience and express popular feelings. Because it was primarily through symbols that the Kaiser communicated emotions in a concrete and broadly recognizable form, the term "symbolic leadership" has been chosen to define this process.

As was the case with Wilhelm's appreciation of the increasing significance of public opinion and press, his appreciation of the impact of symbols on popular feeling was a consequence of the impact that symbols had on him personally. In fact it would appear that for the Kaiser, symbols were not symbols at all. To him they were real—tangible and enduring expressions of feeling that could fulfill his need for constant reassurance. On a personal level, the many honors and titles he bestowed on others and that were bestowed on him were not mere formalities to the Kaiser. They were statements of direct appreciation and recognition. Politically, the state visits and the obligatory decorations and tributes exchanged between heads of state were not mere representations of the underlying state of relations between countries—relations ultimately determined by rational self-interest. For Wilhelm, they seemed at times in and of themselves determinants of the state of relations between countries.

As was the case with his preoccupation with public opinion and the press, Wilhelm's advisers could not understand the vast importance he attributed to what seemed to them to be insignificant symbolic gestures. Bülow, for example, criticized the Kaiser for his tendency "to regard banal civilities and empty phrases as material successes of political consequence."[46] Wilhelm reacted with intense pleasure to such formal honors as being named Admiral of the Fleet in both the Russian and the British navies. To him, these were not honorary titles, but actual commissions carrying great political and military significance. After Queen Victoria had made the Kaiser an admiral in her navy in 1889, he told Bismarck that "he now had the opportunity and right to intervene directly in the construction, organization, and administration of the English Fleet."[47] And intervene the Kaiser did—to the dismay of his advisers and to the indignation of the British.[48] Wilhelm's interventions, although designed to reduce tension, usually had the opposite effect, like that produced by his letter to the First Lord of the British Admiralty, Lord Tweedmouth, in February 1908. At the critical moment during the heated Anglo-German naval rivalry, when the British Admiralty was about to submit its estimates on the rate of German naval development to Parliament as part of its consideration of the naval budget, the Kaiser, in a private letter, sought to assure Lord Tweedmouth that Germany intended no challenge to British naval supremacy. He complained that the admiralty's estimates about the German navy as they had been reported in the papers were erroneous, and he justified his direct involvement in this sensitive matter by virtue of the fact that his letter was written "by one who is proud to wear the British Naval Uniform of an Admiral of the Fleet, which was conferred on him by the late great Queen of blessed memory."[49] As rumors of the existence of Wilhelm's letter began to sweep England, the British press reacted with anger and suspicion. The *Times* editorialized:

> if there was any doubt before about the meaning of the German naval expansion, none can remain after an attempt of this kind to influence the minister responsible for our navy in a direction favourable to German interests, an attempt, in other words, to make it more easy for German preparations to overtake our own.

The article concluded:

> If the complimentary title of Admiral of the Fleet is held to warrant a foreign Potentate in interfering in our domestic affairs by secret appeals to the head of a department on which the national safety depends, the abolition of dynastic compliments of this kind is an urgent necessity.[50]

When the German ambassador in London, Count Metternich, reported the British outrage at the letter to Berlin and expressed his concern that it would increase the mistrust and tension between the two countries, the Kaiser reacted with disblief. "I do not share Metternich's fears," he wrote in the margin of the ambassador's telegram. "The English have not yet become so totally crazy." The *Times'* editorial he could only attribute to the machinations of his uncle, Edward VII, "who is worried that the letter makes such a calming impression."[51]

Even when played out on a political stage, Wilhelm's independent actions contained emotional messages expressed in grand symbolic form. His messianically-tinged journey to the Holy Land in late 1898, his romantically brutal "Hun" speech to the German troops embarking for China during the Boxer Rebellion in 1900, his dramatic alliance with the Czar signed at Björkö in 1905, are all examples of the kind of theatrical epics enacted by the Kaiser which, although serving ostensibly rational political purposes, conveyed an emotional message of mythic grandeur. The political significance of these actions was usually limited to the negative reaction that they produced as the Kaiser's ostentatious dem-

FIGURE 2. Flanked by heralds, the Kaiser crosses the Marienplatz to the Rathaus in Munich.

onstrations of German cultural, diplomatic, or military authority were viewed with alarm and annoyance in foreign capitals. Psychologically, these essentially symbolic actions can be understood on several levels. In the first place, they can be regarded as having served a defensive purpose for Wilhelm. The heroic journeys, the bellicose statements, the bold political initiatives, were from this perspective attempts to mask Wilhelm's chronic insecurity. This, at least, was Bülow's interpretation. "The Kaiser," he wrote in his memoirs, "through loud speeches and strong words sought to deceive others and himself about his inner uncertainty and anxiousness."[52] Secondly, it can be argued that Wilhelm simply lacked the unity of purpose necessary to formulate and consistently carry out clear-cut policies. He did not possess the inner strength to tolerate the tension and uncertainty that accompany the steady and cautious realization of distant political objectives. The Kaiser could only produce sudden bursts of dramatic action designed to effect immediate political change. Finally, it seems likely that on the deepest level these symbolic gestures were yet another manifestation of Wilhelm's driven need for external recognition and appreciation. The dramatic political displays were designed to attract attention and to elicit admiration; they were meant to be awe inspiring. When these actions were not understood or well received, Wilhelm reacted with surprise, anxiety, and depression. After the Björkö Treaty was effectively scuttled by both the Russian and German governments (each recognizing that the treaty was simply not compatible with either Russian or German national self-interest), Wilhelm appeared on the verge of a nervous breakdown. Instead of the acclaim he had expected, he felt humiliated by the treaty's repudiation.[53]

"Fundamentally, the populace *wished* to see itself represented in a proud and magnificent fashion," Thomas Mann wrote in 1905 of the relationship between ruler and subject in his allegorical critique of Wilhelmine Germany, *Königliche Hoheit*.[54] Indeed, it seems clear that in the grandeur of the Kaiser's symbolic leadership a widespread yearning for a sense of national greatness found effective expression. Determining popular attitudes, feelings, and opinions about events, ideas, or individuals is one of the historian's most important tasks. Unfortunately it is a task invariably undertaken with some trepidation, scholarly misgivings, and insecurity. Because of the vital historical importance of this task, however, the historian is obliged to make statements about the popular mood, even with the knowledge that these will be necessarily speculative and tentative and subject to the criticism of colleagues. It is, needless to say, impossible, given present historical methods and the available evidence, to determine scientifically just what the Germans' response to Wilhelm II might have been. Lacking quantitative measures of the popular mood, surveys, or opinion polls, the historian is forced to rely upon qualitative evidence, upon the comments of perceptive contemporary observers, to get a sense of what the Germans thought and felt about their Kaiser.

Clearly, it is impossible to draw general conclusions about the Germans' attitudes, feelings, and opinions about Wilhelm without being subject to a host of legitimate historical criticisms. Specifically, with some notable exceptions, the views of the Kaiser's contemporaries quoted in this article reflect the views of the Prussian establishment, the literati, and the German bourgeosie. Socialists and other political radicals, Jews, and some South Germans had a very different view of Wilhelm II than, say, Thomas Mann or Friedrich Meinecke.[55] Nonetheless, despite the fact that every historical generalization is inevitably a distorted, indeed inaccurate, oversimplified, and limited characterization of the past, such generalizations can also contain a measure of historical truth. As long as these distortions, inaccuracies, oversimplifications, and limitations are acknowledged, there is a place in historical scholarship for the general statement. In the first place, there is ample qualitative evidence (some of which will be cited in the following pages), evidence drawn from both the Kaiser's supporters and detractors, to suggest that for much of his reign Wilhelm II enjoyed significant popularity among large sections of the German population. Furthermore, those observers cited in this article wrote not only as representatives of a specific party, class, or region of the country, but also as Germans. Thus, although opinions about Wilhelm II during the course of his reign differed widely in different parts of Germany and in different segments of German society, there was, one senses but cannot of course prove, an underlying feeling in Germany, experienced by most Germans at one time or another—often against their better judgment—a feeling of proud identification with the heroic image of the German Kaiser. No matter how much they may have detested him as a political leader or disliked him as a man, as the personal symbol of the German nation, Wilhelm II could evoke widespread and intense popular enthusiasm.

Despite the limited political benefit of Wilhelm's symbolic actions, despite their having exposed him to the risk of shattering disappointment, there is ample qualitative evidence to suggest that the Kaiser's emotional message of pride and magnificence was fundamentally in tune with the wishes of many of his countrymen. The sumptuous banquets, the memorable state visits, the impressive parades, the imposing military maneuvers, the decorations and uniforms, all conveyed the simple message of national power and glory the Germans readily understood and appreciated. The spectacular journeys, the fiery speeches, the dramatic diplomatic initiatives all proclaimed to the applause of the enthusiastic nation the importance of Germany's place in the world. Although ill-advised politically, an emotional gesture like the Krüger telegram was extraordinarily popular in Germany. Even a seasoned diplomat like the Prussian minister in Munich, Count Anton von Monts, despite his criticism of nearly everything else about the Kaiser's reign, could write to Bülow one month later: "The only thing that is going well is our foreign policy. The Krüger telegram has my complete approval. If only one doesn't back down."[56] Wilhelm's sense of triumphant satisfaction at the English defeat by the Boers was shared by Monts and many other Germans. Feeling themselves treated with insufficient respect by the British and envious of Britain's mighty empire, the Kaiser and his subjects appear to have identified on some level with the tiny Boer Republic's act of heroic defiance. Wilhelm's telegram to President Krüger gave dramatic expression to this identification with the Boers. It was a symbolic act of emotional defiance of the British paralleling the Boer's military defeat of Jameson's raiders.

If the Germans were a selfobject for the Kaiser, it seems evident by the same token that the Kaiser was a selfobject for the Germans. In an age of nationalism, Wilhelm became a personification of the German nation; he was experienced by his subjects as their representative, as an embodiment of their ideals and aspirations. As Ludwig Thoma, a leading South German liberal and co-founder of the journal *März*, recognized, Wilhelm's glorification of himself served to affirm the glory of his countrymen. Thoma wrote, in 1908:

> It was precisely the remarkable penchant for the operatic that brought our loyal citizenry to see in Wilhelm II the embodiment of its ideal. What epic emotions were unleashed by the monarch's every pleasure cruise. What lyricisms have been written and spoken when he did nothing more than participate in a parade. There was no room for sobriety and nothing could occur in silence. Even the simplest thing took place in a Bengal light. The imagination of the bourgeosie was inspired and aroused daily by the personality of the Kaiser. In every popular court of judgement on him, Wilhelm never found himself opposed, even in those places where he actively searched for opposition.[57]

Through his personality and symbolic actions, the Kaiser held a mirror up to the Germans in which an image of themselves was reflected larger than life. It was for the most part an image they very much wanted to see.

There is one further aspect of Wilhelm's personality which must be considered in the context of the Kaiser's leadership of the Germans: namely, his tendency, described by Eulenburg in 1903 in a letter to Bülow, "to regard and evaluate *all* things and *all* people solely from a personal point of view." Because of his dependence on the responses of his environment, Wilhelm experienced as a personal reaction to himself what to an outside observer might seem an event utterly unrelated to the Kaiser. In the words of Eulenburg's letter to Bülow: "Objectivity is lost completely, and subjectivity rides on a biting and stamping charger." When, Eulenburg continued, news of the failure of the German South Pole expedition arrived, Wilhelm became enraged. "With his tendency to take everything personally, the poor man experiences this expedition as an *insult*."[58]

The Kaiser's rearing subjectivity led him to take a personal view of political life, and, specifically, to understand politics largely in terms of personalities. In part because of their personal authority, in part because of their impact on public opinion, Wilhelm believed other leaders, and especially other sovereigns, to be politically decisive. The symbolism inherent in the Czar's visit to France in 1901, for example, seemed to Wilhelm to pose a much greater menace to Germany than did the formal alliance concluded between France and Russia some seven years before, and he demanded that more forts be built along the Rhine, that more garrisons be sent to Posen and West Prussia, and that the size of the navy be increased.[59]

Consistent with this personalized view of politics, Wilhelm regarded countries as if they were living, breathing, and, above all, emotional individuals. To the Kaiser, countries did not pursue policies determined by their rational self-interest; instead, they were "insulting," "proud," "cowardly," "adoring," etc. From this perspective, policies were organized expressions of feeling, and it was the role of the leader to pursue a course compatible not with the national interest but with the national character. In conducting foreign policy, the statesman was confronted with the difficult task of reconciling the feelings of his own people with the feelings of foreign peoples. In a discussion with Joseph Chamberlain in late November 1899, the Kaiser described the national character of the Germans and advised the British Colonial Minister on how best to deal with them. As Bülow reported the contents of this conversation to Holstein:

> His Majesty added that it would be to the advantage of the English to treat the sensitive, obstinate and rather sentimental Germans with caution, not to make them impatient, but to show them goodwill in little things. The German is "touchy." The more this fact is borne in mind on the English side, the more useful it will be for the relationship between the two countries.[60]

It is striking and significant that the Kaiser's description of his countrymen was also a description of himself. Indeed, there was a subtle blurring in Wilhelm's mind of the distinction between himself and the Germans. Thus, he experienced blows to German national pride as a blow to his own self-esteem. Upon learning that two German missionaries had been murdered in China in 1897, the Kaiser demanded reprisals "that, with total severity and if necessary with the most brutal disregard for the Chinese people, would finally demonstrate that the German Emperor will not allow himself to be trifled with and that it is ill-advised to have him as an enemy."[61] By the same token, Wilhelm experienced insults to himself as insults to the nation as a whole. He reacted to the possible cancellation of the Prince of Wales' visit to Germany in 1902—which, according to Bülow, he would regard "as a slight directed against Him personally"—by threatening "to recall the German ambassador in London."[62]

Ultimately, of course, it was the powerful current of nationalism—of the individual's definition of himself on the basis of the nation to which he belongs—that accounted for the Kaiser's having become, as a symbol of the nation, the focus of popular ambitions and ideals. Nevertheless, Wilhelm II, through his personality and behavior, increased substantially the extent to which he became the personal representative of the Germans. By presenting his subjects with an intensely personalized view of political life, a view that focused popular attention on individual and collective personalities, Wilhelm focused popular attention directly and by implication on his own personality. In his lack of psychological distinction between himself and his subjects, the Kaiser encouraged the Germans to regard him as the personification of their nation. Once again the message was simple, direct, and compelling: politics was essentially an expression of feelings. Again, it was a message his subjects readily understood and accepted. It is easier to consider politics in terms of the influence of an important individual and to consider the relations between states as if they had human personalities than it is to think of politics as the rational competition for subtle economic, diplomatic, or military advantage between value-neutral nation-states. The universal language of emotion is easier to comprehend than is the low-key, complex, and intellectual language of self-interest. Wilhelm II's effective communication of the language of emotion to his subjects can in part be attributed to the fact that it was his native tongue.

Wilhelm's personalization of politics, however, contributed directly to the reactive character of German foreign policy during his reign. Much of Wilhelm's "policy" can in fact be understood as a series of reactions to what he regarded as blows to his own and to his nation's fragile honor. The typical response to such an "insult" was an expression of vengeful anger followed by an effort to restore the self-esteem of Kaiser and country through some bold and dramatic action. When, for example, Wilhelm learned that his envoy in China, Klemens von Ketteler, had been killed during the Boxer Rebellion in June 1900, he demanded a joint European action against the Chinese. He insisted, however, that German troops play the leading role. "The German representative," he telegraphed the State Secretary in the Foreign Office, "will be avenged by my troops. Peking must be razed."[63] The news that the situation in China was being brought under control without any glorious German victories, indeed even before the German commander of the European forces had arrived on the scene, "completely upset His Majesty," according to Eulenburg. "He spoke in the strongest possible terms about Russia and England, who had 'betrayed' him, not even sparing his advisers," and finally demanded that Eulenburg "send a telegram to the Foreign Office ordering the immediate conclusion of a defensive and offensive alliance with Japan, a country which until that time he had held in the utmost contempt." It was only with difficulty that Eulenburg was able to persuade the Kaiser to drop the idea.[64] It seemed to Wilhelm that Germany had lost the opportunity to redeem its honor and restore its strength in the eyes of the world. Feeling exposed and threatened, he reacted with the impulsive desire to find a new ally to support and strengthen his country and himself.

Reflecting the personality of the Kaiser, German foreign policy throughout his reign was characterized by general passivity, punctuated by sudden, frantic bursts of activity. There was no long-range purpose or clear program. Foreign governments were never certain where the Kaiser stood or what he would be likely to do in the future. As a result, they came to mistrust and to fear him. Similarly, in internal affairs, the conduct of government was characterized by a series of crises, scandals, and sudden shifts in direction. This pattern of unpredictability, of successive upheavals on both the foreign and domestic fronts, can be attributed in part to Wilhelm's impulsive, anxious, dramatic reactivity. The Kaiser did not possess the inner consolidation necessary to define a cohesive self-interest either for himself or for his nation. Lacking inner direction and purpose, Wilhelm's course was determined by the buffeting seas around him. His old nemesis, Sir Edward Grey, proved to be prophetic when he wrote at the time of the *Daily Telegraph* affair:

> The German Emperor is ageing me; he is like a battleship with steam up and screws going, but with no rudder, and he will run into something one day and cause a catastrophe.[65]

WILHELM II'S SYMBOLIC LEADERSHIP OF THE GERMANS

In considering Wilhelmine Germany it is easy to overlook the fact that although the concept of "Germany" was old, Germany itself was not. By the time of Wilhelm's accession in June 1888, the German nation had been in existence a mere seventeen years. Without the benefit of a longstanding tradition of national cohesion, the country that Wilhelm led was still attempting to answer such basic questions as: What is Germany? How is it to be governed? Where does Germany fit in with the rest of the world? Not only did Germans have to come to terms with these existential issues relatively suddenly, but they were also confronted with the economic, social, political, and psychological dislocations and divisions brought on by the rapid industrialization that transformed Germany after 1871. As a result of these sudden and sweeping developments, Germans found themselves in profound disagreement over the nature of state and society. Tradition, rather than promoting consensus, tended in fact to promote disunity. Germany was an uncertain aggregate, containing numerous historical tensions that constantly threatened its cohesion. These included: tension between the forces of centralism and those of particularism (Germany was made up of twenty-five heterogeneous states); the heritage of the Prussian-Austrian dualism; tension between Prussian state militarism and the more liberal political tradition in the southern and western parts of the country; tension between authoritarian government and middle class constitutional aspirations; tension among diverse economic interests, tension between the agrarian East and the industrial West; tension between Protestantism and Catholicism; tension between the German majority and Polish, Danish, French, and Alsatian minorities; sharp divisions and antagonisms among various social classes and castes. Despite the conviction of most Germans that they belonged together in a political and psychological entity called Germany, the Reich was a very recent, unstable, and, to a degree, even an artifical creation.

The disjointed state of Wilhelm II's personality made him unusually sensitive to the question of the solidity and durability of German national unity, and he regarded it as his historic mission to increase the cohesion of the German Reich. Wilhelm's concern with national unity was not merely the result of his recognition of Germany's deep internal divisions. Nor was it simply an outgrowth of a general sensitivity to issues of cohesion and coherence. The question of German national unity was so important to the Kaiser because he did not distinguish psychologically between himself and the German nation. In the effort to promote the cohesion of his country, he increased his sense of personal integration; by warding off national fragmentation, he sought to prevent the fragmentation of his self.

As in other areas of his political activity, Wilhelm's promotion of national unity was largely symbolic. With his sensitivity to public opinion, the Kaiser was able to work on several levels to increase the Germans' sense that they belonged together. Recognizing that his subjects needed to have their national identity securely grounded in a sense of historical legitimacy, Wilhelm worked to establish a tradition of a German national monarchy that included the various existing monarchical traditions in a modern national context. The "modern kaiser" as understood and enacted by Wilhelm contained features of the medieval Hohenstaufens, Holy Roman Emperors, and Prussian Hohenzollerns. Nevertheless, in contrast to his grandfather, Wilhelm I, who regarded himself primarily as King of Prussia, and to his father, Friedrich III, who thought of the Imperial Monarchy in romantically medieval terms, Wilhelm, as he would stress over and over again, was first and foremost the *German* Emperor.[66] Where no German Imperial tradition existed, he attempted to create one by glorifying German military victories (against the French in 1870–71) and the "pantheon" of national heroes. Despite the fact that Wilhelm I had only reluctantly assumed the imperial crown and had been deeply averse to the subordination of his title of King of Prussia to the imperial title, his grandson glorified "Wilhelm the Great" as German Emperor. Occasions such as the centenary of Wilhelm I's birth were used to celebrate the German character of the reich and monarchy. Uncomprehending advisers like Chancellor Hohenlohe-Schillingsfürst argued that Wilhelm I's centenary was far less historically important than his accession to the Prussian throne. Wilhelm telegraphed back angrily on December 6, 1896:

> The celebration of the one hundredth anniversary of the birth of the first *German* Emperor of a *German* national Empire from the *German* House of Hohenzollern has a completely different significance for Germany and the whole world than does the coronation of the King of Prussia in 1861.[67]

By communicating to his subjects his sense of personal vulnerability to international "insults," Wilhelm contributed to the climate of anxious and indignant tension in Germany and to the popular perception that Germany was treated with disdain by the other European world powers who were systematically attempting to frustrate Germany's rightful world political ambitions. In no small measure because of the "touchy" and belligerent responses of the Kaiser to these perceived humiliations, Germany came to be viewed in many European capitals as the principal threat to world peace. As England drew steadily closer to France and Russia in their opposition to Germany, Wilhelm and his countrymen began to feel increasingly "encircled" by hostile powers. Although alarmed by Germany's growing international isolation, the Kaiser sought to use the anxiety of his subjects to bring them closer together. In speeches emphasizing the dangers inherent in Germany's geographical position[68] and the need to increase German military preparedness,[69] Wilhelm sought to rally his countrymen behind the defense of the nation's vulnerable independence. In part, the effort to win mass support for the German naval building program was designed to increase national cohesion. "The struggle for the fleet," Wilhelm was utterly convinced, was an ennobling, sustaining, nationally integrative enterprise: bringing together North and South, Protestant and Catholic, capitalist and worker, aristocrat and farmer. The navy was modern and liberal (the fleet had been a favorite liberal cause since 1848), in the economic interests of heavy industry and to a degree of the middle class as a whole. The navy was traditional and authoritarian: the arm of the absolutist-militarist state. Above all, however, the navy was national and monarchical-imperialist (*kaiserliche*). Wilhelm told the British Prime Minister, Arthur Balfour, in 1902:

> Whereas England forms a political totality complete unto itself, Germany resembles a mosaic in which the individual pieces are still clearly distinguishable and have not yet blended together. This is evidenced by the Army which, though inspired by the identical patriotic spirit, is still made up of contingents from the various German states. The young German Reich needs institutions in which the unitary idea of a Reich is embodied. The Navy is such an institution. The Kaiser is its only commander. The Germans from all counties trend toward it, and it is a constant living example of the unity of the Reich. For this reason alone it is necessary and finds a warm supporter in His Majesty.[70]

Ultimately, however, it was less what Wilhelm II did than what he was that made him such a powerful symbolic force for German national unity. As a more psychologically cohesive leader could not have done, the Kaiser was able to personify the often contradictory national aspirations of his countrymen. In what Eça de Queiroz described as his "variety of incarnations of Royalty," Wilhelm symbolically represented many different images of Germany which were only united in the national figure of the Kaiser. Specifically, Wilhelm saw it as his task to integrate for his people the conception of a "glorious past" and an autocratic system of government with mass industrial society. "I have been placed in an infinitely difficult period of history," he told Eulenburg in 1903, a period that requires "the reconciliation of traditional society with modern times."[71] The Kaiser dealt with this task by manifesting features of both past and present in his personality and behavior. The glorification of his Hohenzollern ancestors, the court galas, the monumentality of the Siegesallee in Berlin, the restoration of medieval castles, and the spectacular military parades and maneuvers all testified to Wilhelm's reverence for and rootedness in a romanticized past.[72] At the same time, he became the spokesman of his own Wilhelmine epoch. According to the four volume *Deutschland unter Kaiser Wilhelm II.*, published to celebrate Wilhelm's silver jubilee in 1913:

> In our Kaiser the spirit of the new era expresses itself and in the era the spirit of our Kaiser. No matter how stark the contradictions in the nation may be, how violently opinions may clash in parliament and among the people, it remains an unshakable fact that the Kaiser

and the vast majority of the German people are united behind the goals of the nation. And in many and perhaps in the most important areas it was the Kaiser who won the nation over to his point of view, who taught the nation to believe in his ideas. Precisely those events of epochal significance: the shift from purely continental policies to *Weltpolitik,* and directly related to this: the supplementation of German armed might on the land with the creation of a battle fleet, is based on the idea and determination of Kaiser Wilhelm II.

The author, F. W. von Loebell, insists further that in other areas of contemporary German life—in social, argicultural, commercial, industrial, transportational, artistic, archeological, scientific, technological, medical, and educational developments—the Kaiser had been the dynamic leading force. Von Loebell admits that it is difficult to ascribe these advances either to Wilhelm or to the German people. But, he concludes:

> No matter how diverse the achievements in the individual areas of national endeavor may be, the last 25 years have a special character, and that character could scarcely be more tellingly defined than with the name Kaiser Wilhelm II.[73]

Wilhelm saw nothing incongruous about wearing the traditional Prussian spiked helmet to the opening of a technical college in Breslau, and, even more significantly, neither did many of his countrymen. The German historian Friedrich Meinecke, who was not uncritical of the Kaiser, wrote also in 1913 that Wilhelm

> combines the intense actuality, the sharp purposefulness of the modern man with a glowing veneration of the national past. The grand figures and memories of his forebearers, his state, and his people are transfigured into colorful, gleaming symbols of lasting value. One who focuses on the individual features of his being tends to find a contradiction between his determined modernism and romantic traditionalism. In truth, his historical ideals and symbols are the spiritual tools he uses to inspire the energies of his contemporaries and to keep the surging flow of modern life within wholesome limits.[74]

Meinecke was mistaken. Wilhelm's features were in fact contradictory, and he was unable to reconcile the modern and the traditional. He was, however, able to incorporate elements of both in himself and to reflect them back to his subjects—integrated only insofar as they were fragments of the same disorganized personality.

Not only did the Kaiser's lack of self-cohesion enable him to embody the disparate aspirations of his countrymen, but his grandiose and exhibitionistic behavior tended to focus national attention on his person. Wilhelm's perpetual traveling, encountering spectacular receptions everywhere he went, and his countless speeches to enthusiastic audiences kept him constantly—either through the press or directly—in the public eye. As a figure continuously celebrated and attended to by a captivated nation, the Kaiser became the cynosure of nationalistic strivings, the brilliant symbol of a proud, glorious, and united Germany. Wilhelm himself recognized the intersection of his narcissistic needs and those of a people seeking to have their national cohesion affirmed through the "omnipresence" of their emperor.[75] In an interview with the author Ludwig Ganghofer, published in November 1906, Wilhelm praised the optimistic tone of Ganghofer's books and the virtues of an optimistic philosophy of life. "In politics it is no different," Ganghofer reported the Kaiser to say.

> The German people do indeed have a future, and there is a word that always hurts his feelings whenever he hears it: that word is *Reichsverdrossenheit* [weariness with the Reich]. What advantage is there to be had from *Verdrossenheit*? Better to work and be optimistic. I work without weariness [*unverdrossen*] and believe that I do in fact make progress.
>
> The Kaiser continued by describing in detail the ways and means in which he worked daily and how the profusion and weight of the duties and labors that storm over him are often exhausting. At such times the need always rises up in him to relax and again see a new part of the world, to again meet new people, who again are so stimulating. . . .
>
> The Kaiser described in lively and plastic detail how such a trip gradually has a calming and refreshing effect. . . ."Everything which oppresses Me is gone within a few weeks, and that which gives Me such pleasure other people take amiss frequently. I know that I am called the 'Reisekaiser,' but I have always regarded that as amusing. I don't allow that to take away My pleasure in the world. Travel allows one to make friends, especially in one's homeland. I believe that through travel the feeling of belonging together [*Zusammengehörigkeit*] is strengthened," and, he added, "many Germans do not know at all how beautiful our country is and how much there is to see of it. . . .Such refreshing trips are especially necessary in My serious profession, doubly necessary because one has to fight against many misunderstandings."[76]

From his interview with Ganghofer, one gets a sense of the enormous pressure—both external and internal—on Wilhelm II. Traveling both soothed the Kaiser and allowed him to overcome his underlying depression, the *Verdrossenheit* he was so anxious to deny and allay. The stimulation of new people and impressions restored a measure of psychological balance to the Kaiser and made him feel more internally cohesive. Traveling through Germany, exhibiting himself to his countrymen, increased not only the *Zusammengehörigkeit* of the Germans but that of Wilhelm II as well.

"The German," Wilhelm told Eulenburg in the summer of 1903, "wants to be led."[77] Although the Kaiser does appear to have been in touch with a deeply felt wish of many of his subjects for the autocratic leadership of a great man, it was, as has been discussed at some length, also extremely important psychologically for Wilhelm to appear absolutely sovereign to mask his chronic insecurity. Contemporaries, however, took Wilhelm at his word, and many—both inside and outside of Germany—believed him to be the single most powerful leader in the world. The charismatic and commanding Cecil Rhodes, for example, was fascinated by Wilhelm and recognized a kindred spirit in the Kaiser. After meeting Wilhelm in 1899 he wrote to the Prince of Wales: "the Emperor is really Germany, at least it appeared to me to be so when I was in Berlin, Ministers doing just what he desired and the Reichstag most docile."[78] Instead of appearing increasingly anachronistic, the German absolute monarchy seemed to grow ever more firmly rooted in the national soil, ever more bound up with the national destiny. For many Germans, the kaiserdom appeared to be an institution more of the future than of the past. Writing in 1900, in the psychologically significant first year of the new century, Friedrich Naumann observed:

> In present-day Germany there is no stronger force than the Kaiser. The very complaints of the anti-Kaiser democrats about the growth of personal absolutism are the best proof of this fact, for these complaints are not pure invention but are based on the repeated observation that all policy, foreign and internal, stems from the will and word of the Kaiser. No monarch of absolutist times ever had so much real power as the Kaiser has today. He does not achieve everything he wants, but it is still more than anybody would have believed possible in the middle of the last century. That century, whose middle years echoed with the dreams of a German republic, ended with more power in the Kaiser's hands than even Barbarossa possessed.[79]

The political reality of Wilhelm's sovereignty was rather more equivocal, however, and the historian of the period is confronted with the dilemma of reconciling a Kaiser who could be attacked in a contemporary pamphlet as a "Caligula," that bloodthirsty tyrant who had the audacity to appoint his horse Consul of Rome,[80] with a Kaiser who could feel himself "tyrannized" by his nearly eighty-year-old Chancellor

Hohenlohe-Schillingsfürst.[81] Historians have long debated the question of Wilhelm's "personal regime," and, as was stated at this chapter's outset, have until very recently tended to play down his actual political authority and significance. Within the limits of the present investigation it is not possible, of course, to provide anything approaching a definitive answer to this extraordinarily complex question.[82] Nevertheless, although in theory Wilhelm was an absolute monarch, as a result of his personality and the nature of his position, in practice his political influence was ill defined and seems in fact to have been rather limited. It would serve no useful purpose at this point to go over once again the various features of the Kaiser's personality that worked to reduce his political effectiveness. In general, it would appear that Wilhelm's impact on the political functioning of government was negative. The Kaiser's absolutist pretensions, his attempt to hold all the reins of power, meant in practice that Wilhelm could only capriciously interfere with the affairs of state. His ready reactive tendencies were exacerbated as, in his effort to stay in charge of everything, Wilhelm would shift his attention from one issue to the next. Unable to have knowledge in depth about those myriad areas over which he claimed authority, Wilhelm's absolutism often took the form of rather sullen and stubborn resistance to the plans and programs drawn up by those expert in the area in question. Many of his more impetuous orders were never issued, as his aides—recognizing their potentially catastrophic political impact—would delay sending them off until either the Kaiser's impulse had passed or he could be tactfully persuaded to change his mind. In general, Wilhelm's obstinacy interfered with the conduct of government since so much time and energy had to be expended in attempting to "manage" the Kaiser. Still, despite the difficulties involved, Wilhelm's advisers were usually successful at this task. By flattering the Kaiser into adopting their positions as his own or by threatening resignation, chancellors and ministers were in most instances able to get their way with Wilhelm. Even on those rare occasions when Wilhelm was able to formulate a clear political objective, he was not always able to overcome the opposition of those in the government. One of the most telling such examples of the Kaiser's political and personal weakness was his inability either to convince or to compel the chancellor and other top officials to accept the dismissal of Marschall von Bieberstein—a man whom Wilhelm despised—from his position as State Secretary in the foreign office for almost four years.

Although the Kaiser was far from being a forceful and dynamic political leader, it would be an error simply to dismiss the observations of Rhodes and Naumann. The "personal regime" was not a historically meaningless illusion; it was an emotional and symbolic reality. As the personification of the German nation, as the focus of national pride and popular aspirations, Wilhelm II was truly sovereign. Wilhelm, himself, was certainly aware that as a leader in an age of mass political participation he wielded enormous emotional authority. He wrote to Nicholas II during the waning days of the Russo-Japanese War urging his beleaguered fellow-autocrat to exercise the vast symbolic power at his disposal to mobilize the Russian people and save his crown. "Take your place at the head of your armed forces," the Kaiser told the Czar.

> The European Public as well as the Russian Nation is instinctively looking toward the Zar, and expecting that he will come forth and do something grandly, a great personal act; meant to show that he is the Absolute Ruler of his People and willing to allay their anxieties and pains as far as is in his power.[83]

By communicating symbolically with his subjects, the modern emperor had the ability to mobilize the powerful narcissistic (selfobject) bond connecting him with his countrymen. It was this bond that gave a leader his enormous emotional authority, the authority to save a tottering dynasty, to decide the issue of military victory or defeat. For Wilhelm, at least, his symbolic authority seemed to be of greater consequence than the political authority at his command. And indeed in our modern world, the ability of a leader to achieve the emotional mobilization of his nation may perhaps be even more important than the ability to determine who will be the Secretary of State.

Once again, there appears to have been an intersection between Wilhelm's narcissistic needs and those of his countrymen. On the basis of his own driven personal agenda and his sensitivity to the wishes of his subjects, the Kaiser sought to focus attention on himself as a symbol of national strength and cohesion. The royal "standard waves high in the breeze," he wrote his mother in 1898,

> comforting every anxious look cast upwards; the Crown sends its rays "by the grace of God" into Palace and hut, and—pardon me if I say so—Europe and the world listen to hear, "what does the German Emperor say or think".[84]

Through a shared subjugation to and identification with the Kaiser, Germans were to develop a national group identity bridging social divisions. "*Everyone*, without class distinction," Wilhelm told Eulenburg,

> should stand behind me, should fight beside me for the interests of the Fatherland! No matter what class they belong to. . . . On me, no one exerts any influence; and no one will be permitted to exert any influence on me. *I* am to command.[85]

Not only did Wilhelm's assertion of absolute sovereignty bind Germans together by virtue of the fact that all were subject to his authority—that all, in his words, stood *behind* him—but also, through their shared identification with the grand and imposing figure of the Kaiser—through their sense of fighting *beside* him—Germans experienced their own grandiose fantasies about themselves played out on the stage of world history. As was the case with Wilhelm's need to appear to know everything (the Kaiser's omniscience) and be everywhere (the Kaiser's omnipresence), so too was his need to appear omnipotent fundamentally in tune with the need of many Germans to feel themselves defined and represented by a powerful leader who was firmly in control of the national destiny. As Elisabeth Fehrenbach has written, the Germans, lacking a long established tradition of nationhood, came to see Wilhelm II as the embodiment of "the whole spiritual personality of the nation."[86] But, Fehrenbach continues:

> The Kaiser only became the visible and real symbol of the nation-state by virtue of his personal conspicuousness. The identification of the monarch with the nation was not, it is true, manifested in relation to the Reichstag which, owing to constitutional impediments to parliamentary government and the consequent perception which the parties had of their role, was seen more as a forum for the representation of vested interests than the expression of national unity. This identification occurred as a result of the personalization of the image of the Kaiser in "Wilhelminism." The Kaiser made possible the escape from the labyrinths of mass society; he concentrated people's gaze on the great man, the gifted individual, the embodiment of an historical mission.[87]

According to Maximilian Harden, editor of *Die Zukunft* and one of Wilhelm II's fiercest and most effective opponents, "enlightened" critics of the Kaiser were prepared to tolerate his erratic and impulsive conduct in return for the benefits Germany derived from the fact that "the Kaiser is his own Chancellor."

> All the important political decisions of the past twelve years have been made by him. Changes in trade policy, the build-up of the fleet, the belief in the German Reich achieving *Weltmacht* on an enormous scale, the friendly relations and secret treaties with England, the military campaign in China, all that and a lot more besides is his work. His objectives have been correct almost without exception, but his chosen ways and means have been unfortunate.[88]

In general, even the most committed adversaries of Wilhelm II tended to direct their criticism at the Kaiser's methods rather than at his goals.[89] It would be difficult, however, to characterize the goals of Wilhelm II's leadership (including those cited above by Harden in *Die Zukunft*) as being circumscribed political objectives in the Bismarckian sense of the term.[90] On sober historical reflection, these objectives were not based upon a clear appreciation of Germany's rational self-interest. They were almost all expressions of Germany's fundamental foreign political ambition before the First World War to practice *Weltpolitik*, expressions of the essentially emotional wish that Germany take its rightful place in the world, that it be accorded the international respect that a proud and powerful nation deserved. Harden's "enlightened" critics were correct in attributing these "objectives" to the Kaiser. As has been argued here, Wilhelm's disunity and uncertainty drove him to demand that he be recognized, appreciated, and respected. This goal ultimately formed the basis for his leadership of the Germans. He told Eulenburg in 1903:

> I have never thought about autocracy, but I have long ago made my program of *how* I wanted to be German Kaiser, how I conceived of the German Kaiser: Deep into the most distant jungles of other parts of the world, everyone should know the voice of the German Kaiser. *Nothing* should occur on this earth without having first heard him. His word must have its weight placed on every scale. Well—and I think I have generally held to my program! Also domestically the word of the Kaiser should be *everything*.[91]

The program for the man had become fused with the program for the nation. Internally, the national voice of the Kaiser, it was hoped, would submerge the discordant babble of German voices all speaking at once on behalf of their own narrow interests. It was *Weltpolitik* that provided the principal escape from the domestic din. In this fragmented country, in this recently and insecurely consolidated nation, the emotional goal that the voice of Germany, of the German Kaiser, be listened to throughout the world was perhaps the only goal that most Germans could enthusiastically agree upon.

THE KAISER IN PSYCHOHISTORICAL PERSPECTIVE

After the First World War a number of psychiatric studies were published purporting to demonstrate scientifically that Wilhelm II was mentally ill. *Wilhelm II.: Versuch einer psychologischen Analyse* (Halle, 1919) by Adolf Friedländer is typical of these attempts to diagnose the Kaiser.[92] The author finds that Wilhelm "shows all the indications of overbreeding [*Hochzüchtung*, in the sense of inbreeding] and degeneration."[93] Friedländer continues: "Wilhelm II reveals himself to us . . . as a personality in which the positive and negative hereditary characteristics of his ancestors are present in greatly intensified form."[94] Friedländer's study, like the others published in the aftermath of a bitter defeat, attributes Wilhelm's erratic and extreme behavior to breeding. These studies all share the implicit assumption that part of the blame for the German defeat can be traced to the unstable conduct of the Kaiser, which in turn was a direct result of his hypomania of genetic origin. In the psychiatrist Paul Tesdorpf's *Die Krankheit Wilhelms II* (Munich, 1919), the connection between Wilhelm's "illness" and Germany's loss of the war is made explicitly. "We Germans have lost nothing of our honor and inner greatness. We have emerged internally victorious from this struggle." The author appears to absolve the German people from responsibility for the defeat by attributing it to the Kaiser's sickness:

> The government of Wilhelm II was spurious. It had to collapse. What was to blame for this spuriousness? Was it his will? His will was perhaps noble and pure. But he was sick, sick, as were his thoughts and emotions. . . . For the experienced physician and psychiatrist there can be no doubt that Wilhelm II, already as a youth was mentally ill. . . . The blame for the war which can be attributed to him was the result of this illness.[95]

All the evidence, Tesdorpf concludes, "leads to the natural conclusion that Wilhelm II presents a typical picture of hereditary psychic degeneration."[96]

There are in fact indications that Wilhelm may have had a hereditary predisposition to hypomania, and it is likely that he suffered from congenital hyperactivity.[97] The diagnoses of Friedländer, Tesdorpf, and their colleagues doubtless represent honest efforts to come to terms with a puzzling—and to them historically decisive—personality. Nevertheless, like the veiled ascription of the German defeat to Wilhelm's psychopathology, it seems clear that a diagnosis of inherited "degeneracy" would have suited the needs of many Germans to distance themselves from their Kaiser after 1919. Sigmund Freud, writing in the summer of 1906, noted that such a diagnosis can often be secretly reassuring to us. In his discussion of Wilhelm Jensen's novella *Gradiva: A Pompeiian Fancy*, Freud asserts that because the hero of the novella, a young archaeologist, had developed a delusion about an antique bas-relief of a young woman, an old-school psychiatrist

> would at once stamp him as a *dégénéré* and would investigate the heredity which had remorselessly driven him to this fate. But here the author [Jensen] does not follow the psychiatrist, and with good reason. He wishes to bring the hero closer to us so as to make "empathy" easier; the diagnosis of *dégénéré*, whether it is right or

wrong, at once puts the young archaeologist at a distance from us, for we readers are the normal people and the standard of human- ity.[98]

Although Freud recognized that the diagnosis of hereditary degen- eracy enables us to deny our sense of essential emotional kinship, our empathic bond, with those suffering from psychological disorders, he himself was not immune to the attraction of a popularly held view of the Kaiser that served to increase the distance between the Germans and their leader in defeat. Freud was moved to comment on Wilhelm II's psychopathology by Emil Ludwig's biography *Wilhelm Hohenzollern: The Last of the Kaisers*, which originally appeared in Germany in 1926. For Ludwig, Wilhelm's withered left arm—the result of a birth injury— provided the key to his character:

> Only those who can appreciate this lifelong struggle against the congenital weakness will be fair to him when the future Emperor is seen to strain too far or lose, his nervous energy. The perpetual struggle with a defect which every newcomer must instantly per- ceive and he, for that very reason, the more ostentatiously ignore— this hourly, lifelong effort to conceal a congenital, in no way re- pulsive, stigma of Nature, was the decisive factor in the develop- ment of his character. The weakling sought to emphasize his strength; but instead of doing so intelligently, as his lively intel- ligence would have permitted, tradition and vainglory urged him to the exhibition of an heroic, that is to say a soldierly personality.[99]

Wilhelm's blustering bellicosity and inner weakness are directly at- tributable to his birth defect, according to Ludwig. Indeed, it is implied that a measure of responsibility for both the war and the German defeat can be traced to this "stigma of Nature." The huge success of Ludwig's biography did much to focus attention on the Kaiser's withered arm as a way to understand his personality. It seems likely, in fact, that Ludwig articulated a widely held belief in Germany that attributed the failings and failures of the Kaiser to his physical defect—a defect perhaps the product, according to one popular version of Wilhelm's difficult deliv- ery, of the doctor's having devoted his attention more to the English mother than to her German son. The popularity of Ludwig's biography was such that it came to Freud's attention. Freud invoked it in his "New Introductory Lectures on Psychoanalysis" in 1932 during the course of his efforts to refute Alfred Adler's theory of the inferiority complex. Specifically, Freud criticized Ludwig for having

> ventured on an attempt to erect the whole of the development of his hero's character on the sense of inferiority which must have been

called up by his physical defect. In doing so, he has overlooked one small but not insignificant fact. It is usual for mothers whom Fate has presented with a child who is sickly or otherwise at a disadvantage to try to compensate him for his unfair handicap by a superabundance of love. In the instance before us, the proud mother behaved otherwise; she withdrew her love from the child on account of his infirmity. When he had grown up into a man of great power, he proved unambiguously by his actions that he had never forgiven his mother [in his hostility to her English homeland]. When you consider the importance of a mother's love for the mental life of a child, you will no doubt make a tacit correction of the biographer's inferiority theory.[100]

Freud's interpretation of Wilhelm's psychopathology is important and deserves serious consideration.[101] The subtle shift in emphasis away from Adler-Ludwig's point of view beautifully captures the revolution that Freud brought about in our understanding of human beings. Not the defect of nature by itself, but rather the environment's response to it, is psychologically significant. Nonetheless, Freud has not been able to escape a popular view of the Kaiser in which Germans had an unconscious investment. Freud's interpretation of Wilhelm, while accurate to a degree, is based upon an understanding of the Kaiser derived from the needs of German nationalistic pride, an understanding which again directs responsibility for the Kaiser's psychopathology, for his bellicosity toward Britain, for the lost war, away from Germany, an understanding which attributes Wilhelm II's failings and failures not to his weak and distant German father (or to any other Germans who played a role in Wilhelm's upbringing) but solely to the unempathic responses of the foreign English princess who was his mother.

The diagnoses of the Kaiser suggested by Friedländer, Tesdorpf, Ludwig, and Freud, although explaining circumscribed aspects of the Kaiser's psychopathology, offer a one-sided and convenient picture of his personality and behavior. The continuing popularity of these diagnoses of Wilhelm reflects not only the accuracy of such appraisals, but also their emotional appeal to Germans after the war. By attributing Wilhelm's difficulties to his breeding, his physical deformity, and his English mother, Germans were able to deny their emotional kinship with their Kaiser, their part in influencing and contributing to his actions, and their measure of responsibility for the catastrophe. In the aftermath of a profoundly humiliating defeat, Wilhelm II was made a scapegoat, the target of Germany's own sense of ignominy and helpless anger. In exile in Holland, Wilhelm II in a paradoxical way continued to personify the feelings of Germans about themselves. Now he was not the emodiment of national strength and greatness, but the symbol of national weakness and shame. In a psychological sense, however, the "personal regime" can be said to have continued.

In contrast to the diagnoses of Friedländer, Tesdorpf, Ludwig, and Freud, the view of the Kaiser presented in this article makes a direct connection between Wilhelm's personality and behavior and the needs and wishes of his subjects. Of course the German people were not the cause of Wilhelm's narcissistic psychopathology. His parents and other important caretakers during the Kaiser's childhood, as well as physical and constitutional factors, must bear ultimate responsibility for that. Nonetheless, as a result of the specific nature of his psychopathology, the German nation came to play an important role in determining and directing his attitudes and actions. The weakness and disharmony of Wilhelm's self made it necessary for him to rely on his environment—on selfobjects—to supply him with external support and emotional sustenance. The German nation was such a selfobject for the Kaiser. Without a firmly consolidated inner program of action or set of guiding ideals, he came to base himself to a significant extent on the ambitions and values of his countrymen. Impelled by a desperate eagerness to please and to find external confirmation, Wilhelm was exquisitely sensitive to the responses of his environment, part of which was public opinion as it was reflected in the press. His extraordinary flexibility, the product of his inner disorganization, enabled him to resonate with disparate segments of German society and generally to assume the roles he sensed that his subjects wished him to play.

The connection between Wilhelm II's disjointed personality and the Germans went beyond his ability to recognize the often contradictory and fluctuating popular mood and to adapt himself to it. There can be little doubt that other manifestations of his narcissistic psychopathology were fundamentally in tune with the needs of his subjects. The Kaiser's restless search for admiration and affirmation, his driven need to exhibit himself and his accomplishments, his need to be constantly in the public eye, served to focus the attention of the nation on his person. Often literally donning the garb of a heroic leader, to cover his inner fearfulness, Wilhelm provided his countrymen with a grand and noble figure with whom to identify and around whom the nation could coalesce. His brittle defensive facade of personal absolutism fulfilled the need of many Germans to have a powerful and independent sovereign, a ruler with perhaps a world-historical mission. In the field of foreign policy, Wilhelm's anxious and belligerent insistence that he be listened to and treated with respect paralleled the widespread sense that Germany was entitled to take its place as a world imperial power. Finally, Wilhelm's inner disharmony, his yearning for increased personal cohesion, led him to be particularly sensitive to the issue of German unity and to take steps to promote the consolidation of his young and, in many ways, incoherent nation.

Although Wilhelm's self-pathology allowed him to function effectively as a symbol of the nation and even to be responsive to the emotional needs of his subjects, the Kaiser's central structural weakness and disjointedness made him a singularly ineffective politician. Here, the manifestations of his narcissistic psychopathology—his impressionability, his labile dependence on others to supply him with ideals and directions (on selfobjects that supplied him with conflicting ideals and impelled him in different directions), his tendency to understand and respond to everything personally, his extreme vulnerability, his inability to tolerate criticism or take advice, his impulsive emotionality and reactive character, his lack of diligence and persistence—all prevented him from being able to chart and maintain a steady course. It would be a mistake, however, to assume that because of his political ineffectiveness the Kaiser was politically inconsequential. In domestic affairs, his influence was mostly negative in the sense that his capriciousness and constant meddling interfered with the consistent conduct of government. In foreign affairs, his political impact was even more deleterious. Wilhelm's precipitous shifts in direction and his flamboyant reactive bellicosity alarmed a watching world and contributed directly to Germany's ultimate diplomatic and military isolation. Wilhelm's inability to define a personal self-interest, to decide who he was and what he wanted, found political expression in his inability to determine the self-interest of the nation and to take steps to realize it. In sum, the very psychological incoherence that accounted for the success of the Kaiser's symbolic leadership of the Germans also accounted for his failure as the political leader of his country.

Although we shall never know whether a more psychologically cohesive leader could have created a truly cohesive German national self-interest, it is clear that the Kaiser personified the German nation not only through his effective symbolic leadership, but also by virtue of his very political incompetence. As a total personality, in other words, Wilhelm II characterized a nation and a historical epoch. There is a striking psychological and historical parallel between this youthful, energetic emperor whose internal psychic disjointedness prevented him from defining a coherent personal self-interest and the newly formed, dynamic nation whose economic, social, regional, political, and intellectual disjointedness seems to have precluded the definition and realization of a national self-interest. There is a striking psychohistorical fit between an emperor who covered his profound inner disharmony with a layer of flamboyant, provocative, and even bellicose self-aggrandizement and a nation that covered its profound lack of domestic consensus with a foreign policy of *Weltpolitik*—a policy of flamboyant, provocative, and even bellicose national self-assertion. Both Wilhelm and Germany during his reign sought to escape from internal contradictions with a *Flucht nach vorn*, a "flight to the front." According to a number of thoughtful contemporary observers, the Kaiser as a total personality reflected the "personality" of his countrymen and of his times. Egon Friedell wrote in 1927:

> Wilhelm the Second did in one sense actually fulfill the task of a king completely in that he almost always was the expression of the overwhelming majority of his subjects, the champion and executor of their ideas, the representative of their outlook on life. Most Germans were nothing more than pocket editions, smaller versions, miniature copies of Kaiser Wilhelm.[102]

In his successes and failures, Wilhelm II represented the successes and failures of his countrymen. In their adulation of the Kaiser and in their irritation with him, the Germans were expressing in part their feelings about themselves. As Elisabeth Fehrenbach has written, "criticism of [Wilhelm's] personal rule was usually in evidence when the fiction of the glorious Kaiser threatened to crumble."[103] On the one hand, Wilhelm was criticized when he failed to live up to the idealized expectations of his subjects—when he was unable to realize their glorified image of themselves and of their country. Wilhelm's shortcomings frustrated the wish of many Germans to be led and represented by a monarch who was omnipresent, omniscient, and omnipotent. On the other hand, as was clearly revealed by the reaction of the Germans to Wilhelm after the war, the Kaiser was most bitterly condemned when he personally manifested those features of his countrymen of which they themselves were most ashamed. Wilhelm was adored when he reflected back an image of German national greatness. He was reviled when he reflected back an image of German national disharmony, ineffectuality, and weakness. In their reactions to the Kaiser, the Germans were on some level reacting to an image of themselves.

It is tempting at this point to speculate about the narcissistic disturbance of the Kaiser as a definition of the narcissistic psychopathology of a nation, of a people, and of an era. Despite the host of psychological and historical problems with such generalizations, Nicolaus Sombart's judgment on the relationship between Wilhelm and the Germans should not simply be dismissed out of hand:

> If one wishes to label Wilhelm II as a psychopath, to charge him with Caesarian madness, this conclusion is only correct insofar as the

psychopathological features of the age found precise expression in the figure of the Kaiser. Every society has not only the government it deserves but also the systems of insanity and representative psychopathological figures.[104]

These fascinating and complex issues lie at present on the border of our historical and psychological knowledge. What can be said with confidence today only echoes the voices from Wilhelm's own time, the voices of Walter Rathenau and Friedrich Naumann quoted at the outset of this article. Wilhelmine Germany could hardly have had a more fitting Kaiser than Wilhelm II. Both as a leader and as a man, Wilhelm II was indeed the "mirror image" of his nation. Herein lies his principal historical significance.

ACKNOWLEDGEMENTS

This essay owes its inspiration and many of its conclusions to a lengthy and intense collaboration with an experienced psychoanalyst, Dr. Nathaniel London, and to the Kaiser Colloquium, a gathering of Kaiser Wilhelm II scholars on the island of Corfu in September 1979. The spirit of that meeting on Corfu is captured by an article on the Kaiser Colloquium by Jost Nolte in *Die Zeit Magazin* of 26 October 1979 entitled "Der Kaiser, der ein Spiegel seines Volkes war" (a title very similar to that of this article) and by the book *Kaiser Wilhelm II: New Interpretations* edited by John C. G. Röhl and Nicolaus Sombart (Cambridge, 1982), which contains the papers presented on Corfu. To Dr. London and the members of the Kaiser Colloquium this article is affectionately and gratefully dedicated. I also want to thank Otto Pflanze Lamar Cecil, and Robert G. L. Waite for their help in preparing this article for publication, as well as the Fund which provided for the typing of this article and the Department of Psychiatry of Michael Reese Hospital and Medical Center for help provided in preparation of this manuscript.

NOTES

1. Friedrich Naumann, "Hilfe," January 1909 in *Das deutsche Kaiserreich*, ed. Gerhard Ritter (Göttingen: Vandenhoeck and Ruprecht, 1975), p. 318.
2. Walter Rathenau, "Der Kaiser," in *Walter Rathenau: Schriften und Reden*, ed. H. W. Richter (Frankfurt: S. Fischer Verlag, 1964), p. 247.
3. Fortunately this situation is about to be remedied as Lamar Cecil and John C. G. Röhl are presently preparing just such biographies for publication. The work that comes closest to a scholarly biography of Wilhelm II is Michael Balfour's *The Kaiser and his*

Times (New York: Norton, 1972) which, however, is based exclusively upon published sources.

4. These include: J. Daniel Chamier, *Fabulous Monster* (London: E. Arnold, 1934); Virginia Cowles, *The Kaiser* (New York: Harper & Row, 1963); H. Kurtz, *The Second Reich: Kaiser Wilhelm II and his Germany* (London: MacDonald, 1970); Tyler Whittle, *The Last Kaiser. A Biography of Wilhelm II, German Emperor and King of Prussia* (New York: Times Books, 1977); Alan Palmer, *The Kaiser: Warlord of the Second Reich* (London: Weidenfeld and Nicolson, 1978).

5. Philipp Eulenburg to Friedrich von Holstein, December 2, 1894. Johannes Haller, *Aus dem Leben des Fürsten Philipp zu Eulenburg-Hertefeld* (Berlin: Gebrüder Paetel, 1924), p. 171.

6. F. J. Scherer, *Die Kaiseridee des deutschen Volkes im Liedern seiner Dichter seit dem Jahre 1806*, trans. Terence Cole (Arnsberg: Verlag in Arnsberg, 1896), pp. 5–6. Both this and the preceding quotation are in Elisabeth Fehrenbach, "Images of Kaiserdom: German Attitudes to Kaiser Wilhelm II," in *Kaiser Wilhelm II: New Interpretations*, ed. John C. G. Röhl and Nicolaus Sombart (Cambridge: Cambridge University Press, 1982), pp. 269–85.

7. For further information about self-psychology see, among others: Heinz Kohut, *The Analysis of the Self* (London: The Hogarth Press, 1971); Heinz Kohut, *The Restoration of the Self* (New York: International Universities Press, 1977); Heinz Kohut, *How Does Analysis Cure?* (Chicago: University of Chicago Press, 1984); Paul Ornstein, ed., *The Search for the Self: Selected Writings of Heinz Kohut*, 2 volumes (New York: International Universities Press, 1978); Arnold Goldberg, ed., *Advances in Self Psychology* (New York: International Universities Press, 1980).

8. Those wishing to learn more about Wilhelm's personality and development should see: John C. G. Röhl, "The emperor's New Clothes: A Character Sketch of Kaiser Wilhelm II," pp. 23–62; Thomas A. Kohut, "Kaiser Wilhelm II and His Parents: An Inquiry into the Psychological Roots of German Policy towards England before the First World War," pp. 63–90; and Lamar Cecil, "History as Family Chronicle: Kaiser Wilhelm II and the Dynastic Roots of the Anglo-German Antagonism," pp. 91–120; all in Röhl and Sombart, *Kaiser Wilhelm II.*

9. Bernhard Fürst von Bülow, *Denkwürdigkeiten*, I (Berlin: Ullstein Verlag, 1930), pp. 56–61.

10. Ibid., p. 461.

11. Diary entry, July 9, 1891. Viscount John Morley, *Recollections*, I (London: MacMillan, 1917), p. 272.

12. Speech of August 25, 1910. Karl Wippermann, ed., *Deutscher Geschichtskalender* (Leipzig: W. Grunow, 1885–1934), Vol. for 1910 (II), p. 9.

13. Philipp Eulenburg, "Kaiser Wilhelm II," Bundesarchiv Koblenz, Eulenburg Papers, Vol. 80.

14. For a discussion of the origin of these developmental deficits, see T. Kohut, "Kaiser Wilhelm II and His Parents."

15. Valentine Chirol, *50 Years in a Changing World* (New York: Harcourt, Brace, 1928), p. 276.

16. Bülow, *Denkwürdigkeiten*, I, p. 5.

17. See John C. G. Röhl, ed., *Philipp Eulenburgs politische Korrespondenz*, 3 volumes (Boppard-am-Rhein: Harald Boldt Verlag, 1976–81); Röhl, "Introduction," pp. 1–22; Wilhelm Deist, "Kaiser Wilhelm II in the Context of His Military and Naval Entourage," pp. 169–92; Isabel V. Hull, "Kaiser Wilhelm II and the 'Liebenberg Circle,' " pp. 193–220; all in Röhl and Sombart, *Kaiser Wilhelm II.* See especially Isabel V. Hull,

The Entourage of Kaiser Wilhelm II, 1888–1918 (Cambridge: Cambridge University Press, 1982).

18. Bülow, *Denkwürdigkeiten*, I, p. 140.

19. Herman von Petersdorff *et al*, eds., *Bismarck: Die gesammelten Werke*, 15 volumes (Berlin: O. Stollberg, 1923–33), II, p. 231; XIV, p. 473. Quoted in Otto Pflanze, *Bismarck and the Development of Germany: The Period of Unification, 1815–1871* (Princeton: Princeton University Press, 1963), p. 84.

20. Otto Pflanze, *Bismarck*, pp. 84–5.

21. Petersdorff, *Bismarck: Werke*, XIV, pp. 160–61. In Pflanze, *Bismarck*, p. 79.

22. Letter from Bismarck to Salisbury of November 22, 1887. Bernhard Schwertfeger, ed., *Die diplomatischen Akten des Auswärtigen Amtes, 1871–1914*, 5 volumes with 2 additional volumes (Berlin: Deutsche Verlagsgesellschaft für Politik und Geschichte, 1923–25), I, pp. 288–91.

23. Letter to Hugo von Radolin of November 28, 1889. Norman Rich and M. H. Fisher, eds., *The Holstein Papers*, 4 volumes (Cambridge: Cambridge University Press, 1955–63), III, p. 323.

24. Letter from Wilhelm II to State Secretary in the Foreign Office Marschall von Bieberstein of October 25, 1895. Johannes Lepsius *et al*, eds., *Die grosse Politik der europäischen Kabinette*, 40 volumes (Berlin: Deutsche Verlagsgesellschaft für Politik und Geschichte, 1922ff.), XI, pp. 8–11. This source will subsequently be abbreviated *GPEK*.

25. Wilhelm II's marginalia to report from Monts in Rome to Chancellor Bülow of March 3, 1906; Ibid., XXI(1), pp. 246–48.

26. Telegram from Wilhelm II to Chancellor Hohenlohe-Schillingsfürst of October 25, 1896; Ibid., XIII, pp. 3–4.

27. Telegram from Wilhelm II to Chancellor Hohenlohe-Schillingsfürst of December 2, 1896; Ibid., XIII, pp. 9–10.

28. Bülow, *Denkwürdigkeiten*, I, pp. 164–65.

29. See, for example, after the death of his grandmother, Queen Victoria, in early 1901.

30. Letter in English of May 9, 1909. Isaac Don Levine, ed., *Letters from the Kaiser to the Czar* (New York: Frederick A. Stokes, 1920), pp. 230–34.

31. This was the term used by both Wilhelm and his aides to characterize these periods of intense anxiety and depression.

32. Telegram from von Jenisch to Bülow of November 14, 1908. Bundesarchiv Koblenz, Bülow Papers, Vol. 33. Also: Bülow, *Denkwürdigkeiten*, II, p. 377 and p. 386.

33. Ibid., I, p. 50.

34. Diary entry of November 21, 1904. Graf Robert von Zedlitz-Trützschler, *Zwölf Jahre am deutschen Kaiserhof* (Berlin: Deutsche Verlagsanstalt, 1924), p. 97.

35. Nicolaus Sombart, "Der letzte Kaiser war so, wie die Deutschen waren," *Frankfurter Allgemeine Zeitung*, January 27, 1979.

36. Letter from Hohenlohe-Schillingsfürst to Holstein of May 28, 1896. Politisches Archiv Bonn, Holstein Papers, Vol. 54.

37. Wilhelm II's marginalia to telegram from Metternich in London to the Foreign Office of January 14, 1902. PA Bonn, England 81, Nr. 1b secr., Vol. 1.

38. As, for example, Wilhelm II's marginalia to report from Metternich in London to Bülow of December 27, 1904. PA Bonn, England 78, Vol. 23a.

39. Wilhelm II's marginalia to report from Monts in Munich to Hohenlohe-Schillingsfürst of March 23, 1897. PA Bonn, Deutschland 138, Vol. 10.

40. Letter from Wilhelm II to Eulenburg of August 20, 1897. Bülow, *Denkwürdigkeiten*, I, pp. 137–39.

41. Wilhelm II's marginalia to *The Speaker* of January 25, 1896. PA Bonn, England 81, Nr. 2, Vol. 12.

42. Letter from Wilhelm II to Hohenlohe-Schillingsfürst of January 7, 1896, in Bundesmilitärarchiv Freiburg, RM 2, Vol. 1558. Letter from August Eulenburg to Hohenlohe-Schillingsfürst of January 15, 1896, in Karl Alexander von Müller, ed., *Fürst Chlodwig zu Hohenlohe-Schillingsfürst: Denkwürdigkeiten der Reichskanzlerzeit* (Berlin: Deutsche Verlagsanstalt, 1931), pp. 158–59. Order of January 16, 1896, in ibid., p. 152.

43. Henry Wickham Steed, *Through Thirty Years*, I (New York: Doubleday, Page, 1924), p. 21. Originally printed in *The Times*.

44. Walter Görlitz, ed., *Der Kaiser: Aufzeichnungen des Chefs des Marinekabinette Admiral Georg Alexander von Müller über die Ära Wilhelms II.* (Göttingen: Musterschmidt Verlag, 1965), p. 34.

45. Maurice V. Brett, ed., *Journals and Letters of Reginald, Viscount Esher*, II (London: I. Nicolson and Watson, 1934–38), p. 344.

46. Bülow, *Denkwürdigkeiten*, I, p. 526.

47. Ibid., pp. 93–95.

48. Throughout his reign, the Kaiser sent suggestions to the British Admiralty, Lord Salisbury, and others in England on ways to improve the Royal Navy.

49. Letter of February 16, 1908. *GPEK*, XXIV, p. 34.

50. *The Times*, March 6, 1908.

51. Wilhelm II's marginalia to telegram from Metternich in London to the Foreign Office of March 6, 1908. *GPEK*, XXIV, pp. 39–40.

52. Bülow, *Denkwürdigkeiten*, I, p. 570.

53. Ibid., II, p. 149.

54. Thomas Mann, *Gesammelte Werke*, II (Oldenburg: S. Fischer Verlag, 1960), p. 43.

55. I am indebted to Lamar Cecil for emphasizing to me the importance of this issue.

56. Letter of February 24, 1896. Bülow, *Denkwürdigkeiten*, I, pp. 34–36.

57. Quoted in Friedrich Hartau, *Wilhelm II: In Selbstzeugnissen und Bilddokumenten* (Reinbek: Rowohlt Taschenbuch Verlag, 1978), p. 144.

58. Letter from Eulenburg to Bülow of July 26, 1903. "Nordlandreise II: Psyche." Bundesarchiv Koblenz, Eulenburg Papers, Vol. 74.

59. Telegram from Wilhelm II to Bülow of August 20, 1901. *GPEK*, XVIII(1), pp. 14–16. For a clear exposition of Wilhelm's understanding of politics in terms of personalities see Lamar Cecil, "History as Family Chronicle."

60. Letter from Bülow to Holstein from Windsor of November 24, 1899. Bundesarchiv Koblenz, Bülow Papers, Vol. 91.

61. Telegram from Wilhelm II to the Foreign Office of November 6, 1897. *GPEK*, XIV(1), p. 67.

62. Telegram from Bülow to Metternich in London of January 21, 1902. PA Bonn, England 81, Nr. 1b, secr., Vol. 1.

63. Telegram from Wilhelm II to Bülow of July 19, 1900. *GPEK*, XVI, p. 14.

64. Bülow quoting Eulenburg in *Denkwürdigkeiten*, I, p. 456.

65. Dudley Sommers, *Haldane of Cloan: His Life and Times, 1856–1928* (London: G. Allen and Unwin, 1960), p. 203.

66. For a discussion of the idea of the imperial monarchy, see Elisabeth Fehrenbach, "Images of Kaiserdom" and particularly *Wandlungen des deutschen Kaisergedankens, 1871–1918* (Munich: R. Oldenbourg, 1969).

67. *Hohenlohe-Schillingsfürst*, pp. 285–86.

68. See, for example, the Kaiser's Throne Speech of July 4, 1893.
69. See, for example, the Royal Message of January 18, 1896 on the 25th anniversary of the founding of the German Empire.
70. Telegram from Metternich with Wilhelm II in Sandringham to the Foreign Office of November 9, 1902. PA Bonn, Deutschland 138, secr., Vol. 5.
71. "Ein Zwiegespräch." Bundesarchiv Koblenz, Eulenburg Papers, Vol. 74.
72. Fehrenbach, "Images of Kaiserdom," p. 276. This and the following paragraph generally attempt to paraphrase Fehrenbach's thesis that the Kaiser combined various images of the German Kaiserdom within his person.
73. F. W. von Loebell, "Rückblick und Ausblick." Philipp Zorn and Herbert von Berger, eds., Deutschland unter Kaiser Wilhelm II., IV (Berlin: R. Hobbing, 1914), pp. 1698–99.
74. Friedrich Meinecke, "Deutsche Jahrhundertfeier und Kaiserfeier," Logos, 4 (1913), pp. 171–72.
75. Sombart, "Der letzte Kaiser."
76. Ernst Johann, ed., Reden des Kaisers (Munich: Deutscher Taschenbuch Verlag, 1966), pp. 118–19.
77. "Ein Zwiegespräch." Eulenburg Papers, Budesarchiv Koblenz, Vol. 74.
78. Letter of late March. George Earle Buckle, ed., The Letters of Queen Victoria, 1886–1901, III (New York: Longmans, Green, and Co., 1930), p. 350.
79. Friedrich Naumann, Demokratie und Kaisertun (Berlin: Buchverlag "Der Hilfe", 1904), p. 167f. Translated and quoted in John C. G. Röhl, Germany Without Bismarck: The Crisis of Government in the Second Reich, 1890–1900 (Berkeley: University of California Press, 1967), p. 279.
80. Ludwig Quidde, Caligula—eine Studie über römischen Cäsarenwahnsinn (Leipzig: W. Friedrich, 1894).
81. Letter from Chlodwig Hohenlohe-Schillingsfürst to his son, Alexander, of October 31, 1897. Hohenlohe-Schillingsfürst, p. 398.
82. Those interested in this issue should see Röhl, Germany without Bismarck: and Röhl, "Introduction" to Kaiser Wilhelm II. Röhl makes a compelling case for Wilhelm's ultimate political importance as well as summarizing the historical debate about the "personal regime." See also the contributions of Paul Kennedy, "The Kaiser and German Weltpolitik: Reflexions on Wilhelm II's Place in the Making of German Foreign Policy," pp. 143–68; Kathy Lerman, "The Decisive Relationship: Kaiser Wilhelm II and Chancellor Bernhard von Bülow, 1900–1905," pp. 221–47; and Terence F. Cole, "The Daily Telegraph Affair and Its Aftermath: The Kaiser, Bülow and the Reichstag, 1908–1909," pp. 249–68.
83. Letter of February 21, 1905. Letters from the Kaiser to the Czar, pp. 166–70.
84. Bülow, Denkwürdigkeiten, I, pp. 235–37.
85. "Ein Zwiegespräch." Eulenburg Papers, Budesarchiv Koblenz, Vol. 74.
86. Fehrenbach, "Images of Kaiserdom," p. 277.
87. Ibid., p. 276.
88. "Die Feinde des Kaisers," Die Zukunft, 40 (1902), p. 340. Quoted in ibid., pp. 282–83.
89. Ibid., pp. 269–85. Meinecke, "Deutsche Jahrhundertfeier und Kaiserfeier," pp. 161–75. Meinecke, "Drei Generationen deutscher Gelehrtenpolitik: Friedrich Vischer, Gustav Schmoller, Max Weber," in Brandenburg, Preussen, Deutschland: Kleine Schriften zur Geschichte und Politik (Stuttgart: K. F. Koehler Verlag, 1979), pp. 495–505.
90. With the possible exception of German trade policy, even those goals listed by Harden could hardly be described as being objectives in the Bismarckian sense. In fact they have been considered in the course of this article from the vantage of their emotional meaning.

91. "Ein Zwiegespräch." Eulenburg Papers, Budesarchiv Koblenz, Vol. 74.
92. Adolf Friedländer, *Wilhelm II.: Versuch einer psychologischen Analyse* (Halle: Carl Marold Verlagsbuchhandlung, 1919). See also Franz Kleinschrod, *Die Geisteskrankheit Kaiser Wilhelm II?* (Wörrishofen: K. Neuwihler, 1919); Herman Lutz, *Wilhelm II. periodisch Geisteskrank! Ein Charakterbild des wahren Kaisers* (Leipzig: O. Hillman, 1919); H. Wilm, *Wilhelm II. als Krüppel und Psychopath* (Berlin: A. Gerhard, 1920); as well as Dr. Julius Michaelsohn's article in the *Neue Hamburger Zeitung* of November 30, 1918, Abendausgabe.
93. Ibid., p. 44.
94. Ibid., p. 48.
95. Paul Tesdorpf, *Die Krankheit Wilhelms II.* (Munich: J. F. Lehmann, 1919), p. 4.
96. Ibid., p. 31.
97. See T. Kohut, "Kaiser Wilhelm II and His Parents."
98. Sigmund Freud, "Delusion and Dream in Jensen's *Gradiva*," in Vol. IX of *The Standard Edition of the Complete Psychological Works of Sigmund Freud*, ed. James Strachey (London: The Hogarth Press, 1964), p. 45.
99. Emil Ludwig, *Wilhelm Hohenzollern: The Last of the Kaisers* (New York and London: G. P. Putnam's Sons, 1927), p. 30.
100. Sigmund Freud, "Lecture XXXI. Dissection of the Personality." *The Standard Edition*, XXII, p. 66.
101. For an extensive consideration of these issues, see T. Kohut, "Kaiser Wilhelm II and His Parents."
102. Egon Friedell, *Kulturgeschichte der Neuzeit*, III (Munich: C. H. Beck, 1931), p. 421.
103. Fehrenbach, "Images of Kaiserdom," p. 282.
104. Sombart, "Der letzte Kaiser."

ACHIEVEMENT AND SHORTFALL IN THE NARCISSISTIC LEADER
Gough Whitlam and Australian Politics

JAMES A. WALTER

Conservative parties have dominated Australian federal politics since the Second World War. Coming to power in 1949 under Mr. (later Sir) Robert Menzies, the Liberal-Country party (L-CP) coalition held office continuously until 1972, when it was displaced by the reformist Australian Labor party (ALP) government of Mr. Gough Whitlam. Yet the Whitlam ALP government served for only three years before losing office in unusual and controversial circumstances in 1975, since which time the conservative coalition has again held sway. It is my purpose here to examine the leadership of Gough Whitlam and the effects he had upon the fortunes of the ALP government. But first, it is essential to sketch briefly the political history of the years before Whitlam came to power and the material conditions which the ALP administration encountered, for rarely can the success or failure of an administration be attributed solely to the qualities of an individual. In this case, the contingencies of situation and history were surely as relevant as the characteristics of leadership.

In Australia, the period from the late 1940s until the late 1960s was, in relative terms, a time of plenty. Prices for Australian exports (agricultural and later mineral products) were high, foreign investment in the economy flourished, and Robert Menzies' conservative government capitalized by astutely presenting itself as the beneficent author of these conditions. In reality, the government played little part, and development occurred in a piecemeal and unregulated fashion, while politicians concentrated upon parliamentary politics. Menzies, though indolent and uninterested in economics and administration, was a consummate politician, and maintained a ruthless, sometimes brutal, domination of his party and of the parliamentary forum. His preeminence was assured by the schism which opened up in the ALP opposition in the 1950s—a split which Menzies did all he could to foster and which was the apotheosis of the cold war mentality in domestic politics.

Faction fighting at that time between the left and right wings of the Australian Labor party had its origins in intense and bitter struggles between Catholics and Communists for control of the party-affiliated trade unions in the late 1940s and early 1950s. A Catholic episcopally-backed organization which came to be known as "the Movement" assumed influence in the trade unions and, increasingly, in the Labor party. Meanwhile Menzies, increasingly prone to terrify the electorate with the "red threat" and then promise to save it, set up a royal commission to investigate charges of espionage carried by a defecting Soviet agent, Vladimir Petrov, which seemed to implicate, among others, members of the personal staff of the then ALP leader, H. V. Evatt. Evatt, a prominent barrister, defended his associates before the commission and, in October 1954, released a press statement attacking the Movement for its attempts to subvert the Labor party. The internecine struggle then became public, and the party was irreconcilably sundered. A breakaway group formed a new, virulently anti-Communist, Labor party which was eventually to call itself the Democratic Labor party (DLP). This splinter party's preoccupations remained anti-Communism and a strong forward defense, and under Australia's preferential voting system, the DLP henceforth was able to split the Labor vote by directing all DLP preferences to coalition candidates, and thus to keep the ALP from power. Menzies continued to drum up the Communist specter in every election campaign, with the enthusiastic support of the DLP. The Democratic Labor party maintained its influence in this manner until the apparent certainties of the cold war era were eroded by the debacle of the Vietnam War: it disappeared as a political power in the early 1970s.

Not until the mid-1960s did the Australian Labor party start to emerge from its preoccupation with dissension and faction fighting and to rid itself of aging leaders who forever looked back to the bitter years of the split. Then, in 1967, Gough Whitlam was elected leader of the parliamentary Labor party. Whitlam, aggressive and lively and with a parliamentary manner not unlike (some would say modeled on) a younger Menzies, had won advancement through unremitting work and sheer ability. He, and those whom he had impressed, realized that political success would only be achieved when the party overcame its fragmentation through internal reform and demonstrated its relevance through the articulation of progressive rather than backward-looking policies. They set about this with zeal, and by the late 1960s their success was becoming apparent. Indeed, during those years the Australian Labor party seemed to many the only repository of genuine liberal values, with its newly evident concern for urban reform and enhanced educational facilities, its projected social welfare program, its reasoned opposition to Australia's Vietnam War commitment, its independent foreign policy, its antiracism, and its concern for equal opportunity and human rights.

The changes in the ALP that burgeoned under Whitlam took place against the background of a government of erratic and relatively rapidly changing leadership that appeared increasingly flat and unsure of its direction. Sir Robert Menzies, after seventeen years as prime minister, had chosen to retire in 1966, and the succession of Liberal party leaders thereafter indicated one thing: that in reinforcing his own preeminence, Menzies had, over the years, deposed all potential crown princes, to leave only the untried and the second-rate. His chosen successor, Harold Holt, was beginning to appear an ineffectual prime minister when he disappeared in the sea in December 1967. Holt was followed by John Gorton, who, having come from the Senate, had a tenuous grasp of the forms of the House and whose propensity for unconsidered pronouncements and politically damaging personal behavior lost him the support of his party. Gorton, in the face of an even division on a confidence vote in his leadership in the parliamentary party room, used his casting vote against himself and William McMahon was elected in his stead. McMahon, a diminutive, balding man of poor diction, was an unfortunate contrast to the tall, prepossessing and carefully coiffed Gough Whitlam, then at the height of his oratorical powers. Neither Gorton or McMahon proved a match for Whitlam in the House.

Leadership aside, the increasingly volatile economic climate of the late 1960s and early 1970s, and successive contrivances by the coalition to cope with it, militated against the sort of authoritative impression Menzies had been able to maintain in a more stable climate. It was not that the Menzies policies were seen to fail, but rather than Liberal-Country party by 1971 appeared to be a coalition that lacked policies, in contrast to the detailed articulation of policy by Whitlam and the Australian Labor party. The ALP at last appeared united, offered direction, and promised solutions and optimism.

Thus it was that the Australian Labor party won the federal elections of December 1972, and Whitlam became the first Labor prime minister in twenty-three years. The Labor government carried the hopes of a generation who had known nothing other than conservative rule, and who were persuaded by the ALP campaign slogan: "It's Time [for a change]!" Even conservative commentators hailed Whitlam's accession as "the end of the ice age." These high expectations were to be confounded by the eventful but disappointing record of the Labor government from 1972 to 1975 and the unprecedented manner of its downfall. The debate about what went wrong has continued ever since. It is reasonable to assume that the many articles and books on these events— among them one by this author[1]—were fueled not only by the unusual course of the government, but also by their authors' attempts to come to terms with these disappointed hopes. Certainly, in my own case, this has been a motive, for I was one of those for whom Whitlam's accession represented a better future, and who were disillusioned and baffled by what came to pass.

On one level, the failure of the Labor government can be explained by reference to factors over which it had little control. It was Whitlam's misfortune to be elected on an expansively reformist platform at a time when the world economic climate was beginning to dictate restraint and caution. The blight thus cast on his designs was exacerbated by the structural weakness of the Australian economy, dependent as it is on investment and stimulation from overseas sources, which were then under considerable pressure. Business interests, unchecked during the prolonged conservative rule, were resistant to change and strongly entrenched to defend their practices; business leaders were allied with conservative politicians in questioning the very right of these interlopers to rule. The media, largely owned and controlled by these same business interests, reflected their conservative presuppositions, and, after a brief initial honeymoon, pronounced daily judgments on the "reckless socialists." The federal bureaucracy, habituated to years of conservative caution, was ill suited to managing reform and preoccupied itself with defense of its long-term interests. Under the federal system, the separate state governments—mostly still conservative—were able to impede the implementation of much federal legislation through constitutional challenges, even though the High Court eventually ruled in the federal government's favour in nearly all cases. Most importantly, the Senate, not as directly representative of the popular will as the House of Representative,[2] remained in the control of the conservative parties, served constantly to impede the Labor government's legislative initiatives, and was central to the events which brought the government down in 1975.

On another level, explanation of the fate of the Labor government must take into account the many problems that were of its own making. Once it was clear that Whitlam's great "program" (forged in the 1960s) could not readily be effected in the straitened circumstances of the 1970s, it also became clear that there was no coherent overall strategy uniting the government. Cabinet ministers pursued individual, often conflicting, ends without sufficient consultation. There was much internal squabbling and an embarrassing record of ministers being shuffled and removed. There was notable economic indecision and ineptitude, as the party leadership dithered and divided over whether to pursue its Keynesian economic principles or to accept the Treasury's counsel of restraint. There was serious misjudgment as a cabal of cabinet ministers, unable to realize their dreams through conventional channels, sought massive overseas loans from Middle Eastern sources through covert dealings with a mysterious Pakistani financial intermediary—an exercise which brought ridicule and scorn in equal measure as it was revealed in the most misleading manner by the Australian media. There was, above all, the government's failure to understand that the federal parliament was only one of the sources of power in society, that it had to gain the cooperation of those controlling the economy's commanding heights, that it had to communicate to the electorate through the media, that its measures could only be effected through the bureaucracy, and that inattention to these institutional constraints on the assumption that they could be overridden by "the government" could only lead to disaster.

The events of 1975 can be briefly rendered. The catalyst was the fumbled attempt to obtain aforementioned "Arab petrodollars." Gradual revelation of the nature of these dealings and of the ineptitude of a number of senior ministers—including Gough Whitlam—in these affairs was whipped up by the national media as the "Loans Affair." This scandal was taken by the Opposition as sufficiently "extraordinary" and "reprehensible" to justify the unusual step of blocking the budget through their control of the Senate as a means of bringing the government down. Rather than outright denial of supply,[3] the Senate on October 16, simply deferred voting on the budget. Whitlam decided on a bluff strategy, refusing to call elections and making contingency plans to reach an agreement with the banks and issue government IOUs to Commonwealth workers should supply run out. It was reasoned that the crippling effects of the blocking of supply would be attributed eventually to the Liberal-National Country party (L-NCP)[4] Opposition's intransigence. A stalemate developed, and public feeling on both sides ran high. Whitlam finally decided to compromise to the extent to calling a half-Senate election. However, the Governor-General, Sir John Kerr, decided at the same time that the only solution to the deadlock lay in his hands, and, without prior warning, he dismissed Whitlam and commissioned the Liberal leader, Malcolm Fraser, to form a caretaker government until an election could be held. There was an initial surge of public outrage over this unprecedented and unconventional Vice-regal dismissal, but sympathy for Whitlam apparently faded over the ensuing weeks as people looked at the hard realities of the economy and the blunders of the past years. On December 13, the Fraser-led L-NCP coalition was elected by a landslide.

Whitlam continued as a scarred but tenacious leader of the ALP Opposition until the next federal election in 1977 when, after another resounding defeat of the ALP by the conservative coalition, he stepped aside from the leadership. In mid-1978 he resigned from parliament and took up a position as Visiting Fellow at the Australian National University, a position he still holds at the time of writing.

Gough Whitlam's political career combined unusual achievement with a downfall unparalleled in Australian history. He had been the youngest deputy leader ever elected by the parliamentary Labor party (in 1960, when he was forty-three); he went on to become the longest-serving leader of the parliamentary party (1967–1977); and in 1972 he became the first Labor prime minister in twenty-three years. A brilliant parliamentary Opposition leader, he was justly given a great deal of the credit for the party reform and policy-making drive that transformed the ALP into a credible alternative government by the 1970s. His election as prime minister prompted unusual euphoria in the electorate. Yet his troubled tenure of power, though embattled from without, was also eroded from within by failures of leadership. It ended in a prolonged parliamentary stalemate, whose only solution in the eyes of the Whitlam-appointed Governor-General was the use of "reserve powers"—which had not been used by a British monarch since George III dismissed Lord North—to precipitate a "constitutional coup"[5] and force all parties to election.

The seeming paradox of his career has led observers to write more about Whitlam than about any previous Australian prime minister. Still, he has not been well understood. Generally, commentators, according to their own proclivities, have elected to deal with positive or negative characteristics alone to account for him as a hero or a villain.[6] In the rare cases where both positive and negative features of the man have been acknowledged, they have been juxtaposed to suggest that he was an enigma.[7] Yet even at the simplest level it can be seen that the very practices which served functional ends on the road to power had always contained the dysfunctional elements that would lead to eventual defeat.[8] For instance, Whitlam might be summarily described as a man who lacked self-doubt, demonstrated a strong urge to be in control, was

FIGURE 1. Very much the official image, this photograph appeared in the *Australian Parliamentary Handbook* 1976. When asked if he wanted this picture rerun in a later edition (1978), Whitlam joked, "Why not? I look grand enough don't I?" Later he used it himself on the cover of his book *On Australia's Constitution*. (Source: Australian Information Service)

intolerant of constraint, evidently enjoyed exhibitionistic display, and showed limited empathy with others in interpersonal relations. Such a pattern can be read back into events to show the personal element in both his major successes and failures: it led to a confrontational style of politics in which Whitlam, always convinced of the "right" course, repeatedly gambled for all or nothing and consistently won against opponents who were more consciously divided than he. He himself once described his approach in a sentence which has since become famous: "When you're faced with an impasse, you've got to crash through, or crash." His performance was given an added edge by great ability allied with complete confidence in that ability and an evident enjoyment in the exercise of power. Finally, however, his predilection for crisis, impatience, intolerance of constraints such as those imposed by the necessity of negotiation with others, and his real inability to discern when the tide was running against him led to an impasse where the option of "crashing through" was simply denied him, and he was defeated.

A psychohistorical approach, attempting to show that both positive and negative behavioral characteristics can be understood as manifestations of a recognizable personality structure, promises more than the superficial and selective narratives hitherto offered to account for Whitlam. I will address myself here primarily to the elaboration of what has seemed the best means for understanding Whitlam's adult career in such a manner as to dissolve the paradox baffling previous commentators. This is the chief task. Then I will discuss the likely genesis of his personality in the light of his early life history. Finally, I will remark on the psychohistorical meaning of such a leader.

Whitlam had qualities which could have contributed to success in any sphere. He was physically well-favoured, maturing from a handsome (if rather sleek) young man to a man of commanding physical presence in his prime. Gifted with a strong constitution, he was virtually never ill or indisposed, though he made little effort to exercise and took little care to safeguard his health. The sheer energy Whitlam brought to all of his work gave him a lead which few could match. His intellectual force and marked verbal facility, when combined with a capacity for hard work, great powers of concentration, and a retentive memory, were no small foundation upon which to build a successful career. Such factors cannot be discounted both as potential determinants of personality and as essential to the success of that career.

These qualities were the personal capital upon which Whitlam drew to establish his own idiosyncratic style. A close study of his career and behavior, however, isolates characteristic modes of operation which form a pattern illustrative of personality. To simplify the communication of my findings, let me set out the elements of the pattern here:

- *Pursuit of Knowledge:* Whitlam was driven above all to be "in the know." He also saw knowledge as essential to his work and as the prerequisite for civilization and for all individual action. Special knowledge was the key to his early advancement, a resource he utilized as an advocate within the Party. Wide knowledge was the basis of the generation of policy through which he transformed the ALP in the 1960s. In government, Whitlam could play on the "need to know" principle to conserve his own supremacy in this resource but would also adopt a teaching mode to "instruct" others. He resented and punished cabinet ministers who failed to keep him "in the know." In private, he "kept up" by scanning books, reviews, and indexes. In short, he was characterized by a tremendous curiosity. But in his concern to know everything, Whitlam was apt to confuse "knowing about" with "knowing." He remained unaware of deeper meanings. However, this was obscured for most people by his

- *Professionalism:* Whitlam was clearly committed to his political career, and his work was marked by meticulous preparation, attention to detail, personal consistency, and drive. The application of obvious abilities in such a manner drew attention and gained him supporters. But this professionalism did not extend to the consolidation of initiatives. Whitlam was uninterested in administration or follow-through, and paid dangerously little attention to the manner in which initiatives he had introduced were implemented. This points up the

- *Supremacy of the Decision:* Whitlam was girding himself all the time for the key decisions. Preparation was the crux of effective decision making, and as Prime Minister he took steps to ensure that key decisions (especially in areas of special interest) remained his alone, by setting up competing sources of advice, playing a middle game between disparate interests, and allowing cabinet ministers' interests to devolve upon their own areas so that he alone could know everything. Once a decision had been reached, however, he was prepared to delegate, because he seemed to regard the decision then as something reified and inescapable. At that point his own task was at an end. But, by extension, he was inflexible in his determination that the people had precisely given him a mandate for those decisions encapsulated in the 1972 policy speech, and for a time a list was kept where decisions were crossed off as they were put into effect. Thus Whitlam subscribed to

- *Supremacy of the Settled Program:* Whitlam knew what he wanted for society, and he refused to indulge in politicking about its essentials. This gave him a sure sense of where he was going, which impressed and rallied the less decided. Yet the dysfunctional consequence was that Whitlam had "an intellectual disdain which acts as a barrier to intelligent politics"[9]—he refused to settle for less than he wanted or to bend to the corny or simple effect. Whitlam never acquired the common touch. He could not allow that anyone had a better grasp of policy than himself—after all, he said, "the platform is studded with things I was the first to suggest"—so he would not bend even to the appearance of consultation with his party. Indeed, everything was too urgent to be so diverted, and basic to his style was

- *Impatience:* Whitlam pushed things too fast. Cabinet, according to one participant, was under pressure to make "quick attractive decisions," but "they were coming too fast . . . it was like a flying machine." The Parliamentary Draftsman, although giving credit to Whitlam's grasp of legislation, complained that his office was overwhelmed by bills and could not maintain standards. But as the Manager of Government Business in the House remarked, "Whitlam wanted to have the biggest legislative program, the greatest number of bills . . ." and hardly had one been introduced than he moved ahead to the next, never pausing to consolidate. It was argued by some that Whitlam's generation of policy and transformation of the party before reaching office showed patience. In fact, his achievement at that time was in the proliferation of ideas. It was up to others to attend to the detail of change in the Party and in policy. Whitlam was described from the first as a man in a hurry. An outcome of this persistent urgency was his propensity toward

- *Confrontation:* Nearly every key transformation within the Party was achieved by confronting and "crashing through" opponents—a practice Whitlam took with him into government. It was a strategy that he consciously adopted ("crash through or crash") and was not without planning[10]—yet it was clear that he would not take time to work through conventional forms or to lobby about issues if he could achieve the same end more swiftly by gambling on his position, turning the vote on issues into a vote on his leadership. Fundamentally, it was a tactic of personalization—the challenge was implicitly "do as *I* say, or remove *me*." Likewise, in government, it was a means of raising the stakes, forever forcing the conservative L-NCP Opposition to play for all or nothing. It cannot be denied that for a long time Whitlam won at this game. Yet the recurrence of personal confrontation built resistance, both within the Party and in the electorate, and ultimately—when it fed directly into the 1975 crisis—he was defeated. Nonetheless, it was under the pressure of conflict which he had often provoked, or had allowed to arise, that he reached his apogee—"At his best with his back to the wall," the journalists proclaimed. He was masterful in a crisis, remaining calm "when [in the words of one adviser] an ordinary fellow would be screaming 'Jesus! What'll I do?'" Whitlam thrived under pressure and was clearly energized by these crises. At the same time, he gained notoriety for his

- *Outbursts of Rage:* If he was calm in a crisis, Whitlam was furious when small things went wrong and enraged when someone let him down. Outrage, by his own account, was the affect prompting his entry into politics.[11] In private, his staff were persistently subject to his fearsome temper. In public, a constant level of hostility towards opponents was manifested by verbal aggression, albeit often artfully obscured by

- *Humor:* Whitlam capitalized upon a quick wit, but his jokes were always "tendentious" jokes—Freud's categorization of jokes with a point or an argument. Whitlam's jokes had a target—his opponents—and his specialty was the demeaning and belittling jibe. Hostility was thus transformed into an integral part of the

- *Performance:* He was the public performer above all. He relished the parliamentary chamber, the public meeting and the election campaign. He was always good with people in the mass. Here his exhibitionistic traits were served by linguistic skills which were carefully polished, contributing to his reputation as an orator. Although it was essentially self-serving, one cannot overlook the

- *Importance of Language:* Whitlam was regarded both by himself and by others as a man of words. He was preoccupied by what was said. Care about language contributed to his skill as an advocate. Words gave him power over rivals, were the means by which he maintained himself at the center of attention, and were the tool employed to charm and impress followers. But, if anything, he tended to attribute too much to the power of words. His readiness to speak at length on any subject obscured, from Whitlam and others, the fact that there was a gap between vision and substance, that he was not the man for detailed remedies or meticulous supervision of reform (as his professionalism suggested). Instead, he was a man of

- *Inspirational Leadership:* Whitlam's strength was in constructing a descriptive critique, helping people to recognise how bad things were and at the same time suggesting that reform was possible. By insisting that the state of affairs was parlous, Whitlam provided an imperative for action. By giving definition to the problems Australia faced, he seemed to render them manageable. Thus inspired, others were moved to pick up his lead and to fill in the gaps in what was in reality a simple corpus of ideas. He was a specialist in raising hopes, a mover and a shaker, not a theorist (though one suspects he may have seen himself as one). Thus he recognized the

- *Importance of Allies:* Whitlam was well served by others who were drawn by his drive. Others contributed the things which he could not accomplish. Significant senior figures in the Party saw his promise and promoted him. Pragmatic men backed him for their own motives. His personal staff established links with specialists whose practical contributions to the grand program were essential. Though he was "the leader", he depended on these people. Despite this reliance on others, however, he frequently lacked loyalty, an outcome of his

- *Task Orientation:* Whitlam, it was said, did not lack feeling, but was so committed to the job on hand that people were secondary (further examples of the "supremacy of the decision" and "the program"). Those who had performed a useful service were sacrificed when political imperatives seemed to demand it. Whitlam lacked the skill to let them down gently because of his

- *Uneasiness in Personal Relations:* Whitlam, capable of ready charm at a superficial level (and on first meeting), was uncomfortable with his peers, inept at working closely with colleagues, and even somewhat distant from his fiercely partisan personal staff. Consequently, as a young back-bencher, he was regarded as aloof, and, as a leader, as unapproachable, with a penchant for acting alone. This contributed in no small measure to his

- *Failure to Consult:* Whitlam simply was reluctant to approach others; he was said to prefer poring over papers to the social round, and had no time for courting support on a personal level or for finding out how others felt. He was indifferent to the opinions of others. He ignored or railed against Party opinion and came to rely on allies to liaise with Caucus for him. At the last, he seemed remote even from public opinion, though it was the people of Australia he claimed to trust. Yet, despite the drift towards isolation consequent upon such traits, he retained a certain

- *Outer-Directedness:* Whitlam lived on public reaction and was not an introspective man. As the "peoples' leader" he derived great pleasure from his ability to elicit responses from the mass audience. He sought confirmation from without. Even something as personal as his own language was treated as "out there," something external for others to marvel at. His approach to foreign policy was expansively characterized as an "escape from the inward-looking . . . view."[12] And Whitlam always looked outward to the larger world beyond Australia, enacting this drive through ceaseless travel. Concern for things external personally and nationally (more than with the "inner man" or the "national consciousness") was also manifest in his preoccupation with

- *Image:* Whitlam was clearly conscious of appearances. Always personally well groomed (at the university he had been described as "rather too perfect sartorially")[13], closely involved with the accoutrements of the prime ministership (*vide:* his choice of the purchase of a white Mercedes as his official car), he was determined that Australia should be "well-regarded" internationally.

Whitlam's ideas and habits of thought reflect such traits. In his pronouncement of political philosophy, a drive for equality of opportunity was predicated upon a concern for independence. Independence, for Whitlam, had to do with the realization of powers and (in his words) with "bursting limitations." He spoke, for instance, of the preschool child not being limited in ways which would constrain the exploration through which the child would attain independence. Nor was the nation to be bound by the ties of tradition and loyalty which would inhibit its finding an independent role in the region.

Closely allied with the nation's independent role was Whitlam's notion of interdependence—the individual as an independent unit, but within a responsive community; the nation with a "distinctive" voice, but within a "neighbourhood" or regional community. The individual was, therefore, dependent upon a cohesive, caring community that was not isolated and "peripheral." The nation had to be part of its region (not a European enclave "peripheral" to Asia). Yet Whitlam's propensity to act this out personally led to fundamental antinomies in his behavior. He relied on caring others, such as the allies within the Party and the functionaries on his staff. But he refused to accept constraints and sought freedom in following the line of least restraint. In consequence, instead of cohesion and community, he created the very fragmentation in party and cabinet to which he was philosophically opposed. The corollary, then, was an emphasis on strong, centralized government, on formality, on the rule of law, and even on strong personal leadership as he grasped at external impositions to hold everything together. The man centrally committed to individual freedoms and independence paradoxically entered into politics in response to limitations on the "powers" of a strong central government.

Such antithesis was also apparent in other areas. The man who seemingly defined responsiveness in terms of largesse and benevolence was always slightly apart from and unresponsive to the personal needs of those around him. In the end he could not see the needs of the people. The man whose creed was optimism and the creation of opportunity was alert to the sources of despair all around us and described the careers of our foremost men as ending in failure and frustration.[14] He who stressed order and precision in language was prone to hollow rhetorical flourish. Forever seeking knowledge, he seemed to see everything in concrete and immediate terms and demonstrated an impressive speed in reaching personal conclusions. Similarly, his method of argument was to move outward from the immediate "self-evident" proposition through elaboration to the descriptive critique. Yet this left him prey to his own certainties, peculiarly inflexible and unreceptive to dissonant ideas or the insights of introspection.

One suspects, finally, that the gap between vision and substance could never be bridged without revealing the internal contradictions at the heart of the personality.

As one looks across this checklist of leading characteristics, an initial level of organisation suggests itself. One recognizes that characteristics cluster in certain groups, suggesting particular areas of enquiry as we move from the illumination to the explanation of personality. Thus, as Table 1 suggests, we now turn to biographical materials in search of the sources of the drive for mastery, the intolerance of constraint, an awkwardness with people and emotions, a pronounced exhibitionism, and a certain cognitive limitation.

Whitlam's biographers have rightly emphasized the security and

TABLE 1. Characteristics: A Checklist

Trait	Psychological meaning
Pursuit of knowledge Professionalism Supremacy of the decision Stability of program Paramount importance attached to language Iconoclastic humor (dominance)	Mastery
Confrontation/personalization Impatience/urgency Outbursts of rage	Intolerance of constraint
Inspirational leadership Importance of allies Failure to consult Task orientation (people subordinate to political imperatives)	Uneasiness with people and feelings
Outer directedness (affirmation in mass responses) Emphasis upon performance	Exhibitionism
Commitment to order and logic (external impositions e.g., constitution) Concrete cognition Argument by elaboration from self-evident principles Relative inflexibility (either/or thinking) Failure to link simple ideas	Cognitive limitation

stability of his family background, suggesting that the only peculiarity of Whitlam's childhood—his coming from the relatively privileged middle class—should have led him to a career of social democracy.[15] Graham Freudenberg, onetime Whitlam's personal speechwriter and later biographer, whose closeness to Whitlam might indicate that he was retailing the "authorized" version of his life, takes pains to point out that Whitlam's middle class background cannot justifiably be said to make him the exception as a Labor leader.[16] He argues instead the special case "that of the outstanding Labor leaders . . . Whitlam is the most normal in the sense that there is the smallest gap between his background and his attainments."[17] One can accept that Whitlam's natural endowment and training were conducive to achievement and at the same time take issue over the supposed consonance between background and attainments: there is arguably a large gap between the "normalcy" of the family constellation and upbringing, and the protean qualities of the political career sketched above. That said, however, there can be no cause for suspecting overt manifestations of disruption and trauma within the family nor any reason to doubt that Whitlam had a "terrific, stable home."[18]

Whitlam's father, Harry Frederick Ernest Whitlam ("My father was called Ernest because he was a very earnest baby"),[19] was at the time of Whitlam's birth on July 11, 1916 a "middle-ranking officer in the Commonwealth Crown Solicitor's Office"[20] in Melbourne. In 1918 he was moved to Sydney where, in 1921, he became Deputy Crown Solicitor. In 1928 he transferred to the infant capital of Canberra and in 1936 was appointed Commonwealth Crown Solicitor. He was, therefore, a man of achievement in his own right: a prominent public servant, and a highly regarded one.

Meticulous and thorough in his work, Frederick Whitlam was apparently a discreet and self-effacing man, a model of public service propriety. He became well known in the small Canberra community of that time, however, because of his involvement in community affairs. He was, for instance, prominent in pressing the argument "no taxation without representation" against the Lyons's government's plan to impose a hospital tax upon residents of Canberra in 1933. He was secretary to the Canberra College Association which finally brought the Australian National University into being. He was a member of the ABC concert committee in Canberra and an elder of St. Andrew's Presbyterian Church. "According to contemporaries, in these committee activities he displayed considerable political talent in his ability to smooth over disagreements and avoid problems."[21] Frederick Whitlam also gained distinction in actively pursuing the cause of human rights. Loathing prejudice on the grounds of race, class, or creed, he showed a strong concern for the rights of individuals and minorities and a deep interest in foreign affairs. He was a driving force within the Canberra branch of the Institute of International Affairs. In 1946 Frederick Whitlam was chosen by H. V. Evatt (then attorney general) to attend the Paris Peace Conference as a member of the Australian team. He was also held in high regard by Robert Menzies:

> In 1950 and again in 1954 he was Australia's representative on the United Nations' Human Rights Commission, and after his retirement as Crown Solicitor, he continued to act as consultant to the Federal Attorney General's Department on legal matters involving human rights.[22]

Frederick Whitlam's seriousness and preoccupations were inevitably translated into the family sphere. He "carefully cultivated racial and religious tolerance and a concern for human liberty and equality in his children."[23] and "provided an environment in which they were surrounded by books, encouraged to study, and had few distractions."[24] Indeed, Whitlam's sister Freda[25] remarks "My memory of home is one of books, books, and more books. . . . We didn't have a radio. Father said it wasn't necessary."[26] The picture becomes a rather puritan one: "We were allowed no extravagances."[27] Fairy tales were forbidden—bedtime reading came from Greek and Roman myths.[28] (As something of a classics scholar himself, Frederick Whitlam regretted his lack of Greek, a deficiency he later made sure his son did not suffer from).[29] Slang was banned, idle chatter discouraged, and family conversations centered on serious matters—literature, history, and current affairs.[30] In fact, political science discussion groups met in the Whitlam home, and Gough Whitlam was not excluded:[31] "[My father] had a wide range of friends and they had a wide range of interests. I wouldn't be obtruded into their discussions, but I wouldn't be excluded."[32]

Not surprisingly in the light of the above, Gough Whitlam's biographers tend to speak of Frederick Whitlam as a "dour, scholarly"[33] type, and point out that he was a "somewhat austere Presbyterian whose lifestyle was relatively frugal considering his income and position in the community."[34] Gough Whitlam himself adds to the impression in commenting, "There have been occasions when I could be said to be flippant. He never could be."[35] Yet some qualifications should be noted. Relative personal austerity was offset by a remarkable generosity: his "donations to churches and charities were so large that his public service colleagues wrongly assumed that he had an independent income."[36] Freda Whitlam says, "My parents, without saying anything about it, tithed."[37] Further, the dour, humorless impression has been considerably ameliorated in my discussions with Frederick Whitlam's former colleagues and acquaintances who described him within his own circle as kindly and genial, a man who went out of his way to make newcomers to Canberra feel comfortable. He was "just a very nice, kindly, humorous man" as one put it. A family friend added that he had "an easy temperament. . . . Strict was not my interpretation of Mr. Fred Whitlam—he would be a man to reason with Gough and Freda."

Frederick Whitlam's public career left distinct impressions on the Canberra circle: his wife Martha, apparently almost wholly domestically oriented, left fewer impressions, and they were more disparate ones. She rated only the briefest mention in the Oakes biography, *Whitlam PM*, and was not mentioned at all by Freudenberg. Asked "What about your mother? One very seldom reads about her," Whitlam commented:

> No. I think that probably happens in most families—people take the
> woman for granted. But she was a very lively person, a very good-

> humoured witty person she was. You know her father had come out
> from Shropshire. He was, he was orphaned and came out to the
> colonies.[38]

It has been widely accepted that "Gough Whitlam inherited an
extrovert nature from his mother, Martha, a lively woman with a quick
tongue and a sense of humour."[39] Clearly, however, she was little
known outside the family's social circle, and those I spoke to typically
described her as: "homely—she was more interested in cooking than
anything else;" "I do not remember Mrs. Martha Whitlam having been
involved in . . . activities outside the home. I don't think [she] had a
close circle of friends—the family were her interest;" "I can only ever
remember Mrs. Whitlam in the home context".

One reason that Martha Whitlam's activities were so circumscribed
was her deafness. Thus, it is suggested, Whitlam early acquired the
habit of articulating clearly and precisely, always facing the person he
addressed: "Our mother was deaf and couldn't wear a hearing aid,"
says Freda. "Both of us still speak in much the same way as we did to
her."[40] Martha Whitlam was therefore isolated; as a neighbor and colleague of Frederick Whitlam put it, "Conversation with Mrs. Whitlam
was very difficult . . . she would take you aside, one person at a time.
She could not take part in general conversation."

Something almost universally noted about Martha Whitlam's entertaining was her cooking and social concern. "She was a very excellent
cook . . . [and] entertained quietly at home. Selected friends were welcome at her home;" "There were always great supplies of cream cakes
when you went there. Sometimes she'd been cooking too many . . . she
would feed everyone up too much." "Mrs. Whitlam certainly saw they
all had plenty to eat, whether it was good for them or not." Her family
concurred: "[During the depression] my mother would literally have
given meals to hundreds of people calling at the door."[41] Physical sustenance was apparently a dominant concern, and the daughter of one of
Martha Whitlam's friends adds one detail, "Mrs. Whitlam . . . boasted
that she breast-fed both children until they were the age of two."

The received picture of Martha Whitlam—talkative, humorous,
family centered, and limited by deafness—lacks one dimension. "Tem-
peramentally," remarks her friend's daughter, "Mrs. Whitlam was ar-
rogant, with a great sense of humour and a rather caustic tongue—her
sense of humour made her company interesting." There was, then, a
cutting edge. Comparing Martha Whitlam with her husband, a friend of
the latter remarks that she was much more formidable, overpowering,
sardonic, and ambitious for her son:

> She may have been deaf, but she was a strong and impressive per-
> sonality. . . . She was just very like Gough . . . you know, Gough's

> capacity sometimes to be . . . nasty to people. . . . I never got the
> edge of Mrs. Whitlam's tongue, but I did feel that this was some-
> thing that was there.

It is unlikely, therefore, that Martha Whitlam was a woman who
could be simply "taken for granted" within the family, and in fact Oakes
notes, "When it came to domestic affairs, she dominated her husband."[42]

The interaction between Fred and Martha Whitlam was fundamental to the family climate. It was a very close family—probably closer as a
result of Martha Whitlam's deafness and domestic orientation. Given
her concentration on the family and concern for their sustenance, it
might be assumed that the children would have initially experienced an
intense relationship with their mother but would have early been made
aware of the high standards and concomitantly high expectations of
their father. Gough and Freda were, I am told, "good cobbers [bud-
dies]"—their parents' "first interests were in each other and the children recognized it."[43] (A family friend commented to me, "Mr. Whitlam
adored his wife. In church they always held hands.") Freda was six
years younger than her brother and evidently was dominated by him:

> As a child, I was always in awe of him. You know, he was my big
> brother and all that, but a tremendously strong man intellectually.
> He has a vast fund of general knowledge, extraordinary as a child.[44]

The religious element also played a significant part in the family
climate:

> Although it was so religious, apart from the fact that we said Grace
> before meals, you could be in our home and not realize how we felt.
> We had Bibles, but they were not prominently displayed. I said to
> my father once "I've never seen you pray." He said, "My life is one
> long prayer."Father said that with the self-mocking attitude that is
> so misrepresented in Gough.
>
> Coming from a home like ours, we would have had to go into
> some sort of service to the community. Gough doesn't go to church
> every Sunday but he is completely motivated by our religious back-
> ground; he would not accept that, but it is true.
>
> There was no Bible-bashing in our home; certainly we had many
> clergymen there and I suppose my father had the best theological
> library outside a theological college, but there was nothing dreary
> about it. Of course there was never any drink. We are all very
> puritanical, but it wasn't obviously so. It was the way we lived.[45]

Previous studies of Whitlam have, with some justification, located
the broad outlines of his adult characteristics in the family background
without straining for psychological explanations. Thus, it makes sense

to speak of Whitlam inheriting "his wit and sense of humour from his mother . . . but his attitudes, social concern, thirst for knowledge, cleverness with words, and application to work from his . . . father;"[46] to relate his tolerance, contempt for racial pride, and pursuit of personal excellence to Fred Whitlam's involvement in human rights and personal standards;[47] and to argue that

> in the Whitlam household, words and concepts like peace, honour, efficiency, skills, creativity, and excellence were used with some meaning and without embarrassment.
>
> The household headed by Fred Whitlam was full of good cooking, good books, and good public servants; it was notably lacking in drink, tobacco and profanity. Ever since, Whitlam has been at home with good food, good books, and almost any public servant, and uncomfortable with drinking, smoking and swearing.[48]

Similarly, one can relate his feeling for the central Federal government to his Canberra upbringing;[49] and his rather narrow legal preoccupation with constitutional matters to his father's like interest. ("Fred Whitlam was inclined to be pig-headed about constitutional questions. He had a strong Commonwealth bias, and I felt he was rather narrow in his interpretation.")[50] One might, too, see the seeds of commitment to social democracy in the Christian concerns of the household, although it remains unclear whether Whitlam's politics can be directly related to those of his parents. It is said, for instance,

> Fred Whitlam rarely discussed party politics, but those who worked with him were in no doubt that on most issues his sympathies were with the Labor Party. He is known to have supported the Labor candidate for the ACT . . . in . . . 1951. . . . Another pointer to his views was his high regard for Evatt.[51]

At the same time, I have been informed by a family friend that, in one of her asides, Martha Whitlam had told him, "Gough's politics are not our politics, you know." Whitlam himself has suggested:

> My background in English terms would be that my parents would have been voting not Conservative or Labour, but Liberal. In the Australian context they would vote Labor as the party of change and public responsibility—things being done by elected persons rather than self-perpetuating directorates.[52]

In keeping with the disparate comments noted above, Whitlam here is somewhat equivocal (at least regarding his parents' commitment to the Labor cause), but on balance I would accept Whitlam's proposition that his parents' political sympathies were generally in accord with his: his politics were not taken up as a reaction against the family themes.

In short, I find acceptable such broad conclusions as those relating overt familial features and interests to adult characteristics and preoccupations. At the same time, they present a bland picture which, if stretched, might explain a career of solid, unspectacular achievement (not unlike, say, Fred Whitlam's own) but do little to clarify the impetus which makes Whitlam's own career outstanding in both its highs and lows; it is that which makes him unique. This uniqueness requires a closer analysis of the family patterns outlined above.

There can be no doubt that Frederick Whitlam provided the ideals

FIGURE 2. At the point of defeat: Whitlam listens to the Governor General's Secretary reading the proclamation dissolving parliament on the steps of Parliament House, November 11, 1975. (Source: *Canberra Times*)

and standards taken in by Whitlam in the period of identity formation and expressed in his political philosophy.[53] Nor have observers been in much doubt about the influence of the early closeness between Martha Whitlam and her son. Don Whitington perceptively noted in 1972:

> There seems little doubt . . . that the fact that his father had not become the influence in his life that he did later accounted for Whitlam's developing the slightly impertinent, mischievious, and mordacious manner and speech that can occur in an only boy with an adoring mother and sister but can prove a difficulty in later life.[54]

Interestingly, too, traces of filial conflict recurrently emerged,[55] particularly in the area of religious belief, which was an abiding concern for Frederick Whitlam. In adulthood, Whitlam described himself as, "a fellow-traveller" of Christianity. However, he gave up religious observance at the age of eleven or twelve, asserting independence of his father's beliefs. Yet he continued to compete, remarking, for instance, "I doubt if [my father's] religious beliefs went beyond the most elementary ingredient of Christian belief. He probably believed in the Resurrection, but I would be superior on doctrine."[56]

Although Whitlam added, "he was more of a philosopher than I, and I would be more of a political scientist than he," this was nonetheless a remarkable comment from a man of whom a former aide said to me, "He simply doesn't comprehend religion—he would not know where to locate it in terms of reference"—especially when one recalls that Frederick Whitlam, in contrast, had a large private theological library, a string of clergyman friends, and (in the words of a former colleague) "always showed concern with getting his theological position straight."

Another matter of interest was Whitlam's use of profanity: Whitlam always had a reputation for avoiding profanity and being puzzled and embarrassed by obscene jokes, a reputation which persisted when he was among non-political acquaintances. This avoidance invariably suggested his father's standards in these matters. Yet it was evident in the anecdotes told by his political colleagues that Whitlam had indeed "discovered [profanity] as a means of self-expression (albeit) relatively late in life"[57] and used it liberally not only to amuse, but to (aggressively) shock and disturb his hearers—usage which suggests deliberate contravention of paternal standards. Beyond such particular matters, there were also telling general signs that the filial conflict remained an unconscious personality dynamic. This was clear in his persistence of oral aggression, his failure ever to adopt "idealizing transferences" or to accept anyone as superior, and his implicit denial of the importance of affiliation.

In sum, it might be argued that we find in the continued resonance of the filial conflict the source of those traits on our checklist which seemed to indicate a drive for mastery (competition with his father generalized to dominance of all later rivals). At the same time, some of these characteristics, such as professionalism, the importance of language, and the pursuit of knowledge, were clearly emphasized by the father. The child at one level was socialized into this pattern, though at another level the acquisition of skills in areas important to the father may have been perceived as providing a means to outdo him.

Despite the smooth and ordered flow of family life in the Whitlam household, there is suggestive evidence about the relationship between child and parents (unresolved conflict with father, and a prolonged symbiotic relationship with an ambitious and family-centered mother), which is tied closely enough to psychological theory and clinical work to support the hypothesis that the relationship fostered narcissistic personality traits. Clearly, orthodoxy of the family circle is not predictive of "orthodox" personality resolution, for "it is the child's reaction to the parents rather than to gross traumatic events in the early biography which accounts for the narcissistic fixations."[58] If Whitlam's unconscious, prerational reaction to his parents engendered narcissistic fixations, the conscious apprehension of their care and attention later must have consolidated his sense of uniqueness: why else would mother be so devoted to nurturing, or father so personally involved in setting his child's agenda? And where, so clearly, a great deal was expected of him, it should be no surprise that the child came to expect a great deal of himself:[59] "esteem can be seen as a set of learned expectations that becomes, in later life, a self-fulfilling prophecy."[60] As a first child (by six years) and only son, Whitlam was subject to the concentrated attention and energies of his parents—he was, in Harris's terms, "adult-civilized,"[61] his first and sustained relationships with his parents and their adult friends probably leading to identification with adult values and traditions rather than those of his peers. The cohesive relationships of the close-knit family itself also served as a barrier to the outside world, safeguarding and promoting the effect of family-engendered personality traits at the expense of the ameliorating influence of disparate others, especially contemporaries. In such cases, it often becomes appropriate to note the emphasis with which some families "make" their sons, as studies of John Quincy Adams, John Stuart Mill, and Karl Marx have shown.[62]

In the family, then, Whitlam learned to think of himself as special, but at the same time he developed habits and predispositions which served as a barrier in the transition to extrafamilial relationships, especially with peers. It is a short step from here to the intolerance of constraint and the awkwardness with others that we found to underlie clusters of characteristics in the mature personality.

In important respects, experiences at school and later at the university served to enhance, rather than to ameliorate, the personal style engendered in the family. On entering the outside world, it seemed that the child found himself at a disadvantage in establishing relations with his peers. He could not relate to their values and tended to measure himself against the adults around him. Paucity of contact with other children deprived him of the playing and sporting skills of childhood. At the same time, the literate skills from the association with bookish adults gave him early facility in classroom tasks, which confirmed his sense of superiority over others. He was set apart, thus gaining empirical evidence of his uniqueness. He was teased for being different (he was unusually tall and striking in appearance). He learned to use verbal facility in his defence.

The difficulty of transition from intra- to extrafamilial relationships presumably impelled the formation of a coping strategy. The affective mirroring experienced within the family arguably engendered an imperative to seek similar responses in the larger world. Barriers, such as the failure to achieve satisfactory emotional interaction with peers individually, forced him to turn to other means of eliciting responses: the obvious ploy was to utilize those means which had been successful in eliciting reactions (mirroring) from the mother in an earlier stage—words, clowning, entertaining. Thus, Whitlam persisted with exhibitionism, winning affirmation for his performance and narcissistic supplies from the crowd. At the same time, clowning and attention-getting behaviour was transformed eventually into persuasive skills and charm as the child grew to adolescence and young manhood. Here, then, is the source of those characteristics clustered around the exhibitionism trait in our initial checklist.

We trace above the transformation of narcissism into a workable personality, and later political style. That grandiosity persisted, however, is suggested by Whitlam's continuing conviction of his uniqueness, his expansiveness, his propensity to ignore realistic constraints on action, and above all by his ongoing zest and optimism we find throughout his career. Indeed, we might suppose that the corollary of the ability to maintain the vein of relatively unmodified infantile grandiosity within the mature personality is the ability also to maintain the mood of "elation" which Mahler found dominant in children in the first fifteen months (the symbiotic phase).[63] Thus, with narcissists, we "often . . . find a kind of glow or smile, which gives the impression of smugness to some, of beatific, trusting childlikeness to others."[64] (Just such a glow is frequently remarked about Whitlam, but see specifically the series of photographs in successive editions of the *Australian Parliamentary Handbook.*)

If narcissism dominates, however, it is also true that the push of ambition will outpace the pull of ideals. Intrinsic to Kohut's exposition of narcissism is the idea that ambition is related to the original grandiosity as it is affirmed by the mirroring response of the mother, while idealized goals are implanted by the demands of the father. Where grandiosity prevails, ambition will be superordinate. Freud, in an early formulation of this trait of the narcissistic type, noted, "There is no tension between the ego and the superego . . . the type is not easily overawed . . . [is ready to] break down existing conditions."[65] This, then, provides the stimulus for cultural change, and as Kohut argues, it may be, that "creativity is energized predominantly from the grandiose self, while the work of more tradition-bound . . . activities, i.e., productivity, is performed with idealizing cathexes."[66]

WHITLAM IN PSYCHOHISTORICAL CONTEXT

No other Australian leader has been quite like Whitlam, and Australians have not readily come to terms with him or fully appreciated his qualities. Yet I would suggest that he is of a type that has been recognized for as long as we have had records of human society. The ancients, if they had seen his refusal to accede to the limitations which constrain most of us, would have recognized a touch of the divine in his makeup and may have given him the rights of kingship, but they would have protected themselves through the imposition upon him of rigid and complex rules.[67]

Aristotle might well have seen in him a manifestation of the *megalopsychos*, the great man "who dares to live alone in the secret worship of his own soul."[68] The Greeks, of course, would have recognized the elements of *hubris*, the "failure to recognize the limitations of mortality,"[69] and, recognizing this, may have foreseen the ends to which it would lead. But the psychological truth underlying the classical notion of *hubris* is that we, the followers and spectators, participate in its processes.

Consider the way in which Whitlam drew followers. I have noted the importance to him of allies. Whitlam's sheer energy and capacity drew others to him, who supported and facilitiated his advance. On one level, there were a series of significant pairing relationships with others: with Lance Barnard in the party machine, with Cyril Wyndham in the reform of party structures, with Clyde Cameron in the confrontation with the Victorian ALP left, with Race Matthews in establishing contacts to aid policy reform, with Graham Freudenberg in the expression of "the vision," with Rex Connor on resources policy, with Fred Daly in controlling the House. Interestingly, Bion suggests that in terms of group dynamics, such pairing may be a source of optimism and hope,[70] and optimism and hope *were* characteristic of Whitlam's followers. That aside, beyond such immediate allies, there was Whitlam's intensely loyal personal staff group, who were prepared to be functionaries because Whitlam was "where the action was," and they wanted to be part of the larger enterprise. One actually spoke of it as "like being near a huge generator of power, pumping away." A little further removed were the advisers, various types of people who could fill in necessary details, attracted to Whitlam because he encouraged the belief that through his vision, they could put their own smaller, practical plans into effect. Then there was the parliamentary party, often infuriated by Whitlam, always ambivalent about him, but recognizing the political efficacy of such singlemindedness and the undeniable capacity of the man. Arguably, it was success within these groups that was of primary importance in Whitlam's rise to power, for without achieving on these levels, he would never have come before the electorate as a potential leader. Although the electors in Australia choose parties rather than leaders, parties make some assessment of electorate appeal in choosing their leaders, and clearly leaders generate personal followers (and antipathy) in the electorate at large. On this level Whitlam functioned largely as an inspirational leader, attempting to open people's eyes to how things were, giving expression to grievances, and raising expectations.

The underlying point is that leadership "is a relational process, involving both the leader and the people led."[71] And the corollary is that neither Whitlam nor any other narcissistic leader would have achieved eminence if such leadership did not fulfill certain needs of, or have utility for, those led. What, then, did Whitlam provide, and what may we expect of other such leaders?

Like all strong leaders, Whitlam's gift was an apparent lack of self-doubt. In the complexity of a world where there are many conflicting good ends, the introspective and imaginative are plagued with indecision. The decisive leader, remaining unaware of, or ignoring, potentialities at cross purposes with his own ends "recognizes events as being bounded, often without alternatives and with an imperative to act."[72] If Whitlam was, as I have described him, prey to his own certainties, he nevertheless provided the motive power to mobilize others, perhaps more divided in themselves, in the service of reform. The special edge available to the narcissistic leader is his lack of concern for the radical change in existing conditions,[73] a service which can be of great value. The exhilarating release from indecision and the opening of new avenues for progress can prove a great cultural and political stimulus; certainly Whitlam's accession after twenty-three years of conservative rule had such an effect initially. The paradox, of course, is that without the fervor of such a leader, nothing in particular might be done, yet if we follow him, his narrow judgment might prove mistaken, or his course unproductive.[74] Nonetheless, the people's response to Whitlam and the Labor campaign in 1972 suggests a need for such a stimulus: it was time for a change, time to aim for higher goals to which Whitlam gave expression. Whitlam was a leader appropriate to the salient frustrations of those years, frustrations engendered by years of conservative rule.

The Whitlam case also provides evidence to suggest that the overtly narcissistic leader constitutes a unique focus for the important leadership function of identification. If, as has been argued, the leader is what the followers themselves would like to be,[75] the identification with a narcissistic leader may provide unusual avenues for expansiveness and achievement. Thus, for instance, people with grievances and those with the expertise to propose specific remedies were persuaded, through identification with Whitlam and his vision, that they could achieve society-wide solutions. Instead of tinkering on the sidelines, in isolated specialist fields, each could slot his own contribution into the Whitlam machine. Thus encouraged, people were drawn from disparate settings to approach the government to proffer advice, to participate in committees and commissions of inquiry, and so on: arguably, Whitlam enabled people to contribute in manners of which few had previously dreamed. In another sense, the identification of Whitlam's closer followers with his larger enterprise may have encouraged them to lose the sense of the limits of their own individuality;[76] as functionaries in the group surrounding the leader, they could nonetheless gain intimations of grand potentials unobtainable individually. For those in the electorate at large, most of whom will never see the leader in person, but only through the media, the identification may be less active: they will remain spectators in the main. Yet spectators, too, may take something from the political drama; to use Freud's comments as an analogy:

> Being present as an interested spectator at a spectacle or play does for adults what play does for children, whose hesitant hopes of being able to do what grown up people do are in that way gratified. . . . The spectator . . . has long been obliged to clamp down, or rather displace, *his ambition to stand in his own person at the hub of world affairs;* he longs to feel and to act and to arrange things accord-

ing to his own desires—in short, to be a hero. And the playwright
and the actor enable him to do this by allowing him *to identify himself*
with a hero.[77]

The narcissistic leader, who as the person at the hub of affairs, appears
to feel, act, and arrange things according to his own desires, offers, I
would argue, similar possibilities for identification with a political actor.

Yet it is precisely in the process of joining with the narcissistic
leader in a heightened sense of power and hope that followers and
spectators participate in the *hubris* characteristic of such a leader. The
fact that many join his enterprise serves for such a man as confirmation
of his own grandiosity, encouragement to even greater achievement.
And yet he walks a razor's edge, for just as he attracts intense admiration, so his audience is poised for his failure.[78] The root of our identification with such a man lies in the nostalgic attachment to our own former
narcissism. But our antipathy is aroused since we have had to curb our
own deepest wishes in the interests of living with others, and he who
has *not* allowed himself to be similarly constrained has retained an unfair advantage. Justice demands equal treatment for all,[79] and the man
of hubris must be punished for presuming too much.[80] So, it has been
argued,

> Motivated by unconscious hostility, the populace acclaims its leader
> in such extravagent terms that the leader, maddened with hubris, is
> rapidly induced to ride for a fall by engaging in self-destructive
> adventures.[81]

Whether or not this is the case,[82] we should recognize here that at
the least we ask too much of such leaders. Their purpose is essentially to
express our grievances and to give our aspirations and ideals a new
focus—to restore our sense of purpose. We follow them because they
seem to have a resolve and a drive beyond the normal: they raise our
expectations. But their accomplishment is essentially based on a singlemindedness which ignores the complexities which might sap decision.
To some extent they ignore the full range of reality. Yet we go on to ask
them to be administrators, too, to cope with small (and conflicting)
detail, and to deal with men and events through established systems.
Their grandeur will not be bound by such pettiness, and when they fail
us here we are ourselves unrealistically disillusioned, forgetting their
real gifts in the disappointment of our hopes. For this, if for nothing
else, we punish them.

It is undeniable that a man of Whitlam's psychological nature, with
his talents and capacity, can be a leader of great utility. Let us not
overlook the unique value of a leader of his stamp, in initiating change

FIGURE 3. The almost messianic fervor Whitlam stimulated in his followers is evident here, at the opening rally for Labor's 1972 election campaign. (Source: *Sydney Morning Herald*)

and creativity, in enabling or releasing the potential of others. Nor should we forget the dysfunctional characteristics of such men, which can lead to overreaching and to political downfall. It might be remarked, to return to the initial concerns of this essay, that both functional and dysfunctional features of personality, the strengths and weaknesses that have led to such disparate accounts of the man, can now be understood in terms of a recognizable personality construct. On this account, the very things which led to Whitlam's strength and achievement carried with them the seeds of defeat; yet without them Whitlam would have been less of a leader.

For all of that, in the end one is drawn to concede the wisdom of Riviere's observation that: "The need for power springs . . . from an incapacity to tolerate either sacrifices for others or dependence on others."[83] We may, it seems, be fated to be governed by leaders with wills to power based upon unconscious fantasies of omnipotence; leaders whose conviction can be harnessed to constructive ends, but whose effectiveness is always impeded by the delusion that they, and they alone, can, and *must*, control the work of government.

NOTES

1. James Walter, *The Leader: A Political Biography of Gough Whitlam* (St Lucia: University of Queensland Press, 1980), and see notes 6–8 below.
2. Every state has equal representation in the Senate, giving disproportionate influence to the electors of the least populous States, which are of course also the least industrialized, least urbanized and—some would argue—the least sophisticated. In addition, senators have six year terms, while members of Parliament have three, and only one half of the Senate goes to the polls in tandem with the House of Representatives each time. This can allow for the retention of majorities from a prior government in the upper house when—as happened in 1972—the complexion of the lower house has entirely changed through popular election.
3. The government's legislative appropriation of the money necessary to carry out its functions is called "supply" in the Westminster system. Money bills are known as "supply bills."
4. The rural rump of the conservative coalition, the Country party, made an attempt to broaden its ideological appeal by changing its name to the *National* Country party in 1974 (emphasis added).
5. Constitutional lawyers are still debating the "legitimacy" of Sir John Kerr's action. Opponents of this use of the reserve powers—particularly those prone to conspiracy theories which identified Kerr as a front for more sinister forces such as the CIA— quickly took to calling the dismissal a constitutional coup.
6. For the former account, see Graham Freudenberg, *A Certain Grandeur* (Melbourne: Macmillan, 1977), and for the latter, Alan Reid, *The Whitlam Venture* (Melbourne: Hill of Content, 1976).
7. E.g., Paul Kelly, *The Unmaking of Gough* (Melbourne: Angus & Robertson, 1976).
8. For a fuller account of this thesis, see Walter, *The Leader*.
9. Comment by former speechwriter, Graham Freudenberg: personal interview with the author.
10. See, e.g., Graham Freudenberg, "The Pole Star that Fell to Earth," *The Australian*, February 7, 1977; and Freudenberg, *A Certain Grandeur*, pp. 129–137.
11. Whitlam claims to have been so disappointed by the defeat of the Curtin Labor government's 1944 attempts to gain more powers through referendum for postwar reconstruction, and so outraged by the cynical way the conservatives had treated the proposals, that he joined the ALP. See Walter, *The Leader*, p. 21.

12. Cf. D. J. Murphy, "New Nationalism or New Internationalism: Australian Foreign Policy, 1973–1974," *World Review*, 13 (1974): p. 20.
13. Freudenberg, *A Certain Grandeur*, p. 68.
14. Whitlam provided an extensive list to support the argument that "our chief men and our chief efforts have been singularly associated with failure and frustration;" see his "Introduction" in Irwin Young, *Theodore: His Life and Times* (Sydney: Alpha Books, 1971), p. viii.
15. E.g., Laurie Oakes, *Whitlam PM* (Sydney: Angus & Robertson, 1973); Don Whitington, *Twelfth Man* (Milton, Queensland: Jacaranda Press, 1972), pp. 165–180.
16. Freudenberg, *A Certain Grandeur*, p. 64.
17. Ibid.
18. Freda Whitlam, "Interview," *The West Australian*, January 12, 1977.
19. Freda Whitlam, quoted by Paul Webster, "Interview," *The Australian*, January 1, 1973.
20. Freudenberg, *A Certain Grandeur*, p. 63.
21. Oakes, *Whitlam PM*, p. 6.
22. Laurie Oakes and David Solomon, *The Making of an Australian Prime Minister* (Melbourne: Cheshire, 1973) p. 49.
23. Laurie Oakes, "The Years of Preparation" *Whitlam and Frost* ed. David Frost (London: Sundial Books, 1974) p. 10.
24. Ibid.
25. Whitlam's only sibling, Freda, was six years younger than he, and spoke of having been overawed by him as a child. Freda Whitlam never married but had a successful career in teaching, becoming headmistress of a highly rated Presbyterian girls' school. However, she resigned while the Labor government was in power over irreconcilable differences with the school council. It was suggested that things became increasingly difficult for her with the conservative school council simply because she was a Whitlam.
26. Freda Whitlam, *The West Australian*, January 12, 1977.
27. Ibid.
28. Oakes, "The Years of Preparation," p. 11.
29. Oakes, *Whitlam PM*, p. 10.
30. Oakes, "The Years of Preparation," p. 11.
31. Paul Webster, *The Australian*, January 1, 1973.
32. Gough Whitlam, "Interview," *Australian Financial Review*, May 30, 1972.
33. Oakes, "The Years of Preparation," p. 10.
34. Oakes and Solomon, *The Making of an Australian Prime Minister*, p. 49.
35. *Australian Financial Review*, May 30, 1972.
36. Oakes, "The Years of Preparation," p. 10.
37. Freda Whitlam, "Interview," *Woman's Day*, March 28, 1977.
38. Interview by Lord Chalfont, *The Age*, December 15, 1973.
39. Oakes and Solomon, *The Making of an Australian Prime Minister*, p. 50.
40. Paul Webster, *The Australian*, January 1, 1973.
41. Whitlam, "Interview," *Australian Financial Review*, May 30, 1972.
42. Oakes, *Whitlam PM*, p. 3.
43. Paul Webster, *The Australian*, January 1, 1973.
44. Freda Whitlam, *The West Australian*, January 12, 1977.
45. Freda Whitlam, *Woman's Day*, March 28, 1977.
46. Oakes, "The Years of Preparation," p. 10.
47. Freudenberg, *A Certain Grandeur*, p. 67.
48. Ibid., p. 68.

49. See, e.g., Paul Webster, *The Australian*, January 1, 1973.
50. Remark by a former Parliamentary Counsel; interview with the author.
51. Oakes and Solomon, *The Making of an Australian Prime Minister*, p. 49.
52. Freudenberg, *A Certain Grandeur*, pp. 64–5.
53. Freudenberg, *A Certain Grandeur*, p. 67.
54. Whitington, *The Twelfth Man*, p. 171.
55. Surely, too, Whitlam's depreciation of his father as dour and humorless is at odds with the impression of geniality and concern given by Frederick Whitlam's friends and colleagues.
56. Frost, *Whitlam and Frost*, p. 171.
57. Cf. Freudenberg, *A Certain Grandeur*, p. 68.
58. Heinz Kohut, *The Analysis of the Self* (New York: International Universities Press, 1971), p. 82.
59. I. D. Harris, "The Psychologies of Presidents," *History of Childhood Quarterly*, 3 (1976), 337–350, p. 340.
60. J. N. Knutson, *The Human Basis of the Polity: A Psychological Study of Political Men* (Chicago: Aldine, 1972), p. 51.
61. Harris, "Psychologies of Presidents," pp. 339–341.
62. David Musto, "The Youth of John Quincy Adams," *American Philosophical Society: Proceedings*, 113 (1969), 269–82; Bruce Mazlish, "The Mills: Father and Son," in *Explorations in Psychohistory*, ed. R. J. Lifton and E. Olson (New York: Simon & Schuster, 1974) 136–48; J. E. Seigel, "Marx's Early Development: Vocation, Rebellion and Realism," *Journal of Interdisciplinary History*, 3 (1973), pp. 475–508.
63. M. S. Mahler, F. Pine and A. Bergman, *The Psychological Birth of the Human Infant: Symbiosis and Individuation* (New York: Basic Books, 1973), p. 213.
64. Erich Fromm, *The Heart of Man* (New York: Harper & Row, 1964), p. 70.
65. Sigmund Freud, "Libidinal Types," *Standard Edition*, XXI (London: Hogarth Press, 1960), pp. 217–220.
66. Heinz Kohut, "Creativeness, Charisma, Group Psychology: Reflections on the Self-Analysis of Freud," *Psychological Issues*, 9, Nos. 2–3 (1976): 379–425, p. 388.
67. See J. G. Frazer, *The Golden Bough* (London: Macmillan, 1911), especially Part 2, "Taboo and the Perils of the Soul."
68. R. Payne, *Hubris: A Study of Pride* (New York: Harper Torchbooks, 1960); and cf. Aristotle, *Nichomachean Ethics*, (London: Oxford University Press, 1942), pp. 1124A–1125A.
69. L. Feder, *Crowell's Handbook of Classical Literature* (New York, Crowell, 1964), p. 181.
70. Wilfred Bion, *Experiences in Groups* (London: Tavistock, 1961).
71. D. Katz, "Patterns of Leadership" in *Handbook of Political Psychology* ed. J. Knutson (San Francisco: Jossey Bass, 1973), 203–238, p. 208.
72. P. Haring, *Political Morality* (Cambridge, Mass.: Schenkman, 1970), p. 51.
73. See Freud, "Libidinal Types," p. 218.
74. This sentence paraphrases Haring, *Political Morality*, p. 48, but his observations in "Leaders, Laws, and Justice" (Chapter V) have many remarks of value on this issue.
75. Cf. J. C. Davies, *Human Nature in Politics: The Dynamics of Political Behavior* (New York: John Wiley, 1963), p. 282.
76. Cf. Sigmund Freud (1921), *Group Psychology and the Analysis of the Ego* (New York: Norton, 1959), p. 16.
77. Sigmund Freud (1905–1906), "Psychopathic Characters on the Stage," *Standard Edition*, VII (London: The Hogarth Press, 1960), 305–310, p. 305.
78. Frazer, *The Golden Bough*, pp. 7–8, points out that the homage the ancients paid their

tribal king changed to hatred and contempt at the first sign of failure, and "he is dismissed ignominously, and may be thankful if he escapes with his life." In my judgment, the L-NCP coalition had done so badly in the years after 1975, as to deserve to be returned only by the narrowest of margins in the 1977 elections. Yet the repetition of the anti-Labor landslide a second time suggests that the voters had an unfinished emotional score with Whitlam, who still had to be punished (unrealistically) for presuming so much, for raising hopes so high, and yet for still hanging on as Labor's leader.

79. Cf. Freud, *Group Psychology and the Analysis of the Ego*, p. 52.
80. In psychological terms, the individual experiences social demands in terms of restraint on personal wishes, realizing that the ties which bind the social group require the inhibition of purely personal and instinctual aims (cf. Freud, ibid., p. 72). He who refuses to comply threatens the group on which all depend—the laws of society (the "universe" in which each individual is located) demand his punishment.
81. G. Devereux, "Charismatic Leadership and Crisis," *Psychoanalysis and the Social Sciences*, 4 (1955): 145–157, p. 156.
82. The strength of feeling about Whitlam suggests that it is, and see note 78.
83. J. Riviere, *Love, Hate and Reparation* (London: The Hogarth Press, 1937), p. 40.

LEADERS AND THE ARAB–ISRAELI CONFLICT
A Psychoanalytic Interpretation

MARVIN ZONIS AND DANIEL OFFER

There was a huge wall between us which you tried to build up over a quarter of a century, but it was destroyed in 1973. It was a wall of an implacable and escalating psychological warfare. . .

Together we have to admit that the wall fell and collapsed in 1973. Yet, there remains another wall. This wall constitutes a psychological barrier between us, a barrier of suspicion, a barrier of rejection; a barrier of fear, of deception; a barrier of hallucination without any action, deed or decision.

A barrier of distorted and eroded interpretation of every event and statement. It is this psychological barrier which I described in official statements as constituting seventy percent of the whole problem.

Today, through my visit to you, I ask you why don't we stretch out our hands with faith and sincerity so that together we might destroy this barrier

—President Anwar Sadat, Speech before
the Israeli Knesset, November 20, 1977.

Each change in man's social surroundings confronts him with new adaptational tasks, and that the demands made on him by changes of such magnitude that one can speak of the dawn of a new civilization are, of course, especially great.

It is man's ability or inability to create new adaptational structures (or rather to increase the strength of already existing ones) that
will determine his success or failure—indeed, his psychological survival or death.[1]

—Heinz Kohut

INTRODUCTION

Whether or not the late President Sadat was correct that seventy percent
of the Arab–Israeli conflict is psychological, it is clear that such approaches to the study of that conflict and to its leadership will prove
heuristic both for the study of the conflict itself and for the general use of
psychoanalytic approaches in the social sciencies. This chapter illustrates these notions by examining, in terms of the Arab–Israeli conflict, a
number of models which have been used previously in psychosocial
studies of leaders and followers.

It is clear to us that none of these models is sufficiently well developed to be as precise as we would want them to be in examining different components of the conflict. However, there are sufficient data to
apply to each of the models to make them truly interesting.

What we present as follows are three models which have been used
to study the interactions between the social environment, the leader,
and his followers. We hope to demonstrate how each model may be
most usefully applied to studying leadership and other aspects of the
conflict in the Middle East and the kinds of data which would be necessary for an in-depth application of the models.

The models which we shall examine are the national character
model, the psychopathology model, and the self-system model. The
national character model operates at a different level of abstraction from
the others. National character influences the environment in which the
political systems and peace processes themselves operate. The latter two
models, on the contrary, operate more directly on those processes
through offering the promise of a more immediate understanding of
leaders and their followers.

All three models seem appropriate for studying crucial aspects of
the Arab–Israeli conflict, including the role of leadership in that conflict.
In short, the models are meant to be useful as psychological frameworks
for the study of complex social phenomena.

Jewish-Muslim Relations

Before delving into the complex matter of Middle East leadership, it would be appropriate to comment briefly upon the historical relationship between Jews and Muslims. The relationship was marked by hundreds of years of relative peace and mutual respect. In the Islamic faith, followers of the Jewish and Christian religions are recognized as "people of the book" who are entitled to practice their own religion. Similarly, in the Jewish faith, followers of other religions can have a place in the after life. The Jews are told: "Thou shalt not revile the Gods of other peoples."[2] In contrast with other religions, there is nothing which prohibits Muslims and Jews from relating well to one another.

There have, of course, been problems as Jews have not always been treated with respect in Muslim countries. But for centuries there have been good relations between the observers of the two religions. For example, when the Jews were expelled from Spain in the fifteenth century, they were welcome in the Ottoman Empire.

In the early part of the twentieth century, there were visible signs of Jewish-Muslim friendship. When Theodor Herzl, the founder of Zionism, visited Palestine in 1901, he was greeted warmly by Sultan Abdul-Hamid of Turkey, ruler of Palestine. Two decades later, the Emir Feisal, son of Husain, the Sherif of Mecca, became King of Iraq. He had previously conducted negotiations and conferences with a number of important Jewish leaders. In a fascinating correspondence which he carried on with the American, Felix Frankfurter, Feisal noted,

> We feel that the Arabs and Jews are cousins in race, having suffered similar oppressions at the hands of power stronger than themselves, and by a happy coincidence, have been able to take the first step toward the attainment of their national ideals together.[3]

However outdated those sentiments now may seem in terms of the subsequent political history of Israelis and Arabs in the Middle East, the notion persists that, somehow, both peoples are linked in a special way.

The current Arab–Israeli conflict continues to be described as a Jewish-Muslim conflict. This obscures more than it clarifies. From its beginnings, the republic of Israel had a close and mutually respectful relationship with Turkey, probably the most powerful Muslim country in the world today. There has been no overt hostility between Israel and Afganistan or Pakistan. Currently, with relations between Egypt and Israel more or less normalized, the most powerful Arab-Muslim country has been removed from the conflict.

The central point is that there is nothing inherent in either Judaism or Islam that inspires the conflict. Nor are there doctrinal bases for precluding a settlement. In fact, the basis of the Arab–Israeli conflict in the Middle East has evolved and changed during the past hundred years. An appreciation of those changes is necessary for understanding the conflict and its leadership. Nationalism, religion, race, ethnicity, and class have all played a role in the conflict in differing proportions over time. The conflict of the 1980s is considerably different from that of the 1940s.

THE THREE MODELS OF LEADERSHIP

The National Character Model

National character studies form a rich tradition in cross-cultural anthropology and psychology.[4] Their purpose is to generalize from the psychological studies of individuals within a culture, to the major feelings, customs, and coping devices of a "typical" person within the culture. Despite the relative paucity of significant works in the social sciences on Arab states or Arab culture, there are many studies on Arab national character.[5] Surprisingly, relatively fewer studies exist on the national character of Israel.[6] It may be that this reflects the greater mystery which the Arab world holds for Western social scientists. One cannot help but have the feeling that the psychological study of foreign cultures has been used primarily in instances when those cultures seemed immune to comprehension by more conventional social scientific approaches.

A large number of studies exist which purport to capture fundamental aspects of "the Arab personality."[7] These studies generalize across the entire Arab world irrespective of peculiar historical experiences, national boundaries, or social strata. They explain "the psychology of the Arabs" in terms of the underlying motivations of the Arab psyche, usually through recounting dominant child-rearing practices in the Arab world. Titles of two of the best known examples of genre—*The Arab Mind* and *Temperament and Character of the Arabs*—capture the flavor of these works, and, more importantly, illustrate the entire range of national character studies that have been conducted on the Arabs.[8]

The personality patterns that emerge from these studies of national character of the Arabs tend to identify basic characteristics of all Arabs, such as "free-floating hostility, rigidity, lack of reality testing, and suspiciousness."[9] These so-called character traits are never related to specific groups of individuals, nor is there evidence which would be acceptable to a psychoanalyst or to a psychoanalytically oriented social scientist that such phenomena are useful ways to conceptualize aspects of "Arab personality." Nor are the domains in which these traits are supposed to operate ever identified with precision. Rather, they are simply given and are used to explain virtually every phenomenon which has been identified in the Arab world, from political instability to economic underdevelopment to anti-Western sentiments to the Arab responsibility for the intractability of the Arab–Israeli conflict.

A fundamental shortcoming of the national character studies that have been conducted in the Middle East goes beyond criticisms which may be applied to the genre as a whole. Specifically, in the Middle East, the picture of the "basic personality" has never been derived from the longitudinal study of specific individuals, but has, rather, derived from a composite pastiche which links ethnographic reports of child rearing practices with examinations of novels, myths and folk tales, children's stories, and other ethnographic reports of adults and organizations.

The variety of shortcomings of this approach to explaining personality does not require studied elaboration; those shortcomings are too manifest. Suffice it to list here several objections which are devastating critiques of the way such studies have been conducted in the past.

1. Alternative influences on behavior—both of the individual and of the culture as a whole—have not been elaborated upon.
2. The fit, or lack thereof, between personality and other behavioral determinants has not been systematically examined.
3. The distribution of character traits and behaviors across individuals has not been specified.
4. The psychodynamics of character and the unconscious have never been systematically taken into account when constructing "national character."*
5. The constructs which have been created have never been validated through specific and systematic comparisons with the study of particular individuals.

---

*Most such studies will select one of the many appointed "national character" traits of the Arabs, such as mistrust, but will fail to specify the psychodynamic factors within the individual which produce traits which would be labeled as mistrust, with the result that the investigator has no sense of the conditions under which mistrust would be present. Mistrust is assumed to be a blanket phenomenon which would be seen under all conditions in all circumstances relating to all matters. In the absence of the study of the more fundamental or underlying character traits, therefore, there is very little reliability to the concept of mistrust itself.

These criticisms seem so powerful that one might question the utility of maintaining the national character model as one appropriate for consideration in studying the Arab–Israeli conflict. Despite the stated criticism of this model, future methods might find new uses for this ayproach to studying culture and personality. There clearly are significant generalizations, which those with deep familiarity with both the Arabs and the Israelis are willing to characterize as valid. The extent to which these generalizations have their roots in the psychodynamics of character structure, and, furthermore, play a role in the social and political lives of the people remains open for empirical investigation.

The relation of such characterological generalizations to the study of leadership in the Arab–Israeli conflict has also never been systematically pursued. Given the multiplicity of traits used to describe the "national character" of Arabs and Israelis, there is no obvious connection to any single leadership style.

For at least two reasons, the relationship of a leader to his followers is not defined by the characterological traits articulated by the students of "national character." First, given the absence of any specifications as to the distribution of traits or their saliency, there is no *a priori* reason for assuming that a leader will be successful by possessing any specific trait.

Erikson, in his study of Gandhi, asserted that

> great leaders . . . become great, and they become leaders precisely because they themselves have experienced the identity struggle of their people in both a most personal and a most representative way.[10]

Erikson refers here to a group phenomenon whereby individuals collectively come to define their national character traits. In some unspecified way, an individual becomes a leader because he has specially experienced those same processes which produce national character traits in the collectivity. But clearly, Erikson establishes this "truth" too simply. How and why this process works is unspecified.

A second difficulty characterizes any attempt to establish leader–follower relations through an examination of national character traits. Psychoanalytic theory suggests the absence of any simple correspondence between character and behavior. Similarly, there is no reason for assuming any such correspondence between the behavior of the leader and the character of the followers: that relationship, including the particular resonances of leaders with their followers, needs to be specified with precision. Only then is it possible to begin to understand the relation between the actions and characters of leaders and the characters of their followers.

What is needed is a far more complex study of the leader and the followers and the interactions between the two—behavioral as well as psychological. That will make it possible to understand why the leader is a leader for different sets of followers, for it will be possible to specify those aspects of a leader's style which relate significantly to different sets of followers.

The Psychopathological Model

Psychopathological processes have been used in a variety of ways to study leadership and conflict within or between political systems.[11] Most commonly, the psychopathology of leaders is a highly elaborated and traditional mode of explaining conflict and understanding political processes. Frequently starting with the classical Freudian model, one studies a leader from the vantage point of the interaction of id, ego, superego, and ego ideal, which are carefully scrutinized based on the background of the individual leader and his conscious and unconscious productions, including dreams and fantasies. His childhood, his relationships with his parents, and his relationships with significant objects during his adulthood all are investigated from a psychiatric or clinical point of view. The more overt the psychopathological symptoms of a leader, the more tempting it has been to make clinically based psychiatric diagnoses.[12] What is truly outstanding about such studies, in fact, is the willingness of investigators to make diagnoses on evidence which would not be acceptable in the clinic. Further, the follow-through of linking the diagnosis with subsequent behaviors and emotional states is, all too often, never made. If anything, an attempt is made to link a psychiatrically based diagnosis with an observation of political behaviors, a linkage which itself would not be accepted in the clinic.

At the 1980 meeting of the American Psychiatric Association, an impressive example of this genre was presented. M. N. Walsh, who had studied Rudolph Hess in detail, diagnosed him as schizophrenic.[13] Hess's notorious trip to England was described as a flight into fantasy supported by neither Hitler nor the German High Command.

One need not attempt diagnostics, however, to note what appears to be the role of similar fantasies in the leadership of the current conflict. Prime Minister Begin struck many observers as taking positions based on just such fantasies, in particular fantasies relating to past occurrences which seem not as relevant to the contemporary period as to the age of the Holocaust.

The examples of such thinking are legion. In the midst of the Israeli

FIGURE 1. Menachem Begin, as prime minister of Israel, just prior to the Camp David talks. (Source: A. P. Laser Photo, Sept. 2, 1978)

seige of West Beirut during the summer of 1983, the Prime Minister justified the actions of his army in a letter to President Reagan. It was as if, Prime Minister Begin suggested, the Israelis were beseiging Berlin to liberate it from the Nazis.

A similar example of the Prime Minister's capacity for seeing the past—particularly the Nazi past of the Jewish people—in the present was demonstrated to an American diplomat who, with other American officials, had been sent to Israel by President Carter to salvage the Camp David agreements. After one of the negotiating sessions, Prime Minister Begin was heard humming a song. This seemed odd inasmuch as the session had ended in complete disagreement with the understanding that the Americans would return to the United States to inform President Carter of the collapse of the accords. At a later reception, an American member of the team asked Israeli Interior Minister Burg, who had also heard the Prime Minister humming, what the song was. Burg remarked that the Prime Minister was humming the song which Jews hummed before they went into the gas chambers at Auschwitz, to the effect that while the Germans could destroy the Jews in body, they could never break or destroy the spirit of the Jewish people.[14]

To the extent that Begin meant what he wrote to President Reagan and meant what he was humming, a displacement of emotions from the Holocaust into the conflicts of the Middle East seems present.

The Arab side of the conflict has its own similarly inappropriate elements. The Arab perception is partly based on centuries of humiliation at the hands of foreign powers. The British colonial powers, for example, made it quite clear that they thought ill of their Arab colonies and treated the Arabs as the "feminine" part of the colonized world, versus other, more "masculine" colonized people whom they used to form military regiments for the British armed forces. This type of perception by the Arabs concerning the attitude that the British had toward them was epitomized by Churchill's statement at the time the British withdrew their armed forces from Palestine in 1948. The Arabs threatened to destroy Israel, and Churchill is said to have asked the Chief of Staff of the British Army, General Wavell, what he thought about it. The General replied that there were five times as many Arab as Jewish soldiers, but that since each Jewish soldier was as good as seven Arab soldiers, the Israelis were definitely going to win. It is reported that Churchill replied, "Well then, we have nothing to worry about." The Arabs may have borrowed such British perceptions to construct one component of their own sense of self.

It is clear that the activities of terrorists among the Arabs, in particular the Palestinians, is often directed more at altering the self-perceptions of their fellow Arabs, and especially themselves, than it is aimed at inflicting damage on the Israelis. Thus, a sympathetic treatment of the Palestinian people would approve of the observations of a Palestinian sociologist that the most important component of the Palestinian revolution was, essentially, a change in self-identity:

> The most important thing was that they felt liberated from the daily persecution of the Deuxième Bureau [the Lebanese Secret Police]. They felt more able to defend themselves and to participate more fully in the revolution and take part in the fighting. And they felt more pride. All that came to them from the revolution was a matter of morale.[15]

Certainly, the Palestinians have been the most demeaned and neglected of the Arabs. Their consequent rage can be seen as directed both inward and outward. To understand the self-image of the Palestinians, one might look at the admittedly superficial portrait of the leader of the Palestinian people, Yasir Arafat. In contrast to the more widely accepted bourgeois image projected by such Arab leaders as Presidents Sadat, Hussein, and Assad, Chairman Arafat has made little effort to disguise his paunch; he dresses in the style of the romantic revolutionary and projects an image of neither Arab nor Western models of respectability or power.

It is in this sense that many acts of the Palestinians must be understood—they are frequently the audience as well as the actors. Not that their acutely tuned sense of public relations is not also directed to even wider circles of world opinion. The images which the Palestinians struggle to project are aimed at the Israelis, Europeans, third world countries, the Soviets, and the Americans. But they are frequently aimed, primarily, at themselves. Thus their claims of victory in the Lebanese war and the dramatic, almost conquering style with which they affected their evacuation of Beirut must be understood in that way. Their posturing was also meant to speak to the centuries of powerlessness and lack of recognition which have created their own sense of being demeaned.

Less frequently, psychopathological processes in leaders have been matched with similar processes in their followers to account for the ability of certain leaders to attract mass followings.[16] Psychopathological processes have also been identified in whole societies without specific efforts to link such processes to either leadership or followership.[17] Perhaps the most extreme form of the latter class of psychopathological processes has been made by the analysts Glover and Strachey. Glover sees the notion of political sovereignty, apparently even the existence of the political state, as a reflection of "infantile interests and unconscious psychological factors leading to territorial aggrandizement."[18] Strachey also argues that the state is a "regressive group formation" which by its very nature facilitates pathological processes.[19]

Another major class of pathological processes which have been advanced as an explanation for conflict concerns the splitting-off of aggression for projection onto others.[20] Psychoanalysts and others have frequently noted the widespread nature of this phenomenon, which is frequently explained in terms of the aggression which is generated within the family being projected onto outside groups as a way of preserving the integrity of the family unit.[21] Social scientists have used this observation to explain conflict at virtually every level of social organization. It has been used many times to explain the persistence of the Arab–Israeli conflict when investigators have seen war as one means for preserving the otherwise fragile unity of Israel and of the Arab world. Projecting aggression on to others has been regarded as a way of displacing intense aggression and rage which would otherwise decimate Arab society.[22]

The frequently noted closeness of Muslims and Jews may actually be those presumed displacements of aggression. For example, we have noted the observations of the Emir Feisal on the special relationship between Arabs and Jews. The conflict between Israel and her Arab neighbors appears particularly severe because it occurs between antagonists who do have a special relationship. Some have seen this relationship as so powerful that they have argued for understanding the conflict in terms of family dynamics.[23]

It has often been noted that the most bloody and vicious of wars are civil wars. Nikos Kasantzakis in his book *Pappa Janaros*, describing the Greek Civil War, speaks sardonically about the "sweet pleasure of killing your brother!" Many other writers and historians have also been impressed and astonished by the enormous amount of aggression displayed during various civil wars.[24] It is just such a notion which has been used to explain the intensity in the continuing intractability of the Arab–Israeli conflict.

The "brothers" in this conflict have developed particular animosity towards each other. Thus, it does seem useful to account for the tenacious persistence of the conflict at least partly in terms of the displacement of aggression. Such displacement can be conceptualized in the more conventional fashion as occurring against "outsiders"—whether against Israeli or Arab outsiders—or as a displacement occurring within a larger Semitic family against other "brothers."

The study of psychopathological processes in followers is less developed than is the study of leaders, despite the important beginnings of that enterprise launched by Freud.[25] Frequently, followers, in the psychopathological model, are identified as individuals with diminished or inadequate defense mechanisms who, through the processes of identification, are able to adopt a leader as their own defense structures. The implication of the model is that in moments of economic or political crisis psychopathological leaders are able to emerge because the need for defense mechanisms on the part of the followers is so intense.

Yablonsky's recent study on violent gangs recounted the murder of a polio victim in New York City by a group of young adolescent Puerto Ricans[26] whose gang had been functioning as a group in a relatively healthy manner for many years. Whenever the regular leader of the group left the city, however, whether to look for work or for vacation, the group would commit violent crimes. In fact, when the polio victim was killed, the leader was out of town, and the resulting stress on the gang was so intense that the adolescents adopted a virtually psychotic leader for the two-day period during which their regular leader was gone. It was under his urgings that the polio victim was murdered.

This way of explaining group phenomena has, with considerably less sophistication, been extended to the national level, where the leader is seen as an individual with major psychopathological processes. He is often identified as having overt psychotic or schizophrenic symptoms, or, occasionally, minor symptoms, which result in his inability to make a decision. Before reaching a decision, he may be seen as engaging in obsessional processes—processes which have major political implications for his nation.

Many psychoanalytically inspired investigators have suggested a variety of psychopathological processes at work in the Arab–Israeli conflict. Moses and Moses have suggested projected defense mechanisms, denials, inability to mourn, and the repetition compulsion as major examples of such processes.[27] Schossberger has suggested that the intense search for territory on the part of the Israelis and the Palestinians might be equated with a psychopathological drive to amass wealth.[28]

Another example of such processes is given by Jaffe, who refers to the book, *Siach Lochamim*, which means "talks between fighters."[29] The book contains a record of small group discussions among Israeli soldiers after their return from the 1967 War. What is striking to Jaffe is her realization that during the entire set of discussions which comprise the text of the book, the terms "aggression" and "aggressiveness" never appear. This could be understood as an example of massive psychic denial whereby Israelis come to see their own actions vis-à-vis Arabs as containing no elements of those processes. This negation of aggressive intent seems similarly to be reflected among the Israelis as a whole. Jaffe suggests that aggression is "experienced subjectively by many as a sensation of tension, anger, or covert rage, without being recognized specifically as aggression."[30] In other words, there are massive psychological processes at work among the Israeli population to deny their own aggressiveness and to rationalize it in terms of other phenomena.

An example of psychopathological processes at work among the Palestinian people can be taken from the remarkable autobiographical fragment by Fawaz Turki.[31] Turki, born in that part of Palestine subsequently occupied by the Israelis, spent the majority of his life in exile— in Lebanon, England, and the United States. In one section of his memoirs, he muses:

> Are we cultivating the knowledge that we can ask the world if it is afraid of us? That we have not been defeated by it because we have retained our sanity in our existential perspective?
>
> I hate it. I hated the world and the order of reality around me. I hated being dispossessed of a nation and identity. I hated being the victim of social and political Darwinism. I hated not being part of a culture. I hated being a hybrid, an outcast, and a zero. A problem. Dwelling in a world that suspended me aloft, petrified my being, and denied me a place among men until the problem and I became interchangeable. Where I, the problem, was ignored by some, rejected by others, and derided by the rest.

So I hated. And the world hated me because I hated. It was the circle, vicious and insane, that we lived in. I hated the world for hating me because I hated. I hate not of the self, for I still possess my pride, intellect, and humanity, but one directed at the cruelty of the cosmos and its denizens.[32]

Time and time again, Turki makes clear that it is not necessarily, nor even principally, the Israelis who are the subject of this hatred. Later in his work he mentions, "I hated not only Americans, not only Arabs, not only the Middle East, not only the whole world; I just hated."[33] His words are among the most powerfully articulate examples of the psychological processes which foster the conflict in the Middle East. What is necessary, in this case, is that we understand the mechanisms by which such rage is produced and the processes whereby such generalized personality phenomena come to be manifested in particular political situations at particular times.

Relatively little work has been done in the Middle East on the psychopathological processes among leaders themselves. Some work has begun to appear on Kemal Atatürk, but his irrelevance to the Arab–Israeli conflict makes him of less interest here.[34] There are no studies which speak to the psychopathological processes of leaders central to that conflict.

One potential shortcoming of the psychopathological model has not yet been dealt with satisfactorily, and that is its failure to account for change over time. George and George have demonstrated convincingly that Wilson repeatedly recreated a childhood struggle with his father during certain conflicts of his adult life.[35] Thus Wilson's failures at Princeton and with the U. S. Senate over membership in the League of Nations seem adequately explained by his propensity for such repetitions, the triggers for which George and George attempt to specify.

Short of that one impressive exception, little effort has been made to elaborate the critical combination of events or psychological forces which contribute to the realization in actions of psychopathological processes, whether repetitions from childhood or not. One is left with no appreciation for how basic underlying human psychological processes result in periodic outbreaks of violence or conflict.

The Self-System Model

Heinz Kohut's work on the psychology of the self seems an especially promising approach to the study of the Arab–Israeli conflict. One study of that conflict, based on Kohut's theoretical formulations of self-psychology and the vicissitudes of narcissism, has already been published. The Committee on International Relations of the Group for the Advancement of Psychiatry published an impressive longitudinal study entitled *Self-Involvement in the Middle East Conflict*, which examines questions of narcissism and extended self-objects for the Israelis and the Palestinians.[36] The study is signal demonstration of the potential of Kohut's work for the analysis of group psychology. Here, we focus on two valuable contributions that Kohut's work represents for students of the Arab–Israeli conflict: the concept of the group self and the problems of leadership. The group self is one vantage point from which to examine history.[37] The components of the group self—its commitments, its emotions, its individuality, its ideals and skills—are unique for each group. One may ask if the group self—that idealized conceptualization of the psychological forces operating within a society—is developing toward its optimal capacity. Is the society moving toward a fulfillment of the ideals of the group self? Does it contain regressive elements?

In crisis situations, the group self searches for certainty, cohesiveness, strength, beauty, and truth. The more serious the crisis, the more desperate a larger number of people in a nation become. When a leader gives a significant group that feeling of strength and unity through his own belief in his own invulnerability, a large number of individuals feel good (or whole) as a result. In Iran, for example, throughout the 1970s, individuals were dissatisfied with the Shah. A more flexible and creative monarch could probably have responded positively to that dissatisfaction. Instead, the Shah turned to greater repression. As a result, what had been dissatisfaction became rage against him as his originally idealized and mirrored image showed larger and larger cracks.

Sociopolitical crises often produce strong leaders. It is not by chance that the Iranians turned from the Shah to the Ayatollah Khomeini. Yet in countries where the sociopolitical checks and balances are more institutionalized, mechanisms exist for bringing appropriate leaders to the fore, as well as for replacing them with others as the crisis in the group self alters. Large numbers of Iranians are locked in violent struggle as the original identification with Khomeini has turned to rage against him for his all-too-human frailties. Yet in the United Kingdom, when the crisis of World War II passed, the British people were able to reject the no longer venerated Winston Churchill by failing to reelect him rather than rejecting him through violence.

How the concept of the group self can be developed to prove more useful for studies of the role of leadership and intergroup conflict is one challenge presented by Kohut's work.

The usefulness of the self-psychology model for a better understanding of leadership *per se* is found in the developmental aspects of narcissism. Specific transformations of narcissism from primary to secondary are essential for individuals to function as particular types of leaders. The spectrum of types of leaders that can be observed in the world today, and specifically in the Middle East, is due to a complex interaction of variables that include childhood experience, quality of object relationships, and the ability to transform the primary narcissistic conflicts of childhood to those of more mature realization of the leader's personal needs as well as those of his followers and of his society. The self system is one crucial aspect of the psychological world of the leader. Let us start with an examination of the ideal or wise leader, a moral person who is able to work through his own primary narcissistic needs. He has worked out his inner needs and impulses so that he does not need to act them out through the external world. The following examples are used to illustrate how this process may take place. Either process, or any combination of processes, might take place in the political world. The leader can: (1) have good and personally meaningful relationships with other human beings—relationships which will be meaningful to both the leader and his follower(s), with neither using the other as pawns in a cold game calculated to increase one's power; (2) postpone his own gratification and rehearse in fantasy about future events so that he does not have to act on impulse; (3) appreciate the humor of a situation, which is a way of releasing a considerable amount of aggression. When there is an alternative solution to naked aggression, the ideal or wise leader uses negotiation and conciliation to avoid military confrontation. These are the kinds of factors that we feel, based on the Kohut's theory, a wise leader is able to work through.

Psychoanalytical self-psychology implies a theoretical continuum which begins with the *wise leader* who can rarely, if ever, be found among human beings. A wise leader approximates the ideal description; he is a person who has transformed his primary narcissistic needs. Throughout his infancy, childhood, and adolescence, his instinctual impulses have been worked out enough so that he will not abuse the power entrusted to him. He will use it wisely. Whether the ideal or wise leader also has (or should have) charisma is open to debate. We believe that charisma (that special divine gift) can belong to a person whether or not he is wise. The three other types which we want to discuss briefly are, in order of increasing self-psychopathology, though not necessarily in order of decreasing effectiveness: the impulsive leader, the megalomaniac leader and the messianic leader. These types of leaders are meant to be heuristic rather than an accurate representation of any given individual leader. The examples which we provide for types of leaders, therefore, are to be understood in this context. We do not mean to suggest that any given individual leader is always, or even necessarily usually, a particular kind of leader. Rather, we would select aspects of his or her behavior to exemplify qualities which we think represent significant types of leadership. What remain to be specified, of course, are the conditions under which individuals select or pursue leadership paths which correspond to our typology and the significance for their political systems of these fluctuations.

The *impulsive leader* is a person who, like the immature individual, has a difficult time in postponing gratification. He reacts almost with a knee-jerk reflex to events and is not able to project events or his responses to them onto future situations. He is also a person who has not rehearsed in fantasy forthcoming events. For example, the nonimpulsive leader continuously rehearses in fantasy the possible alternatives that would arise in discussions with another leader before meeting with him—especially an adversary leader of a hostile nation. An impulsive leader could be characterized as one who through misplaced, misguided, or inappropriate self-esteem (or, perhaps, denial) feels no need to engage in such rehearsal fantasies and believes in his own self capacity to respond to that which may arise in a meeting with an adversary leader in an appropriate fashion. These responses would, of course, be primarily affective and intellectual to the extent to which the impulsive leader would be able to generate such inputs on the spur of the moment. At different times in their rule, both Colonel Qaddhafi of Libya and Prime Minister Begin of Israel have manifested qualities which we associate with the impulsive leader. Qaddhafi seems unable to postpone immediate behavioral reactions. Frequently, he seems to generate an almost immediate response on the political or military level, to what he perceives as either an opportunity for, or a need to respond to, an internal or external event. His constant efforts to support terrorists and his attempts to arm and finance those elements of the Palestinian people who are most committed to terrorism as a political goal, seem to be examples of his inability to calculate a considered policy which would be better for the long term interests of Libya and the Arab nations.

Begin, on the other hand, occasionally represented another aspect of impulsive processes. His famous and well-deserved reputation for extemporaneous speaking might have been an example of these processes. For example, his address to the Israeli Knesset on the occasion of President Sadat's visit was made without the aid of notes and yet was an astoundingly fluid speech. Similarly, when the Egyptian prime minister subsequently visited Israel following the precedent-shattering trip of Sadat, Begin once again delivered an extemporaneous speech. In this case, however, the speech proved both humiliating to the Egyptians and

FIGURE 2. Colonel Moammar Qaddhafi, Libyan leader and strongman who has made claims to leadership in the Arab world. (Source: A. P. Laser photo, Sept. 21, 1978)

embarrassing to Israelis. It seems that Begin did not mean his remarks as a calculated insult. Rather, he seems to have been entrapped by his own acting in the absence of sufficient rehearsal in fantasy.

A possible different explanation for Begin's occasional impulsive acts is related to his suffering from cardiovascular problems. It has been suggested that he might have been, at times, under the influence of sedative or hypotensive drugs which are known to cause changes in one's moods and or behavior. The place of manic physical illnesses and their sequels on the behavior of leaders while in office has been discussed in many occasions in the past. For an excellent example of this problem, see Chapter 10 on Wilson in this volume.

An example of the Prime Minister's actions which reveals greater flexibility occurred in 1977 before Sadat made his trip to Israel in search of peace. Israeli intelligence produced solid information that a group of terrorists was going to make serious attempts to assassinate Sadat. The terrorists had been strongly supported by both the Palestine Liberation Organization (PLO) and the Libyan Government. The head of Israeli intelligence presented the information to Prime Minister Begin. Begin was supposed to have said something like, "Why are you showing me this information? Go and talk to President Sadat about it. He is the one who should worry about it." Israeli agents then discussed their data with the Egyptians. A large group of terrorists were captured and detailed plans to bomb the Presidential Palace and assassinate President Sadat were foiled. This example demonstrates the complications of the psychological studies of leaders. Begin, when not under stress, was able to act in a way that many people would feel was psychologically "uncharacteristic" of him. Yet Begin should have his due, because it is very possible that his act of magnanimity not only saved Sadat's life but also started the peace process moving. At the least, Begin's actions made it much easier for Sadat to make his historic trip to Israel.

The immediate responses of the Prime Minister to the Sabra and Shattila massacres were more characteristic of decision making under stress. Following the months of war in Lebanon, the siege of West Beirut, and the assassination of Israel's likely ally, President-elect Gemayel, Begin's first reaction was to stonewall. He and his defense minister, General Sharon, first denied that there had been a massacre, then denied that the Israeli Defense Forces had any responsibility for the killings, and, finally, refused to order a judicial inquiry. Only after the virtually total mobilization of Israeli public opinion and a threat to the stability of his ruling coalition did he concede and appoint a commission with full power to press the inquiry.

One might also question the extent to which the Israeli policy of *lex talionis* is a manifestation of immature processes. The almost instantaneous response to terrorist activities in the form of attacks against Palestinian military and civilian targets outside of the borders of Israel may be an example of a failure to postpone action through an immediate response to a perceived provocation.

The leader we labeled as *megalomaniac* is absolutely certain of his strength and power and of that fact that he knows how to proceed in whatever he is doing. He is also sure that he is better than anyone else on the block.

The *messianic* leader differs from a megalomaniacal leader in that the former is more developed psychologically, having, in Kohut's terms, a greater identification with the idealized self. Both are similar, however, in that they believe absolutely in the rightness of their cause and of their own ability to know right from wrong. They are frequently the leaders who perceive themselves as having come down from the mountain, faced God, and learned the truth. There is no compromising in negotiations with such leaders.

In many ways, traditional monarchs personify the megalomaniac or messianic types of leader. Certainly, the Shah of Iran seems to represent the former. He attempted to project an image of grandiosity and identified himself with Iranian cultural stereotypes of the grandiose self. However, underneath the shell of his charismatic exterior there was very little—widely perceived to be the case by both Iranian followers and international observers. The identification by the Shah with the grandiose self was a faulty one. He was a man left only with his megalomaniacal pretensions and an elaborate public relations bureaucracy. He was a hollow leader.

The Ayatollah Khomeini, on the other hand, is the embodiment of the messianic leader: he has fully identified himself with the idealized superego. In the case of the Ayatollah, this superego is in all essentials an Islamic one. In his remarkable interview with the Italian journalist Oriana Fallaci, Khomeini implied that Islam is perfect and totally com-

FIGURE 3. The Ayatollah Khomeini, addressing a gathering at his residence in Tehran, October 28, 1980. (Souce: A. P. Laser Photo)

prehensive.[38] He also claimed that he personally has never committed a mistake in his life and that he is the embodiment of Islamic wisdom. It takes very little interpretation to suggest that, in fact, Khomeini has blurred the boundaries between the self and the idealized superego, in this case the Islamic faith. There has been a merger between his self and Islam. Such an interpretation is facilitated by the knowledge that Khomeini practices a form of Islam particularly mystical in character. Islamic mysticism stresses the possibility of an individual's merger and identification with Allah. In that case an individual may ascend the "mystical ladder" to heaven and come face to face with Allah. Further attainments of the mystical credo allow that individual to descend the ladder once again and walk the earth as an embodiment of Allah. Clearly, Khomeini believes that he is such a mystic—one who has returned to Iran as the embodiment of the divinity, literally, the Imam.

It is clear that Khomeini's identification with the idealized superego is so powerful that he himself is firmly convinced of the righteousness of his positions. He is seen as no megalomaniacal shell but as a thoroughly committed leader merged with the idealized superego. The thoroughness of his identification is manifest by Khomeini's frequently displayed capacity to compromise with certain of the political realities of Iran which have confronted him since the overthrow of the Shah. In the interests of achieving his long-range goal of transforming Iran to his vision of an Islamic society, he has displayed shrewdness and flexibility over immediate issues. Many examples of his capacity for flexibility in the face of a seemingly overwhelming personal intransigence can be cited. For example, when the women of Tehran protested his order that they appear in "appropriate Islamic garb," he withdrew, not pressing the issue, but allowing the transformation to occur gradually. A less thorough identification with the idealized superego would make such flexibility considerably more difficult.

Other examples of such flexibility abound. One occurred after the Iraqi invasion of Iran in September 1980, when President Bani Sadr learned that certain of the clerics, with whom he was already locked in a struggle for power, had reached an agreement with the Israelis to purchase military spare parts and technical assistance. Bani Sadr was totally opposed to this agreement with Israel, which Khomeini had branded an enemy of Iran second only to the United States, the great Satan. But he saw an opportunity to score points against the clerics when he learned that the Ayatollah knew nothing of the arrangement. Bani Sadr quickly rushed to the city of Qom to inform the Ayatollah. Khomeini listened quietly of Iran's dealing with "the devil" and seemed stunned.

After a few moments of reflection, he asked the president whether

Iran was dealing directly with the government of Israel. Bani Sadr recounted how "dummy" corporations had been established in Cyprus and France to buy the spares from Israel and sell them to Iran. "Good," the Ayatollah is reported to have uttered, "as long as we do not deal directly with the enemy of Islam, whatever is useful to our revolution we should do." Khomeini has always demonstrated such uncanny tactical flexibility while never forgetting his strategic goals.

The wise leader is one who has fully identified himself with the grandiose self. The very conception of the grandiose self needs to be examined in its psychohistorical and psychocultural contexts. Clearly, the wise leader must be set within such a context and, therefore, the nature of identifications will vary accordingly.

President Sadat of Egypt seemed to manifest important qualities of the wise leader. His ability to take decisive and bold action is well known and is exemplified not only by his trip to Jerusalem in November of 1977, but also by his decision to expel the Soviets from Egypt in 1972 (and again in 1981) and his startlingly successful bid for power following the death of President Nasser. His participation in virtually every major event of post-World War II Egyptian history—he was one of the original conspirators with President Nasser in the Free Officers Movement, which culminated in the successful coup against King Farouk in 1952—provided him with ample opportunity to find external validation for his own sense of grandiosity. He not only experienced the primary events of recent Egyptian history from a position of leadership, but he also saw his own sense of political judgment vindicated by his actions.[39]

The far more limited political experience of President Mubarak, irrespective of his character structure, would suggest a lesser capacity for bold action based on a sense of grandiosity. Mubarak reached the presidency by playing second fiddle, as vice president for Sadat as Sadat did for Nasser. But Mubarak had not been a key actor in Egyptian political history, as was true of Sadat. If Mubarak can hold the Presidency long enough, he may acquire the grandiosity-confirming experiences which seem to belong to the wise leader.

The *wise* leader is one who has the energy available to respond to changing circumstances in reasonable ways. He possesses appropriate affect for a variety of social and environmental stimuli. He has the ego capacity to mediate between internal feelings and thoughts and stimuli from the outside world. He does have a system of values which represents a kind of ego ideal. He has a realistic concept of himself so that his self-image is relatively close to his actual capacities.

In many of his relations with Israel, as well as with his own people, President Sadat demonstrated aspects of wisdom. Certainly he had the

FIGURE 4. Anwar Sadat, as president of Egypt, announcing to the press the death of the former Shah of Iran. (Source: A. P. Wire photo, July 27, 1980)

capacity to postpone what he considered to be essential action in the interest of building capabilities so that eventual action would be more likely to be successful. In that sense, his launching of the 1973 War represents what was for him a carefully planned and highly calculated strategy of taking specific and limited military action against Israel. He sought then to achieve important but limited gains rather than, as had been the case under his predecessor, President Nasser, to attempt to destroy Israel through an outburst of military activity. Specifically, Sadat set himself the goals of capturing a limited strip of territory within the Sinai Peninsula and of demonstrating that the Egyptian Armed Forces had the capability to do so and, in the process, to cross the Suez Canal in an impressive bridging operation through a surprise attack. Sadat spent two years preparing the Egyptian Army to achieve that limited set of goals.[40]

On the other hand, he also displayed the ability to act with boldness and decsiveness in order to take advantage of the possibility of success. Certainly his trip to Israel to seek peace embodied an ability to embrace a new set of values with a more or less realistic appreciation of the risks involved and the possibilities of success as well as failure.

Within the concept of the self-system, one can begin to develop issues in the relationship between the narcissistic line of the leader and that of the followers. One can examine aspects of both primary and secondary narcissisms in this regard. Suffice it to say that in the presentation of these models, we have concentrated on the characteristics of the leaders without attention to their interaction with the group self— the problems of followership. Certainly, one can imagine developing lines of narcissism within followers to correspond to characteristics of leaders as we have specified them within the self-system model. When we study the followers in the Middle East, we need to point out that different stresses work on the followers as well as on the leaders. These stresses can come from economic, political, or other sources. The degree and severity of psychological regression which is produced by stress in the individual follower or in the group self is crucial to understanding subsequent follower interaction with the leader. Clearly, different types of leaders may spark different types of reactions in followers who are given similar levels of regression. Beginning in the psychosocial political environment of a particular country, each moment of history brings out different factors in different cultures as well as in different individuals, producing highly various responses in the group self. But commonly in highly stressful situations, or severe crises, there is a failure of the defense mechanisms which protect individuals from the appeal of the empty promises of narcissistically primitive leaders. Such leaders stimulate false hopes in their followers, who then idealize that leader by merging with his supposed positive qualities.

DISCUSSION

These, then, are the three models which we believe useful, under certain conditions, for the analysis of leadership and the Arab–Israeli conflict. A primary concern is that each of the models needs to be clarified both in psychoanalytic and in psychocultural terms. We have only begun here to sketch the components of each model and the dynamics which would make that model a useful tool for conceptualizing and understanding issues of leadership and conflict.

A second concern is to provide the psychological, social, and behavioral data which would make the models work. The lack of necessary in-depth information in each of these three dimensions simply does not allow one to draw meaningful conclusions or to make reasonable inferences based on any of the models, even if they could be highly developed. Moreover, despite the signing of a peace treaty between Egypt and Israel, the Lebanese war, the massacre of the PLO, and the evacuation from Beirut serve as the bases of still considerable obstacles to collecting appropriate data. To do so requires the participation of investigators indigenous to the cultures of the region. At present, the level of mistrust and ill will is so great as to suggest the near impossibility of enlisting such participation. At a recent conference held in England on "The Resurgence of Islam," a number of the participants were Arab social scientists who had been educated in the West.[41] Despite their sharing intellectual theories and conceptual models with Western social scientists, they were unable to transcend the political passions surrounding the Arab–Israeli conflict to apply such models. Rather, they responded to virtually every conclusion or recommendation about the conflict in terms of the motives which they suggested prompted such conclusions. Invariably, they saw such motives as inimical to the interests of Muslims. Western social scientists were accused of attempting to "destroy the unity of the Muslim world," "defame or derogate Islam," "weaken or demean the Arab peoples," etc. They persisted in responding to conclusions different from their own in a defensive and hostile fashion, a stance unlikely to lead to progress on the topic and certainly, if typical, likely to make collecting the kinds of data proposed here nearly impossible.

The data collection problem is especially formidable given that at least four types of data need to be collected:

1. psychoanalysis of individuals in the Middle East
2. careful longitudinal studies on normal samples from childhood to adulthood
3. studies of family dynamics
4. social science surveys based on careful sampling methods to provide accurate perspectives on the attitudes and behaviors of individuals in various Middle Eastern countries.

(Studies of college students from the Middle East now studying in the United States or studying at the American University of Beirut—the two most frequently used sources of such data—are inadequate, to say the least.)

Data for the three models discussed here also need to be collected for the "background" systems of culture, economy, and child rearing practices. These need to be linked to the personal life histories of individual leaders and followers and their relationships.

Besides psycho-socio-political studies of the nature of leadership and followership in the Middle East, there is a need for considerable data on the interaction of these variables and patterns within the systems described. The timing of particular phenomena is of crucial importance. Thus, a particular national character can merge with a leader with certain psychodynamic qualities only if the psychological environment is ready to accept such a leader. A messianic leader would not rise to power in a crisis-free country where democracy has been flourishing.

In order to understand more fully the nature of leadership in modern society, in general, and in the Middle East, in particular, we strongly recommend the clarification of the conceptual bases of these issues and then the collection of appropriate data. At a minimum, intellectual progress needs to be made in the following areas:

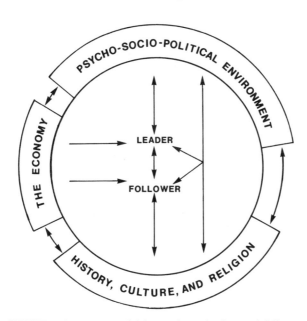

FIGURE 5. A system model for studying leaders and followers.

1. The nature and distribution of attitudes and values in the group
   self concerning the actual and ideal qualities of past, present,
   and future leaders
2. The factors which constitute a crisis for the group self, i.e., data
   which define significant stressors and detail their distribution,
   such as the economy and labor markets; infant mortality and
   general health care; the quality of food, clothing, and shelter;
   literacy and education; the relative size and costs of the armed
   forces; terrorism and internal violence; the vitality and role of
   indigenous cultures, etc.
3. The possibilities and methods for the alleviation of crises of the
   group self
4. The various channels and mechanisms for the expression of aggression, including the cultural values placed on violence,
   humor, the nature of the arts and humanities, etc.
5. The place of war and external conflict in the history of the country and in its culture

These areas are only examples of the large reservoir of socio-politico-
psychological data which are needed to understand conflict and leadership. These data need be distributional in nature and must be collected
from elites, but also from selected non-elite segments, as well.

Several additional observations need to be made about the Arab–
Israeli conflict. These seem obvious. Astoundingly, none seem to have
entered into systematic thinking about the conflict, especially such
thinking employing psychologial models.

The concept of an Arab–Israeli conflict so grossly distorts the phenomena to be investigated as to preclude significant insights. It may
once have been useful to conceive of the struggle between the state of
Israel and other parties as the principal Middle East conflict in terms of
an "Arab–Israeli conflict." But since 1967, the reduction of the conflict to
a dichotomous struggle significantly distorts the factors which need be
understood. In fact, at this time, there are at least four relevant conflicts,
the totality of which can be assumed to constitute what we so loosely
refer to as the Arab–Israeli conflict. These four are the interstate conflict,
the Israeli–Palestinian conflict, the Palestinian–Arab conflict, and the
domestic Israeli and Palestinian political conflicts.

1. There is a conflict between Israel and other states in the region.
Now that Egypt has signed the Camp David Accords, the inter-state
struggle has passed primarily to that between Israel and Syria, with
Lebanon the literal battleground and with Jordan, Iraq, and Saudi Ara-
bia playing secondary roles. This conflict is exacerbated by the conflicts

which exist between the Arab states themselves, for example between Lebanon and Syria, Jordan and Syria, Egypt and Syria, Libya and Syria, Syria and Iraq, and so on.

2. There is a conflict between Israel and the Palestinians which is now at the heart of the overall conflict. This struggle is embodied in the refusal of the Palestinian Liberation Organization to recognize the existence of the state of Israel, even by acknowledging U. N. Resolution 242. It is mirrored by Prime Minister Begin's notorious response to a question posed him at a news conference, "Yasir? Yasir who?" The crucial issue, post-Lebanon, is whether Israel can convert its military defeat of the Palestinians into a political victory over the PLO. The PLO is faced with the seemingly insurmountable challenge of maintaining its political unity given its military defeat and the loss of its political and military base in Lebanon.

3. There are significant and conflictual disagreements between the Palestianian people and other Arab states, both over the role of the Palestinians in the states in which they reside and over the proper strategy for dealing with Israel. Black September—the war between Jordan and the Palestinians in 1970, which resulted in massive loss of life and in the eviction of the Palestinian people from Jordan—is only the first dramatic example of such conflicts. The agonizing 1976–1978 Civil War in Lebanon was another manifestation of the struggle. More recently, Colonel Qaddhafi's 1980 closing of all PLO offices in Libya and the eviction of thousands of Palestinians as a manifestation of his dismay at Chairman Arafat's diplomatic (rather than terrorist) campaign against Israel reflected this same struggle. The continued efforts of Syria to use the PLO as an instrument of Syrian foreign policy and the efforts of King Hussein to use the PLO for his own purposes, against the wishes of the Syrians, are further obstacles to the achievement of Palestinian goals.

4. There are significant conflicts internal to the principal actors in the overall conflict. To focus only on the PLO and Israel is sufficient to make this point. Arafat is literally besieged by Palestinian political opponents seeking to wrest control of the movement enough to change the nature of the struggle with Israel to correspond with their image of a winning strategy. On the Israeli side, there are major disagreements among the coalition partners, among the parliamentary opposition, and among groups not represented in the Government who, nonetheless, wield significant power vis-à-vis Arab policy, as well as among extra-Israeli actors such as the Jews of the diaspora and the United States Government itself. All too often the Palestinians and the Israelis launch actions against each other which are intended primarily as important communications for other actors within their own political systems.

The war in Lebanon has only served to exacerbate such internal conflicts and the predilection of the key actors to communicate internally by speeches and actions which are directed externally.

There are so many sources and modes of conflict among and between these four components of the overall Arab–Israeli conflict that no progress can be made toward comprehending the whole without a disaggregation of the parts and an examination of the separate aspects of the totality.

Yet another issue necessary for understanding the overall Arab–Israeli conflict is the realization of dramatic changes over time. The actors, their positions, and internal and external factors impinging on the conflicts have all fluctuated dramatically. The nature of the conflict of 1948 differed from that of 1955, which, in turn, differed from those of 1967, 1973, and, certainly, 1983. For example, the years following the 1973 War demonstrated the way in which historical facts altered the nature of the conflict between Israel and the Arab states. Then, the manifold increase in the price of Arab oil and the ability of the Arab states, particularly Egypt, to define the outcome of the 1973 War as a dramatic victory for the Arab cause allowed Arabs to develop a greater sense of self esteem and, concomitantly, a more realistic appraisal of the nature of their conflict with Israel and of the state of Israel itself. Megalomania was reduced and substantial progress was made toward moderating the conflict.[42] The superiority of Israel's military, demonstrated so convincingly in the air and on the ground against Syria in 1982, may further moderate the conflict. The large number of Israeli casualties, the loss of any sense of triumph following the wasting siege of West Beirut, and the horror over apparent Israeli complicity in the Sabra and Shattila massacres may reduce Israel's predilection to define further military action as useful for achieving its political goals.

To fail to recognize those major differences is to fail to understand the relevant variables to the point where no cogent analysis can be done. As the report of the Group for the Advancement of Psychiatry concluded, "One of the more instructive observations of this study has been the repetition and subtlety of shifts in the narcissistic configuration of our subjects."[43] The speed and depth of the rapprochement between Egypt and Israel since the signing of their peace treaty bears out this observation. In a short period of time, some twenty thousand Israelis and at least five thousand Egyptians have visited each other's countries with no special controls or supervision. And not a single significant hostile incident has been reported.

It is crucial, then, not merely to recognize the speed and subtlety of change in the Middle East conflict, but also to conduct longitudinal research to measure such change (as the Group for the Advancement of Psychiatry did). Only in this way can the relevance of variables over time become clear.

In addition to an enhanced sense of the complexity of the parties to the numerous conflicts and to the changes in the conflicts over time, it is important to recognize the extent to which each actor is conventionally treated as a single abstraction of what is, in fact, a highly diverse distribution of subsidiary actors. We cannot capture the political and attitudinal spectrum of Israel, for example, if we embody that diversity solely through the views of Begin. This has largely been the approach taken in this paper and in most efforts of psychosocial studies. It is clearly more desirable to treat the conflict system not as made up of univocal national actors, but rather as diverse aggregations of actors within national systems. Doing so enriches the analysis by providing a frame-work to facilitate the analysis of change. Actors can be studied as interacting sets within, as well as between, systems.

It is important, as well, to study the various manifestations of the conflict itself over time. On different occasions, the conflict has entailed a variety of dimensions, from conventional warfare between states, to terrorist and guerilla campaigns, to political contests within the United Nations and with other states, to virtually every conceivable form of political action within the Middle East itself, as well as in most other countries in the world.

Yet another issue to be stressed is the need to focus not on the so-called objective phenomena but, rather, on subjective phenomena, or psychic reality. It is astounding that this point must be stressed to psychologically and psychohistorically sophisticated observers of the Middle East. But somehow it seems that all too often, psychic reality—like political disagreements between America's Democratic and Republican parties—is meant to stop at America's borders. Abroad, we deal with objective realities through a bipartisan foreign policy. Similarly, there is a propensity to deal with foreign conflicts in terms of objective reality, rather than in terms of the psychic realities of the participants.

Perhaps, unfortunately for American analysts, the peoples of the Middle East are as steeped in psychic reality as are we ourselves. We must listen to what people say to understand what they are saying rather than admonish them to pay attention to "reality"—all too often someone else's reality.

A major contribution of Heinz Kohut has been his use of empathy for understanding historical processes—in this case, sociopolitical historical processes. Obviously, the Middle East presents no clinical milieu comparable to that of psychoanalysis. But, at a minimum, the social scientist attempting to apply the psychoanalytic contributions of Kohut and others would want to work in the Middle East with Middle Easterners. By using his empathic understanding of the processes that go on in followers and the leaders, he would be better able to understand the complexities of each conflict situation. One cannot get a meaningful psychological understanding of the Middle East by studying it at a distance, either in the United States or even in the region, for both physical space and psychic estrangement need to be overcome if empathy is to be achieved.

An observation should also be made concerning the increase in a new genre of literature about the conflict. The report by the Group for the Advancement of Psychiatry has provided one example. There are many others, beginning with the important autobiography by Fawaz Turki, as well as this chapter itself. All of these seriously entertain psychological factors as a crucial means of understanding the intensity and intractability of the Arab–Israeli conflict. That such psychological factors can now be seriously examined is an indication that the conflict itself has diminished in intensity.

EPILOGUE

Continuing historical processes coupled with recent events in the Middle East suggest that new opportunities are likely for the resolution of the long-standing central conflicts of the Middle East. Of course, it sometimes takes many generations for an idea to be channeled from a possibility into a reality. Thus, the Jews founded Israel after many hopeless years of striving to be liberated in Europe. The Palestinians, on the other hand, have not yet been able to channel their dreams into a reasonable reality. Their use of violence continues because of the feelings of frustration and rage that they have towards others—their Arab brothers, the Israelis, and the rest of mankind. It is possible that they feel so desolate that in order not to "feel alone" they engage in the various acts of terrorism which, they explain correctly, give vent to how they feel. In order to feel alive and worthy, they have to destroy. It is only when others start taking them more seriously that the Palestinians will develop a better sense of responsibility.

Kohut has stated that narcissistic rage can never be satisfied. Because the original injury remains and cannot be easily repaired, violence may follow. The experiences of the Palestinian people seem to embody these observations. Yet for some other nations of the region, the pattern of rage and violence has proved to be neither perpetual nor inevitable.

Iran was able to negotiate the release of its American hostages. Egypt could sign a peace treaty with Israel that withstood subsequent tumultuous events in the Middle East.

These events suggest that narcissistic injuries need not be expressed through violence, and that the peoples of the Middle East may yet enjoy cooperation, rather than further destruction. A variety of historical processes would seem to be working in that same direction:

1. The intensity of the physical and psychological trauma that the Jewish people suffered in Europe during World War II has diminished. The past will not haunt Israeli leaders with the intensity that it haunts some of its present officials, who, as a result, will be able to study new events fairly and openly. This will both contribute to and be facilitated by a greater sense of security in Israel.

2. The ability of the Palestinians to withstand the Israeli seige of West Beirut may yet prove to be comparable to Egypt's 1973 "victory" in crossing the Suez Canal and holding a strip of the Sinai at the ceasefire, even as their armies faced probable destruction. The ability of the PLO to define the summer of 1982 as a victory while being forced to abandon the military option may lead to a more constructive and diplomatic dialogue between the two parties. Increasingly frequent Palestinaian calls for "simultaneous and mutual recognition" is a step in this direction.

3. The "oil power" of the Arab countries might decrease during the next decade, as more efficient use of energy becomes standard and particularly as alternative sources of petroleum are discovered. The superpowers will be less invested in the region, and it might be easier for the warring factions to settle their conflicts.

4. Members of the PLO are often seen as romantic revolutionaries by the world press. Their self-image is that of freedom fighters. It is probably far more exciting to be a leader in the PLO than to be the "head of road construction in an independent or autonomous West Bank." However, with time and with the defeats of Lebanon, even the glitter of revolutionary struggle subsides and more realistic goals are set. The result will be to allow Palestinian leaders to accept less than their most extreme goals.

Each model presented above has highlighted the importance of leaders in setting the tone for their followers. The need in the Middle East, as well as in the rest of the world, is for leaders who can transcend their own particular sociopolitical culture and tradition and opt for new solutions to old problems. A leader who can see a political conflict only in terms of his own and his people's history and tradition will find it difficult to empathize with the needs, realities, and traditions of other people. We believe that the wise leader can do much to enhance the attitudes and behaviors of his followers. Sadat and Begin took the first step. Their work had just begun when President Sadat was assassinated. The structure for the possible transformation of past hates and fears was, nonetheless, erected. But whether that framework can survive the tumultuous events of the 1982 Lebanese War and President Reagan's new peace initiative remains to be seen. The psychoanalytic processes at work in the key actors would lead to tempered optimism. But in the Middle East, such optimism has all too often foundered on the persistent complications of the conflict.

ACKNOWLEDGMENTS

This work was supported, in part, by the Harold W. Schloss Memorial Fund of Michael Reese Hospital.

NOTES

1. Heinz Kohut, *The Restoration of the Self* (New York: International Universities Press, 1977), pp. 279–280.
2. L. Roth, "Judaism: The Elements," *A Quarterly Journal of Jewish Life and Thought*, 7, No. 1, (1950), p. 11.
3. W. Laqueur, ed., *The Israel–Arab Reader: A Documentary History of the Middle East Conflict* (New York: The Citadel Press, 1968), p. 21.
4. R. F. Benedict, "Psychological Types in the Cultures of the Southwest," *Proceedings of the 23rd Congress of Americanists* (Chicago: University of Chicago Press, 1930), pp. 572–581; A. Inkeles and D. J. Levinson, "National Character: The Study of Modal Personality and Socio-Cultural Systems," in *Handbook of Social Psychology*, ed. G. Lindsey (Cambridge: Addison Wesley, 1954), XI, pp. 977–1020; A. Kardiner, "The Concept of Basic Personality Structure as an Operational Tool in the Social Sciences," in *The Science of Man in the World Crisis*, ed. R. Linton, (New York: Columbia University Press, 1945), pp. 107–122; M. Singer, "A Survey of Culture and Personality Theory and Research," in *Studying Personality Cross-Culturally*, ed. Bert Kaplan (New York: Harper & Row, 1961).
5. H. Glidden, "The Arab World," *American Journal of Psychiatry*, 128, (1972), pp. 984–988; S. Hamady, *Temperament and Character of the Arabs* (New York: J. Wayne, 1960). H. Feldman, "Children of the Desert: Notes on Arab National Character," *Psychoanalysts and the Psychoanalytic Review*, 45 (1958), pp. 40–50; R. Patai, *The Arab Mind* (New York: Scribner's, 1973); M. Zonis, "Some Possible Contributions of the Psychology of the Self to the Study of the Arab Middle East," in *Advances in Self Psychology*, ed. A. Goldberg (New York: International Universities Press, 1980), pp. 439–446.

6. R. Patai, *The Jewish Mind* (New York: Scribner's, 1977).
7. B. Beit-Hallahmi, "National Character and National Behavior in the Middle East: The Case of the Arabs' Personality," *International Journal of Group Tensions*, 2, No. 3 (1972), pp. 19–28; F. M. Moughrabi, "The Arab Basic Personality: A Critical Survey of the Literature," *International Journal of Middle Eastern Studies*, 9 (1978), pp. 99–112.
8. Patai, *The Arab Mind*. Hamady, *Temperament*.
9. Moughrabi, p. 99.
10. Erik H. Erikson, *Gandhi's Truth: On the Origins of Militant Nonviolence* (New York: Norton, 1969), p. 266.
11. H. Lasswell, *Psychopathology and Politics* (University of Chicago Press, 1930); W. C. Langer, *The Mind of Adolf Hitler* (New York: Basic Books, 1972).
12. S. Freud and W. C. Bullitt, *Thomas Woodrow Wilson: A Psychological Study* (Cambridge: Houghton Mifflin, 1967).
13. M. N. Walsh, "Diagnosis and Power Politics: Case of Rudolph Hess," (paper presented to the American Psychiatric Association at its annual meeting in San Francisco, California, 1980).
14. A literary example of the previous anecdote is the recent book by I. B. Singer titled *The Magician of Lublin*. Singer is not direct in his description of the plight of Jews in Europe, but many of his books have a similar message, as follows: the Europeans can destroy the body of the Jews or the Jews in the physical world, but they will never succeed in destroying or even bending their spirit.
15. R. Sayigh, *Palestinians: From Peasants to Revolutionaries* (London: Zed Press, 1979), p. 165.
16. R. Binion, *Hitler Among the Germans* (New York: Elsevier, 1976).
17. F. Fanon, *The Wretched of the Earth* (New York: Grove Press, 1963).
18. E. Glover, *War, Peace, and Sadism* (London: Allen Unwin, 1947).
19. A. Strachey, *The Unconscious Motives of War: A Psychoanalytic Contribution* (New York: International Universities Press, 1957).
20. Robert A. LeVine and Donald T. Campbell, *Theories of Conflict, Ethnic Attitudes and Group Behavior* (New York: John Wiley & Sons, 1972).
21. L. Stone, "Reflections on the Psychoanalytic Concept of Aggression," *Psychoanalytic Quarterly*, 40 (1971), pp. 195–224.
22. Committee on International Relations, *Self Involvement in the Middle East Conflict* (New York: Group for the Advancement of Psychiatry, 1978).
23. H. F. Winnik, R. Moses, and M. Ostrow, eds., *Psychological Basis of War* (New York: Quadrangle Books, 1973).
24. P. Noy, "Cultural Patterns of Aggression," in *Psychological Basis of War*, p. 115.
25. S. Freud, "Group Psychology and the Analysis of the Ego," in *Standard Edition*, XVIII, ed. J. Strachey (London: Hogarth Press, 1921).
26. L. Yablonsky, "Delinquent Gang as Near Group," *Social Problems*, 7 (Fall, 1959), pp. 108–117.
27. R. Moses and A. B. Moses, "Psychoanalytic Perspectives on the Peace Process: Obstacles to Peace with Special Reference to Narcissism" (unpublished paper, August, 1979).
28. J. A. Schossberger, "Another View," in *Psychological Basis of War*, pp. 83–87.
29. R. Jaffe, "Psychoanalytic Implications of Reactions of Soldiers to the Six-Day War," eds. Winnik, Moses, and Ostrow, pp. 89–102.
30. Ibid., p. 94.
31. F. Turki, *The Disinherited: Journal of a Palestinian Exile* (New York & London: Monthly Review Press, 1972).

32. Ibid., p. 77.
33. Ibid., p. 93.
34. D. A. Rustow, "Ataturk as Founder of A State" ed. D. A. Rustow, in *Philosophers and Kings: Studies in Leadership* (New York: Gérge Braziller, 1970); N. Itzkowitz, "Mustafa Kemal Ataturk's Relationship with Women: A Psycho-Historical Inquiry" (paper presented at Princeton University on March 8, 1974 before the Princeton Near East Studies Group and the Task Force on Psychiatry and Foreign Affairs of the American Psychiatric Association); V. D. Volkan, "Immortal Ataturk: Narcissism and Creativity in a Revolutionary Leader," in *The Psychoanalytic Study of Society*, IX, (1978).
35. A. L. George and J. L. George, *Woodrow Wilson and Colonel House: A Personality Study* (Chicago: John Day Company, 1956).
36. *Self Involvement in the Middle-East Conflict, Proc. of the Committee on International Relations, Group for the Advancement of Psychiatry, 1978.*
37. Heinz Kohut.
38. O. Fallaci, "An Interview with Khomeini," *The New York Times Magazine* (Oct. 7, 1979), pp. 29–31.
39. A. Sadat, *In Search of Identity: An Autobiography* (New York: Harper & Row, 1978).
40. For a version of President Sadat's role in the 1973 War considerably different from this widely accepted view, see Lt. General Saad El Shazly, *The Crossing of the Suez* (San Francisco, American Mideast Research, 1980). General El Shazly was Chief of Staff of the Egyptian armed forces at the time of the 1973 War, and he blames the near defeat of the Egyptians to the intervention of President Sadat in military decision making.
41. The Ditchley Foundations Conference on *The Resurgence of Islam*, Ditchley Park, Enstone, Oxfordshire (April 10–12, 1981).
42. Credit must be given to former Secretary of State Kissinger for part of these developments. It was his insistence at the conclusion of the 1973 War that prevented the Israeli Armed Forces from totally destroying the Egyptian armies which they had by then succeeded in encircling. Kissinger realized at the time that the destruction of the Egyptian Army would have prevented their construing the outcome of the war as a victory, precisely what was needed for substantial progress in resolving the Arab–Israeli conflict.
43. *Group for the Advancement of Psychiatry*, p. 489.

PART III

CONCLUSION

REFLECTIONS ON LEADERSHIP

DANIEL OFFER AND CHARLES B. STROZIER

This final chapter presents the authors' reflections on leadership made during the four years of writing and editing this book. Some of the topics to be discussed are the question of psychological evidence, the ethical questions concerning psychohistorical studies of leadership, and the methodology of the behavioral and social sciences as it affects the nature of the evidence. We also consider the psychological qualities which enable a "good" leader to carry out his functions. Finally, we comment on the problems which leaders encounter in the nuclear age.

ON METHOD

There is an obvious limitation to the psychohistorical study of leadership. Having studied leadership historically, we have been able to focus on some interesting psychological characteristics of past leaders, their followers, and the particular socio-historical context in which the events took place. The field of psychohistory has not reached the point at which it can make predictions concerning how future leaders will react in relation to their followers and cultures. Certain leaders function extremely well under adverse conditions, even though they did not seem to have the capabilities necessary to lead successfully. Other leaders, who show tremendous promise, fall apart in crisis situations. In this respect, the field of leadership is no different from the rest of the social and behavioral sciences: we do not possess the knowledge that will enable us to predict who will do what under which circumstances.

In a recent series of longitudinal studies, one of the authors of this monograph followed the development of adolescents from the beginning of high school to one year after graduation from college,[1] and was able to make general predictions about the mental health of the group as a whole. We predicted that stability, rather than change, would best typify our research sample of adolescents. In other words, those adolescents who were well adjusted in high school would continue to be so in the years following high school. The reverse should also be true. Our predictions turned out to be correct. The percentage of mentally healthy young adults was similar to the percentage of mentally healthy adolescents. The same was also true for the disturbed young adults in the sample studied. However, there was no one-to-one correlation between the two groups. In other words, some adolescents who functioned very well in high school showed significant emotional disturbance in college and beyond, and vice versa. We were not able to predict, on an individual basis, who would do well and who would not do well. Other investigators have described similar findings.[2] The social and behavioral sciences have begun to move away from individual case studies and focus more on statistical studies of groups.[3] On the group level we can obtain statistical norms for making group predictions if not individual predictions. Studies like these are still waiting to be undertaken and would not give us specifics concerning individual leaders anyway. They will, however, expand our knowledge concerning leadership in terms of general principles and group norms. Individual case studies of leaders, as presented in this book, are still valid today, despite the problems just described, because we need to know more about the characteristics of leaders intertwined with their followers in particular socio-historical contexts. Better understanding of these phenomena will help us to know more about the specific factors involved and about which leaders do better under what circumstances.

Because we lack the kind of specific predictive power discussed, to us it is absurd to suggest, as Greenblatt has done, that a commission of psychiatrists, psychologists, sociologists, political scientists, and historians should sit in judgment and decide who shall and who shall not run for president of the United States of America.[4] All that society would receive from such a commission would be a highly subjective, politically motivated, and personalized opinion.

An example of a clear misuse of psychiatric data was a survey sent to psychiatrists in 1964 in which a questionnaire asked psychiatrists to state whether they believed that Barry Goldwater would be a "sane" president. As it turned out, Goldwater, whom many considered a warmonger, was not elected, yet Lyndon Johnson, who *was* elected, proceeded to increase America's involvement in the hopeless Vietnam War. Those who responded (a small group of psychiatrists—less than five percent of all members of the American Psychiatric Association) stated, without ever having interviewed Goldwater, that they believed Goldwater was unfit to be President. The American Psychiatric Association has since published a position paper in which the official organization of psychiatrists states in no uncertain terms that this was unethical.[5]

We believe that psychiatrists, even if they were to interview the candidates (as Greenblatt suggests), could not possibly remain objective. The nature of the psychological evidence is such that a person can easily abuse it. As we have stated, the data on which investigators base their opinions is almost nonexistent. These opinions are highly personal and idiosyncratic, and the researcher often has ulterior motives. Psychohistorians can legitimately study leaders they like or dislike.[6] But we believe that psychohistorians and psychoanalysts have many difficulties in studying the leaders whom they either idolize or despise. Examples are easy to come by. Investigators who despised the person they studied include Freud and Bullitt on Wilson and Brody on Nixon. Investigators who either worshipped or were infatuated by the person they studied are Kearns on Johnson and Brenman-Gibson on Clifford Odets.[7] It also seems to us that when one deals with obviously extremely psychopathic leaders like Hitler or Idi Amin, the psychological issues are only part of the total psychological picture. One needs also to understand the psychological nature of the group phenomena (i.e., the followers) and the particular psychohistorical contexts in which the leaders functioned in order to understand why a society allowed them to emerge.

One charge against psychohistory has been that psychohistorians do not possess the richness of associations which are part and parcel of intensive psychotherapy. However, as Klauber[8] has stated, the psychohistorian has the advantage of knowing what actually happened to a leader from childhood through adulthood. In addition to Klauber's comment, it is our belief that psychohistorical studies of leaders will be more meaningful if the researcher will follow these six basic premises:

1. Psychobiographical studies of active and current leaders are difficult to undertake. Bias is almost inevitably present, and, although interesting observations can be made, they usually are more in the realm of psychobiography than psychohistory. It is

our opinion that active and current leaders can be studied when one examines them in their sociopolitical context, as well as in the context of their relationships with their followers. Two examples of such studies of leaders in context are to be found in Chapters 12 and 13 of this book.

2. Psychohistorical studies raise a number of ethical questions of which investigators should be aware. The researcher should avoid studying a leader toward whom he or she has particularly strong negative feelings because of the nature of psychological evidence. The names of the last ten presidents of the United States surely bring forth different images and feelings in most of us. Just listing the ten names in order might suffice: Hoover, Roosevelt, Truman, Eisenhower, Kennedy, Johnson, Nixon, Ford, Carter, and Reagan.

3. Enough time has to pass before we can realistically appreciate a leader's gift of leadership or lack of it.*

4. When we engage in a psychological postmortem, we are able to get a pretty good picture of the individual leader. Interviewing those who know or knew the leader and have worked with him or her, as well as with his or her friends and relatives, can be very helpful. However, the investigator has to remind himself continually that he must get information from all who knew the leader—those who loved him, those who hated him, and those who were indifferent to him.

5. Leaders have to be studied within their psychohistorical contexts, as well as together with their followers. The leaders who have been most frequently studied in the past are the "romantic," "evil," or "dramatic" ones. Hence, there are many studies of Kennedy, Hitler, Napoleon, Lawrence, and Nixon, to name only a few, but there are no full psychohistorical studies of Eisenhower or Truman. Psychoanalysis has focused on studies of deviant personalities and has not, until recently, even attempted to study normal or ordinary individuals.[3] Similarly, psychohistory has not studied the ordinary leader. We need to collect much data on ordinary leaders so that we will have reasonable baseline data on a variety of leadership patterns in modern society.

---

*An example of an absurd case is the recent issue of *Time Magazine* (November 22, 1983) where the journalists stated that President Kennedy can now be studied objectively because he has been dead for twenty years. This is certainly *not* enough time for anybody to gain a true historical perspective. In 2063 this might be possible!

6. The interviews of persons involved with particular leaders have to be performed with relative objectivity. A researcher must develop what we have termed a "research alliance" which will optimize his ability to collect psychological data while minimizing the effect of a potential mini-psychotherapeutic experience. Small variations of interview techniques, personal mannerisms, and so forth, which may seem unimportant to the interviewer, may cause surprisingly large changes in what actually transpires during an interview.[9] Lifton, in his interviews with "historical figures," has faced similar problems.

How reliable is our psychological data? Why should people tell the truth? Individuals often distort their true feelings in order to try to hide them from us, the interviewers. They also, at times, distort events in an effort to please the inverviewers with the type of information they think the interviewers would like. In other words, people do attempt to conceal psychopathology from us because they know that we are interested in their behavior. Can we, the interviewers, change the data? We can, and do, err on the opposite side of our clinical colleagues, causing us to fail to see rampant psychopathology present in our subjects. Clinicians have a tendency, because of their training, to focus on the psychopathology of their subjects. On the other hand, interviewers of nonpatients often err on the opposite side, namely by failing to observe psychopathology in subjects, even when it is obviously present. The interviewer, at times, does not want to press his subjects for more information because, after all, they did not come for psychotherapy. However, as interviewers, we can also tamper with the data by doing some form of psychotherapy, unwittingly entering into a psychotherapist–patient type of relationship with subjects. To be able to attain our goal of a research–interview situation, we need to develop the concept of the "research alliance." It is our belief that the research alliance enables researchers to view the subjects with the least amount of distortion.

We can now return full circle to one of our original questions: What are the qualities of a good leader, with particular reference to the problem of leadership in the nuclear age? The enduring contribution of Freud to the study of leadership is, in our opinion, not his understanding of the psychology and psychodynamics of sexuality, but rather his theory of how early experiences influence the adult behavior of leaders. Erikson has contributed the "great man" theory, in which the personal problems of the leader reflect the general problems of the times, and the leader resolves his own problems by helping to resolve the problems of his culture; examples of this principle are Luther and Gandhi. Kohut has added narcissism as an important new dimension to our understanding of leadership. The transformation of primary narcissism into secondary narcissism is part of normal growing up and maturing.[10] The healthier the leader, the less megalomania (primary narcissism) he has, and the more he or she has transformed original omnipotent feelings (secondary narcissism) into more creative channels and traits (such as the ability to postpone gratification, a sense of humor, etc.).

Freud, Erikson, and Kohut described the leader in terms of personal motivation, but only Erikson and Kohut described the leader also in terms of the motivation and psychology of his or her followers. It seems to us that normal development is immensely more complex than psychopathological development. We need, therefore, to add a third dimension to our understanding of the phenomenon of leadership. This dimension comprises the immediate experience, the skill to perform under stress, and the ability to learn from novel situations. Hence, the Office of Strategic Services (OSS), found, during World War II, that those individuals who did best in training camp (a parallel to childhood experiences) were not necessarily the ones who did best in actual combat behind enemy lines.[11] In other words, one's performance under one set of circumstances did not relate to one's functioning in another set of circumstances. The comparison to leaders is obvious: the leaders with the best past records and potentials are not necessarily the ones who function best once they are in office.

LEADERSHIP: CRITICAL FACTORS

A leader is usually very much aware of the historical moment in which he or she lives. Once elected, most leaders want to leave their personal mark on the history of their nations, or even on the history of mankind. It is clear to anyone who has studied history that those leaders who have emerged as victorious from crisis situations (wars, for example) have usually fared much better in the eyes of their fellow men than have those leaders who sailed the ship of state during peaceful times. Hence, those United States presidents whom we consider the greatest are Washington, Lincoln, Wilson, and Roosevelt. Nothing repels people more than mediocrity. These are at least some reasons why John Kennedy reacted so strongly during the Cuban missile crisis and probably brought us closer to nuclear war than we have been at any other time during the past thirty-eight years. The general principle is that anything grand, if successful, will be remembered as heroic.

Much has been written about how important charisma is for a leader. Charisma is described as a "divine gift" that only a few leaders possess. It is a special talent, which, in the eys of their followers, makes leaders seem particularly able to lead. Although the definition of charisma suggests that one either possesses it or one does not, it seems to us that crisis can breed charisma. Obviously, a crisis situation can also bring out the worst in a leader; in such situations, one often sees a tragic, ineffective, or intolerant leader. Crisis in a cmplex society simplifies the group formations, causes regression among the group members, and brings out the most primitive aspects of the group to the foreground. The more complex and diversified a society, the less likely it is for a charismatic leader to emerge from it. Conversely, the more primitive a society is, the more likely it is to have a leader who "has all the answers." In times of crisis, however, a complex society reverts back to primitive group formation, rallies around its leader, and imbues its leader again with charisma, whether the leader possesses it or not. A stable, prosperous, and well-functioning society seems to also lack charismatic leaders.

The Greeks believed that ambition is a healthy human trait to which leaders should proudly admit. We believe, with Freud, that ambition is a sublimated instinct; we also believe, with Kohut, that ambition is, in part, a healthy transformation of primary narcissism. In either case, ambition is a healthy psychological attribute which leaders should not be ashamed to proclaim. The leaders have to be able, to paraphrase President Truman's words, to take the heat generated from their function as leaders, or they will not be effective leaders.

A listing of the psychological characteristics of a "good" leader is not possible because, as we have stated, there is always an interaction of three major sets of variables: the personality of the leader him- or herself, the needs and aspirations of the followers, and the particular socio-cultural-historical period in which both occur. There are many ways in which personality factors can be studied. Psychoanalysts have used the structural approach to psychological individual psychology, considering the id, the ego, the superego, and the ego ideal.[12] Others have evolved a character topology based on predominant developmental influences in a person's life, and still many other theories have evolved concerning personality and character; it is not our purpose to review them here.[13]

The approach we have elected to use here is the one on which we have elaborated in detail elsewhere.[14] In this approach, the self corresponds to the sum total of perceptions, thoughts, and feelings held by a person in reference to himself or herself. These perceptions, thoughts, and feelings may be more or less clearly articulated into an ongoing self-scheme or self-system in which the self is divided into six different parts, all closely intertwined. These six selves are; the Physical Self, the Sexual Self, the Familial Self, the Social Self, the Psychological Self, and the Coping Self.

The Physical Self. The leader should be in reasonable physical health, so that his or her performance will not be impeded. Much has been written about the problems which Presidents Roosevelt and Wilson encountered because they suffered from ill health.

The Sexual Self. There is no evidence that sexual preference or sexual behavior is related to the ability of a leader to lead.[15]

The Familial Self. Much has been written on this subject, but the last word is not in as yet. There is no question that one's family background is related to one's functioning as an adult. However, exactly how these are related is not clear. Some leaders overcome earlier traumas and conflicts, and others take out their frustrations stemming from childhood on their followers.

The Social Self. The ability to get along with others is important for most persons in office. The leader has to learn how to negotiate with others and how to bring out the best in his or her colleagues. He or she must be able to use interpersonal skills in order to work effectively with diverse, and often hostile, groups.

The Psychological Self. One's inner world—one's fantasies, dreams, or wishes—are important aspects of a person's life. A reflective leader who is free from overt symptomatology has an easier time in office. Psychopathology, as Freud said, is part of everyday life. Leaders are not immune from neurotic conflicts, psychological problems, and, at times, more serious forms of psychopathology such as overt psychosis. There is no question, however, that the less interesting leaders are often also closer to normality. Hence, we are often more fascinated by leaders who have clear and discernible psychological conflicts than by those who do not.

The Coping Self. The leader should be able to handle difficult sociocultural conflicts creatively and to offer new solutions to old problems. The leader should have a reasonable amount of intelligence and knowledge so that he or she can perceive the issues involved. The leader must also have enough confidence in his or her decisions to communicate this confidence to others. Another important aspect of the coping self is the ability of the leader to withstand the stresses and strains of being in office. Stress, as is well known, can manifest itself in many different ways. It can cause severe somatic symptoms, which can seriously limit the abilities of the leader. It can also make for increased rigidity at historically pivotal times, causing a decrease in flexibility and restraint when they are probably needed most.

LEADERSHIP IN THE NUCLEAR AGE: A COMMENT

Our civilization is only ten thousand years old. From the macro point of view, very little time has elapsed for men and women to emerge from a cave mentality to a more civilized one. The evolutionary development toward a more caring and responsible, less violent and brutal, individual is slow. There is some evidence that today's leaders are somewhat more stable emotionally and less impulsive than leaders of the past millennium. Reading Gibbon impresses one with the considerable brittleness of the Roman emperors, who rarely lasted for more than a few years. Assassinations were much more commonplace in Greek, Roman, ancient Hebrew, Hittite, Persian, and Egyptian kingdoms than they are today. Fanatics, who will galdly die for a cause and who believe that their actions will ensure them a seat in their particular heaven, are not unique to any age. It was amazing that the American hostages in Iran, in 1979, were returned unharmed to the United States and not beheaded and shipped back by very different means. Some moderation seemed to prevail.

Because of the potential destructive power of the nuclear age, it seems imperative to any rational person that some compromise has to prevail. It has been suggested by some (Lifton, for example) that the more sanitized means of killing of the twentieth century make it easier to kill. In a sense, we have become less brutal individually because we no longer drive the knife personally into the bellies of our enemies. In addition, it has been questioned whether the technological advances allow for easier expressions of instinctual aggression. It is a question which, in our opinion, is still not fully answered, although by the fiftieth century, it no doubt will have been answered.

Because of the special dangers of the nuclear age, a leader with strong ideological commitments is perhaps more dangerous today than one who is blander and less aggressive by nature. Recent American history would suggest that the world is safer with a Dwight Eisenhower in command than a John Kennedy. On the other hand, Abraham Lincoln undoubtedly excelled whereas James Buchanan, had he been re-elected in 1860, would have performed disastrously. There are no simple answers.

Infantile longings are part and parcel of the human condition. The infant probably has a sense of wonder at the strength of the great and magnificent parent who picks him up, throws him up into the air, catches him, and magically puts him down again without hurting him; the whole experience has been pleasurable and exhilarating. Later on, the child is in awe of the physical strength and the know-how of his parents. Although much disappointment lies ahead for the child (parents are never as wonderful again!), the yearning for leaders who, like the parents of yesteryear, can do anything and solve everything is always within us. It is that yearning for omnipotent leaders which elevates the leaders, in their followers' eyes, to such unrealistic heights. The feelings described above are fundamentally human and the reactions understandable, but the results are often most dangerous.

And yet we strive for inspiration, as reflected in all our institutions as varied as religions and politics. Greatness, in turn, can create an expansion of the self that allows for new forms of creativity in a technological world as challenging as it is complex. But old and familiar ways of working through these psychological needs seem potentially unproductive in the nuclear age. We need Larmarckian change, but history allows only Darwiniam forms.

NOTES

1. Daniel Offer and Judith B. Offer, *From Teenage to Young Manhood* (New York: Basic Books, 1975).
2. Jack Block, *Lives Through Time* (Berkeley: Bancroft Books, 1971); G. E. Vaillant, *Adaptation to Life* (Boston: Little, Brown, 1977).
3. Daniel Offer and Melvin Sabshin, eds., *Normality and the Life Cycle: A Critical Integration* (New York: Basic Books, 1984). See particularly Part III, written by the editors.
4. Milton Greenblatt, "Power and Impairment of Great Leaders," presented as Distinguished Psychiatrist Lecture, American Psychiatric Association Annual Meeting, May 2, 1983, New York City.
5. Task Force Report #11, *The Psychiatrist as Psychohistorian*, American Psychiatric Association, Washington, D.C., June, 1976.
6. Charles B. Strozier, *Lincoln's Quest for Union: Public and Private Meanings* (New York: Basic Books, 1982).
7. Sigmund Freud and William L. Bullitt, *Thomas Woodrow Wilson: A Psychological Study* (London: Weidenfeld & Nicolson, 1967); Fawn Brody, *Richard Nixon: The Shaping of His Character* (New York: Norton, 1981); Doris Kearns, *Lyndon Johnson and the American Dream* (New York: Harper & Row, 1976); and Margaret Brenman-Gibson, *Clifford Odets, American Playwright: The Years from 1906 to 1940* (New York: Atheneum, 1981).
8. John Klauber, "On the Dual Use of Historical and Scientific Methods in Psychoanalysis," *International Journal of Psychoanalysis*, 49 (1968), 80–88.
9. Daniel Offer and Melvin Sabshin, "Research Alliance Versus Therapeutic Alliance: A Comparison," *American Journal of Psychiatry*, 123 (1967), 1519–1526.
10. The detailed discussions of the contributions of Freud, Erikson, and Kohut to our understanding of the psychology of leadership are found in Chapters 4, 5, and 7, respectively.
11. Personal interview with Roy R. Grinker Sr., on James G. Miller, January, 1984.
12. Sigmund Freud, *The Standard Edition of the Complete Psychological Works of Sigmund Freud* (London: Hogarth Press, 1953–1966).
13. One of the best known theories of personality is that by Henry A. Murray, *Exploration*

in Personality (New York: Oxford University Press, 1938). There are literally dozens of theories of personality, each stressing different biological, psychological, developmental, or socio-cultural factors.

14. Daniel Offer, Eric Ostrov, and Kenneth I. Howard, *The Adolescent: A Psychological Self-Portrait* (New York: Basic Books, 1981). See particularly Chapter 1, "The Self: A Theoretical View."

15. This view is in marked contrast to the view expressed recently by Abraham Zaleznik, who stated that true leaders have "wider-ranging sexual appetites than most mortals," in Peter Cowen, "Business Leaders get Poor Grades," *Boston Globe*, February 18, 1983, p. 3.

INDEX

Abdul-Hamid, 267
Abolitionism
  Lincoln and, 83, 85, 86, 87
  pacifism and, 94–95, 102
  "righteousness" of, 101–102
  Southern attitude towards, 96
Abraham, Carl, 30–31
Adams, John Quincy, 93, 253
Adler, Alfred, 23, 26, 27
Adolescence, identity crises of, 50–52
Affect, 46
Aggression
  humor and, 279
  instinctual, 309
  profanity as, 252
  projection of, 274–275
Ahimsa, 112, 119, 124
Alcibiades, 15–19
Alexander the Great, 34–35
Allies, of leaders, 242, 245, 255–256
Altruism, 28
Ambition, 255, 307
Amenhotep III, 30
Amenhotep IV, 30 31
American Historical Review, 52, 81
American Psychiatric Association, 303

Amerindians, 30
Ancient times
  assassination in, 309
  leadership in, 9–19
    Alcibiades, 15–19
    Joseph, 9–12
    Plato on, 13–15
Andreas-Salmoné, Lou, 30
Anne of Cleves, 34
Arab–Israeli conflict, 265–298
  aggression projection in, 274–275, 276
  Arab perception of, 273
  as civil war, 275
  historical processes of, 295
  interstate conflict of, 290–291
  Israeli-Palestinian conflict of, 291
  Israeli perception of, 271–273
  Jewish-Muslim relations and, 267–268
  leadership models of
    data required, 288–290
    national character, 268–271
    psychopathological, 271–277
    self-system, 277–287
  longitudinal research, 292–293
  Palestinian-Arab conflict of, 291
  Palestinian political conflict of, 291

313